D0778977

Village Justice

*The Johns Hopkins University Studies in
Historical and Political Science*

117TH SERIES (1999)

1. Richard K. Marshall, *The Local Merchants of Prato: Small Entrepreneurs
in the Late Medieval Economy*

2. Brendan Dooley, *The Social History of Skepticism: Experience and Doubt in
Early Modern Culture*

3. Tommaso Astarita, *Village Justice: Community, Family, and Popular
Culture in Early Modern Italy*

Village Justice

Community,
Family, and
Popular Culture
in Early
Modern Italy

Tommaso Astarita

The Johns Hopkins University Press

BALTIMORE AND LONDON

This book was brought to publication with the generous assistance of the Georgetown University Gradute School.

The Johns Hopkins University Press
2715 North Charles Street
Baltimore, Maryland 21218-4363
www.press.jhu.edu

Library of Congress Cataloging-in-Publication Data will be found at the end of this book.
A catalog record for this book is available from the British Library.

ISBN 0-8018-6138-1

Contents

Tables and Figures

Money and Measurements

The Neapolitan ducat was usually divided into five *tarì*, each worth twenty *grana*. It could also be divided into ten *carlini*, each worth ten *grana*. The *oncia*, a unit of account used in the *catasto* documents, was worth six ducats and divided into thirty *tarì*.

The following measurements were used in the Kingdom of Naples:

tomolo (for surfaces)	=	0.33 ha
tomolo (for capacity)	=	0.55 hl
rotolo (for weights)	=	0.89 kg
cantaro (for weights)	=	89.09 kg
libbra (for weights)	=	0.32 kg
salma (for wine)	=	1.61 hl

For details see C. Afan de Rivera, *Tavole di riduzione dei pesi e delle misure delle Due Sicilie* (Naples, 1841; 1st ed., 1840); and *Tavole di ragguaglio dei pesi e delle misure già in uso nelle varie province del Regno col sistema metrico decimale* (Rome, 1877), 605–9, for the Reggio Calabria area.

Acknowledgments

I wish to thank the personnel of the Archivio di Stato di Napoli, the Biblioteca Nazionale di Napoli, the Biblioteca della Società Napoletana di Storia Patria, the Biblioteca Universitaria di Napoli, and the Archivio di Stato di Catanzaro. The staff of the Archivio di Stato di Reggio Calabria was very helpful, particularly dottoressa Mazzitelli. I also thank dottoressa Tripodi, of the Soprintendenza Archivistica di Reggio Calabria, and its director, dottor Seminara; Monsignor Lauro, of the Archivio della Sacra Congregazione del Clero (formerly del Concilio); and the staff of the Archivio Segreto Vaticano and of the Archivio dei Redentoristi in Rome. Padre Ferrante and Suor Maria Gonzaga helped me in the Archivio Diocesano di Reggio Calabria.

I am grateful to the Georgetown University Graduate School for a Junior Faculty Research Fellowship in fall 1992, summer grants in 1993 and 1995, and a sabbatical in spring 1996. The staff at Georgetown's Lauinger Library, especially at the Inter-Library Loan Department, was most helpful. I also thank the two readers and Henry Tom and Grace Buonocore of the Johns Hopkins University Press for their advice and suggestions.

I owe thanks, for varied reasons, to Renato Barahona, Giuseppe Caridi, Thomas Cole, Filippo and Babette Faes, Claudio Fogu, John Garrigus, David Gillerman, Francesco Guizzi, Gregor Kalas, Massimo Lo Iacono, John Marino, Richard McCann, Nelson Moe, Giovanna Moracci, Marco and Maria Adele Moracci, Will Morrison, Giovanni Muto, Ugo Piomelli, Bruce Ragsdale, Anna Maria Rao, Scott Redford, Richard Scobey, Scott Spector, and Wendy Thompson. I also thank all my students for reminding me, whenever this project frustrated me, of why I got into this line of work in the first place.

Jim Collins, Alan Karras, Richard Stites, and Jeff von Arx critiqued proposals for this project. John McNeill and Zoë Schneider read parts of the manuscript. All my Georgetown colleagues gave encouragement and comments at two talks I presented. I am very grateful to them all.

Thomas Willette was generous with suggestions; Trevor Burnard was always a source of support; Aviel Roshwald offered me advice and patient listening; John Malloy read most of the manuscript; Francesca Santovetti offered me reassurance, and especially her constant warmth; Laurent Cartayrade helped shape the manuscript's themes; Alessandra Galizzi was the first friend to hear about Pentidattilo and convinced me to pursue this project; Alison Games was generous with encouragement and appropriately ungenerous in her sharp criticisms of my draft chapters. The gratitude I owe all of them for their help with this book is but a small part of my indebtedness to them for their friendship.

My family in Naples followed the progress of this book with enthusiasm. My late grandmother Carmen Grimaldi was always interested and supportive. My brother, Luca, and his wife, Clotilde Pennarola, repeatedly gave me great food, intrigued listening, and their affectionate interest. My mother, Nerina Giuliani, was generous, hospitable, supportive, and, most important, confident in this book and its author.

My maternal grandmother, Mimma Schisano, and her sister, Maria Rosaria Schisano, were the best grandmother and great-aunt a budding historian could have wished for: intelligent, erudite, witty, eccentric, wise, profoundly cultivated, and overall fascinating. My father, Gianni, taught me through his example what joy teaching can bring and always to strive for high standards of personal and professional integrity. Each could be exasperating, but they were all three articulate, original, hardly ever dull, and in love with language and knowledge. They have died recently, and I miss them greatly. This book is dedicated to their memory as a token of my affection and gratitude.

A Village and a Trial

> Pourvu que les paysans ne brûlent pas les fermes, qu'ils n'assassinent pas, qu'ils n'empoisonnent pas, et qu'ils paient leurs contributions, on les laisse faire ce qu'ils veulent entre eux; et, comme ils sont sans principes religieux, il se passe des choses affreuses.
>
> As long as the peasants do not burn the farms, do not murder, do not poison, and pay their taxes, we let them do what they want among themselves; and, since they have no religious principles, horrible things happen.
>
> —BALZAC, *Les Paysans*

Certain notions have long accompanied the image of southern Italian villages in the minds of foreign, and indeed often Italian, observers. Ideas of poverty and backwardness, of isolation and alienness, of illiteracy and ignorance, and of beliefs and ritual practices understandable at best through anthropological analysis have long characterized outside observers' perceptions of rural society in regions south of Rome and Naples. I do not reject all these characterizations, and, indeed, in this book I stress the significance of some of them. I argue, however, that the southern villages were similar to those of many regions of western Europe. More important, although undoubtedly poor and often remote, they were home to dynamic and flexible communities that were able effectively to handle their internal tensions, to maintain a lively and autonomous culture, and to interact frequently and successfully with external authorities. The land was often formidable and the villagers mostly illiterate, but southern Italian rural people were far from passive and fatalistic victims of larger natural or human forces.

This book centers on the village of Pentidattilo, in southern Calabria, at the very southernmost point of the Italian peninsula. Pentidattilo is one of many villages that have largely escaped the attention of scholars. Most historians who have examined the rural areas of the Kingdom of Naples focused on the more prosperous areas, such as the plains of Campania or the plateaus of

Puglia, often characterized by large villages and estates, trade connections and commercialized grain production, complex social structures, and emerging local elites. Pentidattilo—like many other villages in Calabria, Basilicata, and indeed all provinces of the kingdom—was small and remote, with a simple and remarkably egalitarian social structure and traditional economic and cultural patterns that persisted until the late eighteenth century.

Pentidattilo was thus in many ways typical of poor and isolated areas, so that generalizations about communities like it can be drawn. At the same time, the village was distinguished by peculiarities that make its study intriguing and especially revealing. The village was part of a small area with a Greek cultural and linguistic background, and the Greek rites were followed until the seventeenth century. Pentidattilo was thus quite distinctive in its dialect, ritual life, and religious institutions, and this shaped its relationship with the larger world, especially with the Latin Church. The area of Pentidattilo was also affected by substantial, and remarkably rapid, economic transformations in the second half of the eighteenth century, when the local development of citrus fruit production involved it in large trade networks and wrought significant social and demographic changes.

These features make Pentidattilo a useful prism through which to examine the social and cultural history of rural communities. The village became central to my research after I discovered the records of a trial held in the local feudal court in 1710–11. The Pentidattilo records deal with accusations of poisoning, abortion, and adultery and thus give access to crucial themes of village life, such as the status of men and women in the family and the community, the ties that bound villagers together, the hierarchies of village society, and the centrality of family connections, personal reputation and honor, and individual accomplishments in determining each villager's status within the community. The records of this trial, moreover, shed light on the villagers' views of morality, sexuality, and family, and they also provide an example of how justice operated at the local level, how it was understood by the villagers, and how its functioning reflected a broader interaction between villagers and external authorities. The records of this trial serve as a thread guiding this exploration of Pentidattilo's community and its social, economic, and cultural history.

Over the past few decades, many historians of early modern Europe have turned to judicial records, produced by both secular and ecclesiastic courts, not only to study the institutions of justice but also to gain insight into the society and culture of the past. As traditionally marginal groups and individuals, and especially the illiterate rural masses of western Europe, have attracted increasing historiographical attention, judicial sources have emerged as one of the best tools for the study of their lives and ideas. Judicial sources also generally tell specific stories and thus lend themselves well to the renewed interest in narrative and narrative techniques which has characterized much recent historical writing, particularly in microhistorical studies. Many studies have focused on Inquisition records, often approached quantitatively, or on trials for witchcraft, which have revealed with special clarity the tensions and contacts between learned and popular culture. All these developments have been the subject of debate among historians.[1]

The Pentidattilo trial records are complete and include the original denunciation, the testimony of several witnesses, the questioning of the defendants and their torture, procedural matters, and the sentences. Domenica Orlando stood accused of the murder by poison of her husband, Antonino Cuzzucli. Her alleged lover, Pietro Crea, was accused of instigation and complicity, and Domenica's neighbor Anna de Amico was accused of giving Domenica the arsenic used in the murder. As the trial progressed, Domenica was also accused of having obtained an abortion some time previously, and Anna was accused of having managed both that abortion and others for several village women.

Records of trials held in feudal courts are quite rare for the Kingdom of Naples: I have found almost no other examples for the period preceding the end of the eighteenth century, when feudal criminal jurisdiction had been curtailed, at least for the most serious crimes.[2] The kingdom's aristocracy was unique among its western European early modern counterparts in the pervasiveness and extent of its judicial powers. More than three-quarters of the kingdom's population had no access to royal justice, in either civil or criminal matters, until their feudal lord's courts had passed judgment both at the trial level and in the first appeal. Royal jurisdiction was limited to towns that were large or strategic, so that the rural population in particular depended almost exclusively on the system of feudal justice.[3] The records of the Pentidattilo trial represent a remarkable and unusual window into a nearly unknown world of rural courts. They also reveal peasant society's contact and exchanges with the judicial system, illustrating the core of the general relationship between the authority and goals of the state and the values and traditions of the village community.

The Kingdom of Naples was an important center of legal studies and legal innovation throughout the early modern period. Neapolitan jurists were deeply involved in the European jurisprudential discussions of the sixteenth and seventeenth centuries, and Naples was later also an active center of Enlightenment thought, especially in the fields of legal and economic studies. Although the prestigious history of Neapolitan jurists and law has been extensively studied, we still know very little about how the mass of the kingdom's population encountered and perceived the justice system. The records of the Pentidattilo trial display how the illustrious legal and judicial traditions of Naples operated in practice, and especially how they interacted with the culture and experiences of the rural masses of the kingdom in a system that led to negotiation, cooperation, and mutual influence.

The Pentidattilo trial records also reveal much about peasant culture and society and about the structures of village life. In addition to the trial records, I have utilized all available fiscal, notarial, ecclesiastic, and administrative documents concerning the village to reconstruct the social, economic, and cultural networks in which all participants in the trial operated and to analyze the functioning, culture, and character of a peasant community in the south of Italy. There are few studies of village communities for the early modern Kingdom of Naples, and they focus almost exclusively on demographic history and economic issues such as land management and property, which will be secondary in this study.[4]

The Pentidattilo trial occurred at the start of profound transformations for the rural communities of the kingdom, and indeed of much of western Europe. The first half of the eighteenth century marked the beginning of demographic and economic growth in many areas of the kingdom, and by midcentury new social realities came to the fore as villages became increasingly differentiated in their social structures and integrated into larger economic networks. The early eighteenth century was also the time when new ideas about the law and the functioning of justice germinated and later led to Enlightenment reforms, in the Kingdom of Naples as elsewhere in Europe. Finally, in the region of Pentidattilo these decades also witnessed the final steps in the long transition from Greek religious traditions to the dominance of a more assertive Latin Church led by Counter Reformation bishops and staffed by better-trained clerics.

In this study, then, I examine the workings of the judicial system in the countryside, the village's social and economic life, and rural morality and religion. Linking together these topics is also the interaction between the rural, remote, and mostly illiterate world of the people of Pentidattilo and the outside world and written culture of the state, the church, and the feudal lords and their representatives. The trial of Domenica Orlando is just one example of the frequent presence of the law and the state in the village and of the contacts between local and outside views and realities. Pentidattilo, in spite of its distant location and small size, had frequent and extensive contacts with larger forces and outside authorities and with their different culture. The village was an active participant in these interactions, which reveal the initiative and shrewd agency of both the villagers and their community. The state, the church, and the justice system could not have operated as they did in the vast rural world of the kingdom without important exchanges with, and the active contributions of, both villagers as individuals and the village community as a whole. No justice, no administration, no moral and religious control would have been possible without a process of negotiation and mutual influence between outside forces and village culture, as appears in the records of the trial of Domenica Orlando, in the production itself of most sources about the village, and in the village's life in general.[5]

Pentidattilo presents an example of a vibrant community whose life was marked by clear values and organizing principles. Local clans were settled and supportive of their members. The village had regular contacts with the larger world, but within the community outsiders remained rare, marginal, and, in time of crisis, vulnerable. The villagers shaped a lively, autonomous culture, which long maintained its own values, rules, and traditions. Personal honor and achievements, which were reflected in each villager's reputation, remained more important than inherited wealth or status within the local community.

The village's culture was also reflected in its moral and spiritual life. The period from the end of the sixteenth through the mid-eighteenth century witnessed an increasingly aggressive struggle of secular and ecclesiastic authorities, in both Catholic and Protestant Europe, against a variety of popular views and behaviors. The rising administrative states and the post-Reformation churches were concerned with the threat to hierarchy, stability, and authority which they came to perceive in much unfettered popular behavior. The fight took place especially in the areas of justice and moral control, and it involved an expanding criminalization of behavior, the increased severity of laws and tribunals, and the church's battle to reform the clergy and to instill in the laity a new ethics of self-control and discipline. This struggle sought to break the circularity of exchanges and influence which had characterized the relationship between learned and popular culture and fully to separate the two. Particularly in the rural world, as we shall see in Pentidattilo, the success of these policies was limited until at least the end of the old regime, and, while the contrast between learned and popular culture grew, popular views never became subordinate to official ones.[6]

The fight to establish and strengthen political, social, and religious control took particular aim at the moral and sexual behavior of urban and rural masses. The well-disciplined, patriarchal family was increasingly envisaged by secular and clerical leaders as the core structure symbolizing and ensuring the stability of social order and of monarchical and ecclesiastic institutions.[7] State and church focused on the condemnation and repression of what was now defined as illicit or deviant behavior, and jurists, judges, confessors, and bishops gave particular attention to sexual crimes and sins. This concentration on sexual behavior led, by the early eighteenth century, to increased awareness of the contradictions and tensions inherent in the judicial procedures prevailing in western continental Europe and thus to the first impulses for legal and judicial reforms. Because the system of secular and ecclesiastic justice played a crucial role in this confrontation between the authorities and the general illiterate population, judicial records often constitute the main sources we have in seeking to understand popular, and particularly rural, behavior and beliefs.

Judicial sources, of course, reflect, and operate within, a power relationship in which the defendants had much the weaker position. The illiterate speak in judicial records in distorted ways, mediated through the conceptions and the aims of clerks and judges. The defendants, as well as witnesses and denouncers, also pursued their own goals and attempted to manipulate the system in which they were caught, so that their statements do not always directly reveal their actual thoughts or actions. Nonetheless, judicial records are among the few sources that allow historians to gain any sense of peasant agency, of the motives and rationales of the illiterate and the less powerful, and of what has been called the "verbal agency" of women. Although these sources, then, express the prevailing power structure, the dialogic format produced and required by judicial procedures also makes visible, and gives us access to, an alternative "cultural reality."[8]

Judicial sources have also proved especially interesting to social and cultural historians because of the similarities and reciprocal influences between judicial and historical methods and goals. From this point of view, too, the late seventeenth and early eighteenth centuries constituted an essential formative period. It was in those decades, as discussions on the character and method of all sciences took place throughout western Europe, that jurists delved most deeply into the problems of proof presented especially by moral and sexual crimes; it was also during this time that the pursuits of jurists and the concerns of historians came to resemble each other. History, like jurisprudence, medicine, and other "humane" forms of knowledge, centered on questions of evidence and proof and increasingly relied on conjecture, speculation, and deduction. By the later eighteenth century the works of great historians, like the decisions of great judges, hinged on what Carlo Ginzburg called the "evidential paradigm."[9]

The records of early modern justice have been the basis in particular for most microhistorical analyses. The dependence of these studies on judicial sources has caused difficulties relating to the distortions inherent in judicial records, the often random nature of the surviving evidence, the definition of the relationship between the information available through judicial sources and larger social and cultural contexts, and the typicality of the cases analyzed. Microhistorical studies have been the object of severe criticisms for their real and alleged failures to address these issues. Nonetheless, this approach has certainly brought previously neglected subjects within the scope of historical inquiry and broadened our knowledge of early modern society and culture, especially of the illiterate population of early modern Europe. Microhistorical studies have enriched our understanding of popular culture, social relationships, and power structures; they have allowed us to see old subjects, such as the rise of the modern state, in new light; and they have creatively investigated and illustrated the boundaries between individual freedom and action and social structures and constraints.[10]

Because they rely extensively on judicial sources and on the detailed reconstruction of the individual lives that appear in them, however, the authors of microhistorical studies have often given relatively limited attention to the larger social and economic context of their analysis. Works that have focused on specific rural communities, on the other hand, have often stressed economic, demographic, and social structures to the detriment of issues of popular culture, local religion, or communal life.[11]

By employing judicial records alongside other sources and within the context of a full community study, it is possible to unite these approaches fruitfully, to address both social and cultural issues more thoroughly, and to understand better the whole of local experience and rural life in the old regime. By investigating in detail the village of Pentidattilo, and by using the trial of Domenica Orlando in that investigation, I hope to bridge the gap that often still exists between legal history and social and cultural history. Balancing a microhistorical perspective on the trial with an exhaustive community study enlarges the microhistorical scale and makes it possible to discern more fully the interrelations between the operation of the judicial system at the local level, village social and economic patterns, the structures of peasant families, and the cultural, moral, and religious life of rural communities. By balancing the ordinary and the extraordinary, I use the village and the trial as entries into a comprehensive analysis of rural community, culture, and life.[12]

Studies that concentrate on judicial sources have also made historians more aware of the construction of narratives, of the telling of stories, which takes place within judicial documents, as well as in other types of sources.[13] This attention to the narrative strategies and techniques employed both by the writers and by the other, mostly illiterate, participants in the production of sources as texts also brings to the fore the process of cultural interaction that is reflected in, and therefore can be reconstructed from, judicial and other sources. These sources, which report, however mediated, the voices of illiterate people, could only come to existence as texts with the contribution and through the collaboration of both official and popular culture.

The narrative elements present in many sources thus employed are also connected to the narrative strategies chosen by historians. Some scholars, such as Carlo Ginzburg, make the reader an apparent participant both in the construction of the object of research and in its interpretation, which are presented almost in the style of a detective novel. Others, using an openly more authoritative voice, locate the story told by their sources in a general context they draw from broader historical works. Others still, especially if working with more personal documents than judicial sources, place their sources in the foreground and limit themselves to brief commentary to "illuminate" the sources.[14]

I have combined elements of these approaches. This book contains six chapters plus a prologue and an epilogue. Each chapter is introduced by analyzing a section of the records of the trial of Domenica Orlando and the issues it raises about the operation of both justice and the village community; these issues then lead to an examination of different aspects of rural life and of the relationship between the village and the larger world. Chapter 1 examines the location, demographic evolution, history, and administration of Pentidattilo, defines the characteristics of villages like it, and analyzes its relationship with the state administration and the role of literacy within village society. Chap-

ter 2 aims to understand the system within which the records of the Pentidattilo trial were produced and examines the workings of the judicial system in
the countryside and the interactions between feudal justice at the local level,
royal legislation, and the learned traditions of continental western European
jurisprudence. Chapter 3 addresses the village's economic and social life, the
characteristics of its agriculture, its social hierarchies, and the character of its
local elite. Chapter 4 studies the family structures and residential patterns that
defined the villagers' private life and the various social ties that held their
community together. Chapter 5 analyzes the crisis of traditional judicial ideas
in the eighteenth century, the reforms that ensued, and the role of questions
pertaining to moral and sexual crimes—and to the position of women—in
this transformation. Chapter 6 deals with the spiritual and moral aspects of
village life, in particular the role of the parish clergy and the bishops and their
confrontation with popular culture, and the views of villagers and their community in regard to reputation, honor, gender, and the cycles of family life.

Finally, I need to comment on the text and reliability of the trial records that
are an important source for this work. The feudal court in which the trial was
held was headed by a local governor appointed by the feudal lord. The governor was assisted by three other men, a legal counselor, a scribe, and a court
messenger. The governor, the counselor, and the scribe signed most trial documents, which were written by the scribe himself, as was the case with all documents emanating from the court. The full competence of the feudal court
extended not only to criminal cases but also to civil disputes, to suits involving the village and its neighbors, and to the certification of important moments in the life of the feudal family, such as testaments and successions.[15]

    The court documents are only one of the sources in which the words of the
villagers are recorded. Villagers, both literate and illiterate, frequently testified
in inquiries of various types, and the community was never without at least a
few villagers capable of producing written documents in which the local
dialect intermingles with the different constructs and vocabulary of a bureaucratic language. All these sources make it clear, from the occasional glimpses
of actual dialect that appear in them, that we rarely, in fact, read the villagers'
own words reported directly and that a process of mediation and interpretation, if not of translation, takes place when the villagers' speech is transposed
onto the documents. This process took place all over Europe, especially in
areas where the local dialect was quite different from the official national language.[16] The dialect of the Pentidattilo area is the Calabrian dialect, with the

additional presence of Greek influences, which are evident in both vocabulary and orthography. The Greek linguistic influence began to wane only in the second half of the seventeenth century, at about the same time that Greek religious traditions lost their prominence.[17]

The fact that the language used in the documents does not precisely reflect the words spoken by the villagers raises the question of the reliability of all documents pertaining to the village—and in particular of the trial records, which include the testimony of several villagers—as sources for the actual words and thoughts of the people of Pentidattilo. In reporting the testimony of villagers, it is clear that the scribe adjusted their words to express them in a language more acceptable to a written and legal culture. This is evident not only in syntax and orthography but also in the frequent use of indirect dialogue. All studies that use early modern judicial documents, and in particular microhistorical studies, need to assess the impact of this adjustment of spoken words.

The translation of the witnesses' words is, however, not complete, and the scribe himself, in the trial analyzed here as in many others, is not simply a representative of an abstract written culture and language. Court scribes were both audience and authors, both readers and interpreters. In most cases, the scribe, like local priests or administrators, was rooted in the local culture and language as well as more or less well versed in the language of the bureaucratic state. The written trial records, like other village documents, were produced within a predominantly oral culture, ruled by custom, which shaped their format and language. Virtually all documents pertaining to the early modern Kingdom of Naples are indeed written in a combination, and reflect the influences, of official Italian, Spanish, Latin, and Neapolitan dialect. The documents produced at the local level add local dialects to this cocktail.

The Pentidattilo scribe, for instance, often adapted the witnesses' words to the patterns of indirect speech. This was required by the format and procedure of the inquiry itself, which consisted of a series of questions and answers between the governor and the witnesses, the text of which was written by a third, supposedly neutral, observer, namely the scribe. The scribe often maintained the first-person narrative spoken by the witnesses, and on a dozen occasions during the trial of Domenica Orlando, for instance, he even reported direct dialogue in the first person. The scribe seems to have been conscious that these were slight violations to his rules, and in about half of these cases he included the reported dialogue in parentheses.[18] While all the testimonies were written down in reasonably official orthography and syntax, the scribe made no attempt to free the language he transcribed of the vocabulary of dialect, with which both he and the governor were obviously fully familiar. Dialect terms appear repeatedly and very frequently in the records, especially to refer to objects of common use, such as pitchers, aprons, furniture, clothes (and poisons), and to frequently occurring actions—in particular, in Domenica's trial, abortions.[19]

In addition to few cases of first-person direct dialogue, still reported in the hybrid language of all documents, only once in the entire trial records did the scribe transcribe the exact words spoken by a witness in the original dialect. This happens in the course of Domenica's confession, and the pivotal moment in her narrative at that point perhaps explains the scribe's decision. Domenica reported a conversation with Anna, her neighbor and alleged accomplice, in which Domenica complained of the mistreatment she suffered at her husband's hands and of the failure of previous attempts to poison him. Anna allegedly replied: "You want me to make your husband die." The scribe, in a moment we can perhaps label as literary, left these words with the full effect of their dialectal power.[20]

While certainly an adaptation, the text of the trial records is therefore definitely not a full translation of the villagers' words, and much of the dialect survives at least in the vocabulary of the records. In fact, the frequent use of dialect terms indicates that the scribe made only a limited effort to Italianize the vocabulary spoken by the trial participants and that only a narrow cleaning up of the sentences actually spoken was felt to be necessary. The scribe, the governor, and the trial's protagonists spoke largely the same language, although the first two also knew the rudiments of another. Moreover, although later supervision was not entirely impossible, it was unlikely that these records would ever be read by anyone not connected with the village and unfamiliar with its parlance. Additionally, the fact that the records include contradictory testimonies and contrasting opinions and judgments points to very limited editorial interventions on the part of the scribe. The records, then, do not faithfully reflect the actual words of the villagers, but they come as close as possible, and certainly closer than any other written source could, to allowing us a glimpse of their thoughts and opinions.

Thus, this close study of the village of Pentidattilo and of the trial of Domenica Orlando discusses the mechanisms and operation of the feudal justice system, the structures and values of rural family and community life, the relationship between village culture and the institutions, policies, and views of both the early modern state and the post-Tridentine church, and the role of women—and of relations between women—in village life. These are all subjects on which little historical work exists for the south of Italy,[21] and they are not always well known for other areas of rural western Europe. I am hopeful that what emerges here is a picture of the legal, social, and cultural order of the old regime, analyzed at the start of its waning decades and by means of the example of a remote rural community as it grappled with crucial issues and transformations.

Village Justice

The Story

Domenica Orlando and Anna de Amico were more than just neighbors. Their homes in Pentidattilo were contiguous, and an opening through a shared wall made communication, exchanges, and awareness of—and often involvement with—each other's life even easier than with most good neighbors. The two women were not the same age—Anna was about a decade older than Domenica—but their life situations were nonetheless similar. In particular, both had been unlucky in their marriages. Anna's husband had long ago abandoned her, leaving her alone and without ties in a village of which she was not a native. Domenica's husband, Antonino, had also left her alone for long periods of time, beginning shortly after their marriage, in order to live with other relatives in a nearby village. When he lived with her, Antonino frequently quarreled with Domenica and mistreated her—or so she told Anna (who knew much anyway through that opening in the wall) and other village women.

It is not surprising that Domenica and Anna became close. They often chatted and gossiped together, bemoaned their fate, cooked with and for each other, and appealed to each other for help. Their bond probably started when Domenica found herself pregnant during one of Antonino's prolonged absences and, as had other village women, used Anna's knowledge of roots to cause an abortion. After the two women became neighbors and friends, Domenica reciprocated by assisting Anna with an abortion when Anna also became pregnant. Finally Anna, older, more industrious and talented, and, as an outsider to Pentidattilo's old clans, more used to being independent and to relying on her own wits, urged Domenica to remedy her unhappy conjugal situation. When Domenica took a fancy to Pietro Crea, Anna offered the lovers counsel, hospitality, and encouragement. As the lovers conspired to murder Antonino, it was natural that they appealed to Anna and her knowledge of poisons, and Anna obliged. The accomplices succeeded in their goal.

This is the basic plot of the story that emerges from the records of the criminal trial of Domenica, Anna, and Pietro, which was held in the feudal court of Pentidattilo in 1710 and 1711. The events came to light when Antonino's brother denounced his sister-in-law and her accomplices to the local judge, and the latter began and conducted a thorough and well-recorded investigation. Because physical evidence was limited and no more than suggestive, as was often the case in early modern murder trials, numerous witnesses, of both genders, of all ages, and of varied status and occupation, were called upon to give their knowledge of the events and their views of the character of the people involved. Rich information came forth, not only about Domenica and Antonino's married life and the latter's death but also about Domenica's abortion and the several others Anna had managed for various village women.

Eventually, the two women whose destinies had hitherto been so intertwined were separated by the crisis the trial created in the village's ordered life and by their different positions within village society. Domenica's local roots and the inevitable slowness and inefficiencies of early modern courts helped her escape with her life: she fled the village jail and was never sentenced. Pietro, himself protected by village ties, also avoided punishment. Anna, on the other hand, became the trial's main defendant and scapegoat and received a harsh sentence.

The story of this trial is simple yet powerful, and through it we learn much about situations that seldom appear in historical documents and about people the details and texture of whose lives are rarely recorded. The next chapters offer a detailed examination of the developments of this trial to reveal the characteristics and structures of rural society and culture in the early modern Kingdom of Naples.

The Village of Pentidattilo, Its Lords, and the State

> The appearance of Pentidattilo is perfectly magical.
> —E D W A R D   L E A R, *Journals of a Landscape Painter in*
> *Southern Calabria*, September 2, 1847

The village of Pentidattilo today is almost deserted. The people who had remained until a few decades ago were dislodged by the earthquakes that have plagued the area for centuries and by the increasing danger from falling rocks and have moved somewhat lower down the hill. This gives the village perhaps an even more magical aspect than when Edward Lear, led by a taciturn muleteer, made his way there. A few houses are still in partial use, and there are plans to revive the village as a tourist attraction. The ruins of the old castle and of most buildings, however, seem to blend in with the dry and forbidding rocks from which they spring. The sight everywhere of wild prickly pear trees, growing in the most unexpected places and in the most peculiar shapes, adds to the eerie beauty of the place. It takes more imagination now than in 1847 to see a gigantic hand in the huge rock that looms over the remains of the village, and access is thankfully somewhat easier, but the rest of Lear's description could be penned today:

Having gained the high ground opposite, the appearance of Pentidattilo is perfectly magical, and repays whatever trouble the effort to reach it may so far have cost. Wild spires of stone shoot up into the air, barren and clearly defined, in the form (as its name implies) of a gigantic hand against the sky, and in the crevices and holes of this fearfully savage pyramid the houses of Pentidattilo are wedged, while darkness and terror brood over all the abyss around this, the strangest of human abodes. Again, a descent to the river, and all traces of the place are gone; and it is not till after repassing the stream, and performing a weary climb on the farther side, that the stupendous and amazing precipice is reached; the habitations on its surface now consist of little more than a small village, though the remains of a large castle and extensive ruins of buildings are marks of Pentidattilo having once seen better days.[1]

The appearance of Pentidattilo thus was, and certainly still is, quite unusual. While many southern Italian villages developed in forbidding and remote locations, few could claim quite so challenging a terrain and difficult an approach as Pentidattilo. Yet in numerous ways the village was similar to many others in the Kingdom of Naples. It was small in size, as its population never reached one thousand. Its social structure was simple, and no stable and clearly defined local elite developed until the late eighteenth century. Its economy was also rather simple, poor, and centered on a limited area around the village, at least until the production of raw silk, and later of citrus fruits, brought it into contact with distant markets and larger trade networks.

The traditional image of the southern Italian peasantry is one of economic backwardness, social stagnation, and cultural primitiveness, as compared, for instance, with the wealthier countryside of early modern Tuscany or Lombardy, let alone of France or England. Villages such as Pentidattilo, however, were far from passive and retrograde communities and shared much with their richer counterparts elsewhere. Even though their village was remote and poor, the people of Pentidattilo engaged in frequent and diverse contacts with the outside world, formed a fluid and remarkably egalitarian society, developed a vibrant community that ably protected the villagers' interests and arbitrated between them, and successfully negotiated with external forces without ever passively surrendering to outside goals, influences, or orders.

Pentidattilo was also representative of most villages elsewhere in the kingdom, indeed in Europe, in the daily life of its inhabitants and the character of their community. Most villagers received much of their sustenance from the land they owned or worked. The family played a crucial role in the life of all residents. The community was tightly knit and cohesive and exercised a significant degree of control over the lives, decisions, and actions of its members. Outsiders were rare, and they did not enjoy the same supportive networks and protections as the more settled inhabitants. Religion was a strong force in the ritual and spiritual life of both individual villagers and the community, as well as through the property and influence of the clergy, although here Pentidattilo differed from most villages because of the heterodox ritual heritage of its religious institutions and traditions.

The village community was not only the center of much of the life of its inhabitants but also the locus of their competing interests and often the mediator between them. While the conflicts of rural life could at times explode with violent force, the themes of those conflicts were as complex and varied as anywhere else in early modern Europe. Additionally, after the mid-sixteenth century, when the Spanish government consolidated its political authority over the kingdom and attempted to reinforce its control throughout the provinces and the Counter Reformation church sought to change the quality of the rural clergy and the religious life of its flock, the village was the focus of a struggle by external forces to assert their influence and regulatory power on rural life.

The villagers and their community had a clear understanding of their status and conditions, and they were able to shape their individual and collective destinies. Their determining input, which reflected their values, traditions, and beliefs, is evident in the gradual transformations that in the late seventeenth and eighteenth centuries affected the rural economy, village society and life, and local religion and culture. Certainly the people of Pentidattilo belonged to a Christianized world, and they were governed as part of a comprehensive state apparatus and a sophisticated judicial system. Yet neither the Counter Reformation church nor the early modern state could have developed and functioned as they did without engaging in a constant process of negotiation and collaboration with the communities of villages like Pentidattilo, and that process of interaction is revealed also in the production and character of the very sources historians use for the study of village society and culture.

The Easter Massacre of 1686

> È succeduto un caso strano e compassionevole in Calabria.
>
> A strange and pitiable affair happened in Calabria.
> —CONFUORTO, *Giornali di Napoli*

In 1686 dramatic events occurred in Pentidattilo which gained the village brief notoriety even in the distant capital, and the memory of these events, magnified and dramatized in popular and erudite tales, became part of local folklore, appeared in local proverbs and songs, and survives to this day. The violence of the events was extreme and shows how high the potential for violence remained in the rural society of the Kingdom of Naples even after almost two centuries of Spain's rule. It also reveals the continuing opportunities for murderous resolutions in local disputes, even in those affecting the highest levels of feudal society on the local scale. In addition to its indubitable gothic fascination, the "Easter massacre" of 1686 can serve as an introduction to the village and to many themes of village life. The underlying motivations of the violence, which centered on gender roles, property concerns, and the relations of villagers to their lords, were issues of constant importance in rural society. The unfolding of the events, though difficult to reconstruct exactly, also opens a window on the local role of church and state and on the deep structures of the community.

The Alberti, marquis of Pentidattilo, had a longstanding dispute with the lords of the neighboring community of Montebello, the barons Abenavoli del Franco. The Abenavoli, though not titled, were an old baronial family from the area, and indeed they had ruled Montebello, with a few interruptions, since 1507. The village's territory, like Pentidattilo's, extended to the sea, and its economy relied on traditional agriculture complemented by the production of raw silk. Montebello was larger than Pentidattilo, and it had counted more than three hundred households in the mid-sixteenth century, though by the late seventeenth century it had declined to just over two hundred. When the fief was sold in 1693, its feudal income was assessed at 1,200 ducats and its value at about 27,000 ducats, which made it worth almost one and a half times the value of Pentidattilo at that time.[2]

The "public enmity" between the neighboring lords was personal, but it also involved the two communities, which quarreled over boundaries, pastures, and the use of border waters. Villagers of both communities had also rebelled against their lords during the revolt of 1647–48. In 1675, during a brief reconciliation between the two lords, Bernardino Abenavoli had served as godfather to Domenico Alberti's son Francesco, but disagreements had soon flared again, and in 1682 the dispute came to the attention of the highest authorities in Naples. When Domenico died in 1685, however, the two families were apparently seeking a permanent accord, and Bernardino wanted to marry Antonia Alberti, the eldest of Domenico's four daughters. According to most sources, he had received assurances about the intended union from the marquis Domenico before the latter's death.[3]

At this point the Alberti's changing ambitions, and perhaps the inexperience of the young new marquis, Lorenzo II, led to tragedy. The Cortes, a prominent ministerial family, came to the village for the marriage of Lucia Cortes to the young marquis. Escorting the bride were her mother, Agnese, and brother, Petrillo, and the latter developed an interest in the marquis's sister. The possibility of strengthening the Alberti's connections in Naples appealed to the family, and Lorenzo approved the marriage of his sister Antonia to his own brother-in-law, thinking it "of advantage to his house." Lorenzo ignored warnings not to offend the baron of Montebello, because he believed that the enmity between the two families had ceased with the death of the old marquis. As the news of the impending marriage reached Bernardino Abenavoli, however, he assembled 150 armed men and, thanks to contacts with disgruntled servants of the Alberti, was able, on the night of April 16, 1686, to enter Pentidattilo and take the castle without a fight.[4]

A remarkable slaughter ensued. Bernardino personally shot the young Lorenzo and then stabbed him fourteen times. He threatened to kill the marquis's young wife but spared her after Lucia and Antonia swore that the former was not pregnant with an Alberti heir. Then Bernardino personally killed the marquis's old mother, Maddalena, as she wept on her slain son's corpse. The ten-year-old Simone, brother of the marquis, was also killed, as was, according to one source, their other brother, Francesco, to whom Bernardino had served as godfather eleven years before. As Anna, another of the marquis's sisters, tried to flee, Bernardino ordered Giuseppe Scrufari, a citizen of Pentidattilo and thus a traitor to his feudal lord, to kill her, which the latter did by both shooting and stabbing her. The two youngest sisters were saved, eight-year-old Teodora supposedly thanks to the entreaties of her sister Antonia, and five-year-old Giovanna because she was hidden by a nurse and because the chicken pox from which she was suffering disfigured her enough to avoid recognition. Several servants and other members of the Alberti households were also killed during the slaughter. According to some sources, Bernardino also raped Antonia in the presence of her intended husband, Petrillo Cortes, and, after spending two days terrorizing the castle residents and the entire village, he returned to his fief bringing with him both Petrillo and Antonia. There he and Antonia were married by the *dittereo* (second priest) of Montebello, in the presence of the local head priest and the baron's mother.[5]

The horror of the massacre stunned contemporaries, as is evident in the shocked report given by the Naples chronicler Confuorto. Moreover, the Cortes family was in a position to push the government for swift and decisive reaction. One of the provincial judges was in nearby Melito at the time of the massacre. He quickly alerted the governor of Reggio and the *preside* (provincial governor) and then went to Pentidattilo. The *preside* went to Reggio and started on an expedition to bring Bernardino to royal justice. Bernardino, however, escaped from a skirmish with the royal troops and had fled his fief when the *preside* took the local castle and freed Petrillo Cortes. Eight of Bernardino's men were captured; six were executed and their heads exposed on the walls of the Pentidattilo castle, and two were condemned to the galleys.

Two other culprits were quartered and pieces of their corpses displayed in both villages. The traitor Scrufari was also killed and his head exposed on the spot where he had killed young Anna Alberti.

From Naples, where the news had arrived within a week, the viceroy dispatched ships and soldiers to prevent Bernardino's escape. The latter was, however, not without friends. He went to Reggio, where he entrusted Antonia to a convent (in some accounts through the intervention of the archbishop), and then, with the apparent complicity of the governor of the city, took refuge himself in a Capuchin monastery. There took place the most rocambolesque episode of the whole story, as the *preside* came to search the monastery and was guided by a hooded friar, who—it later became known—had been none other than Bernardino himself. That Bernardino had prominent supporters is also clear from the fact that shortly thereafter the viceroy dismissed and replaced the Reggio governor, who was suspected of engineering Bernardino's escape.

Bernardino, disguised again as a Capuchin, fled to Malta first and thence to Vienna, where he was later supposedly recognized and denounced by a former vassal from Montebello but pardoned by Emperor Leopold I, who had heard of the tragedy at Pentidattilo. The baron became an imperial captain and died during a naval fight against the Ottomans in the summer of 1692. His actions had nearly destroyed the Alberti rule in Pentidattilo and also led to the end of the Abenavoli rule in Montebello. Bernardino's heir, his aunt Maria, contracted large debts in order to repair the castle and village after they were taken by the royal troops, and in 1693 she had to sell the fief.[6]

The Alberti, in the meantime, attempted to rebuild their shattered family. Francesco Alberti, uncle of the slain marquis, became the guardian for his nieces and reached an agreement with the Cortes family for the restitution of Lucia's dowry and for the payment of other obligations. He also sued to have the marriage of Bernardino and Antonia rescinded, and he remained as guardian of young Teodora after Antonia died in 1691, after five years spent in convents in Reggio and Messina. Despite their early agreement, Francesco also later fought a legal battle with the Cortes over the dowry payments and over valuables that Lucia and her mother had allegedly stolen from the castle after the slaughter.[7]

The shocked reaction of contemporaries and the fact that this story became part of local folklore show that even at the time such actions and events were seen as extraordinary. The Pentidattilo Easter massacre, nonetheless, reveals a world of rural violence and brutality, the persistent potential for a high degree of feudal anarchy, and the difficulties of bringing outside justice to the countryside. Nearly two centuries of Spanish rule, the development of centralized institutions and tribunals as essential elements in a bureaucratic state, and well over a century of attempts by the Counter Reformation church hierarchy to regulate rural religion and morality and to encourage the disciplining of emotions had done little to make tragedies like the Alberti's impossible, or even to bring their perpetrators to justice or repentance. The episode also reveals much about attitudes towards women and family and about the perceptions of communities and outsiders, which were crucial issues in rural society.

The events of 1686 also show elements of a two-tiered expression, perception, and repression of violence. Bernardino is shown in the various versions of the events to have acted, for the most part, according to a code of feudal violence and to have been motivated by offended honor. His men, and especially Scrufari, whose role is amplified in some versions almost as an alternative protagonist to Bernardino, act as brutal peasants who express a beastly hatred for their betters, which is made especially horrific in Scrufari's case by his betrayal of his feudal master. The murders they commit, especially Scrufari's murder of Anna Alberti, are more barbaric than Bernardino's and their motivations even less honorable than his. The punishment of these men, of course, is also much more violent and complete than their leader's. This intermingling of class, justice, reputation, and violence will also be evident in the trial of Domenica Orlando and in many other aspects of village life.[8]

Geography

> Kennst du das Land, wo die Zitronen blühen?
>
> Do you know the land where the lemon trees blossom?
> —GOETHE, "Mignonslied"

What was the setting of such horrors? Pentidattilo is in Calabria, the southernmost region of the continental south of Italy. Originally named Brutium by the Romans from the name of a local Italic population, the region, under the name of Calabria, was part of the Norman Kingdom of Sicily established in 1130. After the Sicilian Vespers of 1282 it became part of the Kingdom of Naples, in which it remained until Italian unification in 1861. Duke of Calabria was the title of the heir to the Naples throne. By the sixteenth century the kingdom was divided into twelve provinces, two of which made up the modern

FIG. 1.1. The Kingdom of Naples

region of Calabria. Calabria Citra (or closer to Naples) consisted of the north-
ern half of the region, and its capital was in Cosenza. Calabria Ultra (or farther from Naples) consisted of the southern half of the region, and its capital
was, most of the time, in Reggio, though for a while it was in Catanzaro. Today
Reggio, on the coast opposite Messina and Sicily, is the regional capital.[9]

Pentidattilo, in Calabria Ultra, sits under its threatening five-fingered rock a few kilometers from the southernmost coast of the Italian peninsula, and the village enjoys a spectacular view of rapidly descending hills and distant sea. The rock is surrounded by the valleys of two streams, the Annà and the Sant'Elia, completely dried up in the summer but at times dangerously over-flowing in the winter. Coming from Reggio, about thirty kilometers up the coast, one leaves the coastal road just before arriving at Melito (the full name of which is Melito di Porto Salvo) to climb towards Pentidattilo on a narrow road. Olive and citrus fruit trees are the main crops in the narrow plains, but the land quickly becomes very dry and almost barren, except for the omni-present wild prickly pear trees. A little before arriving at the old settlement one passes the recent village, on a small hill to the right. The road ends at the southeastern corner of the old village. From there one climbs the last few meters and enters the narrow stone roads and dirt paths that wind through the old ruined buildings.

The little church of San Pietro, in the middle of the village, looks in rea-sonably good shape from the exterior, but it is no longer used. A few houses

F I G . 1.2. General view of Pentidattilo (*photo by the author*)

FIG. 1.3. The parish church of San Pietro in Pentidattilo (*photo by the author*)

are somewhat modernized and inhabited mostly by a small community of artists. The rest of the buildings are ruined to various extents, some maintaining their roofs and windows, others surviving only in their walls. The walls of the houses at the lower level blend in with the rock. A few larger and more elegant houses appear as one climbs towards the summit of the village. There lie the imposing but scarce ruins of the castle, in a crevice in the vertical rock that looms over the village. Behind the castle, looking away from the sea, the hill's descent is forbidding, as is much of the vast countryside below. The remains of a wall circle the rock behind the castle, part of what was probably a full circle of walls surrounding the village. A path circles the rock and allows one to leave from near the castle and return to the other end of the village.

Pentidattilo was one of the many *università* into which each province of the Kingdom of Naples was divided. These were administrative units consisting of a principal settlement, which gave its name to the università, and a specific territory, often including smaller settlements as well as scattered habitations. The modern commune of Melito, which represents the old università of Pentidattilo, covers 37.3 square kilometers from the coast to the inland mountains. The old università was bordered by the sea and the università of San Lorenzo to the north and east and by Montebello to the north and west, both of which were larger in population than Pentidattilo in the early modern period.[10]

Pentidattilo was probably settled in the Byzantine period, as war and depopulation afflicted the Italian peninsula and malaria became a common scourge of the plains. The religious divisions of the Mediterranean, and the fact that the Calabrian coast was one of the boundaries of those divisions, made the coastal areas not only unhealthy but dangerous and the frequent victim of pirate and military raids over ten centuries or more. A small settlement may have existed earlier on the coast, and a small landing and later a few religious buildings were maintained there, but it was only in the seventeenth century that the coastal village of Melito developed. In the eighteenth century the old settlement of Pentidattilo began to lose population to the now safer and healthier coastal plain, and later the administrative center of the area was officially relocated to Melito. Pentidattilo suffered greatly from the earthquakes that plague the region, and after the catastrophic 1783 quake the rock began to crumble, and the old village became increasingly dangerous. Only in the last twenty years or so, however, was the old village virtually abandoned.

The retreat of settlements to high hills, in search of the inaccessibility that would grant protection from diseases, foreign enemies (and often domestic ones as well), and outsiders in general, was a common occurrence in medieval southern Italy and is responsible for the landscape of many of the poorer areas of the Kingdom of Naples, such as Basilicata or Calabria. Southern Italian villages of this type were not only remote but also concentrated in their population, and scattered habitations in the countryside were quite rare.[11]

Calabria shares with other areas of the Italian south an ancient myth of its fertility and plenty. As late as 1770, Domenico Grimaldi, while detailing the dire poverty of the region, claimed that Calabria had "the sweetest and most beautiful" climate in Italy and that it was the very fertility of the land which made men lazy and content with primitive tools and low yields. The reality, however, is quite different, and the region has perhaps even more challenging natural features and climate than the rest of the old Kingdom of Naples, although geographers and visitors were fond of praising at least the "good air" of mountainous villages such as Pentidattilo and its neighboring communities.[12]

Although no part of Calabria is more than fifty kilometers from the sea, the region has few plains. The often menacing hills and mountains, especially in its southern part, produce irregular streams and rivers, many of which, like the two streams around Pentidattilo, bring more damage than support to agriculture. Summers are very hot, and winters cause violent storms and winds. Rainfall is scarce, and the weather is so rarely moderate that the region has been said to have "only two seasons." Ever since late antiquity the region has also suffered from deforestation, which has increased the danger of floods when storms come. Earthquakes in Calabria have been the most damaging among the many that afflicted the kingdom over the centuries. Moreover, good harbors were very few, and as late as 1860 most country roads were extremely arduous; despite the vaunted Royal Road of Calabria, in that year it still took eight days to travel by land between Naples and Reggio, a distance of about five hundred kilometers. Only in this century have roads and railroads made access easier, at least to the coastal areas of Calabria.[13]

Especially until the narrow coastal plains became widely used once again in the late seventeenth and eighteenth centuries, agriculture in southern Calabria struggled to contend with these natural conditions and with the additional difficulties posed by the feudal system that involved more than 80 percent of the region's territory. The more mountainous areas such as Pentidattilo, while largely feudal in jurisdiction, saw few large estates. Small peasant holdings, owned or more frequently rented, were the most common form of land exploitation. Latifundia were rare and all in the coastal plains. Small peasant holdings tended to concentrate on intensive crops in the land nearer the villages, especially on a mixture of grain production and olive or fruit trees, or sometimes mulberry trees for the production of raw silk. Livestock was not a substantial part of the area's economy. Finally, fishing was important in the economy of the coastal settlements.[14]

Since the late eighteenth century the small area around Pentidattilo, and in particular its coastal sections, have benefited from the cultivation of citrus fruits. This cultivation requires intensive labor, especially for its high water needs, and the relatively dense population and fragmented property of the area made it easily available for it. Additionally, the hot climate and the scarcity of fog are local conditions that facilitated the new cultivation. The Reggio area has very hot weather, with average temperatures in January as high as 11°C and average temperatures from June to October between 20°C and 26°C.

The previous cultivation of mulberry trees also allowed for the transition to citrus fruits, since the production of raw silk had required the development of a transformation agriculture oriented to commercialization and especially export. The presence of foreign merchants in the area was as crucial to the production of raw silk as to the new citrus fruits. The transformation occurred around the end of the eighteenth century, as more English, Dutch, and American merchants came to Sicily and Calabria, as lemon came to be used widely against scurvy, and as all citrus fruits were used in the perfume and pharmaceutical industries. Various descriptions of the kingdom around 1800 refer both to mulberry trees in the Pentidattilo area and to new citrus fruit production. By the 1950s, the area of Reggio including Pentidattilo and Melito produced 83 percent of the lemons and 89 percent of the bergamots in the whole region, much of that in the Melito plain, and the local perfume industry produced for a national and international market.[15]

Population and Its Evolution

> Quelle laideur dans les femmes! Quel air stupide et grossier dans les hommes!
>
> What ugliness in the women! What an air of stupidity and coarseness in the men!
> —CASANOVA on the Calabrians (1743), *Mémoires*

There are few indications about the population of Italy in late antique and early medieval times. In the half century before the Black Death the Kingdom of Naples had about 2.8 million inhabitants, and by the start of the fifteenth century the population stood at about 2 million. Growth continued slowly through the fifteenth century, with 2.2 million inhabitants in 1444, and intensified in the sixteenth century, especially in the first two-thirds of the century. Much growth took place in the city of Naples itself, which, with more than 300,000 inhabitants in the early seventeenth century, was one of the three largest cities in western Europe at the time. High levels of population continued until the devastating plague of 1656, which killed at least one-fourth of the kingdom's population and half of Naples's inhabitants. Slow recovery followed in the kingdom to more than 4 million inhabitants, until the famine of 1764, after which the kingdom's population grew from 3.8 million in 1766 to 4.8 million in 1797. Growth continued in the nineteenth century and into the twentieth, and in 1961 the old kingdom's area had 12.4 million inhabitants, or 25 percent of the national Italian total.[16]

Calabria participated in these general developments, though the sixteenth-century demographic expansion stopped in the region somewhat earlier than in the kingdom as a whole. Until the fifteenth century Calabria was depopulated, and livestock was then much more significant in the regional economy than in later centuries. According to census data, the region doubled from about 50,000 households in 1505 to more than 100,000 in 1561. Between that year and the 1595 census the population of Calabria Citra stagnated, while Calabria Ultra grew by about another 10 percent. In the first half of the following century, according to the 1669 census, the region as a whole lost 27 percent of its population, in line with the kingdom's loss of 29 percent, but again Calabria Ultra, losing 24 percent of its population, fared somewhat better than Calabria Citra, which lost 31 percent. Calabria Ultra, however, later suffered in the Messina war of 1674–78, and the whole region found itself in a marginal position by the eighteenth century.[17]

At the end of the eighteenth century Calabria had about 850,000 inhabitants. By this date the migration towards the plains had begun, although by 1793 less than 30 percent of the kingdom's population lived in the plains. The last Ottoman raid on the Calabrian coast took place in 1815, and the plague no longer visited the kingdom, although cholera epidemics occurred throughout the nineteenth century. In the forty years or so before the Great War many southern Italians left the country, including more than 300,000 Calabrians, most of them from the mountain settlements. Overall, about 27 percent of the southern Italian population has left the south since 1871, for a total of more than 3 million people, including almost 800,000 from Calabria. Finally, at the start of the twentieth century, with the building of the coastal roads and rail-

TABLE 1.1
Population of Calabria in the Sixteenth and Seventeenth Centuries
(number of households)

Province	1505	1561	1595	1648	1669
Calabria Citra	21,287	51,322	50,216	46,636	34,791
Calabria Ultra	28,506	54,859	59,498	56,850	46,851

SOURCES: Galasso, *Economia e società*, 111–12, and Da Molin, *Popolazione e società*, 55–60 (with slightly different figures for 1595).

NOTE: The census records for the sixteenth century are considered reliable indications of population trends, though they cannot be taken as completely accurate. The later censuses are less reliable. See the discussion in Galasso, *Economia e società*, ch. 3.

road and the draining of coastal marshes, the population of the south generally moved towards the coasts, the plains, and the larger cities.[18]

Pentidattilo's population was never large, although there is evidence that the village was more populated in the late medieval period, probably before the Black Death. The Counter Reformation archbishops mentioned the presence in the village's territory of several ruined churches and chapels, which hints at a large earlier population, but these mentions disappear from the records after the mid-seventeenth century, and the old village never needed any additional ecclesiastic constructions.[19]

Pentidattilo's growth in the first part of the sixteenth century was less pronounced, and its subsequent decline more so, than for the province as a whole. Calculating the average size of a household at 4.5 people, the village went from about 550 inhabitants at the start of the sixteenth century to about 750 in 1561, and possibly 800 a few years later. Though this is a considerably smaller increase than the doubling experienced by the province of Calabria Ultra, it represented a strain on the village's resources, and between the 1570s and the early 1590s the village engaged in a series of disputes with neighboring communities over the control of border pastures and lands. While these disputes certainly display the new eagerness of the Spanish authorities to impose the state's role as mediator, they also indicate the hunger for land resulting from increased population in the area. There were fewer such disputes in later years. Another sign of the village's relative expansion is the presence there in the 1580s of a notary, the last one to reside in Pentidattilo until the 1740s.[20]

This expansion was short lived. According to census records, Pentidattilo had declined to about 450 inhabitants by the start of the seventeenth century. Later censuses are less reliable, but episcopal visits report a stagnant population of about 400 souls in the early seventeenth century, increasing to between 500 and 600 at the end of the century. While the official population of

TABLE 1.2

Population of Pentidattilo, Sixteenth to Twentieth Century

Settlement	Date	Households	People
Pentidattilo	1532	124	
Pentidattilo	1545	138	
Pentidattilo	1561	167	
Pentidattilo	late 16th c.	177	
Pentidattilo	1592	99	
Pentidattilo	1597	100	400
Pentidattilo	1648	99	
Pentidattilo	1669	116	
Pentidattilo	1683		622
Pentidattilo	1686	174	590
Pentidattilo	1690	150	500
Pentidattilo	1693	160	536
Pentidattilo	1729		766
Pentidattilo	1745	108	479
Pentidattilo	1759	106	423
Melito	1759	50	212[a]
Pentidattilo	1794–95		626
Melito	1794–95		551
Pentidattilo	1804		900
Melito	1804		600
Melito	1815		2,074
Melito	1825		1,745
Melito	1849		2,702
Melito	1861		3,050
Melito	1901		5,277
Melito	1951		8,717
Melito	1971		6,693
Pentidattilo	1971		602
Whole commune	1971		8,769

SOURCES: Giustiniani, *Dizionario,* for the 1532, 1545, 1561, 1592, 1648, 1669, and 1804 figures; Mazzella, *Descrittione,* 165, for the late sixteenth-century figure; ADRC, the 1597 visit report of Archbishop D'Afflitto for the 1597 figure; ASV, the *relationes ad limina,* for the 1683, 1686, 1690, 1693, and 1729 figures; ASN, Catasto Onciario 6090 and 6091 for the 1745 and 1759 figures; Galanti, *Giornale di viaggio,* for the 1794–95 figures; and Valente, *Dizionario,* for the other figures.

NOTE: Until 1745 the population figures are for the whole università, under its name of Pentidattilo. Beginning in 1815 the population figures are for the whole commune, under its name of Melito, except for the 1971 figures.

[a] The 1759 census also lists 22 households and 113 people living in Corio, a new hamlet in the università's territory.

the village after 1669 remained fixed at 116 households (or a little over 500 people), the archbishop counted more than 750 inhabitants in 1729. In 1732 the village was assessed fiscally for 153 households, though this calculation was soon reduced to 125. In the 1745 and 1759 censuses the università reported 108 and 178 households, and 479 and 748 inhabitants, respectively. The fast growth between these two censuses probably reflects the losses in the local plague epidemic of 1744, which would have affected the 1745 data.[21]

Pentidattilo thus remained a small village of at most about 700 people, and probably fewer, until the late eighteenth century. The village also remained smaller than its neighboring communities. By the middle of the eighteenth century the population, however, was no longer concentrated in the old settlement under the rock, and in the 1759 census Melito was home to almost half as many people as old Pentidattilo. Melito continued to grow, as appears also from the increasing amount of business transactions stipulated there. By the end of the century, in addition to Melito and the hamlet of Corio, on the road to San Lorenzo, there was also a "population dispersed in various places" numerous enough to merit the appointment of an itinerant curate to minister to its spiritual needs. This was a recent development, as in the 1745 census only 5 of the 108 households had lived scattered throughout the università's territory.[22]

Like all of the kingdom, and indeed of Italy, Pentidattilo grew in the last third of the eighteenth century, and in 1795 its population was assessed at about 1,200 people, evenly divided between the old village and Melito. Giustiniani in 1804 ascribed 900 inhabitants to Pentidattilo and 600 to Melito. In 1807 Melito, thanks to its location on the coast, became the district capital for an area covering also San Lorenzo and Montebello, and in 1811 Pentidattilo officially became administratively dependent on Melito. After that Melito eclipsed its predecessor and grew steadily in population and importance. In 1860 Garibaldi landed there from Sicily to launch his advance into the continental kingdom. Despite emigration the commune grew from 3,050 inhabitants in 1861 to 5,277 in 1901. By 1951 the commune had 8,717 inhabitants, 4,342 of them in Melito proper, and in 1971 the commune had 8,769 inhabitants. Of these, 4,738 lived in Melito proper and only 602 in the Pentidattilo subdivision of the commune. The old settlement under the rock by this date had dwindled to 192 inhabitants.[23]

The village of Pentidattilo was always a small settlement, continuously challenged in its growth by the poverty of the land around it, by the difficulties of life in the hills and the dangers of life in the plains, and by larger and stronger neighboring communities. As we shall see, the lords of Pentidattilo in the Spanish period were not powerful or wealthy enough steadily to support any substantial increase in the numbers or prosperity of their vassals. Even the sixteenth-century expansion remained limited and was quickly stifled by the scarcity of natural resources in the area. When sustainable growth came, in the second half of the eighteenth century, it largely bypassed the old mountain settlement to the benefit of the now much more hospitable, and soon even relatively prosperous, coastal plains.

One last characteristic of the population of Pentidattilo remains to be mentioned, namely, the presence in this area of Greek and Albanian minorities. In the century and a half after the Black Death, the Angevin and Aragonese kings of Naples supported and encouraged the migration of people from the Balkans into their depopulated kingdom. Many of these migrants settled in their own new communities, but many also settled in existing villages, and Calabria received substantial numbers of these new inhabitants. Most Greek and Albanian settlements were in Calabria Citra, but Pentidattilo was one of only two villages in Calabria Ultra in which the king's new subjects came to reside. Pentidattilo was well suited to this influx of new people, owing to the Greek heritage of its culture and religion. Greek names for people and places remain in the area—starting with the village's name itself, of course—and documents show Greek spellings and pronunciations common into the seventeenth century. Even in the mid-eighteenth century one scholar reported that in Pentidattilo and Montebello "the Greek language prevails over the Italian," while both were spoken in Melito and San Lorenzo. A Greek dialect continued to be spoken in the area around Pentidattilo until this century, if not this day. As we shall see, the village was part of an area that followed the Greek rites until well into the seventeenth century, which also affected its relationship with ecclesiastic authorities.[24]

History

> L'Europe finit à Naples et même elle y finit très mal. La Calabre, la Sicile, tout le reste c'est de l'Afrique.
>
> Europe ends at Naples and it ends there quite badly. Calabria, Sicily, all the rest, that's Africa.
>
> —CREUZÉ DE LESSER (1801), cited in
> F. von Lobstein, *Settecento calabrese*

Little is known about the history of Pentidattilo in the early Middle Ages, from its Byzantine foundation to the Norman kingdom. The oldest churches in the village dated from these obscure times. In the troubled years between the late thirteenth and fifteenth centuries, when the Kingdom of Naples was frequently torn by civil wars and the ambitious Angevin and Aragonese monarchs warred with the kingdom's Christian and Muslim neighbors, Pentidattilo's strategic location at the bottom of the Calabrian peninsula and the presence in the village's territory of important fortifications led to its appearance in the chronicles of royal history. As we have seen from the archbishops' reports, there are also indications that the village was somewhat more populated in the late Middle Ages than in the early modern period.

The castle of Pentidattilo was already in existence in 1276 and played a role in the War of the Vespers (1282–1302) and in the later plans of the Angevin kings of Naples for the reconquest of Sicily. The enemies across the Mediterranean also could not be ignored, and in 1282 the village was briefly occupied by Arab troops. In 1323 King Robert strengthened the Pentidattilo fortress after receiving a papal authorization, necessary because the village was then a church fief. The area of Pentidattilo was at this time home to several Basilian monasteries, and indeed a local monk who died in the fifteenth century, Pietro Vitali, was beatified, joining in the local pantheon the earlier, and probably mythical, Saint Ursula of Pentidattilo. The village was prosperous enough in the early fifteenth century to justify a permit, granted in 1428 by King Louis III, to hold a fair on May 1 of each year. No traces of this fair remain in later documents, and it was probably discontinued because of the village's decline in population later in that century. The decline was accentuated when, as a consequence of the 1462 baronial revolt against Aragonese rule, Pentidattilo was sacked by Alfonso of Aragon, son of King Ferrante I.[25]

Under the Aragonese begins also the known feudal history of the village. Many of the kingdom's università were given as fiefs to noble lords by the late medieval kings of Naples, perennially in need of cash and military assistance, and by the fifteenth century titles began to be granted as well, so that the baronage came to be structured into a complex feudal hierarchy. Feudal lords in the kingdom enjoyed a wide array of powers, jurisdictions, and economic rights, so that fiefs were eagerly sought by ambitious and successful individuals and families. The Spanish monarchy, after acquiring the kingdom in 1503, greatly expanded this policy of granting fiefs and titles, thus creating, by the middle of the seventeenth century, a situation in which more than 75 percent of the kingdom's population lived under feudal rule.[26]

In 1477 Pentidattilo became a fief of the Letizia family; little is known about their rule there, and by 1509 the fief of Pentidattilo with all jurisdictions had passed to the Francoperta family. The Francoperta belonged to a secondary level of the feudal nobility and had ties of clientage with prominent titled families, such as the dukes of Montalto.[27] During the Francoperta's feudal rule over Pentidattilo the village found itself on the front of Christian Europe's struggle with the Ottoman Empire. It was in the mid-sixteenth century, for instance, that the coastal tower of Pentidattilo became an important defensive

structure, as is shown by the frequent investments in repairs and by the attention given by the Naples government to its proper maintenance. The Francoperta were directly involved in this struggle, and the lord of Pentidattilo participated in the battle of Lepanto with a ship armed at his expense. The village
also suffered from Ottoman and pirate raids, which would continue over the
following centuries, while the tower near Melito remained ready for defense
well into the eighteenth century.[28]

Pentidattilo grew in population in the sixteenth century, and as a result its
feudal revenues increased, probably keeping ahead of the inflation that characterized the century. The Francoperta, however, did not prove skillful managers of their fief, and by the end of the century the village's feudal income of
more than 600 ducats a year was burdened with substantial debts. The last
Francoperta barons were overwhelmed by their family's debts, and the fief
was eventually confiscated by the royal government and put up for auction in
order to satisfy the barons' creditors.[29]

The fief was sold for 15,180 ducats—implying annual revenues of about
600 ducats—to Simonello de Alberti, a merchant and landowner from nearby
Messina in Sicily. Simonello's grandfather Filippo had been the first member
of the family to move to Sicily, and he had descended from the Florentine
Alberti. The Messina Alberti had acquired substantial possessions in the city
and its environs, and their purchase of Pentidattilo presumably stemmed
from a desire to gain the status of barons. The merchant Simonello, however,
did not abandon his activities, and he seems never to have resided in his new
fief. In his will of 1601 Simonello left much capital invested in businesses in
Messina, in addition to houses, shops, and land in and near that city.[30]

The seventeenth century was as difficult a period for Pentidattilo as for the
kingdom as a whole, with economic and demographic stagnation or decline,
epidemics, and the revolt of 1647–48. Pentidattilo was also afflicted by frequent
Ottoman raids, especially in the 1660s. The income of many feudal revenues
was tied to the population of each fief and therefore tended to stagnate with
it. The feudal income from Pentidattilo, which had increased until about 1620,
declined sharply by the 1640s and continued to stagnate until the 1680s, when
the area's economy began again to improve. Nonetheless, unlike many other
feudal families, the Alberti were apparently able to preserve some financial stability through the century, although this result was not always achieved without friction with their vassal community. The Alberti also gradually changed
during the century from a merchant urban family to a titled, landed, noble
line, as evidenced by their residence patterns and marriage alliances.[31]

TABLE 1.3

The Feudal Lords and Marquis of Pentidattilo, 1509–1806

Ferdinando Francoperta (1509–36)
Giovan Michele Francoperta, grandson by son Giovan Nicola (1536–58)
Giovan Giacomo Francoperta, son (1558–85)
Giovan Battista Francoperta, brother (1585–89), fief sold

Simonello Alberti (1589–1602), married Caterina Alberti
Giuseppe Alberti, son (1602–26), first marquis 1619, married Antonia Saccano
Lorenzo I Alberti, son (1626–48), married Giovanna Mancuso
Domenico Alberti, son (1648–85), married Maddalena Vannechthoven
Lorenzo II Alberti, son (1685–86), married Lucia Cortes
Antonia Alberti, sister (1686–91), married Bernardino Abenavoli
Teodora Alberti, sister (1691–1758), married Francesco Ruffo and later Nicola Caracciolo di Brienza
Litterio Caracciolo di Brienza, grandson by daughter Imara Ruffo (1758–59), fief sold

Lorenzo Clemente (1759–90)
Alessandro Clemente, son (1790–1806), feudal system abolished

N O T E: The dates indicate the period of feudal rule.

When he succeeded his father, Simonello, in 1602, Giuseppe Alberti claimed not to know much about the revenues from Pentidattilo, because he did not reside there and was busy with other affairs in Messina. He became, however, increasingly involved with the fief during his rule there. In 1619 Giuseppe obtained the elevation of his Calabrian fief to a marquisate, and later the family also began to claim the title of duke of Melito, though I have found no evidence of the granting of this title. In 1620 Giuseppe also obtained the privilege known as *camera riservata,* which exempted Pentidattilo from military billeting, and in the 1620s he had a mill and a press built in the village. Giuseppe did not reside regularly in the village and continued to spend most of his time in Messina, though he actually died during a stay in his fief.[32]

Giuseppe's son and successor, Lorenzo I, married Giovanna Mancuso, the daughter of a Sicilian baron, who brought a dowry of more than 15,000 Sicilian scudi. By the time of Lorenzo I's death in Messina in September 1648, the relationship between the baron and the villagers of Pentidattilo was strained, following disputes over the baron's payment of the *bonatenenza* (the local tax on nonfeudal holdings), over the università's debts to its lord, and especially over the behavior of the vassals during the revolt just ended. At one point Lorenzo had asked the central government for assistance in forcing the people of Pentidattilo to obey his authority and fulfill their customary obligations. Shortly before his death, the marquis had agreed to a set of capitulations with the università, settled most of the outstanding financial disputes, and offered "a universal pardon for the uprising in his village." Despite the tension, Lorenzo had given, in any case, clear signs of his interest and involvement in the management of Pentidattilo by organizing several parcels of land and a few buildings into the start of the new settlement of Melito on the coast.[33]

In her book on the 1647–48 revolt in Calabria Ultra, Carmela Spadaro interprets the Pentidattilo capitulations within her argument that the revolt was led by discontented elites trained in the law who found themselves shut out of local power by entrenched oligarchies. While this may be a valid analysis for the larger towns in the province, it makes little sense in the case of Pentidattilo, where no closed ruling group existed and where in 1648 there was no elite trained in the law. Spadaro's interpretation of the 1648 agreement, then, as a series of damaging concessions to which elite villagers forced the marquis seems to me profoundly vitiated, though certainly the marquis's authority was strongly challenged and possibly somewhat weakened as a result of the upheaval.[34]

The events of 1648 may have been one of the reasons why the new marquis, Domenico Alberti, became ever more directly involved in the life of his fief. Under his rule the Alberti shifted their residence to Pentidattilo and oriented their interests and attention away from Messina and towards Naples and their fief. Domenico first made a successful marriage, when in 1652 he married Maddalena, daughter of Ettore Vannechthoven, a "Flemish merchant and Messinese nobleman." Ettore was the Flemish and imperial consul in Messina, and his father, Cornelio, had been a general under Emperor Rudolf II. Maddalena, elder of Ettore's two daughters, brought a dowry of more than 23,000 Sicilian scudi, most of which was in cash and precious objects and the rest in solid Sicilian tax farms. The Alberti still owned property in Messina, though the income was mainly devoted to the upkeep of elderly uncles and aunts in holy orders, the proliferation of whom is another indication of the family's new aristocratic identity.[35]

Domenico and Maddalena soon began to take more interest in their feudal seat. They gave donations to Pentidattilo's churches and chapels and became involved directly in the management of the fief, and by the 1660s the marquis was claiming a special ceremonial for the masses he attended in his village. The couple's first son and heir, Lorenzo, was born in Messina in 1661, but by the 1670s the family had moved to Pentidattilo. Domenico and Maddalena's last four children were born and baptized in the village between 1675 and 1681, and the whole family was living there, as is shown also by the birth there of young Lorenzo's own two illegitimate children. Domenico's brother Francesco was also residing in the village.[36]

In 1674 the city of Messina, for fiscal and administrative reasons, rebelled against Spanish rule and appealed for French help. It took the Spanish government until 1678 to reassert its control, and these troubled years greatly damaged Messina's trade and prosperity. These events most likely encouraged the Alberti's relocation and their embrace of their new primary role as barons and landlords. In the 1670s and 1680s Domenico built several houses in Melito to be used for raising silkworms, and the marquis was instrumental in the development of the production of raw silk in the fief. Both Domenico in his will of 1674 and Maddalena in hers of 1678 left several bequests to benefit pious foundations in the village as well as individual villagers, and Domenico also released the università from a debt of 728 ducats. Domenico's will was drafted in the Pentidattilo castle and witnessed by the two local parish priests and several other prominent villagers. The feudal administration thus increasingly engaged in cooperation and mutual support with both the village community and the more established village clans, especially at the time of transitions within the feudal lords' family, as we shall see later in this chapter.[37]

The family's orientation towards a different role and identity is apparent also in Lorenzo's 1685 marriage to Lucia Cortes, daughter of Pietro, counselor of the Sacred Royal Council and a prominent Spanish minister in Naples. This marriage brought a dowry of 4,000 ducats, the relatively small size of which indicates the value the Alberti placed on this alliance with the high ranks of society and government in Naples, where the family had no previous connection. Shortly after this marriage was agreed upon, Domenico died and was buried in the parish church of the village that had become his home. In May 1685 Lorenzo II was marquis of Pentidattilo, presiding over a family that consisted of his mother, wife, one brother, and four sisters. Soon the Easter massacre decimated the family.[38]

After the turmoil that followed the 1686 events, the fief and its title passed to Lorenzo's sister Antonia, and at her death in 1691 to their younger sister Teodora, who was living, like her sister, in a Messina convent under the guardianship of her uncle Francesco Alberti. By the 1690s the economy of the Pentidattilo region was improving, its population again increasing, and the value of the fief consequently grew. Teodora Alberti was an heiress, and in 1695 she married Francesco Ruffo, nephew of the duke of Bagnara and a member of the greatest family in Calabria and one of the noblest in the Kingdoms of

Naples and Sicily. Teodora's younger sister, Giovanna, married Aurelio Landolina, baron of Carcicera, and spent much of her life in Naples, engaging in a long lawsuit with her sister over the complex inheritance that had resulted from the slaughter of the sisters' family.[39]

Teodora Alberti, perhaps as a result of the trauma of 1686, proved a remarkably resilient woman. She managed her fief with a strong hand, which alienated some of her vassals, and she continued to reside there after the death of her husband, shepherding the village through the troubled early years of the eighteenth century, when war again came to the Calabrian shores and the kingdom passed from Spanish to Austrian rule. In 1722 she arranged the marriage of her only surviving daughter and heir, Imara Ruffo, to Domenico Caracciolo, marquis of Brienza and prince of Atena, of an established and prosperous branch of one of the two greatest clans in the Neapolitan nobility. The new couple lived for some time in Melito, where the family had by now an agreeable villa that offered an alternative to the old and imposing castle in Pentidattilo. In 1724 the forty-six-year-old Teodora married Nicola Caracciolo, her son-in-law's penniless thirty-year-old brother, but the young man's likely hopes for a nice settlement were dashed when he himself died four years later, to be survived by his wife for another thirty years.[40]

Teodora lived in her fief until the 1740s, when she moved to Naples. In 1740 she rented the fief for 1,500 ducats a year (plus a few contributions in kind) to a neighboring baron. In 1754 her daughter died, and Teodora's heir became her grandson Litterio Caracciolo. By the time of her death in 1758, at the age of eighty, Melito had become a prosperous village, the first citrus fruits had made their appearance in the economy of the area, and Pentidattilo was increasing in population and value. The village was again home to a notary and had access to a medical doctor, and its society was beginning to diversify and become more complex. Teodora still engaged in the patronage and paternalistic activities that her ancestors had practiced, and in her old age and in her will she donated money to various pious foundations in her fief. When she rented the fief in 1740, she had insisted that the tenant employ the services only of her vassals. In her will she released the università from some outstanding debts and ordered grain to be distributed to the villagers from her warehouse.[41]

By midcentury, moreover, a clear and wealthier village elite appeared in Pentidattilo. The università became in these years more assertive in its relationship with the feudal lords, perhaps also because of Teodora's absentee management in her final years. In the 1740s, disputes over debts occurred between Teodora and the community, and a long fight started over the community's rights of access to, and use of, the baronial forest and other land in the village, which would continue until the end of the feudal system in the early nineteenth century. Although his newly acquired fief was undoubtedly valuable, Litterio Caracciolo decided nonetheless to sell it, to strengthen his financial situation and better maintain his paternal family's ancestral fiefs. Pentidattilo was "too distant from his other fiefs," and it was "therefore very inconvenient to go there for the good management of the fief and its revenues."[42]

The sale was quickly concluded, and at the end of 1759 the fief and all the Alberti assets there were sold to Lorenzo Clemente, marquis of San Luca, who owned other fiefs in Calabria Ultra. Litterio Caracciolo maintained possession of the old Alberti property in Messina, and the title of marquis of Pentidattilo was declared extinct. The price for the sale of Pentidattilo was 68,000 ducats, indicating likely annual revenues of 2,720 ducats. The new lord never resided in the fief, and his rule, and that of his successor, in an age of increasing opposition to the feudal system, was characterized by continuous disputes with both the università and individual villagers. The disputes also became the focus of inquiries and lawsuits during the complicated procedures that followed the 1806 abolition of the feudal system.[43]

Although its new lords thus found Pentidattilo to be a troublesome fief, the village itself was experiencing a prosperous time in the second half of the eighteenth century. Melito had become the leading settlement in terms of economic and demographic growth. The coastal village had been established in the mid-seventeenth century, as we have seen, and in 1682 the marquis Domenico Alberti completed construction of the local church. By 1754 the dittereo left his traditional church of San Costantino in the old village and settled in Melito. By the turn of the century the new village, now about as large as the old one, was home to its own medical doctor. Although a notary operated again in Pentidattilo at the end of the century, in 1794 the old village had some difficulty obtaining a replacement for its deceased *arciprete* (head priest). In 1811 Melito became the head of the commune, and in 1845 the title of arciprete for the commune passed to the Melito parish priest, while the parish priest in Pentidattilo became the dittereo. By 1800 also citrus fruits had become an important source of local prosperity, and a structured and diverse local society developed, with many new family names appearing in village documents, something virtually unknown in the previous two centuries.[44]

Before the end of the eighteenth century, however, the village, like the whole of Calabria Ultra, went through perhaps its greatest crisis, namely, the devastating earthquake of February 1783. The quake struck primarily the western parts of the province, where it killed more than 30,000 people, or 10 percent of the province's population, but it severely damaged buildings and natural structures throughout the province and beyond it. Bagnara, the center most hit, lost more than 3,000 people. The royal government, under the influence of Enlightenment thought, responded not only with assistance but also with a broad plan for the reform of agriculture and property in the area, to be achieved through the expropriation of ecclesiastic property and its redistribution in small parcels to new owners, whose entrepreneurship, it was hoped, would stimulate the region's economy. The result was a large shift of landownership to a recent and growing rural bourgeoisie that did not necessarily manage its new assets with an eye to the general welfare of the region's economy and population.[45]

The area of Pentidattilo and Melito was not among the most severely affected, and no deaths were reported in the villages. Damages were substantial, however, and indeed the rock on old Pentidattilo, "almost out of its perpendicular, threatened to fall on the village." All the houses in the village were damaged and several ruined. Damages were estimated in Melito at 25,000 ducats, in Pentidattilo at 20,000, and in nearby Montebello, "the name of which [did] not correspond to the unhappiness of the houses and of the site," at 30,000 ducats. For the whole province damages were estimated at 31,250,000 ducats, plus more than 600 dead and almost a million ducats in damages in Sicily.[46]

Although the royal representative who toured the area found that in Pentidattilo there were still enough people to cultivate grains and beans and produce raw silk, all habitations were deemed dangerous, and a plan was proposed to abandon the old village and relocate the inhabitants to Melito and the coast. A report described Pentidattilo as "one of the most unhappy and pitiable villages of the province" and "most beaten and hurt by the harm and negligence of its baron." A project was prepared for the building of new houses in the coastal area, and more than ninety villagers put their name or cross, "with jubilant spirit," to a petition to relocate the village. The project, however, was poorly planned and financed, and the baron opposed it, because of its costs and allegedly because the new settlement would have occupied baronial land on which mulberry and citrus fruit trees were cultivated. Despite the claim that "the villagers live always with death staring them in the eyes," by 1788 the new mayor sided with the baron's arguments, and the project was dead.[47]

This project may indeed have been popular with the villagers at one point, but the sources, inspired by antifeudal rhetoric, probably exaggerate both the benefits of the plan and the power and motives of the baron's opposition. The old village never regained its previous role within the università even when later the commune and Melito continued to grow, but Pentidattilo maintained its population level well into the nineteenth century, and even after the devastating earthquake of 1908, which destroyed most of Reggio Calabria and Messina. But ultimately, after a gradual decline, the beautiful and majestic rock that had given the village its name and its protection for centuries led to the final abandonment of Pentidattilo by its inhabitants, leaving the old settlement to its prickly pears and its breath-taking views.

Administration

> Facinorosi . . . rozzi, queruli di mala fede, spergiuri, denunzianti, calunniatori . . . indocili
>
> Litigious . . . uncouth, whiny in bad faith, trustless, prone to denunciation and slander . . . untamed
> —G. M. GALANTI on the Calabrians,
> *Della descrizione* (1794)

Pentidattilo throughout the early modern period was a feudal università. As such it had two parallel administrative structures, one representing the community and the other the feudal lord, who in his fief operated as the delegate of the sovereign, in terms of the judicial and some of the economic management of the community. Two separate hierarchies of officers, therefore, existed in the village, each regulated in its handling of its tasks by the laws and traditions of the kingdom. Local administration was thus the locus of intense interaction between the state, the feudal lords, and the village community.

The major differences among the kingdom's università, from the point of view of local administration, depended less on whether jurisdiction in the community was feudal or royal than on the size and wealth of each community, and consequently on its degree of internal social differentiation. Larger università during the early modern period tended to abandon traditional democratic institutions and to move instead to oligarchic structures. In particular, the old community parliaments, gatherings of all male heads of households to elect local administrators and address issues of common concern, tended to disappear by the end of the sixteenth century from all large centers in which a clear elite had developed and gained the ability to control local

affairs and to establish privileged contacts with sympathetic central administrative organs.[48]

Pentidattilo, on the other hand, like many other small centers, did not de-
velop a hierarchically structured society until well into the eighteenth century. The traditional parliament survived, though none of its records do—if
any were ever kept. The capitulations between the village and the marquis
after the 1648 revolt, for instance, make no mention of separate orders of citizens. The earliest mention of a division of citizens into separate orders occurs
in the documents relating to the 1745 and 1759 Catasto Onciario, and on that
occasion the division may have been mandated by government rules about
the drafting of these documents. The division does not appear in any other
document until the nineteenth century.[49]

The village was administered by two mayors (*sindaci*) and four or five aldermen (*eletti*), who all served one-year terms, starting in September of each
year, and were elected by the assembled community. The blind, the deaf, the
mute, the imbecile, the "longtime" infirm, minors, bastards, Jews, heretics,
criminals, and women were excluded from these positions. On the other hand,
literacy was not among the skills necessary or even particularly desirable in
village administrators, as the services of a chancellor (*cancelliere*) sufficed for
the village's needs for written documents. The administrators were primarily
responsible for the università's finances and budget, for the management of
the università's property and of common lands, for the defense of its traditional liberties and privileges, and for its relationship with the state and with
its feudal lords.[50]

Income or indirect taxes and occasional excise and other fees constituted
an università's main revenues. They were used primarily to make the payments imposed by the royal government, which were levied based on each
community's assessed population. These taxes, and their collection from the
università, were often farmed out by the government to its own creditors or
to other private businessmen. The other major expense for the università consisted of payments, in money or kind, to the baron for various feudal rights
or privileges. The università's excess revenues could be used to pay local salaries (especially to the chancellor), religious expenses (such as the salary for
a preacher or communal charity), the community's debts, and especially the
lawyers' fees and other legal costs incurred in the course of the many lawsuits
in which università were often involved, like everyone else in the litigious
kingdom.

In addition to their primary responsibility for the università's payment of its taxes and debts, local administrators were also charged with the community's myriad contacts with the central authorities. The upkeep of the tower in Melito, the management of censuses, and the enforcement of royal edicts on various matters were tasks that brought all villagers, and especially the administrators, in contact with the state and its provincial representatives. The state also required information—for instance, on local prices—that the administrators had to gather, attest to, and transmit to the relevant royal officers. All villagers, and especially the administrators, also frequently interacted with the state and its agents during disputes with neighboring villages or with the feudal lords. All these situations implied the recording and formalization of villagers' opinions and testimonies, as did each passage from one feudal lord to another.

Although the frequency and variety of these occasions for contacts between villagers and external authorities make it clear that no village, however poor and small, was totally isolated, at the same time traditional rules for participation in public life point to stable communities in which outsiders were rare and regarded as different. In order to be a "citizen" of any università one had to have been born there, and a permanent mark remained on any residents who had moved to the community. The latter were identified as "foreigners," their fiscal responsibilities were different, they did not vote in local assemblies, and they were not eligible for local offices. The distinction was not purely legal but affected public perception of the "foreigners." In the trial of Domenica Orlando, her alleged lover, Pietro Crea, strengthened his claims of ignorance of the events and principals of the case by reminding the judge that he was not a citizen of Pentidattilo. The alleged abortionist, Anna de Amico, was immediately suspect to the Pentidattilo witnesses, they claimed, not only because of her activities but because she had been born elsewhere. In speaking of Anna's husband, who had left her and Pentidattilo, one witness stated that he could not even recall the man's name "because he was a foreigner in this village."[51]

The feudal lord was in theory enjoined from interfering in the università's own administration. Barons were forbidden from influencing the election of local administrators or the functioning of local institutions, and the capitulations between a lord and his fief detailed the limits of the baron's role and curtailed his ability to usurp powers and rights belonging to the community. The many lawsuits between università and their lords which occupied the kingdom's tribunals and the vast jurisprudential literature on these matters indicate that abuses of all sorts of course occurred, indeed frequently.[52]

Another source of conflict and potential abuse was the presence in each fief of a separate set of administrators, appointed by the baron and charged with the exercise of his judicial and economic prerogatives. The administration of the baron's economic interests, which included the exploitation of the baron's land and the management of the many feudal rights pertaining primarily to the economic life of the community, was entrusted to individuals chosen among the vassals. The rights, in particular, were usually rented by the baron's administrators to the highest bidders, who then exercised them year by year. Often each fief was responsible for providing its feudal lord with his managers, and usually there were two each year, known as the *erario* and the *conservatore*, respectively responsible for revenues in money and for those in kind. These managers could also be placed under the supervision of a general agent appointed by the feudal lord. Since baronial rights affected many aspects of public life and comprised the imposition of fines and the adjudication of many disputes, these administrators played an important and delicate role within each feudal università.[53]

Finally, the baron appointed officers charged with the administration of justice in each fief, who became the representatives of baronial authority and the delegates of royal sovereignty in the community. The principal one was the governor of each fief, who served as the judge in the feudal court. He was assisted in his duties by a legal counselor, when the governor was not a law graduate, by a scribe, and possibly by a servant, a jailer, and one or two guards. The court often also had available the services of two lawyers entrusted respectively with the defense of the indigent and with the legal support of plaintiffs. These officers, and especially the governor, could not be citizens of the università in which they served or vassals of the lord they represented. Their salaries were fixed and supposed to come exclusively from the proceeds, such as fines and fees, of their offices. These stipulations, honored in many cases in the breach, were meant to prevent undue partiality, involvement in village factions, and outright abuses or corruption.[54]

Even a small community like Pentidattilo had a complex administration and hosted a plethora of officers, in charge of various aspects of public life. In fact, this very mixture of jurisdictions, responsibilities, and interests could and often did result in litigation and increased the possibility of conflicts and problems landing in one of the many available courts. As the early modern period progressed, the Spanish government increased the state's concern for the proper administration of even the remotest communities, and state regulation of the behavior of both the università's and the lord's officers became more articulate and detailed. This led to ever more frequent contacts between every village in the kingdom and outside authorities, although the success of the latter in shaping village life and culture remains very much open to question. In increasing the complexity of administration and the number of rules affecting it, the early modern state, in Naples as elsewhere in western Europe, also attempted to limit opportunities for violence and upheaval and to broaden its own role as mediator of disputes and adjudicator of litigation.[55]

The close attention the state paid to local administration and the constant interaction between state agents and rules and the local community brought larger trends and issues to bear on local life, but villagers managed this relationship without abandoning their own values and practices. The autonomy and traditions of village culture, and the centrality of oral communication within it, survived centuries of state building.

Village Life and the Written Word

> Non vi sono negotii né si fanno troppe scritture.
>
> There is no business and few acts are written down.
> —Archivio di Stato di Napoli, Relevi 367.6 (1694)

Villagers were not passive recipients of the will, and objects of the actions, of the early modern state. The very production of virtually all documents about village society reflects the interaction of peasant values and state (or church) needs, of oral tradition and written culture, of local concerns and the aims of external authorities. An autonomous sphere of village values and practices continued to shape community life and the functioning of local administration.

Throughout the early modern period, few people in rural areas were literate, in the Kingdom of Naples as in most of Europe. The development of centralized states, however, meant that even the most remote villages were ever more frequently obliged to deal with written documents and the written culture of an increasingly bureaucratic central administration. The residents of Pentidattilo and other similar villages learned to recognize and respect the authority of the written word. While the community as a whole had to interact with the world of writing, however, within village society literacy remained only one source of influence and prestige, and illiteracy did not prevent many villagers from attaining, and successfully exercising, positions of authority and responsibility. Other factors, such as age and personal reputation, remained determining factors in a villager's status within the community.

The goals and needs of the state meant that the village, acting in its legally constituted identity as an università, often had to report to or inform the central authorities about a variety of aspects of its life. The royal government, on the other hand, had to rely on the cooperation and compliance of the villagers to achieve its aims and enact its decisions, so that most resulting documents are the fruit of this cooperation. Even aside from extraordinary and major demands of the government, such as the Catasto Onciario of the 1740s and 1750s, the village of Pentidattilo frequently communicated with provincial or central authorities, for fiscal, military, or administrative reasons. All these exchanges took place in written form, and in them the villagers had to attest to, and guarantee the truth and accuracy of, the information they provided to the authorities.

The università was responsible for regular communication with the royal administration regarding the size of its population and its tax responsibility. The central financial administration also requested regular statements of the prices of agricultural products current in each region and università. Moreover, Pentidattilo, which was home to a coastal tower, had to report to the military authorities on a monthly basis about the defense readiness of the tower, the skills of the captain and guardian there employed, and the punctual payment of their salaries. All these communications were prepared by the università's scribe and signed (or marked with a cross) by the village administrators.[56]

Another frequent reason for written communications between the village and the royal authorities was presented by feudal successions. Whenever the feudal lord died, villagers partook in a series of ceremonies recognizing the passage of lordship to the heir, which included both public rituals and the recording of statements by respected villagers acknowledging the heir as legitimate and accepting him or her as the new lord.[57] While this part of the transition took place in the village context, within a year the payment of the feudal succession tax involved the villagers in another exchange with the central authorities. The inquiries regarding the relevio brought representatives of the Sommaria, the kingdom's central fiscal court, to the village, where they questioned feudal administrators and other villagers on the extent of feudal land, the revenues of feudal assets, and the general accuracy of the income declared by the new lord.[58]

The village mayors and aldermen were therefore frequently called upon to attest to the truth of communications with the government and to the statements and quality of their fellow villagers. The administrators were rarely literate themselves. Illiteracy was no obstacle to achieving wealth or reaching prominent and respected positions that gave their occupants important responsibilities and influence in village life. Although over time it became more common for village administrators to be literate, this was still far from the norm at the end of the eighteenth century. At the end of the sixteenth century virtually all local administrators were illiterate, and, for instance, in documents from that time pertaining to the coastal tower they jointly stated that the certificates were "underwritten of our own hands, with the sign of the cross by us who do not know how to write."[59]

The mid-seventeenth-century documents show an increase in the literacy of village administrators, but the process was slow. Only one of the seven administrators who concluded the village's 1648 agreement with the marquis could sign his name. In the 1680s one of the erari was illiterate, even though his job responsibilities included bookkeeping. Five of the thirteen administrators and evaluators who prepared the 1745 catasto could not sign their name, and they included one of the deputies for the "middle" estate and the notary's own father. As late as 1759 and 1782 Pentidattilo had illiterate administrators, and in 1759 even the sons of a former chancellor could not sign their name. At the time of the 1759 census, 18 out of 178 heads of household could sign their name. Nor was this situation unique to Pentidattilo. A study of more than one hundred università in the early eighteenth century has shown that only about one-third of mayors could sign their name.[60]

Even though village administrators, and villagers generally, rarely knew how to read and write, written documents were crucial to the village's interaction with the state. In each generation at least a few villagers who had command of the written word were necessary to produce written documents, both to fulfill the requirements of the royal government, thus limiting its interference in village affairs, and to ensure the validity of transactions of special importance in the life of the community or sometimes of individual villagers. Although the content itself of what was written down in almost every case was shaped by the testimony and cooperation of illiterate village administrators and witnesses, the village needed a trustworthy source for the production of these written texts. There were several options available to the village community for this task.

The most obvious method to produce legally valid written documents was to employ a notary. The marquis and their family often did so, summoning notaries from Reggio or Messina, when they needed to draft wills or other important family documents. Few other people in Pentidattilo, however, felt the need to give the business they conducted the formal character of a notarial act. In fact, only three notaries were based in Pentidattilo in more than two centuries: Nicola Maria Pannuti, who was also the village scribe, at the end of the sixteenth century; Francesco Celia, also at times the chancellor, in the 1740s and 1750s; and Francesco Familari in the 1790s.[61]

In Naples and in other cities notaries might specialize in specific types of acts or work primarily for particular clients who needed their services on a regular basis, but in Pentidattilo they had to seek work where they could, and in fact they acted more often for the community as a whole than for individual residents. Celia, for instance, drew up only a handful of acts relating to the transfer of property during his eight years of recorded activity, and most of these pertained to property owned by clergymen, which needed more formalities. Celia also drew up only three wills and two marriage contracts in Pentidattilo. Property exchanges and family affairs in Pentidattilo rarely called for formal written records. The bulk of Celia's activity in the village consisted of notarizing agreements that involved several citizens, the feudal court, or the community as a whole and in drafting certificates of good conduct for local clerics, the occasional military officer, and once the governor himself. In these cases the notary really served as the scribe of a community action, writing down the statements of prominent villagers and feudal officers.[62]

For most of the early modern period there was no notary active in Pentidattilo, an absence often noted in the royal inquiries concerning the relevi payments. The villagers seem to have easily made do without one. In the absence of notaries, there were two men residing in the village who could be called upon to produce written papers of some legal validity. One was the *mastrodatti,* the holder of the feudal office of the *mastrodattia.* This office, which was rented out by the feudal lord, entitled its holder to issue official acts for citizens of the village in the name of the feudal court and to charge fees for them. The mastrodatti also served as the scribe for the feudal tribunal, as did Giulio Guerrera in the trial of Domenica Orlando. As a feudal officer, the mastrodatti often provided whatever formalization was deemed necessary for feudal rents and contracts and was in charge of the archive kept by the feudal court. His role extended beyond the service of the marquis, and the community recognized his potential usefulness for all villagers. Thus, for instance, in 1654 the mayors issued a formal certificate of praise for mastrodatti Domenico Costarella, "a legal person, faithful in his writings, which are authentic."[63]

The other officer who could produce legal written records was the università's chancellor or scribe. The chancellor was an officer of the community, appointed by the mayors, and the 1648 agreement between Pentidattilo and its lord stipulated that the marquis could not give the mastrodattia to the same man who held the position of chancellor. The chancellor was responsible for the preservation of community records and drafted most of the documents the università exchanged with the central government.[64]

In the actual life of the village, however, these offices often overlapped, given both the scarcity of literate villagers and the small income available from the production of written documents. Relevi documents, for instance, show that for much of the time between 1692 and 1696, "since there [was] no public notary," Paolino Malavenda was both the mastrodatti and the università's chancellor; in 1692 he was also one of the village's mayors. Malavenda himself testified that he had long been the mastrodatti, though the scarcity of business meant that he often failed to earn the 25 ducats that renting the office cost him.[65] This overlap of functions and positions was quite frequent in Pentidattilo and is further evidence of the limited need for formal written documents. As we have seen, the marquis at times appointed erari who were illiterate and who relied on the mastrodatti—or even on the marquis himself—for whatever writing their job required. On some occasions, when the erario was literate, he also held some of the other writing positions in the village. Notary Celia, who had already been the università's chancellor at the time of the 1745 catasto, by 1757, his notarial practice presumably abandoned, was serving the marquis as erario.[66]

The village, therefore, was never without one or two men capable of producing the necessary legal written documents. Yet literacy never became a precondition for village leadership or other important local positions, which presented a conflict between the hierarchies and values of the village community and the requirements of the state. The people of Pentidattilo resolved it by accepting, within limits, the function of written documents but also by maintaining alternative sources of authority and knowledge.

Written documents took on indeed a peculiar significance when few could read them. Texts were perceived as objects that were meant to be read but which also operated as symbols, representing in fact the very might of all powers extraneous to the community itself. That written documents were seen as powerful and important tools of the authorities is reflected in their fate in the 1647–48 revolt. In 1654 the two mayors and three aldermen—only one of whom was literate—declared that in 1647 "all the written papers which were in the castle of the Illustrious marquis of this village together with all the other papers written by the village scribes were burnt and set on fire by some rebellious and violent men who lived at that time."[67] The 1710 trial records themselves in a sense had a similar symbolic function. Although record keeping was required by laws and procedures, it was unlikely that anyone outside the village would desire or need to read the records of local trials. Yet the formalization of what the court did and of what the witnesses said made the events, and the conclusion reached by the court, official in the eyes of all villagers, literate or not, thus giving a symbolic legitimation to the community's judgment.

The written word was not the only means the people of Pentidattilo employed or recognized to organize reality and establish fact. In a community in which literacy remained very rare and the production and preservation of written documents were limited, the way things had been, or could be claimed to have been, in the past—the old ways, in short—maintained a strong probatory power and remained an essential argument for continuing current practices. The old ways were not based, in large part, on written evidence but on memory and oral tradition. There was thus less an evolution from an oral to a written culture than a system in which the two were complementary and parallel: truth and proof were based on both written and oral evidence. In cases in which the two were in contradiction, the authorities could use their strength to impose a resolution based on written documents, but the villagers were skilled at exploiting their own role in the production of those documents and the state's own respect for custom and precedent. Therefore, in the rural world, elite monopoly over writing did not exclude the illiterate majority from public power or influence.[68]

The people of Pentidattilo were aware that their way of doing things and of establishing proper procedures was an alternative to the written culture of the larger world around them. In several documents villagers pointed out that, within their community, there was little need for written evidence. In the 1655 relevio, for instance, the 1648 erario noted that he had had written documents prepared to guarantee the rents of feudal property only a few times, because such transactions involved "vassals" and "matters of little consequence." The 1655 erario in the same document stated that he had never had any rents written down, because with these "subjects" there was "no need for much formality in order to receive payments." In 1686, in listing the feudal assets, a later erario noted that the mill, like other property, was rented out "without any written act, but with a verbal agreement, as [was] usual in this fief." In 1694 the village scribe stated that his office provided him with little income, because in Pentidattilo "there [was] no business and few acts [were] written down."[69]

Oral tradition and the ways of the past were not, however, left to chance, and the villagers recognized the need for reliable criteria to establish truth, especially when faced with challenges from outsiders. The age and reputation of individuals and their skills and qualifications were crucial in determining their veracity and the value of their word, within the community and particularly in conflicts opposing the community to its lords, neighboring villages, or the central authorities. Old age in particular was an essential element of an individual's reliability and of his potential usefulness as a witness, and it provided an alternative to literacy as a source of prestige and influence. The respect and trust accorded to old villagers gave them a special place in matters of public concern. In some cases old age even overcame the customary exclusion of women from the role of witnesses and sources of information in public disputes.

Pentidattilo was frequently involved in disputes with its neighboring villages concerning the control of waters, the exact boundaries of each università's territory, and fishing rights and privileges. In all these cases it was essential to demonstrate to the provincial or central authorities called upon to resolve the disputes that the village's rivals were attempting innovations, which the state, no less than the villagers, deemed illegitimate, if not outright dangerous. Given the rarity of written documents, the testimony of respectable old people—and by contrast the vilification of rival witnesses—were the main weapons available to each community to triumph in this discourse of respect for the past.

This respect accorded to the old ways and by extension to old people is clearly articulated in the 1654 relevio inquiry. In order to establish the amount of feudal revenues, two old illiterate villagers, Gregorio and Menelao Squillaci, brothers aged eighty-four and eighty-seven and described as "ancient persons and of grave age," were questioned. Their testimony is followed by a sworn statement by the village's two mayors (only one of whom could sign his name) that indeed the two brothers were "persons worthy of trust, and truthful, and as such they [had] always been esteemed and held by this entire università." A similar declaration follows the depositions of two only slightly younger, and also illiterate, villagers.[70]

Other examples abound. In 1592, for instance, the village complained to the

Sommaria that the baron of Montebello had been attempting to stop the people of Pentidattilo from sharing pastureland, a privilege the Pentidattilesi had
enjoyed for "such a long time, that there [was] no memory of it being otherwise." In 1662 three old illiterate villagers, one of them aged ninety-seven,
testified that the salting of sardines fished in the area had been reserved to
Melito, in Pentidattilo's territory, "for as long as the world has existed." In
1669–72 a dispute over pastures and control of a stream opposed the village
and its marquis to the lord and the people of the neighboring fief of San Lorenzo, and again several old illiterate villagers testified not only about the
boundaries and the use of the waters and pastures that the people of Pentidattilo had traditionally enjoyed but also about the moral failings of the rival
lord's witnesses. One of them, the Pentidattilo side argued, was "a poor peasant" and had a wife who was "a public whore who [had] had many bastard
children," while another stole animals and had "a wife and daughter who
[were] public whores."[71]

Old people could also be questioned about private matters concerning their
fellow villagers. In the early eighteenth century, when the age of villagers involved in various disputes had to be ascertained, several times the consulta-
tion of parish documents was complemented by the questioning of aged villagers. Similarly, in other villages, old people were employed alongside parish
documents to establish family genealogies and the need for marriage dispen-
sations.[72] The specific qualifications of individual villagers could also offset
their illiteracy and make them authoritative witnesses. The evaluators who
assessed real estate at the times of the catasti and those who assessed church
land for the 1780s sales were all illiterate, but their testimony served a crucial
function in the village's economic life.[73]

The testimony of illiterate villagers was thus accepted and necessary to ascertain facts and events, despite the fact that such testimony lacked in preci-
sion when it came to matters of time. The age itself declared by witnesses was
often imprecise, as the parish records show, and there are many cases of ages
given in the 1745 census which do not match the ages given by the same individuals in the 1759 census. In peasant life, the season and the work cycle mattered far more than the calendar year. Thus, in the trial of Domenica Orlando,
her abortion was dated by different witnesses to three to six years before
the death of Domenica's husband, but they all agreed it had occurred in September. Other events were dated to the Carnival or harvest time. This vague
chronology was, of course, not unusual in rural experience, and it did not
diminish the value of testimonies.[74]

Arguments based on precedent and the testimony of old witnesses continued to have strong probatory power throughout the eighteenth century, when
access to written documents was becoming more common. In 1708, for instance, an agreement was reached to solve a longstanding dispute over pastures between Pentidattilo and Montebello. The two main witnesses for Pentidattilo were Giovanni Cancelleri and Domenico Manti, whose ages were
given as ninety-nine and ninety-seven, though they were more than matched
by Marco Schirrica of Montebello, aged one hundred.[75] Furthermore, when
in 1759 the università claimed that the marquis had usurped parts of the communal forest, at least thirty-eight witnesses testified, of whom only eight were
literate. These witnesses included several villagers in their seventies and eight-
ies and seven women. The women were all illiterate and either quite old themselves or able to report what their older female relatives had told them about
the village's history. The women witnesses in particular spoke of the villagers'
suffering under the marquis's extortions, especially the plight of widows, and
stated that, without proper relief, all of them would have to flee the village.[76]
The villagers were thus able to exploit the state's reverence for precedent and
to appeal to the rhetoric of the old ways and of the poor, small settlement
under attack by stronger neighbors or by its own vicious lords. The testimony
of old people, including women, was crucial to establish the truth, or at least
the credibility and reliability, of the community's position and statements in
these disputes.

The written word, then, did not dominate the village's public life, which
was characterized by the central role of custom, established through oral tradition and complemented by written texts. The village's small size and its simple social structure meant that documents were rarely written or preserved,
nor did they need to be. A village elite developed late and slowly in Pentidattilo, and literacy did not become a significant marker of community status.
Within the community, and in the production itself of most written documents about the village, oral traditions remained central, and the often illiterate villagers who were seen by their neighbors as the most fit to guarantee
and maintain them continued to play a major role in the public life of the
community and in its relationship with the outside world. Old age, specific
skills, and one's general reputation continued to be at least as important as literacy in shaping individual citizens' status, their influence, and their ability to
play a role in the community's public life.[77]

At the same time, the interplay between village traditions and external pressures meant that many villagers became used to offering formal testimonies

in diverse matters and circumstances and to seeing their statements transferred to the medium of written texts. This interaction also meant that villagers, and village communities, were far from unskilled, unprepared, or out-
maneuvered when they confronted other villages, feudal lords, or outside
authorities in the many struggles and litigations that formed the texture of
much early modern public life.

Pentidattilo was a fairly typical rural community of the early modern Kingdom of Naples. Like many villages, its location was not easily accessible, its
economy was closely linked to its ungenerous natural surroundings, and its
agriculture was traditional. Slowly, the development of raw silk production
brought some prosperity to the area, which increased when citrus fruits became the main local crop. Pentidattilo's population followed the general demographic evolution of the kingdom, which was not unlike that of much of
southern Europe. Geographic isolation and economic difficulty remained
constraints on population growth until the end of the old regime. Local society was simple and local culture mainly oral and traditional. Individual reputation and achievement remained crucial elements of local status.

Nonetheless, early modern Pentidattilo was increasingly integrated into the
larger worlds of the early modern state, the Mediterranean economy, and the
Catholic Church. By the late sixteenth century, if not already before, the village was forced to deal with feudal lords who often resided and had interests
elsewhere; with the administrative, fiscal, and military demands of the Spanish government in Naples; and with a committed Tridentine episcopate. The
values, traditions, and autonomy of the village community were affected by,
and responded to, these outside influences and, through a process of continuous negotiation and collaboration, shaped the developments that gradually
transformed village life in the eighteenth century.

Jurisprudence and Local Judicial Practice

The records of the trial of Domenica Orlando and her accomplices do not report events as extravagantly dramatic as those of the Easter massacre of 1686, but they offer a rare window into the functioning of justice at the local level and the life of ordinary villagers. The events reported in the records, and especially the detailed depositions of defendants and witnesses, give us insights into the village's economic, social, and cultural structures which richly complement the information available from other records. These trial records are a particularly enlightening source because they bring us close to a worldview articulated by the villagers themselves, and in particular by those, such as women and the illiterate, who were often not among the village's leaders or wealthier citizens. Although the trial records do not give us the direct and unmediated voice of the villagers, they reflect it more than other sources. More important, given the nature of the alleged crimes, the procedures of early modern justice, and the way in which the trial records were put together, the very process of the trial and its outcome reflect the values, beliefs, and attitudes of the village community in which it took place.

The records of most trials represent, of course, a narrative of events, endowed with and shaped by the court's interpretation of the meaning and repercussions of those events. Especially in the rural world, and particularly with moral and domestic crimes such as those of which Domenica Orlando and her accomplices stood accused, justice would, however, have come to a standstill if the prosecution had not also operated in the context of what villagers felt to be just, true, and convenient. The narrative that is the trial thus did not come only from the court but resulted from the contributions of and the cooperation between the court and the community. This creative interaction was the basis of the functioning of the judicial system. It does not much matter, in a sense, whether the story the records tell is a true one or not; in order to be told at all, it had to reflect what both the villagers of Pentidattilo and the men charged with administering justice among them found believable, likely, and acceptable. The story's effectiveness was founded on its plausibility within both judicial and village culture. This narrative, then, is imbued with, and hence reveals, the expectations, values, and perceptions of the villagers and their community, as well as the concerns, aims, and needs of the judicial authorities, and it provides access to both popular and learned ideas and views.[1]

In addition to the interplay of judicial and village values, the trial records also reveal the centrality of individual honor and reputation within the village community, the network of links between local women, the respective position of insiders and outsiders in village society, the expectations placed on men and women within the family and the community, and the fluidity, vibrancy, and relative egalitarian character of community life in Pentidattilo. The trial also occurred at the start of a period of transformations for the village economy, for its social and demographic structures, and for judicial institutions and practices.

The Trial Begins

> Plus est hominem veneno occidere, quam gladio.
>
> It is worse to kill a man with poison than with the sword.
> —Early modern jurisprudential commonplace

On Tuesday, March 18, 1710, Giovan Domenico Cuzzucli, also known as Lofaci, a native and resident of Pentidattilo, appeared in the local feudal court to make a denunciation regarding the death on the previous day of his brother, Antonino Cuzzucli, also nicknamed Lofaci. Thus began this remarkable trial that would involve many villagers from families both prominent and undistinguished in village society. It would also present the court with difficult issues pertaining to women's status in the village and in the family, sexuality and reproduction, the operation of the justice system, and its interaction with the networks and the culture of peasant society.

We do not know whether Teodora Alberti, marquise of Pentidattilo, and her husband, Francesco Ruffo, were in the village when the trial took place. The case would, however, prove so interesting that its records were kept by the feudal administration and, moreover, were preserved by the later masters of Pentidattilo even after they sold the fief in 1759, when they otherwise only kept records that had some bearing on family properties or ongoing litigation.[2]

Giovan Domenico claimed that his brother "had always enjoyed the most perfect health" but a few days before had experienced sudden "stomach pain with continuous vomit, and an inflamed belly," which eventually had caused his death. These symptoms, said Giovan Domenico, "evidently demonstrate[d] that they [were] caused by poison." Giovan Domenico's suspicions did not stop there, and he went on to accuse Domenica Orlando, his brother's widow, of the poisoning, alleging that she had acted in complicity with Anna de Amico and Pietro Crea, the latter a native of nearby Motta San Giovanni residing in Pentidattilo. The motive, according to the accuser, was an illicit relation between Domenica and Pietro. Giovan Domenico stated that Domenica "let herself be carnally known by Pietro." Anna had aided and abetted this relation, and she had given the adulterers "the comfort and the place to sin carnally" in her house, which was adjacent to Domenica's.[3] Pietro, the accusation went on, had promised, in the presence of Anna, to marry Domenica should she be free.

The accuser proceeded with an accusation only indirectly related to the murder of his brother. About four years earlier, he alleged, during a prolonged absence of Antonino, who had lived with his brother in nearby Montebello, Domenica became pregnant by an unknown man and obtained an abortion, in the fifth or sixth month of her pregnancy, with the help of the same Anna, a "woman little fearful of God." Abortion was a capital crime—as, of course, was murder, especially domestic murder—so Giovan Domenico's accusations were very serious indeed. Since all of this resulted "in significant ignominy, damage, and interest not only of the denouncer, but also of the entire people of this village," Giovan Domenico asked the court to proceed, investigate, and gather information, and he urged the jailing of the three accused "so that they be severely punished as the laws command for these most enormous crimes."[4]

Neither the denouncer and his deceased brother nor any of the three defendants belonged to wealthy families, and none of them enjoyed a prestigious position within the Pentidattilo community. They all, however, had a clearly defined station in the village, and they all, in different ways, were involved in a web of connections with their fellow villagers. Those connections would become evident during the trial and would greatly affect the trial's progress and outcome. Before examining village relationships and the structures of the local community, it is necessary to analyze the judicial institutions and legal traditions that provided recourse and attempted to exercise authority and control when local life was disrupted by events and disputes such as those concerning Antonino's death.

Following Giovan Domenico's denunciation, the circumstances and consequences of the death of his brother Antonino left the sphere of the household and family and became the concern of both the local court and the village community. The trial of Domenica Orlando and her alleged accomplices
took place in a traditional rural society, but one that would soon face significant economic, social, and demographic transformations. The early eighteenth century was also a time of increasing difficulties within the established
legal and judicial system, which were joined, in Naples as in much of Europe,
to new concerns about the rationalization and fairness of justice and the need
to mitigate both unnecessary cruelty and the arbitrary decisions of judges.
Indeed, cases such as the Pentidattilo one would provide one of the main
stimuli for substantial changes in judicial methods and principles.

The trial also illustrates an essential area of involvement and collaboration
between villagers and external forces. The procedures followed by the court
immersed the judge and his staff in a process of negotiation with the witnesses, the defendants, and village notables, which alone made it possible to
bring the trial to a conclusion. The Pentidattilo trial thus represents a rare and
detailed example of how a local judge and court dealt with the peasant society around them as well as with the large questions of early modern European
jurisprudence: how to reconcile the tradition that required a full and free confession or undoubted proof for unmitigated conviction with the difficulties
of ascertaining the truth about so-called hidden crimes, such as abortion,
adultery, or domestic poisoning; whether, when, and to what extent to apply
torture and what use to make of its results; how to question and evaluate witnesses. In short, the trial records show us how justice operated at the local
level.

In particular, because the Pentidattilo trial took place in the village's feudal
court, its records offer a rare example of the principles and methods that
guided what was, for a majority of the kingdom's population, the main, and
often the only, arena for justice. At the same time, these courts were bound
and regulated by the broader doctrines and practices defined by the traditions
of the kingdom and by Roman law, prescribed by royal edicts, and discussed
in painstaking detail in the myriad treatises penned by the many jurists in
which the early modern Kingdom of Naples (not unlike the modern Italian
south) was notoriously fertile. Since the kingdom participated fully in the general tradition of Roman law and jurisprudence, it differed but little, in its laws
and judicial system, from the methods and the doctrines obtaining in most of
Europe. Indeed, early modern Naples was an active center of legal studies and

later also of Enlightenment thought, and conclusions drawn from this study have a broad application.

One of the features of early modern Continental jurisprudence is that its authors, more so than their late medieval predecessors, overwhelmingly came from the growing numbers of judges and lawyers who staffed and practiced in the expanding courts of the early modern European states.[5] Therefore the question of the actual relationship between doctrine and judicial practice became an important subject of reflection and study. The study of legal treatises combined with that of any trial records offers the opportunity for testing this relationship in detail. The Pentidattilo case is a particularly useful vehicle for such a study, because this trial presented many questions that were of special concern to early modern jurists and to the states that employed them, including problems of proof, the status of women in law, and the treatment of sexual crimes.[6] This little court in an isolated village in a remote region of a relatively minor state was dealing—on the whole, effectively and intelligently—with issues and questions that represented central preoccupations whenever justice was discussed in early modern Europe.

Feudal Courts: Competence

> Imperandi, regendi, et iustitiam ministrandi
>
> Ruling, governing, and giving justice
> —CAPOBIANCO, *Tractatus* (1622 ed.)

In 1710 the feudal governor of Pentidattilo was one Giovan Andrea Amodei, who was not a law graduate and therefore was advised and aided in all legal aspects of his task by a counselor, Fabio Nesci. The court staff also included a scribe, Giulio Guerrera, to whose diligence, knowledge of procedures, and neat handwriting we owe the clear and complete records of the Pentidattilo trial. Guerrera belonged to a local family, but neither the governor nor his counselor, in keeping with laws and traditions, was a native of Pentidattilo or belonged to village families.[7] These were the men in charge of determining what had happened in the death of Antonino Cuzzucli and what response to give to his brother's denunciation. In their actions, these men operated within the limits of what the people of Pentidattilo were willing to help them to do, but at the same time they represented the feudal lord's authority, royal sovereignty, and the learned early modern conception of justice.

The definition of what constitutes criminal behavior, and the attempt to prevent, control, adjudicate, and ultimately punish such behavior, represent one of the main areas of state power and activity throughout European history. In particular, the fulfillment of these tasks was extremely important to the early modern process of state building, in Italy as in the rest of western Europe. The development of judicial and punitive institutions designed to deal with crime and the training and employment of the growing numbers of lawyers, jurists, and judges produced by European universities occupied much of the attention, and certainly spent many of the resources, of early modern governments. This applies perhaps more than elsewhere to the Kingdom of Naples, which was home to a notoriously litigious population and whose robe elite—the *togati*—achieved during the seventeenth and eighteenth centuries great wealth, influence, and power.[8]

The functioning of justice, however, was far from being an area of undisputed state power. At least partial management of justice had long been entrusted to landlords, clerics, or urban governments, though the state regulated the conditions of its exercise. The European monarchs of the Renaissance and early modern periods sought to expand their control over the territory and population they ruled and to limit the traditional powers and rights of forces such as the church or the aristocracy, at both the central and local level. The process of absolutist state building undoubtedly changed the relationship between the monarchy and its subjects and expanded the role of the state. Since the 1970s, however, historians have called into question the success of these policies. Historians of Italy's regional states in particular have pointed to the persisting strength of local elite groups and traditional institutions and to the continuing dialectic relationship between center and periphery. This is especially true of the judicial function, which the state strived to control and centralize. The aristocracy lost much of its political power as an alternative to monarchical power, and in Naples this process was accelerated by the entrance of the kingdom into the Spanish imperial system. But the economic and social prominence of the aristocracy, and its local power, remained largely undisputed well into the eighteenth century.[9]

Like many noble landowners throughout Europe, Neapolitan lords enjoyed the right of jurisdiction over practically all inhabitants of the villages and towns enfeoffed to them. Until the abolition of the feudal system in 1806, the term *vassals* was indeed used for all those subject to their lords' jurisdiction in the Kingdom of Naples. The Neapolitan feudal lords (known also as the barons) were, however, peculiar both in the extent of their jurisdictional powers and in the percentage of the kingdom's population subject to those powers. Until the end of the eighteenth century, more than 75 percent of the kingdom's population consisted of the vassals of feudal lords, and nearly all barons enjoyed full civil and criminal jurisdiction through the first appeal (what was known as the first and second instance), with many also possessing the right of second appeal (the "third causes"). This meant that, especially for the rural population, access to royal justice was so difficult and expensive as to be virtually impossible. Although feudal jurisdiction did not provide its holders with significant revenues in and of itself—the profits of justice in the form of fees and fines were usually estimated to pay for the costs of justice but no more—it represented a most important element in the panoply of feudal rights and powers and a crucial factor in the continuing strength of the barons' position in the kingdom until the early nineteenth century. The royal government made only modest efforts to limit these powers until the mid-eighteenth century, and even then the impact of Bourbon reforms was narrow.[10]

Feudal jurisdiction was broad and substantial, at least since the fifteenth-century concessions made to the Neapolitan barons by King Alfonso the Magnanimous. It was not, however, unregulated, and the kings of Naples issued twenty-seven edicts between 1466 and 1772 dealing directly with the powers and rights of feudal lords, many of which applied specifically to feudal civil and criminal jurisdiction; many other edicts regulating justice in general further defined the extent and the limits of the barons' power.[11] To analyze these edicts, a whole subgenre of legal treatises was published in Naples which discussed the mutual rights and obligations of barons and their vassals, with special focus on feudal jurisdiction, and the competence and personnel of feudal courts.[12]

The most important function of feudal courts was the administration of justice, both civil and criminal, for all the vassals of any given village or town constituting a fief. King Alfonso had granted almost all barons extensive jurisdiction, which found expression in the three formulations of *merum et mixtum imperium, gladii potestas,* and the "four arbitrary letters." Like any other feudal right, these supposedly had to be spelled out in the documents of formal investiture for each fief in order to be exercised lawfully by the barons, but in reality a strong presumption existed that all barons enjoyed these powers, and it was most rare for the vassals to succeed in challenging their possibly illegitimate use.

The first two formulations sanctioned the vast extent of feudal jurisdiction. They granted the barons the exercise of high and low jurisdiction, both civil and criminal, including the power to inflict the capital penalty. As de Angelis put it, the barons' jurisdiction "is called fullest and general . . . and it is circumscribed by no limits, but it grants the vastest power of giving justice." The baron enjoying these powers could "erect gallows," though he could not keep them standing except when needed for executions.[13]

The "four arbitrary letters" granted more specific powers, of varying importance. The barons who had received them could compose crimes the composition of which was usually reserved to the crown (such as the bearing of illegal weapons or certain grave forms of murder, but excluding the crimes of blasphemy and sodomy—held to be even graver);[14] they could proceed ex officio (i.e., in the absence of denunciation or complaint) also in crimes that could result in the death penalty or in mutilations and in cases of injury to the protected categories of widows, orphans, and ecclesiastics; they could punish the most heinous criminals without observing the regular forms of the law; and, finally, they could order the torture of highwaymen during the holiest feast days, and even at Easter.[15]

Feudal criminal justice was obviously not unlimited; there were crimes that it could not prosecute (most notably false coinage and the many forms of lese majesty), its procedures were occasionally controlled by royal courts (especially in the eighteenth century and as they pertained to the prosecution of murder cases), and, of course, in theory appeal was always possible to the provincial and then to the central royal courts of the kingdom. There was also, as in all of Europe, a parallel justice system in the church courts, which at times clashed with the secular system, particularly over so-called mixed crimes, such as blasphemy, adultery, and a varying number of moral crimes (heresy was indisputably reserved for inquisitors and bishops).[16] But in the rural world, where the only clerics usually were poorly educated scions of local families, the power conferred on the barons by feudal jurisdiction was indeed substantial, and considerable—and virtually unchallenged—its impact on the life of the vassal population.

No thorough modern study exists of the civil and criminal jurisdiction of Neapolitan barons, and records for feudal courts are rare and often unexamined. There are, however, substantial records for the activity of the feudal courts of the four main fiefs of the Caracciolo Brienza at the very end of the feudal regime. By this time the barons had faced a narrowing of their jurisdiction with regard to violent crime and particularly to murder, which was mostly reserved for royal justice after the midcentury, but the available information for the feudal courts of Atena, Brienza, Pietrafesa, and Sasso still provides an interesting and reasonably broad survey of the competence of baronial justice.[17]

Records survive of 328 cases, both criminal and civil in nature, which led to action in the feudal courts of these four fiefs between 1780 and 1806 (with one dating to 1774). These records range from complete trial records to just a sheet or two describing specific actions taken by or in one of the courts. In addition, there is a register containing a summary description of cases tried in the four feudal courts between 1742 and 1792, which offers minimal information about 180 cases not included in the 328 for which specific records survive. In total, it is possible to know the crime or matter at hand in 508 cases spanning the period between 1742 and 1806.[18] The resulting data are presented in table 2.1.

Although obviously the absence of murder trials weakened the role of feudal courts (there is only 1 case among the 508, in 1755 in Sasso), these data portray, even at the end of the feudal regime, an active system of feudal justice, not so much in the absolute number of cases with which it dealt (which average to about 12 a year for the four fiefs together in 1780–1806) but rather in the variety of the behavior and activity it sought to control and adjudicate. All types and manifestations of conflict within the community came before the feudal court; the sexual, moral, and religious behavior of the vassals was regulated; and disputes of a civil nature often found in the feudal court an arbiter accepted by the parties. Since the cases of disputed jurisdiction include examples of resistance to ecclesiastic tithes and to municipal authority, it appears that even the clergy and the università had recourse to the feudal court for the enforcement of their own rights and privileges.[19]

The many categories in table 2.1 can be further grouped depending on which aspect of community life they affected. Thus 213 cases, or 42 percent, related to personal violence and conflict (categories 1–2); there were 81 cases of theft, or 16 percent; another 81 cases, or 16 percent, resulted from disputes over property (categories 4–6); 73 cases, or 14 percent, arose from trouble in civil life (categories 7–10); 32 cases, or 6 percent, dealt with the religious and moral life of the community (categories 11–12);[20] 18 cases, or 4 percent with economic life (categories 13–14); and in 10 cases, or 2 percent, the court offered a recourse for the most diverse problems affecting the community, from the profanation of a tomb to the presence of a quack doctor, from a violation of paternal power over unemancipated children[21] to a dispute between a pharmacist and a doctor over the right to sell medicines.

While the specific characteristics of these four fiefs certainly affected the

TABLE 2.1
Cases Tried in Feudal Courts
(Caracciolo Brienza fiefs, 1742–1806)

Category[a]	No. of Cases	Percentages
1. Wounds, fights, insults, threats	208	41
2. Libel and defamation	5	1
3. Theft	81	16
4. Disputes over property[b]	38	7.5
5. Illicit cutting of trees	28	5.5
6. Arson and damage to property or animals	15	3
7. Disputed jurisdiction[c]	48	10
8. False deposition or falsity in official acts	12	2
9. Illegal weapons	7	1
10. Judicial actions[d]	6	1
11. Blasphemy	17	3
12. Sexual/moral crimes[e]	15	3
13. Fraud	9	2
14. Usury	9	2
15. Miscellaneous	10	2
Total	508	100

SOURCE: ACB, 94–108.

[a] The classifications are my own and often involved arbitrary decisions. Many cases include elements of different crimes (e.g., wounds may include insults or illegal weapons; rape may include attempted abortion); I have assigned each case to the category that seemed to represent its main feature.

[b] These include the violation of boundaries between landholdings, the usurpation of lands, illicit appropriations, etc.

[c] See discussion of these cases in text.

[d] These were not trials but judicial acts (such as a deposition, the record of an arrest, etc.) that were kept in individual files.

[e] These include rape (7), concubinage (2), the abduction of women (2), and one case each of sodomy, abortion, infanticide, and pimping.

activities of their feudal courts, there is no reason to doubt the general picture these records present of the workings of feudal justice. Feudal jurisdiction played a central role in community life, and its interplay with the villagers' attitudes, behavior, and beliefs was frequent and varied. Indeed, jurisdiction was a crucial element of community life. Villagers understood, and were familiar with, the local judicial system and were able to use it, and often to manipulate it, for their own goals and needs.[22]

The feudal court's function and competence did not stop at the administration of criminal justice. Civil jurisdiction involved the feudal court and its personnel in all aspects of the daily life of a fief's population and ranged in Pentidattilo, for instance, from disputes over property to paternity suits.[23] The court's main officer, the governor, by his presence gave validity to notarial contracts whenever a specialized *giudice a contratti* (contract judge) was not available. In a mostly illiterate world, the court also sanctioned and pro-

vided legitimation for important moments in the life of a village and its population. The court, like the università, was responsible for an archive of documents pertaining to the community. When a feudal lord died, it was the
court that kept and opened his testament and publicly declared and recognized the succession of his heir.[24] In small fiefs the court was also responsible
for the collection of seignorial revenues, another task that placed it at the center of community life.[25]

The baron, of course, could be, and often was, in conflict with his vassals
over the precise extent of his powers and jurisdictions. In these cases, litigation took place in the royal courts, and these suits could represent a heavy financial burden for both sides. Jurisdiction could also be the focus of heated
struggle between lords and vassals, as was the case in Pentidattilo and throughout the kingdom in 1648. But feudal jurisdiction could also be of benefit to the
vassals. An example is provided by the privilege (known as the *pescato*) enjoyed
by the people of Melito that all sardines and bluefish caught in the waters
around it should be salted in the village. This financially benefited both the
village and the baron, and the feudal court pursued violators of the village's
privilege. In these as in other cases, the governor added to his usual powers
that of acting as delegate of the Sommaria, the central royal court responsible
for the oversight of feudal monopolies and revenues.[26]

Feudal jurisdiction included the right to keep a prison in the fief, at the
expense of the baron, who was also required to provide food for indigent prisoners. The feudal prison was also the object of regulations and occasional
conflict, and it certainly added to the power of the feudal lord and his representatives. Disputes centered on the quality of the prison (which should not
be "dark, subterranean, or fetid"), its financing (often barons tried to shift the
cost onto their vassals), the abuse of prolonged detention, and the existence
of separate prisons for civil and criminal delinquents and for men and women.
One Neapolitan jurist worried that a feudal prison was an "evil house, horrible and filthy place, home of the devil, consumption of the good, solace for
one's enemies, trial for one's friends, tomb for the living, correction of sins,
similitude to death, tearing of the body, harsh torment, squalid, form of torture and slavery, worse penalty than working in the fields."[27]

The università of Pentidattilo had reached a comprehensive agreement
with its lord in 1648 that included a pledge "that women may not be jailed in
the criminal prison, except in capital cases, but otherwise they should be confined to their own home after posting bail." Moreover, the università could

build and keep its own prison for civil delinquents and choose its warden, by paying the marquis sufficient bail to prevent (or cover) escapes and losses. Wherever the lord had an old castle to use as residence and administrative center for the fief, as was the case in Pentidattilo, the prison traditionally was part of it. By the eighteenth century there were prisons in both the castle in Pentidattilo and the smaller, more modern residence the marquis used when in Melito, although by the early nineteenth century—when, with the abolition of the feudal system, they ceased to be necessary—they seem to have been both damaged.[28]

Feudal jurisdiction was therefore very extensive, and it affected the life of the vassal population in many different ways. The baron, through his court, was a judge, a mediator, a facilitator of the community's public life, an enforcer of the community's moral values, a potential helper, but also a potentially oppressive jailer, and he could have the power of life and death over his vassals. Undoubtedly, jurisdiction greatly strengthened the influence, control, and power—and could add to the revenues—of feudal lords and was arguably the most crucial element in the continuation of the feudal system in the Kingdom of Naples until the start of the nineteenth century.[29]

Feudal Courts: Personnel

> Nisi essent doctores mundus esset in tenebris . . . suntque doctores veluti stellae in firmamento coeli.
>
> If there were no lawyers the world would be in darkness . . . and lawyers are like stars in the firmament of heaven.
>
> —DE ANGELIS, *Tractatus*

Lawyers, jurists, and royal administrators spent considerable time defining and regulating the identity and qualifications necessary in the personnel staffing feudal courts. The main officer of the fief, as of any royal town or city, was the governor, also known as the captain because of the military origins of the office. In the fiefs the governor was the baron's delegate in regard to the administration of justice, and barons were required to appoint a governor, to delegate to him their full jurisdictional authority, and not to interfere at all in the administration of that authority.

Even a baron who resided in his fief could not exercise his jurisdiction in person. Although he could occasionally attend the feudal court, which usually met in the feudal castle, the baron was barred from attending specific judicial actions such as the questioning of witnesses or the infliction of torture, at which the governor's presence was required. The main reason for this regulation was in the potential conflicts between the lord and the vassals, in dealing with which the governor was expected to play a neutral role. The governor was in fact appointed by the baron but was responsible to royal justice for his behavior and observance of the laws of the kingdom and was subject, at the end of his term, to an evaluation period (called the *sindacato*) during which the villagers could bring grievances against him.[30]

Laws and jurists' opinions spelled out several requirements and qualifications for the baron's choice of governor. The two main concerns were to prevent the venality of offices and to make the governor as neutral a member of the community as possible. The barons were repeatedly enjoined from selling the office of governor and other judicial offices in their purview. The governor, like the court's other officers, was to be paid a salary drawn from the profits of justice, but he was not in theory to have other opportunities to benefit financially from his office; as de Angelis put it, "the magistrature ought to be a burden, not a benefice." Therefore the power to compose suits was limited, in order to prevent the barons or their officers from selling justice. The fact that these prohibitions had to be repeated by successive Spanish viceroys points to the persisting abuses inherent in the system due to the weakness of royal central control.[31]

The governor served for one year, beginning in January. He could not be a native of the fief or a vassal of the baron appointing him, so that he be as free as possible from undue influence of the lord and from familial or other local obligations and ties. There was great concern lest justice be affected by the powerful ties created by family, clan, and other forms of social relationship, and the governor was forbidden from marrying in the village during his tenure and barred from becoming the godfather of a local child.[32] The baron could also not appoint his own relatives or any foreigners (Spaniards were not considered foreigners in the kingdom).

As another remnant of the military roots of the office, the governor was not required to have a law degree (though it was held to be advisable that he be literate); if he did not have a law degree, the baron had to appoint a counselor who did, and the counselor would have to attend all judicial actions taken by the court and advise the governor in all legal and judicial matters. De Angelis also asked himself the "elegant question of whether offices can be conferred upon women," since, after all, women could hold fiefs in their own right in the Kingdom of Naples and appoint governors and were therefore not inherently incapable of exercising jurisdiction; he concluded, however, that the honesty and modesty of women argued against appointing them to judicial and other offices.[33]

No study exists of the feudal governors as a group, but in many cases (though not in 1710 in Pentidattilo) they seem to have come from the large ranks of provincial lawyers eking out a living by serving feudal justice across the kingdom. The profits to be made from these offices were small and probably declining in the eighteenth century, but the barons—who were allegedly more jealous of jurisdiction "than of the honor of their wives"—were ready to accommodate any available candidates.[34]

The doctrine of the jurists and the laws of the kingdom were thus designed to make the governor a neutral arbiter and judge for disputes both within the community of the fief and between members of the community and the baron. Their success in doing so is open to question. In almost all cases of conflict between the lord and the vassals, the governor could be found on the baron's side. In 1621 in Pentidattilo, for example, the marquis refused to pay his local tax to the università, and the governor not only sided with his employer but threatened "with armed men and without fear of God nor of justice" the representatives of both the central and provincial courts who came to Pentidattilo to try to resolve the dispute. In many cases, however, in which the baron had no personal interest or potential gain, the governor's short tenure and lack of local ties probably made him as impartial a judge as might have been possible.[35]

The baron also appointed a number of other judicial officers. If the baron enjoyed second-degree jurisdiction, and most did, he had to appoint an appeals judge who was to reside, if at all possible, within a few miles of the baron's fiefs, so as to reduce the cost of appeals to the vassals. The governor had a small staff serving under him, also appointed by the baron. The counselor when necessary, the mastrodatti, a servant, a jailer, and one or two guards usually composed the entire personnel of the court. The mastrodatti was also not supposed to be a native of the fief where he served, though this requirement was waived in small fiefs, as it was in Pentidattilo, and the fees he could charge were to be carefully specified to avoid graft and corruption.

There were two other members of the feudal court. Like all royal courts, the baron was obliged to provide a defense counselor for indigent defendants, though, as we shall see in Pentidattilo, this help could be given in a supremely negligent and reluctant manner. The baron was also allowed what was technically called a *coadiutor curiae* (helper of the court), who acted as a prosecution lawyer. Royal courts had a *procurator fisci* to guard the interests of the treasury (*fiscus*), but, since feudal courts had no treasury of their own, they were not allowed the exact equivalent. The coadiutor supported plaintiffs and presented the case for the prosecution, but, unlike his equivalent in royal courts, he could only join the proceedings after the court had gathered the evidence from documents and witnesses and formally charged the defendant. To protect the formal equality of the parties before the court, the defendant and the plaintiff with his coadiutor were supposed to see what information the court had collected at the same time.[36] This situation resulted from the confusion due to the court's role as both prosecutor and judge, typical of the inquisitorial procedure, which I shall discuss further below.

These officials, who were, or became, well known to villagers, served to root local justice deeply in rural communities. As we saw in Chapter 1, the università also appointed officers of a more or less legal character, such as the chancellor. The baron was not supposed to interfere with their appointment and duties, and they received their salary from the università, but they often interacted and cooperated with the feudal officials.

In conclusion, while abuses and corruption could and frequently did take place, feudal courts labored under the control of royal laws and tribunals. Their sphere of competence and the qualifications and activities of their staff were carefully defined in edicts and in the jurisprudence, and these definitions were largely obeyed. The result was to create a system of feudal justice which operated under much the same standards and rules as the system of royal justice (which, of course, was itself far from immune to corruption and abuses). This result was reinforced in the area of procedures and methods, in which the same principles and theories drawn mainly from Roman law directed the workings of all tribunals in the kingdom. These doctrines and procedures, however, given also the weaknesses of documentary evidence in the early modern period, forced all courts, and particularly those charged with the administration of justice in the rural world, constantly to gain the cooperation of the population in whose midst they operated.

Judicial Procedures and Methods

> Facilius est captum liberare quam liberum capere.
>
> It is easier to free the captured than to capture the free.
>
> —AMBROSINO, *Processus*

With the decline in late antiquity and the early Middle Ages of Roman law and imperial institutions, judicial practice in western Europe came to be characterized by oral procedure and direct confrontations between the parties. Trials could only begin with an accusation lodged openly by an accuser (hence the name of accusatorial procedure by which this system is known), and decisions often depended on the result of ordeals and other nonjudicial methods. The system could not easily detect crimes that had no witnesses and left no visible victims or traces. The church began early on to criticize the use of ordeals on moral grounds. By the thirteenth century, faced with a wave of heretical movements,[37] the church also became increasingly preoccupied with the repression of what it saw as highly subversive and dangerous beliefs and behavior that the existing system was largely impotent to suppress. The result was the development of an alternative procedure, applied first in canonical courts. This inquisitorial procedure gradually spread to the secular courts of the newly strengthened Renaissance states. It was codified in the Holy Roman Empire with the *Constitutio Criminalis Carolina* of 1532 and in France with the Ordinance of Villers-Cotterets of 1539.[38]

The spread of the inquisitorial procedure was accompanied and often preceded by the renewed intellectual interest in Roman law, which became the focus of most continental European jurisprudence in its analyses of both canon and secular law. Italian universities were an early center of the new legal studies, and by the fourteenth and fifteenth centuries most Italian states were changing from old communal and private systems of justice to a codified inquisitorial procedure. In the Italian regional states as in all of continental Europe, the new procedure contributed to the centralization and the more public character of justice as a fundamental attribute of the early modern state.[39] The attempt of Renaissance and early modern states to assert and establish a monopoly on justice, or at least the supremacy of royal justice, is evident also in the creation of a complex system of appeals from inferior jurisdictions to royal tribunals and in the spread and publicity of executions.[40]

The inquisitorial procedure was a written one, and it became increasingly a secret one, in which the rights of the defendant were ever more severely curtailed. Although the guarantees of freedom and fairness which both Roman law and medieval tradition had included never disappeared entirely from the theory and even from the practice of justice in continental Europe, there is no doubt that the repression of crime became the overwhelming preoccupation of secular and church courts in all states, much to the detriment of the ability of defendants to make, let alone prove, their case. Indeed, paradoxically, some of the old guarantees of fairness resulted in doctrines and practices concerning proof which made the inquisitorial procedure ever harsher to modern eyes and which led, by the eighteenth century, to calls for significant change and reform.[41]

One of the main novelties of the inquisitorial procedure was the very mechanism that set it in motion. Rather than proceeding solely on the basis of open accusations, the new procedure could be, and in most cases was, started by secret, even anonymous denunciations, as well as by the ex officio initiative of the magistrate. The judge himself ceased to be the arbiter between the parties he had been in the old procedure and joined in his person the functions of both prosecutor and evaluator of the evidence he himself had gathered. In the case of collegial magistracies an individual judge would usually gather the evidence to prosecute, and then the whole body would assess it and pronounce the sentence. As the jurists put it, the judge was not only the judge of the law but also the judge of the fact, two functions that remained separate in the English system of trial by jury, in which the jury judged the facts, while the judge served as an arbiter during the trial and pronounced the sentence at its end.[42]

If the denunciation was found to have some merit, the judge proceeded with the gathering of evidence, the so-called *processus informativus* (investigative process). This started with an examination of the corpus delicti (the "body of the crime"), namely, the corpse of a murder victim, the wounds of an assault or rape victim, or any other material evidence that may have been left behind by the criminal. In this examination the judge should have recourse to the advice of experts, in most cases physicians, and in fact the evolution of the inquisitorial procedure stimulated the development of legal-medical studies on the Continent.[43] Further evidence could then come from documents or objects, but in the great majority of cases it came primarily from the testimony of witnesses.

The judge thus proceeded to the calling and questioning of witnesses. These were chosen among the defendants' and plaintiffs' neighbors, friends, or relatives, or others who may have information about the matter at hand; each witness was also asked to name other possible witnesses. The interrogation, usually under oath, began by asking the witness for his name, age, occupation, and family.[44] Jurists insisted that the questioning not be leading or in any way suggestive and that witnesses always be asked *de causa scientiae,* that is, how they knew what they knew. The standard example of how this question worked was the case of witnesses testifying to nocturnal events, whose deposition would be suspicious if they did not say that there had been a full moon.[45]

The "quality" of the witness weighed very heavily in the assessment of his testimony, and indeed "vile" or "infamous" witnesses were not to be given much importance, if they were to be heard at all. These categories included those who had been declared "infamous" by previous condemnations and entire groups of people considered unworthy by definition, such as prostitutes and their protectors, guards, Jews, grave diggers, or butchers.[46] The testimony of others might be invalidated, or at least weakened, by their relationship with the defendants; this applied to servants, relatives, enemies, and so on. Other categories were suspect for reasons of sex or age. Usually the testimony of those under a certain age carried limited weight. In the Kingdom of Naples the testimony of children under eighteen years of age was considered weak, and those under ten and a half did not take an oath at all, though their testimony could be used to strengthen circumstantial evidence, as we shall see in the Pentidattilo case. If there was any suspicion of complicity or reluctance on the part of the witness, and if the gravity of the crime justified harsh measures, witnesses could be tortured at the discretion of the judge.[47]

Thus the doctrine on witnesses, and the practice of courts, gave great weight to their group and individual identity. In particular, personal reputation and honor were crucial in determining the authority of each witness's words, as we have seen in Pentidattilo also outside the court system. Witnesses were definitely not all equal, and in the context of a closely knit village the court was bound to take into account all villagers' status and reputation in deciding whether and how to question them, what to ask them, and what significance to give to their testimony.

After the gathering of evidence the judge decided on the arrest of the defendant, although, in cases of heinous crimes or whenever the judge had reason to fear that the defendant might escape, the arrest could be ordered even before the examination of the corpus delicti, as was indeed done in Pentidattilo.[48] The next step in the procedure consisted of the examination of the defendant in prison. The procedure until this point had been, in theory, completely secret, so that the defendant might well have no idea of why he had been arrested. Since he was to be denied any contact with the outside world until formally charged, all he could learn of the trial depended on what the judge allowed him to know, although it is unlikely that this secrecy was always effectively maintained.

The judge was supposed to make good use of the defendant's ignorance. The first question, after self-identification, was to be what the defendant thought might be the reason for his arrest, in the hope that he might reveal crimes or accomplices hitherto unknown to justice. The laws required the investigating judge to conduct all interrogations, which had to be faithfully transcribed by the attending scribe, as was the case with all witnesses. Again, no leading or suggestive questions were allowed, and the judge's goal was to corroborate the evidence already at his disposal and to gain a confession. At the judge's discretion, the defendant might be confronted with the witnesses' depositions. Ambrosino recommended, before doing this, asking the defendant for his opinion of the character and truthfulness of both the witnesses and other acquaintances and about his relationship with them, so that the judge might find out possible enmities that would invalidate or vitiate some depositions.[49]

The interrogation of the defendant concluded the gathering of information. Torture was not applied during this phase, except for the growing number of crimes held to be particularly grave. At this point the defendant could be formally charged with the accusation, the truth of which became the official position of the court. This was known as the "publication of the trial," since only at this point was the defendant supposed to learn all that the court knew, and many jurists referred to it as the "beginning of the fight" between the defendant and the prosecution. If the defendant had not confessed and there was as yet no full proof, the defendant was held to have "contested" the case, as happened in the Pentidattilo trial.[50] The witnesses now had to repeat their depositions or take an oath in front of the defendant as to their accuracy, a step known as the confrontation.[51] The defendant was at this point given the "terms of defense," which consisted in a number of days (usually three) during which to prepare his case with the aid of his lawyer. The court provided a lawyer for indigent defendants. The judge and any accusers used the same time to strengthen (or "fatten"—*ad impinguandum*) their case.

The defense could present new witnesses who testified to the character or the actions of the defendant and attempt to weaken or invalidate the court's evidence, especially by presenting arguments for the rejection of the prosecution's witnesses. The defense witnesses could also be rejected by the plaintiff, though not by the court itself, and a few days were allowed for this.[52] When, as in most cases, the defense failed to sway the court, and when the crime was punishable with corporal or harsher penalties (which was the case with a large number of crimes), the judge could order the torture of the defendant in order to obtain a confession. The use of torture was justified not only by the concern with the repression of crime but also by the very emphasis on avoiding the arbitrary decision of the judge and on creating absolute, objective standards of proof. Torture was carefully regulated in law and doctrine, as to duration and method. Unlike its twentieth-century incarnation, early modern torture was a regular, thoroughly structured part of criminal procedure. Because it could not simply be applied until the defendant confessed, torture could therefore be resisted.

The defendant was to be encouraged and threatened until the very last minute before torture and throughout its duration, in the hope of diminishing the infliction of pain. A medical examination was necessary before torture could be applied, and a physician was to attend the torture, in order to prevent life-threatening pain. To avoid excessive pain and vomiting, torture had to be inflicted several hours after the defendant had eaten. Certain categories of defendants, such as the old, the infirm, the very young, or pregnant women, were exempted from torture, as were, at least for most crimes, privileged groups such as priests, nobles, and—perhaps unsurprisingly—judges and "illustrious jurists."[53]

By the sixteenth century most types of torture had become obsolete, and the forms of torture most commonly used in western Europe were the compression of limbs and the suspension. In the latter, which was used in the Pentidattilo case, the defendant's arms were tied behind his back, and he was then tied to a rope, suspended in the air, and left hanging for a duration not to exceed one hour, "except in the most enormous crimes." In the case of heinous crimes, and rarely by the late seventeenth century, the torture could be hardened by hanging weights from the defendant's feet, by whipping him while he hanged, or by suddenly dropping him until he almost reached the floor, thereby dislocating his joints (the *strappado*).[54]

Torture could usually be applied up to three times in separate days, though again for grave crimes it was possible to continue further. A confession given under torture had no validity unless ratified the next day by the defendant. Refusal to ratify, however, usually resulted in renewed torture. Although we do not know much about the effectiveness of torture, it seems to have been, if not a "relatively mild ordeal," certainly not as effective as legislators might have hoped. Cardinal de Luca believed that suspension had become "very familiar, and easy to sustain": "The larger part of the tortured sustains it without difficulty." The rate of confession under torture in France went apparently from 10 percent or less in the sixteenth century to less than 3 percent in the following century, and confessions were rare also in Habsburg Spain, though rates of 40 to 90 percent have been reported for the Holy Roman Empire.[55]

After torture and possibly confession the defendant had a last chance to defend himself against his own statements. Finally came the sentencing. Apart from capital sentences, punishments included corporal penalties, banishment or exile, service in the galleys, pecuniary penalties and fines, or, increasingly by the seventeenth and eighteenth centuries, imprisonment. While prison terms were used as forms of punishment in canon law, most jurists until the seventeenth century stressed that prison was not to be used as a punishment but only to detain the defendant during the trial. There was special concern, therefore, that prisons not be too harsh, since they were not meant to be a punishment in themselves, and in the Kingdom of Naples, as we have seen, the quality of feudal prisons was frequently the object of conflict between the barons and their vassals. Gradually however, because of the spread of galley service and of workhouses for the poor and vagrant, which employed detention as a punitive measure, prison terms came to be used as penalties, usually accompanied by hard labor.[56]

All the aspects of this procedure applied, with small variations, throughout continental western Europe and to all tribunals. In the Kingdom of Naples there was, however, a significant difference between the central royal court of the Vicaria in Naples and all other courts. The Vicaria had the special privilege of torturing defendants in grave cases during the processus informativus, that is, even before the publication of the trial. Since this meant torturing before having given the defendant a chance to present a defense, it could be done in theory only in the presence of "evident, clear, urgent, legitimate, and probable" clues, such as no defense could likely refute; even a single clue could suffice, provided it was "urgent, nearest, certain, and undoubted." As the vagueness of these words itself suggests, in practice this privilege was widely applied and probably widely abused. Its usurpation by provincial royal courts and by feudal courts was strenuously resisted by the Vicaria and by Neapolitan jurisprudence, though gradually some of those courts came to enjoy the same privilege.[57]

The inquisitorial procedure was thus secret, written, biased against the defendant, and favorable to the centralization of justice. However, it also de-

pended very heavily, in order to operate and to achieve convictions, on confession and especially on the testimony of witnesses. Given also the prevailing
theory of proof, witnesses were an essential basis of the justice system. Public
opinion and the reputation of defendants and witnesses within their community were of crucial importance. This made, as happened in Pentidattilo,
the cooperation of the community with the judicial authorities critical to a
successful investigation and trial. The relationship between individual witnesses or defendants and the justice system was mediated through family and
community, and witnesses in particular often expressed, and were expected
to express, less their own views than those of their community. Thus many
crimes went unreported, and many criminals were not prosecuted, or fled
prison or otherwise escaped conviction and punishment, because local opinion did not condemn them. This meant that outsiders of all sorts were frequent targets of criminal inquiries and that they were disproportionately represented among criminal defendants, especially among the convicted, as was
the case with Anna de Amico in Pentidattilo.[58]

The Pentidattilo Witnesses

> Intesi parlare et io per coriosità mi avicinai.
>
> I heard talk and out of curiosity I drew nearer.
>
> —VITTORIA VERNAGALLO, in the
> records for the trial of Domenica Orlando

Early modern jurists produced many treatises, both prescriptive and descriptive, to consider the inquisitorial procedure and its implications and to discuss in great detail the varieties of circumstances that, in the ingenious imagination of these writers, could affect the application of the procedure. We do
not know how the prescriptions of jurisprudence reached rural areas. It is
doubtful that anyone involved in the Pentidattilo trial, except counselor Nesci
and the lawyer advising the plaintiff, had received any formal training in the
operation of justice. Yet it is clear that several villagers were familiar with the
workings of judicial procedure and that all were accustomed to the process of
giving testimony and of interacting with the language and rituals of the law.

The procedures the feudal court of Pentidattilo followed in the 1710 trial,
and the depositions it gathered, give us an opportunity to see how jurisprudence became judicial practice. They also reveal much about a rural commu-

nity's involvement with and understanding of the judicial process. The villagers knew how central their role was in shaping the outcome of the trial, and it is evident that each of them brought to his or her participation in this trial a specific judgment of the events and of their protagonists, at the same time as they all brought to it their community's sense of the events' meaning and impact. The records make plain the pivotal role of individual reputation and honor within village society and the community's protection of its settled members to the detriment, if necessary, of outsiders, even those who had temporarily earned a useful role in the community's life.

Immediately after Giovan Domenico Cuzzucli's denunciations, the trial records list eleven witnesses to be questioned by the court about the case. The same day, March 18, 1710, the court issued a more formal order—solemnly headed by the names of King Charles, Francesco Ruffo, marquis of Pentidattilo, and Governor Giovanni Andrea Amodei—to twenty-four people in Pentidattilo to appear as witnesses in the trial. Scribe Guerrera noted that Giovanni Remansi, the court messenger, testified to having delivered the summons to all witnesses, either in person or to their habitual domiciles. Twenty-two of the listed witnesses, and an additional one, did appear, and their testimonies constitute the bulk of the trial records. They included members of practically all of Pentidattilo's large clans, and nine of them were women. Their depositions were taken beginning the next day, March 19, and this business kept the court occupied until March 27.[59]

The immediate concern of the court, mirroring standard jurisprudential advice, was to investigate the circumstances of the death of Antonino Cuzzucli. This entailed the examination of his corpse (quite literally the corpus delicti) to ascertain any evidence of foul play. On March 19, therefore, the court heard Francesco Giannetti, one of its most useful witnesses, one of six who were able to sign their depositions (the six would all be men—and one of them was barely capable of this feat).

The interrogations assumed a standard format, which followed established rules of judicial practice. In the presence of the governor and the scribe, both of whom signed each deposition, each witness first identified himself (or herself) by giving (with few variations) name, place of birth, place of residence, age, and often occupation—or, in the case of women, marital status. The witness then took an oath and began to answer the specific questions posed by the court. The records are mostly written as if they were verbatim transcripts, though scribe Guerrera obviously polished the dialect of the actual statements. At the end of each major subject of questioning the witness was asked

about how he or she knew what he or she had just stated, though this was invariably reduced to a formula. The last question required the witness to name
co-witnesses to what had emerged from the testimony. The witness's signature or cross closed the record of each testimony.[60]

Francesco Giannetti, the trial's first witness, was a native of Messina, aged
about sixty, who declared he had long lived with his family in Pentidattilo,
where he was "barber and expert in surgery." He had long been active as such
in the village, and his services were appreciated.[61] He was questioned in the
parish church of San Pietro, where the corpse of Antonino Cuzzucli had been
brought for examination. Since no medical doctor resided in Pentidattilo at
the time, Giannetti was the best the court could do for the forensic analysis.
The good barber obliged. First of all, he recognized the corpse as Antonino's,
who in life had been well known to him. Examining the naked corpse, though
without an actual autopsy, Giannetti noted it had many black spots, on the
neck, chest, and above the heart; foam was oozing from the mouth, and the
hair and beard fell when pulled even lightly. The face and flesh were jaundiced,
and the nails black. These symptoms were among those listed by many juridical treatises as possible proofs of poisoning, as the barber and the court counselor likely knew. Giannetti concluded: "Through these signs I have judged
and judge and hold for certain as someone experienced in such examinations
that Antonino died of poison." This conviction was strengthened by the fact
that two days earlier the barber had been called to visit the suffering Antonino,
who lay in bed complaining of intestinal pain and whose body had been exud-
ing pus. Giannetti signed himself "*mastro.*"[62]

This report was substantiated for the court by the added testimony the
same day of two prominent villagers, Antonio Foti and Bartolo Battaglia, both
literate, who witnessed Giannetti's examination of the corpse and agreed to
his conclusions. Their presence and testimony are the first indication of the
court's desire to confirm and validate its actions through the stamp of approval
of respected villagers.[63]

Having dealt with the pressing business of examining the corpse, the court
waited until March 24 to resume questioning witnesses. By this date the three
defendants had been arrested (which was customary for heinous crimes such
as poisoning) and were detained in the prison in the imposing feudal castle,
where the rest of the court's business would be done. From now on, all witnesses took their oath in the presence of the three defendants and were then
questioned without the defendants present.[64] This oath, as we saw above, was
a procedural shortcut: it allowed the defendants to learn the identity of the

witnesses, but it rendered unnecessary the later repetition of the deposition after the court formally charged the defendants. In a small village, where the defendants were likely anyway to know more than the court may have wished, the benefits of this step probably outweighed its risks.

The first group of witnesses heard by the court on March 24 consisted of four women and a young girl, who provided the judge with plenty of material about both the murder and the other accusations. The first woman was Vittoria Vernagallo, wife of Giovan Battista Corso, who declared her age as thirty-five and was from a large and prominent village family. She, like several other witnesses, was a neighbor of Domenica and Anna, and, like all other women involved in the trial, she could not sign her name. She could talk, however, and her deposition, the longest in the trial except the defendants' own, covers all aspects of the case. She twice refers to her own curiosity that led her to eavesdropping and to close observation of her neighbors' movements. As a neighbor, she had also been present when Antonino had been ill and at his death.[65]

From Vittoria's testimony, and that of the witnesses who followed her, the court learned more about the chronology of Antonino's sudden illness. She stated that she had seen Pietro "frequenting" Domenica and her house all too often during the winter, and she reported several incriminating conversations between the three defendants on the subject of Pietro's and Domenica's illicit relationship and of the means to rid themselves of Antonino. She described the symptoms of the quick deterioration of Antonino's health, which matched the signs found by Giannetti on the corpse. Vittoria also offered a new angle to the investigation. Like Anna de Amico, she had been in the house during Antonino's last moments and for a while afterwards, helping his sisters and brother take care of him, and she reported that Domenica had shown no sign of the sorrow expected in a young woman whose husband is dying a painful death. Domenica had spent time weaving while her husband died, she had never cried, and the next day when Vittoria had "admonished" her that her behavior was wrong, Domenica still had "shed no tears."[66]

The conversations overheard and reported by Vittoria pointed to the complicity of the three defendants in the poisoning of Antonino and placed the responsibility for providing the poison—identified as arsenic—squarely on Anna's shoulders.[67] The judge then asked another question obligatory in these circumstances, namely, "of what reputation is the said Anna," an essential clue in judicial practice intended to help the judge assess all other information about a defendant (or a witness). Vittoria did not mince words. "[Anna is] a person of bad life and reputation, who does nothing but pimpings in this village, and is even a public concubine, and even often arranges abortions for women"—as she had done with Domenica herself a few years before. Anna had used a poisonous root, and Domenica's abortion had taken place in the house of Mariuzza Schirrica. With the same root, Vittoria alleged, Anna had managed at least another six abortions for four village women. "All this," said Vittoria, "I know because I have heard it said publicly."[68]

Vittoria named twelve other villagers as co-witnesses for her statements and added, concerning the abortions, "Since it is publicly known, all the people of this village can attest to it." It is plain here that both the court and the witnesses placed great importance on reputation and on the community's knowledge and judgment of each individual's behavior. These criteria had probatory value in the eyes of both judges and villagers, and the latter found here one of their main instruments to affect any trial's progress. It also appears from Vittoria's deposition that both the likely adultery and the abortions had been known to many in Pentidattilo well before Antonino's death. As was often the case with moral crimes, villagers had not reported or pursued these illegal actions. Antonino's virtual abandonment of Domenica may well have justified, in her neighbors' view, her seeking companionship elsewhere, and Anna's services were obviously useful to several village women. Things changed when Antonino's death started a murder trial.

The court immediately pursued some of the threads contained in Vittoria's long deposition. The next witness, thirty-year-old Agostina Palomara, took her oath in the presence only of Anna, since her deposition concerned not Antonino's murder but one of the abortions in which Anna was now implicated, one of two she had supposedly arranged for Antonia Crea. Agostina also stated that Anna had been "a concubine for many years, and [was] of bad life and repute and [had] no fear of God nor of her conscience."[69]

The next witnesses on March 24 allowed the court to pursue the matter of the arsenic used to kill Antonino. The sixty-year-old widow Antonia Tropea was also present at Antonino's death and testified to his symptoms, some of which she had not actually seen but rather learned from Antonino's sisters, Mattia and Angiolella, who seem to have been in charge of the house at their brother's death. Antonia Manti, aged thirty-two and wife of Giacomo Costarella, revealed the source of the arsenic. She testified that Domenica had asked her to send her daughter to Domenica's sister-in-law Mattia to ask her for some arsenic, "because rats were damaging her things." Domenica allegedly had said that she could not go herself because she had already asked Mattia for arsenic recently. Antonia also testified that she had witnessed Antonino's death and Domenica's indifferent behavior on that occasion.[70]

This busy day ended with a special testimony, that of eight-year-old Gratia Costarella, daughter of Antonia Manti. The careful procedures for the questioning of children mandated in jurisprudential literature were scrupulously followed. Gratia did not take an oath; she was escorted by scribe Guerrera to counselor Nesci (rather than the governor), and her answers were reported by Guerrera in the third person. Gratia related her conversation with Domenica and Anna and her expedition to receive the arsenic, which was given to her by Cola de Amico, Mattia's son, because his mother was not at home. She had given Cola bread and olives as a gift allegedly from her own mother, and she brought back to Domenica and Anna a quantity of arsenic as large as a walnut, wrapped in paper.[71]

The following day, March 25, the court heard three more witnesses. One was Cola de Amico, a twenty-five-year-old farmer, son of Mattia Cuzzucli and nephew of the victim, who confirmed what the court already knew about the arsenic.[72] Another was Domenico Malavenda, of a prominent family. Domenico, aged twenty-eight, was a farmer and could sign his name. He testified to having frequently observed the goings-on between Domenica and Pietro—including an occasion when the two had danced together at a gathering at the house of Vittoria Vernagallo and her husband—and to having at one point spied on them. He also saw the dead Antonino, and, like Cola before him and many other witnesses, he testified that the village rumor was that the defendants had indeed poisoned the victim.[73]

The most interesting witness of the day, however, was Mariuzza Schirrica, whose testimony concerned Domenica's alleged abortion managed by Anna. Mariuzza had been baptized on October 12, 1683, and had been married to Giuseppe de Amico, possibly a relative of Anna's, with whom she had had at least a daughter, Anna Maria, born in 1702. By the time of the trial she was a widow and twenty-six, though she declared her age as thirty. It was in her house that Domenica had actually had her abortion, about six years before, with the help of both Anna and Domenica's own mother, Francesca Familari.[74]

The judge's pointed questions led Mariuzza to the three or four years when Antonino had inhabited Montebello leaving Domenica alone in Pentidattilo. Asked whether Domenica had been pregnant during that period, Mariuzza cautiously replied that she "only knew that," on a September night about six years before, she had been awakened by knocking at her door, and, after recognizing them from the window, she had let in Domenica and her mother, Francesca. The latter asked Mariuzza to keep Domenica hidden in her house, and Mariuzza, who had already heard from her cousin Domenico Tropea that Domenica was pregnant, agreed to do so. The next morning Anna de Amico came to Mariuzza's house and asked to see Domenica, who was staying in a dark room on the ground level of the house, because, so Anna had allegedly said, Domenica was "all swollen in her belly" and needed help. Anna repeated her short visit the next day, and at night Domenica came up to see Mariuzza and told her that Anna "had placed inside her vagina a root which she still kept in there."

The next night Domenica also came up to sleep near Mariuzza, but this time she experienced great pain in her belly, and "after a while she gave birth to a male child," which Mariuzza baptized and wrapped in clothes but which died shortly thereafter. Mariuzza went to inform Francesca of the event, and on her return, she and Domenica, who carried the dead child in her apron, went to Francesca's house. As they encountered Francesca halfway, Mariuzza left them and went back to her own house. Asked for the age of the fetus, Mariuzza estimated it at "six or seven months, because it had hair on its head, and because soon after Domenica gave birth to it, it made itself heard by crying." Asked about Anna's reputation, Mariuzza said that she "had heard it said publicly by the people and among the people of this village that she arranged abortions for other women as well, and [was] of bad life and repute, and even a public concubine." Besides her cousin Domenico, Mariuzza did not cite any other co-witness who had not already testified.[75]

The next day, March 26, the court heard from three other witnesses. The focus of the interrogations had by now decidedly shifted from the murder of Antonino to the abortions, and the major blame was also being shifted away from Domenica (and even more so from Pietro) and onto Anna and her activities with poisons and roots. Pietro was not present when these three witnesses testified, and two of them took their oath only in the presence of Anna. The first witness was Francesco Tropea, a forty-five-year-old farmer, who was able, with much apparent difficulty, to sign his name.[76]

Francesco stated that he, too, had been involved in Domenica's abortion, though it is not clear why Domenica and her mother had sought his help. He testified that one late night in September, six years before, he had been awakened in his house by the two women, who had asked him to accompany them to their house because Domenica had had an abortion. Francesco had been aware that Domenica had been pregnant, and, seeing the bundle Domenica was carrying, he had suspected it contained her aborted fetus. After a short walk, Domenica put her bundle on the ground and left the other two for a moment, during which Francesco "knelt and looked subtly and recognized clearly that it was a child." Domenica returned with a flask, and the three resumed walking towards Domenica's house. There the two women told Francesco to leave them.[77]

On further questioning, Francesco confirmed that Domenica's husband had been away in Montebello when the abortion occurred and for a while before then. He also stated that a few days later he had talked to Mariuzza and learned of the circumstances of Domenica's abortion, though not of the specific method employed by Anna to induce it. Last, Francesco testified that he "had heard it said publicly" that Anna had arranged abortions for several women, that she was a "public concubine," and that "for this reason her husband, whose name, since he was a foreigner in this village, [he] could not remember, had left Anna and gone away." It is again evident from these depositions that both Domenica's presumably illicit pregnancy and Anna's management of abortions had been well known and even the topic of several village conversations, though neither had thus far resulted in denunciation or prosecution.

The next two witnesses on March 26 both took their oath only in the presence of Anna. The first was Caterina, called Cata, Vazzani, a native of nearby Motta long since residing in Pentidattilo, aged twenty-three. Her testimony concerned only Anna's abortion activities. Cata testified that three years earlier she had visited Anna to ask her to cut some cloth. Anna evidently added to her medical talent sartorial skills, and the occasion was perfect for the exchange of information. Cata indeed went on to say: "Since I had heard it said that the said Anna had arranged abortions for some people, out of curiosity I asked her, saying to her, 'Oh Anna, I hear that you have the power to induce abortions.'" Anna had replied that she could confide in Cata, since the latter was a "secretive person," that she had indeed induced abortions for Domenica Orlando, Antonia Crea, and Lucretia Condella. Cata then had asked Anna what "medication" she used, and Anna had replied that it was "a certain root." The cloth having been cut—and her curiosity sated—Cata left "on [her] own business." No other witnesses had been party to this conversation, but Cata stated that the abortions were "a public thing" to which everyone in Pentidattilo could attest.[78]

The next witness was twenty-six-year-old Sicilia Zuccalà, presumably unmarried like Cata and who herself was supposed to have had two abortions with Anna's intervention.[79] Sicilia was, however, not questioned about her own alleged abortions but about those of Domenica Orlando and of one Antonina Flachi, who made thus her first appearance in the records. Sicilia reported that a year earlier she had gone to converse with Anna, whose house neighbored her own, "as was usual that [she] always went." The two women talked about the recent return of Domenica's husband, Antonino, from Montebello, and Anna allegedly said: "Oh Sicilia, Domenica was crazy to want an abortion." On Sicilia's eager question as to how the abortion had happened, Anna replied that she had placed a root in Domenica's vagina, as she had done to Antonina Flachi.[80]

Sicilia also testified that she had gone to visit the sick Anna on another occasion, this time only two months before the trial, adding, "since she is my friend." Anna was in bed and said she had great pain in her belly. Sicilia, aware that Anna was pregnant, told her to call the midwife. When the midwife came, she told Anna to stand up from her bed. "Anna got up and as soon as she sat down she ejected from her vagina a piece of coagulated blood, and standing up again she went back to bed," and Sicilia "saw with [her] own eyes the said piece of coagulated blood, and attached to it two small bits of roots." Sicilia was not asked any other questions, and she cited only the midwife as a cowitness. Indeed, Sicilia was the only witness who openly spoke of her friendship with Anna—though certainly not the only one who engaged in friendly exchanges with her—and remarkably she was not asked to testify about Anna's reputation, indicating perhaps that by now the court wished for no interference with the likely conclusion of the trial.

On the next day, March 27, the court heard from its last two substantive witnesses. First came the sixty-year-old widow Maria Romeo, who performed the "exercise" of midwife in Pentidattilo. Since the early 1690s, before she became the village midwife, Maria's name appears in the baptismal records of Pentidattilo as the godmother of two foundlings and illegitimate children, a role that often pertained to midwives. Maria belonged to a large clan and was the only woman whose occupation was reported in the records. Midwives were traditionally recognized as expert witnesses, and their testimony was, of course, especially valuable in trials for abortions and rapes, in which they played a role similar to that performed by doctors—or barbers—in murder trials.

Maria testified to the events narrated by Sicilia on the previous day. She had been called by Domenica Orlando, and she had found Anna in bed with pain in her belly and bladder. Maria had told Anna to stand up and insert her hand in her vagina. When Anna did this, Maria saw "immediately that Anna ejected from her vagina much blood . . . and [Maria] soon saw and observed that in the said blood there were two small pieces of flesh, and attached to them two small bits of roots, so that [she], as a midwife and an expert soon judged that the said Anna was pregnant, and had had an abortion because of the said roots."[81] Maria ended her brief testimony by saying that Sicilia Zuccalà and Domenica Orlando had been present on this occasion. Sicilia, perhaps to cover her friend, had neglected to mention Domenica's presence.

The next witness was Domenico Tropea, a thirty-six-year-old farmer, cousin of Mariuzza Schirrica. He testified that six years earlier Domenica had asked him to help her, since she was pregnant, her husband was away, and she "was afraid of her relatives." Domenico stated that Domenica had asked him "if [he] knew of some woman who had some remedy to get an abortion" and that he, "having heard it said" that Anna had arranged abortions for "other people," went to her and asked her to help Domenica. Four days later, Domenico had asked his cousin Mariuzza to "do [him] a favor and keep Domenica secretly in her house." Another four days later, Domenico ran into Anna and asked her what had happened, and Anna told him that Domenica had had an abortion in Mariuzza's house. On his asking her how the abortion had been induced, Anna talked of her root and said that Domenica had given her "as a gift" 10 or 12 *carlini*.[82]

The feudal court in Pentidattilo proceeded in a manner entirely consonant with the general procedure and jurisprudence applied throughout much of Europe. This correspondence between the dictates of learned writings and what happened at the village level is not just a sign of the centralizing power of early modern states. It also shows that the justice system fulfilled a recognized function in the life of village communities and that villagers both accepted its presence among them and facilitated its working. After all, as noted above, most early modern jurists were not pure theorists but had direct experience of how justice could and did operate. They knew, and acknowledged in their treatises, that the judicial process, in order to function at all, needed the cooperation of the population whose behavior it sought to control and adjudicate.

This collaboration, along with the mutual benefits it implied, was inherent in the inquisitorial procedure, as we can see in the gathering of evidence and depositions in the Pentidattilo trial. The inquisitorial system was undoubtedly harsh and severe towards the defendant, but it was based on a clear and specific theory of proof and punishment which had its own logic and rationale and which was rarely, if at all, questioned until the eighteenth century. This theory of proof relied fundamentally on the interaction between learned and popular notions, between institutional and popular culture. This was even truer with crimes of a sexual and moral nature, and it would be in dealing with these crimes that the difficulties of the inquisitorial procedure would become obvious in the course of the eighteenth century. The Pentidattilo trial offers an early example of those difficulties, and indeed, as we shall see in Chapter 5, the Kingdom of Naples would be among the first European states to confront the need for new theories of proof.

In addition to offering a detailed example of the cooperation between judicial authorities and rural communities, the Pentidattilo trial also reveals many aspects of village life and customs. Individual reputation, as assessed by and within the community, determined the force of each villager's words and opinions, and often the consequences of his or her actions. Outsiders were marginal and dispensable figures within village society. The community of Pentidattilo was knit together in a thick web of mutual relations and exchanges of information and favors. Villagers knew and discussed the behavior of their relatives, friends, and neighbors. They judged it, too, according to their individual and collective moral sense. Yet they avoided bringing external forces to bear on their fellow villagers' actions unless unforeseen events threatened the stability and well-being of their community.

THREE

Economic Structures and Social Hierarchies

Village culture and village society conditioned the control and punishment of crime as much as, if not more than, royal laws and jurisprudential doctrines. Rural society was not, however, always the same in all villages, nor was it unchanging within any specific village. The Pentidattilo trial illuminates several aspects of village society and can be used as an introduction to its structures and their eighteenth-century evolution.

Pentidattilo as it appears in the trial records was a traditional stable village, yet the events of the trial showed contradictions and instability within its society, especially with regard to the position of outsiders and the marginalization of villagers who did not belong to the more established clans. Although the trial ended with and through the reaffirmation of local practices and established social structures, within a generation or two this peasant community confronted significant changes in its economy and social life.

The progress of the trial raises questions about the functioning of village society. The community of Pentidattilo had its social hierarchies, which were reflected in the operation of the justice system. There was clearly a village elite, consisting especially of native citizens belonging to the more established clans. Its members enjoyed prestige and respect within the village, and the lord's court recognized their status. This status was, of course, linked to economic factors. Yet the village economy, while not rich, was relatively egalitarian. Thus elite status in Pentidattilo was not based solely on economic standing but also on family and personal reputation and individual achievement. Village society was therefore fluid, and elite status could shift as generations succeeded one another.

This chapter and the next focus especially on the life and character of the village community. Issues of property, inheritance, and marriage are relatively secondary, in part because they are less directly related to my main interest in the local community, its evolution, and its relationship with outside forces and pressures, but also because of the limitations of the available data. The available sources are of different types and span a time of more than a century, from the baptismal records of the late seventeenth century to the trial records of 1710, from fiscal surveys and notarial acts for the mid-eighteenth century to records of the sale of ecclesiastic property at the end of the old regime. The sources are not optimal, but it is possible to glean evidence from them about the characteristics and transformations of village society and the village community.

Pentidattilo in the early eighteenth century was, compared with other villages of the Kingdom of Naples and of other areas of western Europe, small and remote but not overly poor. Its inhabitants lived in a traditional community held together by solid links of family, godparenthood, neighborhood, and friendship. Economic disparities were not pronounced in the village, though they would become more so as the century advanced. By the end of the century the village and its population would become more integrated in large commercial, economic, social, and administrative networks.

As is true of the trial records themselves, the sources available for a study of village economy and society resulted from frequent and fruitful contacts between the official, written culture of early modern authorities on the one hand and village, mostly illiterate, culture on the other. The fiscal surveys, in particular, were the product of an interaction similar to that which produced the trial records, and they offer access not only to the villagers' financial situation but also to elements of their own view of their economic and social organization.

The Role of Elite Witnesses

> Se non fusse stato verità non si haveria detto.

> If it had not been the truth it would not have been said.
> —GIOVAN BATTISTA CORSO, in the records
> for the trial of Domenica Orlando

Most of the witnesses the Pentidattilo court questioned about the murder of Antonino Cuzzucli and his wife's abortion testified to specific events in which they had participated or which had occurred in their presence (or earshot). But on two occasions the court also had recourse to witnesses who contributed differently to the case. These witnesses, all men, brought to the proceedings their individual prestige and trustworthiness and served to reinforce the legitimacy of what the feudal judge and his staff were doing. Their testimony gave a stamp of community approval to the trial's development and conclusion.

The first instance came at the start of the trial, after the barber Giannetti examined Antonino's corpse. The court called two supporting witnesses, also questioned in the presence of the corpse, Antonio Foti of Reggio, long residing with his family in Pentidattilo and belonging to an old local clan, aged fifty, and Bartolo Battaglia, native of the village, who gave his age as thirty-five. Neither gave his occupation. Their depositions add nothing to Giannetti's; they simply repeat what they had seen the barber do and the symptoms they, too, identify, on Giannetti's authority, as those of poison. Their testimony thus has a very different function than his, as it attests not to what had been done but to the fact that what had been done was appropriate. Both Foti and Battaglia signed their names. Both belonged to wealthy and prominent families in the village.

Bartolo Battaglia in particular came from the largest and most important Pentidattilo clan, one that claimed six households in the 1745 census and nine in that of 1759 (including two listed with the honorific "Don"). The clan had been prominent since the late sixteenth century: its members had frequently rented feudal rights and large areas of feudal land; they had been omnipresent for two centuries among the village's elected officials and feudal administrators, serving at various points as mayors, aldermen, and erari; they had been witnesses in important disputes and notarial acts and witnesses for the marchional family in important moments. In a remarkable number of these cases they had been able at least to sign their name. Bartolo was throughout his life a major presence in Pentidattilo in many capacities, and he was still testifying in defense of the village's interests in a dispute with the marquis in 1759.[1]

The testimony of a man like this, the governor surely felt, would get the trial off to a good, solid start. The same motivation appears in the last witnesses the court heard, seven men whose testimony ended the gathering of depositions. Their statements marked the return on the scene of Pietro Crea, since they all took their oath in the presence of all three defendants. All gave short depositions (a page each, including the various formulaic passages), all but one were *massari* (substantial farmers), all were adults of respectable age and status, one of them could sign his name, and their statements added precious little to what the court knew about the case. Their role was not to offer the court any real enlightenment as to the facts of the case but rather to provide a sense of the general opinion in the village on the matter under trial. Public opinion and the reputation of the parties involved in a crime were, as we have seen, essential elements in early modern judicial practice. It is therefore significant that, while women witnesses had reported much of what was known about Antonino's murder, Domenica's abortion, and Anna's activities, when it came to the final assessment of what the events had meant the court turned to the men of Pentidattilo, to solid citizens, to give confirmation and legitimation to, and offer a commentary on, what the court had done and learned. In this sense, these seven witnesses played a role not unlike that of a Greek tragic chorus.[2]

The judge asked them what they knew about Antonino's murder, and, with small variations, they all replied that they had heard it said in the village that Domenica had poisoned her husband in order to marry her lover, Pietro, and that Domenica's "great friend" Anna had participated in the murder. Molé stated that "this public rumor began immediately after Antonino's death and has lasted until today," which presumably made it stronger as evidence. Palumbo, Costarella, Ficara, and Corso stated, each in slightly different language that may have been suggested or adjusted by the scribe, that "more so [they] believe[d] [the rumor] because if it had not been the truth it would not have been said."[3]

The ties of friendship, neighborliness, and complicity between the three defendants were variously stated by these witnesses. In particular, some of them stated that Anna had lent her house to the two lovers for the consummation of their illicit relationship. The witnesses variously used the term "friend" to define both the relation between Domenica and Anna and that between Anna and Pietro. These seven final male witnesses, like many of the other men questioned, also tended to ascribe a more important role in the planning, determination, and execution of the murder to the single male defendant, Pietro Crea, than would seem warranted by the depositions of other witnesses. At the same time, they all confirmed Anna's complicity and her earlier facilitation of the illicit relationship. Domenica, the only defendant who was a native of the village, assumes an almost entirely passive role in the description of the events offered by these final witnesses.

Village Economy and Finances

Paga con puntualità il suo annuo debbito . . . alla Regia Corte.

[The village] punctually pays its yearly due . . . to the Royal Court.
— Archivio di Stato di Napoli,
Tesorieri e Percettori 4292/684 (1694)

These witnesses represented the village's public opinion. They performed that role because of their gender, their age and occupation, probably their family connections and level of economic comfort, and their personal respectability and credibility. They were, in short, solid citizens, members, in various ways, of the village elite.

The economy of the Pentidattilo area centered on the higher lands, and local agriculture concentrated on grain production, with the addition of some vineyards and olive trees and of livestock breeding.[4] The prevalence of intensive agriculture and livestock breeding is apparent in how important common pastures and waters were for the survival of many villagers. The availability of feudal land and especially of the feudal forest for economic use by the villagers was at the center of disputes between Pentidattilo and its lords all the way through the eighteenth century.[5] Land management in Pentidattilo, as in many other villages in the kingdom with remote or mountainous locations and relatively poor land, was characterized by small units exploited by individual peasant families, and by widespread peasant ownership of, and access to, land. *Latifundia,* or large estates often run through large-scale management and the employment of landless rural labor, prevailed in many areas of the kingdom, such as in the plains of Terra di Lavoro near Naples, the Puglia plateaus, and the more fertile low-lying areas of Calabria itself. In this system, which has received much scholarly attention, villages, which tended to be large in population, were characterized by substantial wealth disparities between their inhabitants, large numbers of landless or almost landless peasants, large-scale seasonal migration of rural labor, highly commercialized production, or sometimes large-scale, long-distance pastoralism. None of these traits is found in Pentidattilo or in many other areas of the Kingdom of Naples.[6]

The feudal lords of Pentidattilo did not reside in the village until the mid-seventeenth century. Although they held an extensive amount of land in their fief, local agricultural and geographic constraints did not favor large-scale direct management, and throughout the early modern period the feudal lords rented out their land in small parcels to Pentidattilo's peasants, in most cases in exchange for rents in kind. The lords also levied a *terraggio* (the feudal lord's share of the harvest of all feudal land) of one-fifth, which was higher than in other, poorer areas of the kingdom.[7]

The Alberti marquis, beginning in the early seventeenth century, took a more active role in the economy of their Calabrian fief. In the 1620s Giuseppe Alberti built a mill and an olive press in the village, and in the following decades his son Lorenzo played a central role in joining several parcels of land and scattered settlements in the coastal area to form the new village of Melito. By the midcentury the marquis also began to shift some of their land from grain production to the growing of mulberry trees for the feeding of silkworms and the production of raw silk. This change required a substantial investment of capital on the part of the Alberti: in particular, in the 1670s and 1680s the marquis Domenico built twenty-four houses in Melito to be used for raising silkworms. Mulberry trees and silk production were then widespread throughout the area near Reggio. In Pentidattilo, various villagers worked the land used for silk production, and two-thirds of the product went to the marquis. By the end of the century Pentidattilo's castle was not only the lords' residence but the center of a growing agricultural enterprise.[8]

Virtually all villagers lived off the land, and even those engaged in various crafts continued to engage in farming as an important complementary activity. Silk production, if it was to be more than a limited complement to other agricultural activities, required substantial capital, and only the marquis was in a position to provide the necessary investment. Although the marquis pocketed much of its profits, silk production also benefited the villagers, by providing an additional source of income to poor peasant families, by offering employment for marginal labor within the peasant household, and more generally by opening the village to contacts with outside markets. By the mid-eighteenth century these changes would be evident especially in the activities of the residents of Melito. By the second half of the seventeenth century Pentidattilo was no longer very poor or isolated, as was true of many other small villages the dire economic conditions of which historians have tended to exaggerate.[9]

Silk production remained for more than a century a central element of local agriculture. In the eighteenth century it began to be replaced by the production of citrus fruits, which has remained to this day the main specialty of the region. Though a few citrus trees appeared on the lord's land as early as

1704, they remained rare, and in 1745 the two citrus tree orchards owned by Teodora Alberti were intended primarily "for pleasure." By the end of the century, however, the transformation of the area into an orange and lemon grove was well under way. Silk, grains, and livestock remained in any case strong features of the local economy. By the late eighteenth century the production of raw silk and especially of citrus fruits involved Pentidattilo in large commercial networks unlike any the area had previously known. In the 1770s Henry Swinburne, for instance, commented on the village's relative prosperity.[10]

The general economic development of Pentidattilo mirrored fairly closely that of the kingdom as a whole. The evolution of feudal revenues, village finances, and local prices shows rapid growth, accompanied by high inflation, throughout the sixteenth century and until the 1620s. There followed a substantial slowing down in the local economy, aggravated by the 1647–48 revolt, the 1656 plague, and the 1674–78 revolt of Messina, which hurt the economy of all of southern Calabria. By the 1680s it was increasingly difficult to find villagers willing to rent feudal land and rights. The relevio paid by the lords, for instance, grew much more than tenfold in nominal terms between 1536 and 1628, from 36.1.17½ ducats to 598.2.14⅓ ducats, but then declined to about 300 ducats by the end of the seventeenth century. Prices, on the other hand, increased by only three to five times between 1536 and the 1620s and then stayed fairly stable until the middle of the following century.[11]

Specific sources of feudal income show a similar evolution. The *bagliva* and the mastrodattia were feudal offices that the lord rented out and the revenues of which were closely tied to the population level and general economic health of the village. Their income stood at a high of 100 and 42 ducats, respectively, by 1627, but plummeted to 40 and 12 ducats soon after the 1647–48 revolt. The rents grew again to 70 and 25 ducats by 1691, and the bagliva alone yielded 128 ducats in 1695. By 1704 the two offices brought in 134.50 and 52.20 ducats. The *fondaco* of Melito (a fee levied on local food sales) and the lord's share of the fishing catch in Melito also remained stable in the late seventeenth century but rose substantially during the eighteenth century, from the 40 ducats they produced in 1691 to 115 ducats in 1745. As these examples show, the turn of the eighteenth century, when the trial of Domenica Orlando took place, marked the start of a period of growth for Pentidattilo.[12]

The eighteenth-century growth is also apparent in the village's finances. As we have seen in Chapter 1, the università of Pentidattilo enjoyed the administrative autonomy customary in the kingdom's old villages. There are few records of the università's finances for Pentidattilo, but their evolution likely mirrored that of the local economy. The università was indebted to the marquis in 1648. In his 1676 testament, the marquis Domenico released the università from 728 ducats it owed him, "the better to show the usual beneficence and love that [he] ha[d] always felt towards [his] vassals." The università again owed money to Teodora Alberti in 1749, when an agreement was reached for the payment of 819.64½ ducats over the following ten years. But there is no evidence of other significant indebtedness, and by the later eighteenth century the finances of Pentidattilo were in reasonably healthy condition.[13]

In 1718 the village's budget included expenses for 1,058.91⅝ ducats. This would make Pentidattilo's operation a rather inexpensive one, compared, for instance, with the larger budgets of the Caracciolo Brienza fiefs in Basilicata, but the lack of significant debt arrears bespeaks on the other hand financial stability. The village was not in a position to indulge in luxuries. Like many others, it employed no physician and had no school. Only 92.50 ducats of the expenses were used to benefit the local economy (including license fees to the government related to the silk trade), 122 ducats went to pay local officers and lawyers in Reggio and Catanzaro, and 64 ducats were spent in religious and other public celebrations. The rest, or nearly three-fourths of the budget, consisted of tax payments, debt service, and the military expenses required by the government.[14]

The village was even more frugal in later decades. In 1745 the budget called for 1,049.00⅓ ducats in expenses, including 30 in salaries, 12 in religious expenses, and 70 for other local expenses; the rest, or almost 90 percent, went into taxes, debts, and military expenses. In 1759, of the 956 ducats of expenses in the università's budget, 60 ducats were in salaries to local officers and 37 in religious expenses, again leaving about 90 percent of the budget to tax and debt payments and military expenses. Pentidattilo was not rich, but it was not badly administered—in comparison, the much larger and more fertile fief of Corigliano, for instance, had managed to accumulate debts for 74,000 ducats in the decades around 1700.[15]

In the mid-eighteenth century, then, Pentidattilo was certainly still a small and needy village. Its budget was not large, and local economic activity was not sufficient to give much work to the local notary. The village was, however, far from destitute: the community had few debts, and the local economy was expanding. Indeed, in 1759 Litterio Caracciolo Brienza fetched 68,000 ducats when he sold the fief he had just inherited from his grandmother to Lorenzo

TABLE 3.1
Communal Finances of Pentidattilo, 1718, 1745, and 1759
(in ducats)

1718		
Category of Expenses[a]	Amount	Percentage
Military expenses	156	14.8
Tower	32	3
Royal taxes	477.61⅚	45.2
Debt payments	110.80	10.5
Local officers	98	9.3
Lawyers	24	2.3
Local economy	92.50	8.8
Religious expenses	24	2.3
Public celebrations	40	3.8
Total	1,058.91⅚	100
1745		
Military expenses	234	22.5
Tax and debt payments	693.00⅓	66.5
Local officers	30	2.9
Religious expenses	12	1.2
Extraordinary expenses[b]	70	6.9
Total	1,049.00⅓	100
1759		
Military expenses	216	22.3
Tower	42	4.3
Tax and debt payments	611	63.6
Local officers	60	6.1
Religious expenses	37	3.7
Total	956	100

[a] Military and tower expenses consist of the salaries of local cavalry and tower guardians, which the università was required by the royal government to pay. Royal taxes (*fiscali*) were actually paid in large part directly to the government's own creditors (the *fiscalari*). Religious expenses include the salary to a preacher and the costs of religious feasts. Public celebrations were also mostly of a religious nature, but they are not always specified in the documents. The categories are not the same in all documents.

[b] These are unspecified local expenses.

Clemente, a price that, at the customary capitalization rate of 4 percent, suggests expected annual revenues for the new lord of 2,720 ducats, a solid increase over past years and a significant figure for a small fief.[16]

There are no fiscal surveys after 1759, but other sources show the continuing growth of the local economy. In the 1780s the property of many ecclesiastic institutions in Calabria was sold by the royal government to raise money for the region's reconstruction after the devastating earthquake of 1783. The sale of church land in those years in Pentidattilo and Melito shows the respectable wealth of the local church and the liveliness of the local land market. By that time Melito, strengthened by the prosperous silk and citrus production of the coastal area, had become the main center of population, and it would also soon be the local administrative center.[17]

Melito was increasingly integrated in active commercial networks, and its society and population were becoming more complex, stratified, and diverse. The università's only inn was in Melito, where travelers would have been much more likely to stop. While the two mills were in the old settlement, both in 1745 and in 1759 the università's only two greengrocers lived in Melito, showing that the latter's inhabitants did not cultivate most of the food they needed but were more specialized in their activities and engaged more frequently in market exchanges for basic necessities. The 1759 muleteer also resided in Melito, where his transportation services were presumably more needed. Documents from the 1780s and 1790s show further developments in Melito's society, also through the high frequency of honorific labels used to describe numerous wealthier citizens.[18]

Economic growth meant more peaceful relationships between the università and its lords and between the village and its neighbors. Pentidattilo had been involved in disputes with the marquis, primarily over the latter's payment of local taxes and over pastures, during part of the seventeenth century. The village had also been bitterly fighting the neighboring villages of San Lorenzo and Montebello over their respective borders and over rights to highly necessary pastures and waters for more than a century. But evidence of such struggles becomes meager after the beginning of the eighteenth century.[19]

The early eighteenth century, then, was an important transition period for Pentidattilo's economy and finances. The village was more prosperous and peaceful than it had been in previous decades, and the whole area was entering a phase of expansion which would last for the rest of the century. Changes were coming to the village, especially in regard to population growth and the movement of population towards the coastal area. The economic and social fabric of village life reflects a community on the verge of substantial changes.

The Catasto Onciario

Suggellato coll'Universal suggello

Sealed with the università's seal
— Archivio di Stato di Napoli, Catasto Onciario 6091 (1745)

The most important source for the economic and social makeup of Pentidattilo is the great fiscal and population survey ordered by the Bourbon government, carried out by all università throughout the kingdom in the 1740s and
1750s, and known as the Catasto Onciario (the *oncia* was a unit of value used
to assess wealth). Two surveys survive for Pentidattilo, one drawn up in 1745
and the other in 1759. The catasto was carried out by the local administrators
assisted by two evaluators from nearby communities and was then assessed
by the Sommaria. Each università elected deputies and evaluators to compile
lists of all households and to assess the capital value of all real estate and animals owned by each household. The catasto assessed the property not only of
local citizens and residents but also of the feudal lord, all ecclesiastic foundations (though these were subject to a different fiscal regime), and any nonres-
idents who held property in the village. The result is both an invaluable source
and a monument to eighteenth-century administrative rationalization.[20]

Like the documents for the relevio, the text of the catasto results from the
interaction between the goals and policies of the state authorities as they were
conveyed to all village administrators and the understanding and views of each
community's inhabitants. Pentidattilo's elite citizens were prominent in the
drafting of all these texts and operated as mediators between the state and their
fellow citizens. But all citizens participated in the preparation of the documents, and many poor and illiterate villagers occupied important positions of
responsibility in that process. The drafting of the catasto was a collective event,
and discussions regarding it were largely oral. As with the trial records, the
Catasto Onciario as a text tells a story that reflects both official and village
culture.[21]

An example of this contact between different notions is the definition of
the village's social hierarchy. The two surveys are the only documented occasion when the population of Pentidattilo was formally divided into three separate estates, and this division reflected royal instructions and preconceptions
more than the reality of village society. Deputies were elected in parliament
for the "better," "middle," and "low" estates, and four appraisers, two from

the village and two from outside, were also chosen. The mayors and aldermen, who were not elected according to estate, cooperated with the deputies in drawing up the surveys. In 1745 only half the men involved in drafting the survey were able to sign their name. In 1759 four of the eight village administrators but only two among the eight men who served as deputies or village appraisers could.[22]

After stating the prices and values to be used in the survey to assess property and animals, the deputies collected the *rivele* (declarations and estimates for each household). Each rivela includes a list of household members with their names, profession if any, tie to the head of the household, and age. There follows an assessment of the head tax (1 ducat for able-bodied heads of household under the age of sixty) and of the *once d'industria,* or capital value assigned to the earning capacity of each able-bodied adult male in the household. This assessment allowed for three levels, depending on the occupation, namely 16 *once* for the higher taxable professions (pharmacists or the lower levels of legal occupations), 14 for several skilled crafts and occupations, and 12 for most other workers. The learned professions were exempted from this assessment, as was anyone described as noble or "living civilly" (*civil vivente*). In Pentidattilo there was nobody in the 16-*once* category, and only those described as massari (wealthier farmers) and the two barbers of 1759 were assessed at 14 *once*; all others (mostly *bracciali,* or field laborers) were assessed at 12 *once.* The very elderly and the disabled were exempted from this assessment, and boys between fourteen and eighteen years of age were assessed at half the rate of adults.[23]

The rivela continued by estimating the *once di beni.* First, mention was made of whether the household owned its lodging or paid rent. No tax was levied on houses used by their owners for their own habitation. After this, all other real estate was assessed, by estimating its annual revenue and then arriving at its capital value in *once.* For most land or houses the capitalization rate was set at 5 percent. Payments to the feudal lord (*censi*) owed on parcels of land were deducted from the income before capitalization, as was 25 percent from any rent drawn from houses to allow for repair costs. Finally, the value of all animals was assessed. The deputies set at the start of the catasto the expected income from each type of animal, and the capitalization rate for income from animals was set at 10 percent, to allow for the aging and losses that were more likely than with real estate. Horses and occasionally mules "for personal use" were assigned no taxable capital value.[24]

Although the catasto remained, of course, inequitable, especially in the taxing of the *once d'industria*, it had a great potential to provide for more fairness in the fiscal system of the kingdom, in that it was founded on direct taxation and established uniform criteria for the assessment of most property. The royal government set the amount of taxes due by each università on the basis of its population, as determined in the most recent census. Each università then chose how to levy that amount, plus any other tax revenue deemed necessary for local expenses. Since the late sixteenth century many università, though most likely not Pentidattilo, had turned to indirect taxes as the main form of local taxation, which greatly favored wealthier citizens. The Catasto Onciario, by requiring that all communities levy most of their taxes on the basis of property held and its income, allowed for less regressive taxation, which was, together with securing and stabilizing fiscal revenues for the state, one of the main reasons for the reform instituting the new system.[25]

After the taxable *once* for all citizens were assessed, the deputies proceeded with all other categories of property owners. Widows sometimes constituted a separate category. Other groups included citizens who no longer resided in the community and noncitizens who held property there, be they resident or not; resident noncitizens paid a *jus habitationis* (resident fee) of 1.50 ducats a year. Finally, as a result of the 1741 concordat between the Bourbon government and the papacy, the catasto also assessed the property of various categories of ecclesiastic owners. Local priests paid taxes on property above a set diocesan standard, and ecclesiastic foundations and institutions (except the parish churches) paid tax on half the net value of their property. All clergy was exempted from any personal head or *industria* levy.

After the *collettiva*, or final general assessment, was established, the total liabilities of the community were calculated. These included all taxes owed to the central government and all local expenses. The contributions of ecclesiastic and nonresident owners were determined, taking into account their various exemptions from specific payments and taxes. The income from the head tax levied on all nonexempt citizens was also calculated and deducted from the communal expenses. The rest was divided by the total *once* of the citizens to arrive at the tax rate for all citizens. It was the hope of the central government that this rate would not exceed 4½ *grana* for each *oncia* of value, or 15 percent of taxable income, though in many villages this rate, in fact, had to be exceeded in order for all liabilities to be met.[26]

We know, therefore, quite a bit about the economic situation of the citizens of Pentidattilo in the mid-eighteenth century. Although certainly not a wealthy community, the village was reasonably secure. In fact, most of its citizens owned taxable property and animals, and almost half of them owned the house in which they lived. Economic disparities within the village, despite the catasto's separation of the inhabitants into estates, were limited. The separation itself was primarily a matter of administrative definition and indeed is never mentioned in the individual citizens' rivele.

Sources and Levels of Wealth

> Dice viver del suo.
>
> He says he lives off his assets.
> — Catasto statement for "civil" people

In 1745 there were in Pentidattilo 108 households headed by lay citizens, including 4 headed by widows, plus 6 households headed by local priests (3 more local priests did not reside in the università), for a total of 114 households and 494 people.[27] The average household size, not unusual for small villages in the kingdom, was 4.33, ranging from 3 people living alone to 2 households of 10 members. All 114 households were assessed. The 6 priests were assessed for *once* 16.15, after deducting the income allowed under the diocesan standard. Of the remaining 108 households only 7 were found to have no taxable income or assets. These included the 4 widows, whose households accounted for 9 people. Only 1 widow had any net revenue, but it was below the taxable minimum for widows. The other 3 households without taxable assets were headed by an elderly and disabled hermit who lived with his widowed sister (the little property they owned belonged to the widow and was therefore exempted as well); a disabled man suffering from dropsy who lived with his wife and had no assessed property; and a man who "lived civilly" and therefore paid no tax on his labor and who lived at the expense and in the house of a brother in holy orders.[28]

The citizens were assessed for a total of 2,278.05 *once,* of which 1,704, or about 75 percent, were *once d'industria* and 574.05, or about 25 percent, were *once di beni.* For the 101 households with taxable assets the average was 22.16 *once* and the median 18.03 *once.* In 1759 the average for the 144 households (out of 158) with taxable assets was virtually unchanged and stood at 22.18 *once,* though in the later survey the total *once di beni* were almost equal to the total *once d'industria.* In 1745 the total taxable assets ranged from the 3.10 *once* of 2 households headed by disabled men to the 74.15 *once* of a massaro whose

TABLE 3.2

Owners and Value of Assets in Pentidatillo Recorded in the Catasto Onciario,
1745 and 1759

(in *once*)

	1745			
Category of Owners	*Once d'Industria*	*Once di Beni*	Total	Percentage
Resident citizens[a]	1,704	574.05	2,278.05	64.5
Nonresident citizens[b]	78	58.25	136.25	4
Local clerics[c]		16.15	16.15	0.5
Local ecclesiastic foundations[d]		2.16	2.16	0.1
Lay noncitizens[e]		702.29	702.29	19.9
Outside ecclesiastic foundations[f]		389.06	389.0	11
Total	1,782	1,744.06	3,526.06	100
	1759			
Resident citizens	1,671	1,583.10	3,254.10	50.1
Nonresident citizens	84		84	1.3
Noncitizen residents[g]		49.20	49.20	0.8
Local clerics		411	411	6.3
Local ecclesiastic foundations		74	74	1.1
Noncitizen resident clerics		34	34	0.5
Lay noncitizens		425.20	425.20	6.5
Feudal lord		1,622	1,622	24.9
Outside ecclesiastic foundations		553.15	553.15	8.5
Total	1,755	4,753.05	6,508.05	100

[a] These included 108 households, of which 101 had taxable assets.

[b] Five households totaling 14 people, all living in nearby San Lorenzo; there were also 6 individuals who were living in nearby villages and had been counted among Pentidattilo's inhabitants in the census of 1732 but who had not paid anything to the università for a long time (ASN, Catasto Onciario 6091, fol. 29v).

[c] These figures include only the revenues above the limit set by the diocesan standard for resident clerics.

[d] Only one local ecclesiastic foundation was assessed as having any net revenue from property; the figure was halved for the catasto, according to the terms of the 1741 concordat.

[e] These included the feudal lord, assessed for 277.22 net *once*; only the lord's allodial assets were counted for the catasto; feudal assets were listed, and most of them were assessed, but they followed a different fiscal regime.

[f] In this case, also, the net revenues were assessed at half value, following the concordat.

[g] These include 4 of the 22 Corio households, which are taxed only for *once di beni*. The document is somewhat confusing, in that 2 other Corio households, also headed by noncitizens, are nonetheless listed and counted among the citizen households and taxed for both *industria* and *beni*; hence the totals in the resident-citizens category refer to 158 households, 142 of which are taxed (the remaining 16 were headed by 13 widows, an elderly unmarried woman, and 2 "civil" men).

household included three able-bodied sons. The assets held by citizens had by far the largest taxable value in Pentidattilo. Another 136.25 *once* were held by nonresident citizens. Ecclesiastic owners held a total of 408.07 taxable *once,* and lay noncitizens, including the feudal lord, owned 702.29. The resident citizens owned therefore 64.5 percent of the taxable assets in the village, a high percentage compared with nearby Motta and with the villages analyzed by

TABLE 3.3
Total Taxable Assets of the Citizens of Pentidattilo, 1745
(in *once*)

Amount	Number of Households
Less than 10	5
10.01–15	30
15.01–20	21
20.01–25	13
25.01–30	12
30.01–35	4
35.01–40	6
40.01–50	6
50.01–60	2
More than 60	2
Total	101

Pasquale Villani in his study of the Catasto Onciario. As Villani observes, this high percentage bespeaks relative social stability and balance.[29]

Of the 101 citizen households with taxable assets, all but 8 were assessed for *once d'industria.* Four of the 8 were headed by disabled individuals; the other 4 were "civil" and hence exempted from paying for their labor. Only 1 of these was reported as having an occupation, namely, as castle and prison warden for the lord. Pentidattilo was home to 6 other taxpayers described as "living civilly," but 5 of these were assessed for the *once d'industria* of other members of their household, such as servants, apprentices, or relatives.[30]

We would expect almost all villagers, and certainly the poorer ones, to be assessed for their labor, but it is remarkable that 70 of the 101 households assessed for any tax in Pentidattilo were taxed for *once di beni,* that is, for real estate and animals producing net revenues, leaving only 31 households without any taxable property beyond the labor of their members. This was a rather high percentage of property owners compared with other villages and towns of the kingdom, and this percentage obtained also in 1759, when 110 households out of 158 held taxable property. The property distribution in the village was also more egalitarian than in other centers.[31] In 1745 the taxable property of these 70 villagers ranged from the 0.04 *once di beni* of a field laborer to the 34 *once di beni* of notary Francesco Celia. The average taxable property for these 70 villagers was 8.06 *once* and the median 5 *once.* The spread of taxable assets for total *once* and for *once di beni* is reported in tables 3.3 and 3.4.

It is difficult to define what these assets meant in terms of living standards in the mid-eighteenth century for what was a small village in a remote area of the kingdom. In the same period in Naples, where life was certainly more ex-

TABLE 3.4
Taxable 'Once di Beni' of the Citizens of Pentidattilo, 1745
(in *once*)

Amount	Number of Households
Less than 0.15	8
0.16–1	4
1.01–2	3
2.01–3.15	13
3.16–5	7
5.01–10	12
10.01–15	11
15.01–20	6
20.01–30	4
More than 30	2
Total	70

pensive than in Pentidattilo, salaries for the least skilled members of an aristocratic household staff were below 10 ducats a year, plus lodging and some food. In the Calabrian village of Nicotera field laborers and harvesters in 1630 were paid between 1 and 2 ducats a month. In the early eighteenth century landless rural laborers in Corigliano, also in Calabria, were paid about 1.70 ducats a month, plus some bread and wine, in the months when they were employed. This was roughly the equivalent of one *tomolo* of wheat a month.[32] Although assets of 5 *once*, the median in Pentidattilo, would mean income of only 1.50 ducats a year, we must remember that the catasto does not represent a complete survey of all the wealth in the kingdom, especially given the predominance of the feudal system.

As was typical in areas of relatively poor agriculture in Mediterranean Europe, the land that peasants owned represented in fact only a small part of the land they could and did cultivate and use. Common lands and seignorial lands were also largely accessible to peasants. In fact, frequently, as in Pentidattilo, peasants' direct ownership of land was concentrated in small parcels of land, often orchards and vineyards, rather than arable land used for cultivation of grains or pasture. Most villagers in Pentidattilo supplemented the income of their own property by renting and farming parcels of feudal land, and therefore we cannot consider the data presented here as a total picture of the income available to the people of the village. The only prices we have from the survey are those of agricultural products on the regional market, but it is not known how often and at what prices food was bought or sold among the villagers, who themselves produced most of what they needed. The absence of food vendors and shopkeepers in the old village of Pentidattilo indeed points to largely self-sufficient households. The catasto offers a picture of the relative economic standing of villagers compared with each other, but it cannot yield a portrait of their absolute standard of living.[33]

More than two-thirds of the households of Pentidattilo, then, or 70 out of the 101 with taxable assets, owned land and animals in the village. They included villagers with all types of occupations, from "civil" people to field laborers. Sixty-six households owned one or more parcels of land, including those headed by 7 "civil" people and by 35 of the 55 field laborers in the village. Eighteen households owned houses in addition to the one in which they lived, and 55 households owned animals. The total taxable assets in real estate were assessed at 171.15 *once*, those in animals at 405.20 *once*.[34] The citizens owned a total of 74 bovine animals, primarily oxen used for plowing, 108 sheep and goats, only 3 sows, and 44 horses, mules, and asses. Most of the equine animals were not taxed because they were reserved "for private use."[35]

Although most of the villagers owned taxable real estate and animals, nobody in Pentidattilo had much property. Only 3 parcels of land, all described as gardens, gave net revenues of 3 ducats or more, with the highest net revenue at 5.55 ducats for the garden belonging to the tenant farmer Domenico Zampaglione.[36] Apart from a few gardens, the most common parcels of land were vineyards and land with fruit trees, and parcels described simply as arable land were rare. This again shows that villagers tended to rent arable land from the feudal lord while they devoted the land they owned to more specialized agriculture. Only 12 villagers owned animals assessed at more than 10 *once*, and only 2 of those owned animals assessed at more than 20 *once*—the innkeeper, with 3 carting mules, and a massaro, with 4 oxen and a cow.

The survey data from Pentidattilo, then, reveal limited economic disparities. Unlike other villages, such as nearby Motta, all social groups in Pentidattilo had access to property, and no villager, or category of villagers, owned substantially more or less than their fellow citizens, with the exception of households headed by widows, which were generally the poorest. The local economy was characterized by a mixed labor-intensive agriculture, in which villagers exploited small parcels of land which they owned or rented (in addition to any feudal land to which they could gain access) to produce grains, fruits, wine, oil, and silk and used most of their animals to assist them in laboring on their fields. The few villagers whose primary occupation was not in agriculture also often owned land and animals.[37]

Relative economic equality is also evident in the high number of villagers who owned their own home. Forty-four of the 108 households in Pentidattilo lived in lodgings they owned, and these included representatives of all local occupations. Three of the 4 widows owned their own house, as did 21 field laborers, 12 massari, and 4 of the "civil" people. The homeowners included households at all levels of taxable assets. Fifty-five households lived in rented lodgings, although 26 of these actually paid no rent. Twenty-four of these 26 lived in houses owned by the feudal lord in Melito, and 20 of them worked there for the lord in the production of silk; 3 more were "at the service" of the lord, and 1 massaro paid no rent for unspecified reasons.[38] In fact, Melito in 1745 was still mostly a community of silk producers working for, and living in houses provided by, the feudal lord. Only 1 of Melito's 30 citizen households, headed by a field laborer, lived in a house it owned.

The 9 remaining households also paid no rent, though formally they did not own their houses. Two of these, the tower custodian in Melito and the castle guardian in Pentidattilo, paid no rent to the feudal lord for the lodgings that came with their occupations. The third was a hermit, and the fourth was a field laborer working for the feudal lord and living in a house in the countryside for which he paid no rent. Another 5, 4 of whom were "civil" households, lived in houses belonging to relatives in holy orders. It is, of course, most likely that assigning the ownership of the house to the family member who was an ecclesiastic was intended purely for fiscal reasons.[39] Only 29 households, therefore, or 1 in 4, paid rent for their lodging. Only 5 rents were higher than 2 ducats a year. One of these was paid by the notary, who presumably used a large lodging for his office, too, and rented two houses from the feudal lord for a rent of 7 ducats. Another was the captain of the tower, who paid 3 ducats, and the last 3 were the 2 millers and the innkeeper, who paid the feudal lord high rents for the businesses that functioned also as their lodgings.

As Melito grew, the situation would change somewhat by 1759, but the low percentage of renters in the università continued. In the later survey, 65 of old Pentidattilo's 106 households lived in lodgings they—or their relatives—owned. Thirty-eight, including the 2 millers, paid rent, while 3 more paid no rent for their lodgings. Of Melito's 50 households 24 worked and lived rent-free in the marquis's silk houses, 15 owned their lodgings, 7 paid rent, and 4 had various rent-free arrangements. By the time of the later survey the università also included 22 households in the hamlet of Corio, 8 of which owned their lodgings, 6 lived and worked in rent-free silk houses and gardens, and 8, in a sign of the fragility and novelty of the settlement, lived in haystacks.[40]

While some of the people of Pentidattilo lived more comfortably than their fellow citizens, according to the fiscal data no social group was excluded from access to property or from a comfortable economic situation, at least relative to the village as a whole. Indeed, field laborers, the poorest of the occupational categories used in the catasto, were well represented among property owners. Categories such as those used in the catasto are, in fact, often misleading in Pentidattilo, and the structure of wealth of each household, and the access to and use of the land by its components, were remarkably mixed and generally not determined by these social definitions. Although an elite group did exist in Pentidattilo and was growing more separate from its fellow villagers in the course of the eighteenth century, the level and sources of its wealth differed little from those of many other villagers.

The Village Elite

> Civile e poverissimo
>
> Civil and most poor
> > —From the 1759 rivela of Ugone Guerrera

Even when economic differences were limited, however, occupations and life-styles could differ substantially, with significant impact on each villager's status. The notarial contracts drawn in Pentidattilo in the 1740s and 1750s, when the two surveys were conducted, shed light on these and other factors.

According to the catasto survey, there were citizens of Pentidattilo worthy of being described as "better" than other villagers. The individual rivele do not specify which estate each household belonged to, but in 1745 ten households in the village were headed by men who were described as "living civilly," which meant not engaging in commoner occupations, such as farming or manual crafts. Only two of these men, in fact, reported an occupation, namely, the guardian of the castle, Girolamo Vernagallo, and the notary, Francesco Celia. The level of wealth, the standard of living, and the social function of these men can be explored to verify and analyze the significance of social hierarchies within the village.

The ten include the two deputies elected for the "better" estate, Bartolo Battaglia and Nuntio Palermo, and one of the two deputies elected for the "middle" one, Giuseppe Scrufari. In the 1759 survey the heads of thirteen households were listed as *magnifico,* a title of honor which denotes elite status, including four of the same men who were listed fourteen years earlier and the sons of three others.[41] Of the remaining three "civil" men from 1745, one was no longer included among the village elite, while the status of the widows of two others is not clear.[42]

Who were these men and what distinguished them from their fellow citizens? Five of the ten "civil" citizens of 1745 belonged to four of the larger clans in the village (Battaglia, Domenico Romeo, Scrufari, and Girolamo and Giuseppe Vernagallo), whose last names appear again and again in the history of Pentidattilo. Theirs are the names we find most frequently among the witnesses and tenants who testified in the relevi investigations since the late sixteenth century. Two of the oldest men, Battaglia and Domenico Malavendi, had been among the witnesses at the trial of Domenica Orlando thirty-five years before, when they both were already respected citizens and among the witnesses able to sign their name. Apart from family tradition, men who had elite status often had connections to the clergy. Four of the ten lived in houses owned by relatives who were priests, while Malavendi's son had taken minor orders. These men were also older than their fellow villagers: their average age was fifty, whereas for all heads of household in the village it was forty-three. The age factor also indicates the importance of individual achievement in determining elite status.

Other factors include education and standard of living. Eight of the ten men (all those for whom we have this information) were able to sign their name, though the notary's father was not, despite being labeled "civil." In 1759 ten of the thirteen magnifici were able to sign their name, though only two of the eight additional "civil" men were. Three of the 1745 men (Girolamo Vernagallo, Palermo, and Pietro Catanoso) had young sons who were attending school outside the village.[43] Three of the "civil" households (those of the notary, Antonio Amato, and Palermo) also kept servants, something only two other households in Pentidattilo did. Amato also owned one of only three horses kept in the village for private use. As we have seen, only the castle guardian and the notary did not live in houses they owned, though they both owned other houses. Finally, these men were tied together by family connections. While three were widowers, two of the others were married to women who bore the family name of two other men in the group, and after 1745 Giuseppe Vernagallo married a daughter of Pietro Catanoso.

Elite status was, however, not cast in stone. While the notary's father and Romeo's son are also described as "civil," Battaglia's son is listed as a massaro and one of Malavendi's sons as a field laborer, and as such they are taxed for their *industria*.[44] If we compare the 1745 and 1759 surveys, we can see both social ascents and descents. Giuseppe Vernagallo—who in 1745 at thirty-seven years of age owned nothing and lived at the expense of his brother Antonino, a priest—by 1759 had married a woman much his junior, had three children and two servants, owned property assessed at 22.25 *once*, and was elected one of the "better" deputies. On the other hand, in the later survey Giuseppe Scrufari was no longer a member of the village elite (he was, in fact, again elected as one of the "middle" deputies and was labeled neither magnifico nor "civil" but a field laborer). Moreover, the widow of Antonio Amato had lost her servant and was instead burdened with seven children, and Antonino Palermo, son of Nuntio, despite having gone to school, was not listed as a magnifico. Another example is Giulio Guerrera, the scribe of the 1710 trial, who appears as a magnifico in notarial papers of the early 1740s: in 1759 his two sons, Ugone and Marco Antonio, though "civil," were not magnifici, and, rather surprisingly for the scribe's sons, they were illiterate.

Prestige was more a matter of individual achievement than a transferable resource, even for members of established clans. It was not automatically transmitted to one's children, and even individual status, such as Giuseppe Scrufari's, could fluctuate within fifteen years. Nor was elite status closely tied to the level and sources of wealth of each household. Five of the "civil" men of 1745 paid taxes on the *industria* of sons, other relatives, and servants or apprentices, and this added to the taxable worth of their households. Still, only four of these ten men had taxable assets above the village median, and the average of their total taxable assets was below the village average. Two (Battaglia and Giuseppe Vernagallo) owned no taxable property. Of the eight who were taxed for *once di beni*, three (Malavendi, Palermo, and Girolamo Vernagallo) owned less than the village median of 5 *once di beni*, and Scrufari barely surpassed it with 5.05 *once di beni*. The remaining four all owned respectable patrimonies, including animals. However, the average *once di beni* owned by these ten men was only about 40 percent larger than the average for the seventy villagers who owned such taxable assets beyond their labor. Therefore, while three of these elite men were among the six villagers with more than 20 *once di beni* and indeed the notary owned the largest amount of taxable property of any citizen in Pentidattilo, elite status was not synonymous with substantial wealth, nor was substantial wealth sufficient to gain elite status (see tables 3.8 and 3.9 below).

It is possible that fraud occurred in 1745 to underreport the elite's wealth, and the recent epidemic may also have skewed the 1745 data. In the middle decades of the century demographic and economic growth resulted, as elsewhere in the kingdom, in the solidification of the status and wealth of local notables. The 1759 survey offers a rosier picture of the elite's wealth than the earlier document: the average for the eighteen "civil" households taxed for *once di beni* (27.08 *once*) was almost double the average for the village as a whole (14.20 *once*), and only five non-"civil" households had taxable property assessed at more than the "civil" average. Still, wealth was not equivalent to membership in the elite, and one of the three villagers with taxable property above 50 *once* was an illiterate field laborer (see tables 3.8 and 3.9 below). It would be only at the very end of the century, particularly as a result of the sale of church land in the 1780s, that a local notability established itself firmly as a social and economic elite.[45]

If, at least until the later decades of the eighteenth century, wealth was not the determining factor in establishing a citizen's elite status, did the men identified as members of the elite play any particular role in village society which expressed their different status? As we saw with the specific role of some witnesses in the 1710 trial, some village men enjoyed a particular authority in the community's public life. The surviving papers of notary Francesco Celia for the years 1740–54 help clarify the meaning of elite status within the village. Pentidattilo itself did not provide enough business for the notary, and Celia's surviving papers, which contain seventy-seven documents covering eight non-successive years, show that he had to travel frequently to neighboring villages and occasionally even to Reggio Calabria in order to find business. Only thirty-six of the surviving acts Celia drew up were prepared in Pentidattilo, though often his fellow villagers were parties to the acts he drew up elsewhere, and acts drawn up in Pentidattilo involved parties residing in other villages. Although these documents are too few to offer much detailed information on the economic life of the village, they allow us a glimpse at the structures of village society.[46]

Even with a small sample, the notarial documents reflect many types of transactions, from sales of houses or parcels of land to wills, from marriage contracts to agreements solving disputes, from certificates of good behavior to appointments to ecclesiastic benefices. Many of the contracts dealing with land (six out of nine) involved ecclesiastic property, which was subject to more stringent regulations. As we saw in Chapter 1, often land changed hands in Pentidattilo without a notarized act. Even when such an act was drawn up and a price named, the exchange often took, at least in part, the form of barter.

None of the elite men in Pentidattilo are among the primary parties involved in the notary's acts, but they all play a significant role as witnesses and guarantors, in various ways, of the accuracy and legitimacy of important moments in the lives of their fellow villagers. Seven of the ten men listed as "civil" in the 1745 survey appear repeatedly as witnesses to acts drawn up by the notary, who was himself also among the ten. The two exceptions are the castle guardian and Giuseppe Scrufari, whose elite status, as we have seen, was the weakest in the 1745 survey. All of the men listed as magnifico in the 1759 survey also appear as witnesses to acts drawn up in Celia's later years of activity, with the exception of one who would have been too young. The notary's father, Antonino, also listed as "civil," serves as witness to several acts and once as "expert appraiser of land" in a sale contract; his illiteracy was no obstacle to performing this function.[47]

Some of the elite men played an even more prominent role as keepers of public faith. The village did not always have a contract judge (a minor official whose presence and signature were required in notarized acts), and often the feudal governor replaced him. However, the governor himself was at times absent, and in these cases someone from the village served as the governor's lieutenant for the purpose of approving contracts. Domenico Malavendi and Pietro Catanoso held this position, in 1741–42 and 1747–48, respectively. Giuseppe Vernagallo was among those attesting to the good behavior of the tower captain in Melito in 1747, and in 1751 he was serving as the agent of the Chapel of the Holiest Sacrament when a parcel of its land was sold.[48] In 1759 two magnifici served as representatives of village ecclesiastic foundations in the drafting of the catasto, and another was the marquis's erario.

These men, identified in the fiscal surveys as the village elite, thus played an essential role in the public and social life of the village. As prominent, respected citizens, and probably consequently also as the notary's friends, they lent their own respectability to verify, guarantee, and strengthen important moments in the common life of the village and in the private affairs of many of their fellow citizens. In this their role was matched only by that of the parish priests (often these men's relatives), who also appear frequently as witnesses in the notary's acts. While the feudal governor served only one year and was often either absent or little known to most villagers, these men provided the continuity and stability crucial to a peaceful village life. Though they were not necessarily wealthier than their fellow villagers, their education, family connections, age, and personal reputation and accomplishments established their prominence within village society. Their function in the mid-eighteenth century was quite similar to that we have seen served by the final male witnesses in the trial of Domenica Orlando.[49]

The "Middle" and "Low" Estates

> Con quella pompa funerale conveniente al suo stato
>
> With that funeral pomp suitable to her condition
> —From the 1751 will of Lucretia Foti

What, then, of the rest of Pentidattilo's citizens? Apart from a few elite men, the solidity of one's position as a resident of Pentidattilo was linked less to one's economic situation than to one's membership in one of the established village clans and to the cycles of one's family life. Even the "low" citizens enjoyed a stable, secure status in the village if they were linked to the older, larger clans; the true outsiders, as the trial of Anna de Amico illustrates, were those without such connections. It is the names of these clans, wealthy or not, which recur many times in all the documents relating important public moments in Pentidattilo's history.

The census categories of "middle" and "low" citizens are not specifically defined in the records. Through the fiscal survey we can, however, analyze occupational divisions within the village, which are more significant factors in determining levels of wealth. In 1745 eight households were headed by men without a recorded occupation, and four were headed by widows. Three more were headed by men described as disabled, without any reported occupation. The great majority of the remaining ninety-three households were headed by men engaged in agriculture. These were described as bracciale, *forese* (tenant farmer), and massaro. Together these three occupations employed seventy-eight of the heads of households.[50]

Although these three categories were not strictly parallel to amount or type of property held, their levels of wealth were quite different. Twenty-two of the fifty-five field laborers owned no taxable assets beyond their labor, and the average total taxable wealth of their households was 19.19 *once*, below the village average of 22.16 but above the median of 18.03. The five *foresi* were not in very different circumstances, as two of them paid no *once di beni* and their average total taxable wealth was 22.20 *once*. The massari, on the other hand, were obviously the village's agricultural elite. Their main characteristic was that they all owned taxable animals, and this resulted also in high totals for their taxable assets. Their average total taxable wealth came to 34.15 *once*, or one and a half times the village average and by far the village's highest for any occupational category. Their average *once di industria* was also the village's

TABLE 3.5

Occupation of the Heads of Household in Pentidattilo

(from the 1745 fiscal survey)

Occupation	Number of Cases
Field laborer (*bracciale*)	55
Farmer (*massaro*)	18
"Living civilly" (*civil vivente*)	8
Tenant farmer (*forese*)	5
Widow	4
Disabled	3
Guardian of cattle	2
Fisherman	2
Miller	2
Greengrocer	2
Innkeeper	1
Hermit	1
Captain of the tower in Melito	1
Custodian of the tower	1[a]
Castle guardian	1
Notary	1[b]
Ironsmith	1
Carter	1
Total	109

[a] The custodian was also listed as a field laborer, hence the total of 109 households instead of 108.

[b] The notary and the castle guardian were also defined as "living civilly."

highest, and their average *once di beni* was again one and a half times the village average and among the highest in the village. In 1759 the massari again had the highest average total taxable assets of any category in the village and the second highest average *once di beni*.[51]

Again, however, these occupations did not represent insurmountable social barriers. In several cases, the sons or brothers of heads of households who were massari were described as field laborers, and this was true also for one of the sons of Domenico Malavendi, who himself "lived civilly." The reverse was also sometimes the case. Tables 3.5 and 3.6 report the occupations recorded in the 1745 fiscal survey for all the people of Pentidattilo. The village economy offered little opportunity beyond agriculture, and pastoralism was not a primary occupation in the village. There were few artisans in Pentidattilo, and, with the exception of the innkeeper's son-in-law, who was a carter, no secondary household members were working as artisans in 1745. Most of the few local artisans, as was true in much of Europe, complemented their craft with farming, and several owned land or animals. The presence of an inn and of a few greengrocers and carters shows that there was some trading and marketing in the area, but probably not yet sufficient as a full-time activity. Yet Pentidattilo's population included more occupational diversity than bigger villages, such as nearby Motta: there field laborers constituted four-fifths of the population, and artisans were less numerous than in the smaller Pentidattilo.[52]

Two examples drawn from notarial acts allow us to analyze closely the standard of living and social life of nonelite households in eighteenth-century Pentidattilo. What emerges is a relative level of economic comfort, to be expected from those—quite few in Pentidattilo—who felt the need to use a notary, strengthened through the connections of extended families. We also find no firm barriers to social contacts between villagers of different occupations and economic situations within the small-scale and tightly knit village society.

The first example comes from a milieu close to the village elite but confirms the fluctuating nature of status, the importance of clan connections, the open social contacts of village life, and the effects of the cycles of family life. The earliest and one of the last surviving acts notarized by Celia regard a branch of the omnipresent Battaglia clan. On January 16, 1740, the notary drew up the will of Giovan Battista Battaglia, in his two-floor house near the main parish church. Attending were seven worthy witnesses, including the arciprete Giuseppe Palermo, the subdeacon Giuseppe Battaglia, two other priests (of the Vernagallo and Squillaci families), the magnifico Nuntio Palermo, Filippo Foti, and the magnifico Antonino Celia, father of the notary. The governor was also in attendance, serving as contract judge.[53]

TABLE 3.6

Occupation of Other Members of Households in Pentidattilo

(from the 1745 fiscal survey)

Occupation	Number of Cases
Field laborer	40
Domestic servants	6[a]
Farmer	4
Tenant farmer	4
Apprentice (*garzone*)	4[b]
Cleric	4[c]
Cattle farmer (*massaro di bovi*)	3[d]
"Living civilly"	2[e]
Carter	1
Total	68

[a] Four women and 2 men.

[b] Two of the *garzoni* lived with the notary; the other 2 lived with a *massaro* and with a *bracciale*, so they were probably farmhands rather than apprentices.

[c] These were all young men who had received minor orders. One, Paolino Malavendi, was a "married cleric."

[d] These were people who rented oxen belonging to others and shared the product with the animals' owners.

[e] The notary's father and the son of Domenico Romeo.

TABLE 3.7

Occupation of the Heads of Household in Pentidattilo

(from the 1759 fiscal survey)

Occupation[a]	Number of Cases			
	P	M	C	T
Field laborer	27	25	8	60
Farmer	16	9	8	33
Widow	28	4	0	32
"Living civilly"	17	3	0	20
Guardian of cattle	4	2	4	10
Tenant farmer	7	1	0	8
Miller	2	0	0	2
Greengrocer	0	2	0	2
Barber	1	1	0	2
Military	0	1	1	2
Hermit	1	0	0	1
Guardian of pigs	1	0	0	1
Notary	1	0	0	1
Scribe (*mastrodatti*)	0	0	1	1
Tailor	1	0	0	1
Muleteer	0	1	0	1
Unmarried woman	0	1	0	1
Total	106	50	22	178

NOTE: "P" stands for Pentidattilo proper, "M" for Melito, "C" for Corio, and "T" for the total for the entire *università*.

[a] The notary and the scribe were also included in the "civil" category, which thus numbered 22.

Giovan Battista was a member of the most prominent village clan. Though he was not labeled magnifico himself, his wife, Felicia, was the daughter of the "civil" Bartolo Battaglia, presumably a relative and one of the most respected citizens of Pentidattilo, though, as we have seen, hardly a wealthy one. The Battaglia also had another mark of distinction, a family tomb in the main parish church. It was there that, after the customary invocations, Giovan Battista directed that his body be interred. He further left 10 ducats, to be obtained through the sale of the next harvest on his land, for masses to be offered for his soul. He stated that he had left further instructions with the dittereo Salvatore Gangemi and another priest.

The bulk of his estate, which was not detailed, Giovan Battista left to his daughter, Margherita, under the guardianship of her mother, Felicia. Should Margherita not reach adult age, the estate was to be divided between Felicia and Giovan Battista's brother Giovan Maria. Five years later, at the time of the catasto, Felicia and Margherita (then twenty-eight and eight years of age, respectively) were living with their widowed father and grandfather, Bartolo, sixty-five years of age, and his two other children. As we have seen, Bartolo's

TABLE 3.8

Taxable Assets by Occupation, Pentidattilo, 1745

Occupation	No. of Households	*Once*	Percentage	Average
		Total Taxable *Once*		
Civili	10	181.23	8	18.05[a]
Massari	18	621.01	27.3	34.15
Foresi	5	113.08	5	22.20
Bracciali	55	1,079.18	47.4	19.19
Artisans[b]	9	224.05	9.8	24.27
Others[c]	5	58.10	2.5	11.20
Village[d]	102	2,278.05	100	22.16
		Once di Industria		
Civili	5	64	3.7	12.24
Massari	17	396	23.1	23.09
Foresi	5	78	5	15.18
Bracciali	54	960	56.2	17.23
Artisans	9	170	10	18.27
Others	3	36	2	12
Village	93	1,704	100	18.10[e]
		Once di Beni		
Civili	8	117.23	20.7	14.21[f]
Massari	18	225.01	39.4	12.15
Foresi	3	35.08	6.1	11.22
Bracciali	33	119.18	20.3	3.19
Artisans	4	54.05	9.5	13.16[g]
Others	4	22.10	4	5.17
Village	70	574.05	100	8.06[h]

[a] The *civili* heads of households were not assessed for their own labor, though 5 of them were assessed for the *once di industria* of other men in their household. One of the 10 was not assessed for any taxable assets at all, but I have included him in this table in order to gain a complete picture of this particular category, formally the village elite.

[b] Two millers, 2 greengrocers, 2 fishermen, a carter, an innkeeper, and an ironsmith.

[c] The captain of the tower, 2 guardians of cattle, and 2 men described simply as disabled (and hence not assessed for *once di industria*).

[d] The remaining 6 households (of the 108 secular ones in Pentidattilo) were headed by the 4 widows (none of whom owned any taxable assets), an old hermit, and a disabled man, both of whom owned no taxable property and were not taxed for their labor.

[e] Nine of the 102 households were not assessed for any *once di industria*: 5 of the *civili*, 1 *massaro*, 1 *bracciale*, and 2 others (the non-*civili* ones because they included no able-bodied male). The average *once di industria* if one counted all 102 households would be 16.26.

[f] The average for all 10 *civili* households would come to 11.24 *once di beni*, but 2 of them were not assessed for any.

[g] The innkeeper, with 30.10 *once di beni*, raised the average for this category considerably.

[h] Thirty-two of the 102 households were not taxed for *once di beni*; this did not mean that they owned no property but that they received no net taxable income from any property they might own. They included 2 *civili*, 2 *foresi*, 22 *bracciali*, 5 artisans, and 1 other. The average *once di beni* if one counted all 102 households would be 5.20.

TABLE 3.9
Taxable Assets by Occupation, Pentidattilo, 1759

Occupation	No. of Households	Once	Percentage	Average
		Total Taxable *Once*		
Civili	21	516.26	15.9	24.18[a]
Massari	26	952.08	29.2	36.19
Foresi	8	132.22	4.1	16.18
Bracciali	53	965.20	29.7	18.07
Artisans[b]	8	174.10	5.4	21.24
Others[c]	9	215.21	6.6	23.29
Widows	19	296.23	9.1	15.19
Village	144	3,254.10	100	22.18[d]
		Once di Industria		
Civili	2	26	1.5	13
Massari	26	463	27.7	17.24
Foresi	8	120	7.2	15
Bracciali	52	697	41.8	13.12
Artisans	6	82	4.9	13.17
Others	9	157	9.4	17.13
Widows	11	126	7.5	11.14
Village	114	1,671	100	14.20[e]
		Once di Beni		
Civili	18	490.26	31	27.08[f]
Massari	26	489.08	30.9	18.25
Foresi	3	12.22	0.8	4.06
Bracciali	31	268.20	17	8.21
Artisans	8	92.10	5.8	11.15
Others	8	58.21	3.7	7.08
Widows	16	170.23	10.8	10.20
Village	110	1,583.10	100	14.13[g]

[a] One of the *civili* is reported with no assets, and the information on another is missing from the document. I have included these two in the table in order to assess the village elite as a whole.

[b] Two millers, 2 greengrocers, 2 barbers, a tailor, and a muleteer.

[c] Seven guardians of animals, a hermit, and a soldier.

[d] The remaining 14 households (of 158 secular ones in the two villages) were headed by widows. If one counted all 158 households, the average for the village would be 20.18 *once*. In this table I am including in the households of Pentidattilo and Melito two noncitizen households residing in Corio (a *massaro* and a *bracciale*) but which for unclear reasons are counted in the document among the citizen households. Only 4 other Corio households held any taxable assets, for a total of 49.20 *once di beni*; see table 3.2.

[e] A total of 44 households were not assessed for *once di industria*: 19 of the *civili*, 1 *bracciale*, 2 artisans, and 22 widows. The average *once di industria* if one counted all 158 households would be 10.17.

[f] The average for all 21 *civili* would come to 23.11 *once di beni*, but 3 of them were not assessed for any.

[g] Forty-eight households were not taxed for *once di beni*; this did not mean that they owned no property, but that they received no net taxable income from any property they might own. They included 3 *civili*, 5 *foresi*, 22 *bracciali*, 1 other, and 17 widows. The average *once di beni* if one counted all 158 households would be 10.01.

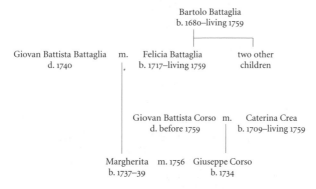

FIG. 3.1. The family of Margherita Battaglia
Note: In this and the other genealogical charts, the dates are drawn from baptismal records, fiscal censuses, and trial records. The discordances in dates are due to discrepancies between the 1745 and 1759 censuses.

son, in 1745 a *massaro di bovi,* did not inherit his father's status, and in 1759 he was living—not a magnifico—with his own wife and three children, while the very old Bartolo by that time lived alone.

Margherita Battaglia did live to adulthood, but in her case, too, we see an example of the tenuous nature of local status, despite respectable wealth. On February 22, 1754, notary Celia drew up a marriage contract between Felicia Battaglia, acting for her daughter (then about sixteen), and Giuseppe Corso, whose title of "mastro" defines him as an artisan. The contract was concluded "through common acquaintances, friends, and relatives" and in the presence of the contract judge and three witnesses, including magnifico Paolino Pangallo and Antonio Battaglia. The dowry included 50 ducats in cash, a two-floor house with two ground-floor rooms, four cows and a heifer, a full bed with two mattresses and pillows, and a long list of clothes and housewares. Margherita's trousseau included blankets, linen of various types and qualities, a bridal dress with a damask girdle (this item was described as used), four silk and four canvas veils, shirts and jackets, tablecloths, and coats. It also included a garnet necklace with eight gold buttons, pearl earrings, a gold ring with a turquoise stone, a crown with a silver medal, two silver buttons, plus eight tomoli of wheat, six chairs, and several pans, skewers, grills, and candlesticks of copper and tin.[54]

This dowry was considerable, though, as was common in the kingdom but odd for an only daughter, it included no land. The house objects and especially the linen bespeak comfort and even luxury for a rural family anywhere in Europe.[55] In exchange Giuseppe offered all legal guarantees to return the dowry and pledged a *dotario* (the husband's gift, to be paid at the husband's death) of one-third the value of the dowry. The marriage was to be celebrated after two years, though the animals were to change hands immediately. In the 1759 survey Giuseppe Corso, then twenty-five years of age, is indeed listed as married to Margherita Battaglia, then twenty years old, and his trade is identified as tailoring. It seems that most of his tailoring actually took place in Reggio Calabria, and he is therefore not taxed for *industria*. His taxable property, all consisting of animals, is assessed at 12 *once*.[56]

This alliance seems lopsided. Margherita's dowry was substantial and her family connections prestigious. Giuseppe, on the other hand, belonged to a small family, fairly new to Pentidattilo. He was probably related to the field laborer Giovan Battista Corso, who had been born in Reggio but who lived in Pentidattilo when he testified at Domenica Orlando's 1710 trial and had married Vittoria, from the established Vernagallo family. But, while a Francesca Corso was the wife of a field laborer's son in 1745 and a Maria Corso the wife of another, no household headed by a man with that name was in the village in 1745, and only Giuseppe's was listed in 1759.[57] Giuseppe was a young artisan about whose previous fortune we know nothing. Margherita was, however, the daughter of a widow, and her most prominent relative, her grandfather Bartolo, was by the time of her wedding well into his seventies and neither a wealthy nor a healthy man (he had been described in the 1745 census as "disabled in half his body"). This marriage reinforces the conclusion that status and prestige in Pentidattilo were neither tied primarily to wealth nor easily transmitted across generations and that social contacts remained fluid and could fluctuate according to individual achievements and the vagaries of the family cycle.

Similar conclusions can be drawn from a document concerning another family, one not included in the village's elite, though clearly a settled one in Pentidattilo. This is the will of Lucretia Foti, drawn up by the notary on November 7, 1751, in the two-floor house where Lucretia lived and which she owned. An array of seven villagers, including two Battaglia (one of them Bartolo), a Vernagallo, and a Palermo, witnessed the act along with the contract judge. The dittereo Gangemi was named testamentary executor.[58]

We know a fair amount about Lucretia and her family. The Foti were one of the largest clans in the village, accounting for four heads of household in the 1745 survey and three in 1759. They appear in many documents about Pentidattilo over at least two centuries, and Antonio Foti had been a prominent

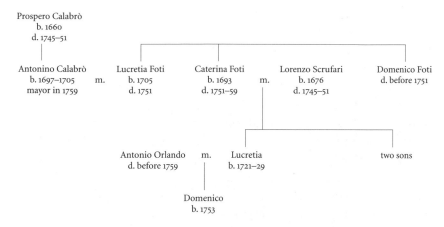

FIG. 3.2. The family of Lucretia Foti

witness at the trial of Domenica Orlando. Although they were not wealthy—
all four Foti households were headed by field laborers in 1745—their position
in the village was a secure one. Lucretia was married to Antonino Calabrò, of
another well-established local family, with three households in both 1745 and
1759. In 1745 Antonino and Lucretia still lived with his aged father, a field
laborer, but Antonino was a massaro, and the household owned a very respectable 18.05 *once di beni*. Antonino and Lucretia, both reported as forty
years old in 1745, had no children. In 1759 an Antonino Calabrò, probably the
same man, was one of the village's mayors, was assessed for 32 *once di beni,*
and, now married to a thirty-year-old woman, had two small children. He
was, however, illiterate.[59]

Lucretia was not a member of the village elite, but her place in Pentidattilo's society was a solid one. She had brought to her husband a substantial
dowry and, since she had no children, was able to bequeath it freely. After an
elaborate religious invocation, her will stipulated that her body be interred in
the parish church in the tomb of the brethren and sisters of the confraternity
of the Holiest Sacrament "with that funeral pomp suitable to her condition."
She then named her sister, Caterina, widow of Lorenzo Scrufari, as her universal heir. The Scrufari were also a large local clan, with four households in
1745, including the "civil" Giuseppe and a miller. In that year Lorenzo was still
alive, and he and Caterina (then aged sixty-nine and fifty-two, respectively)
had three children, among them a daughter named Lucretia, like her aunt.

Lucretia, however, left most of her estate (the greatest part of which had

been her dowry) to the church. Most of what she owned was to be sold in order
to pay for masses for her own soul and that of her late brother Domenico. Her
husband was to be given the chance to match any offered price for the real
estate and animals, but he received no other mark of preference in Lucretia's
will. Her house, a vineyard, an ox, a heifer, seven goats, and five tomoli of wheat
were to be sold, along with several articles of clothing and jewels. Lucretia
owned a gold ring and gold earrings with pearls, a garnet necklace, a silk dress,
hemp clothes and house linen, a cotton blanket, a mattress, and other linen.
Her sister received two jackets, a shirt, a tablecloth, and one tomolo of rye; her
niece and namesake, a shirt and a girdle; and a nephew and a grandnephew,
one tomolo of wheat each. This bequest may have helped young Lucretia in
finding a husband, for she appears in the 1759 census as the widow of an Antonio Orlando.[60] By that time her mother, Caterina, must also have died.

What we have here is a significant dowry for the wife of a massaro and the
sister-in-law of a field laborer, though clearly not as large as Margherita Battaglia's (and including no ready cash). Like Margherita, and several other
women in Pentidattilo, Lucretia lived in a house she owned. The fact that
almost the entire estate is represented by Lucretia's dowry points to the difficulty for a married woman to acquire any property fully her own, but the
dowry itself points to a relative level of comfort. Lucretia was also evidently
well integrated into a network of family links and religious structures that
helped define her position within Pentidattilo's society. In many ways, her situation must have resembled that of Domenica Orlando, whose family, while
not as numerous as the Foti, also had a long, stable, and respected presence in
the village and who also probably owned the house in which she and her husband lived during their unhappy union.

These two examples shed light on the factors that shaped social hierarchies
in Pentidattilo and confirm that the village preserved an atmosphere of relative equality and communal unity. Clans, with their connections and established positions in village society, were essential in defining the status of individual villagers at all social levels, as was the specific family situation of each
individual. Wealth played a limited role in determining the villagers' social life
and contacts, and indeed poor, nonelite villagers had a secure function in the
village's administration and often were engaged in stable and equal relationships with those nominally their betters. There certainly were poor citizens in
Pentidattilo, and they were more likely to be found among the bracciali than
among other occupational categories. But members of all such categories
could and did attain economic comfort and social respect. Villagers who be-

longed to established families and kin groups also participated actively in the web of ties created by godparenthood, neighborhood, and friendship.

In Pentidattilo, as in most European villages, the truly marginal villagers were those without established connections. Such was Anna de Amico, as is shown by her trial, and such were some of the women who were widowed or abandoned by their husbands. The 1745 survey lists 45 heads of household (out of 108) whose family name appears only once in the document. When, however, we eliminate those whose family name appears more than once in the 1759 list, those whose last name is borne by wives in the two surveys, and those whose families appear frequently in other village documents, we are left with only 10 men without apparent local connections, all rather poor (only 1 massaro among them, and not a wealthy one). Furthermore, 6 of these men were married to women with prominent village names and lived in Pentidat- tilo proper. The last 4 (2 fishermen, a massaro and a bracciale) all resided in Melito, which is where one finds most of the new family names in local doc- uments.[61]

Even before contacts with wider markets began to affect the area's economy, Pentidattilo was never fully isolated from connections with the outside world. Neither the isolation nor the poverty of even small, remote villages should be exaggerated, as David Vassberg recently observed for early modern Castile. Villagers always knew about the outside world, interacted with it, and re- sponded to its influence, while maintaining their traditions and their distrust of outsiders. Pentidattilo was neither large nor wealthy, but it was far from immobile, and its society was always fluid, dynamic, and remarkably egalitar- ian. By the mid-eighteenth century, however, profound changes began.

Melito, barely a hamlet at the end of the seventeenth century and still a small community in the 1740s, would by the 1750s and 1760s become the focus of local growth and change. As the eighteenth century progressed, the new settlement on the coast attracted a growing population, much of which came from outside the old village, owing not only to the new safety of the coast but especially to the new economic circuits in which the local economy began to operate. These new inhabitants formed in Melito a different kind of society than the one that characterized the traditional, small settlement high on the rock. There clan connections mattered less and personal wealth and entrepre- neurship more. Economic and social disparities became more pronounced— as seen in standards of living, economic dependence, demographic and resi- dential patterns—and began to have a greater impact on the village's social hierarchies and life. Melito, as we shall see in Chapter 4, was also home to different households, generally poorer and larger than in old Pentidattilo, and many of the old customs that had distinguished local communal life began to disappear in the new village.

The trial of Domenica Orlando presents an image of a cohesive peasant community, and indeed the trial ended with the reassertion of established social patterns. The outsider was condemned and expelled, the defendants belonging to old families escaped punishment, and the solid citizens of Pentidattilo cooperated with the court and maintained their role as the community's spokesmen and guarantors. Yet, just as the judicial system at work in the 1710 trial would soon be substantially critiqued and reformed, within a half century Pentidattilo's economy and social life would be irrevocably altered.

FOUR

Family, Household, and Community

The death of Antonino Cuzzucli obviously awakened suspicions and revealed a tense and difficult family situation. The union of Antonino and Domenica Orlando was of course not a typical one. Domenica was twenty-three at the time of the trial, and, given the dating of her alleged abortion to at least four, if not six, years earlier, she must have been quite young when the couple had married, younger than was usual for rural women in the Kingdom of Naples. Whatever the reasons for Antonino's frequent and prolonged absences from the village, that they occurred so soon after he and Domenica had married indicates a union unhappy from the start. Yet, at the same time, the trial records, when examined along with other documents, can yield information about what marriage meant within village society, how families and households came together and operated, and how all families in each village were tied together through numerous relationships, rituals, and practices.

A careful reading of the details of the trial depositions sheds light on local social practices and illustrates the strength of the links that bound together the people of Pentidattilo. Village society was fluid and vibrant, as we saw, and the villagers were connected to one another in an intricate network of mutual obligations. The specific position and role of outsiders and insiders, the respective responsibilities and commitments of men and women within the family sphere and in the public life of the community, the forms of social interaction between the sexes, and the different patterns of sociability followed by women and men can be explored by analyzing daily life in the village as reflected in the trial records.

All villagers, no matter their means, age, and gender, engaged in frequent and fruitful contacts with their fellow residents, and the links of godparenthood, neighborhood, and friendship crossed economic, social, and gender lines. Men and women imbued these ties with different meanings: men's social connections were often associated with economic relations and public issues, whereas women's focused on the domestic sphere and the cycles of family life. But no villager, especially if connected with the established clans, was isolated from intense and useful exchanges. Outsiders had to struggle more to earn a place in these social networks, but in normal situations they could and did find significant functions to exercise.

Although these traits distinguished the traditional society of Pentidattilo, in this respect, too, we find that the mid-eighteenth century brought new developments and substantial changes in social organization. The census records show that Melito not only evolved a different economy from that of the old village but was also home to different kinds of citizens, who established different living arrangements.

The Trial's Principals

> Cu ammazza u porcu è cuntentu n'annu, cu si marita è cuntentu nu jornu.
>
> Who kills a pig is happy for a year, who gets married is happy for a day.
> — Calabrian proverb

Who precisely were the protagonists of the Pentidattilo trial? The first person to appear in the trial records was Giovan Domenico Cuzzucli, the dead Antonino's brother. The Cuzzucli clan was a large one in the area of Pentidattilo, though not a wealthy one. Its name was typical of Pentidattilo and nearby Montebello and San Lorenzo, and its Greek origin bespeaks its ties with the older history of the area.[1] Giovan Domenico had been baptized on September 21, 1682; his and Antonino's parents were Giovan Battista Cuzzucli and Antonia Familari. Since Domenica's mother was also named Familari (not one of the most common names in the village), Antonino and his wife may have been cousins, perhaps even first cousins. Moreover, in the generation of their parents, one Antonio Orlando had married Sicilia Cuzzucli and one Francesco Orlando Portia Cuzzucli, so that Antonino and Domenica's marriage might have been one of those cases—frequent in early modern southern Italy—of marriage among cousins with the purpose of returning and circulating dowries within the same clans.[2]

The Cuzzucli clan was present in both Pentidattilo and nearby Montebello, where Antonino and his brother had lived some years before the trial. Al-

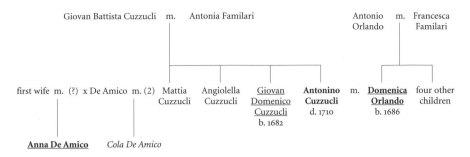

FIG. 4.1. The Cuzzucli and Orlando families
Note: Defendants' names are underlined and in bold; witnesses' names are italicized; victim's name is in bold; denouncer's name is underlined. The "x" indicates an unknown first name.

though not among the most prominent clans in Pentidattilo, to judge from their rare appearances among the village's administrators, the Cuzzucli were not insignificant figures, and men of this name were active in the village's economy throughout the seventeenth century. One Antonino Cuzzucli (probably not the murder victim) had been a village alderman in 1694. At the turn of the eighteenth century, therefore, the clan was established in the village economy and society, although its level of wealth had declined compared with a century before.[3] After the time of the trial, the family became less prominent in Pentidattilo. By the 1745 census only 1 of the 108 households in Pentidattilo was headed by a Cuzzucli (a laborer). At the time of the 1759 census, only 1 household in Melito was headed by a Cuzzucli man, and a few other men with the name of Cuzzucli appear in mid-eighteenth-century documents about the coastal village.[4]

The clan, on the other hand, was always prominent and numerous in nearby Montebello. Around 1600 there was in that village a church called Santa Maria dei Cuzzucli, indicating a position of wealth and prestige for the clan. In 1648 Antonio Cuzzucli was one of the leaders of the local revolt against the baron. Other Cuzzucli were prominent there in the early eighteenth century. The clan had long gravitated around Montebello, which helps explain Antonino's prolonged stays there, and its social and economic status within Pentidattilo was declining by the late seventeenth century. The murder of Antonino coincided with the Cuzzucli's near complete abandonment of Pentidattilo.[5]

At the time of the trial, therefore, the murder victim and the plaintiff were not members of a prominent clan in Pentidattilo, and in fact, members of their clan were becoming less numerous in the village. While the three defendants were also of humble status personally—and, in the case of Anna de Amico, a woman living alone and not a local native, marginal to village society—they were better integrated within the older and larger families of Pentidattilo, and this may have been one of the factors that ultimately protected Domenica and Pietro from the direst consequences of the crimes of which they stood accused. In the small world of the village, and in a justice system that granted community values and concerns an essential role, belonging to an established and numerous clan was a decisive advantage.

Domenica was a native citizen, while Anna and Pietro had been born elsewhere, in Montebello and Motta San Giovanni, respectively. Like the Cuzzucli, all three clans were more prominent in the village and the surrounding area in the seventeenth than in the eighteenth century, though the Crea were at all times more numerous and prosperous than the other two. The name Orlando was typical of the Pentidattilo area, while Crea (of Greek derivation) is found more widely in southern Calabria.[6] Domenica Orlando had been baptized on October 17, 1686, the daughter of Antonio, son of Leonardo Orlando, and his wife, Francesca Familari. Domenica was therefore twenty-three years old at the time of the trial, though she declared to be twenty-six. She had an older sister and three younger brothers, and the godparents of all the siblings belonged to old Pentidattilo families. At the end of the seventeenth century there were at least three Orlando households in Pentidattilo.[7]

The earliest documented member of the family was Francesco Orlando. In 1646–49, along with others, he rented 150 tomoli of some of the best feudal land in the village, for an annual rent of 165 tomoli of wheat. Francesco was very prominent in Pentidattilo: in 1648 he was one of the two village procurators in negotiating with the marquis the capitulations that followed the 1647–48 revolt. The following year Francesco, who was illiterate, was elected as one of the two village mayors. In 1670, by now eighty years old, he acted as a witness in Pentidattilo's quarrel with nearby San Lorenzo over the villages' borders, a role that indicates that he was viewed with great respect in the village.[8]

The clan grew in numbers, and in 1663 Giovan Battista Orlando was the village's dittereo, usually the next in line for the position of head parish priest. Several Orlando men rented feudal land in the later seventeenth century. The family declined somewhat in the following century. In 1745 the census listed only two Orlando as heads of households, and both were field laborers. For the 1759 census Stefano Orlando, the only head of household by that surname to remain in the village, served as one of the two deputies of the "low" estate, while another Orlando household was in Melito. The family was still present in Pentidattilo at the end of the century.[9]

Domenica Orlando's mother, Francesca Familari, still alive at the time of the trial and living in Melito, also belonged to an established Pentidattilo family. Familari men were engaged in the local agriculture and testified in relevio investigations throughout the seventeenth century. Though only one Familari household appears in the 1745 and 1759 censuses, others with that name lived in Montebello in the eighteenth century. Santo Familari was a respected and wealthy priest in Pentidattilo in the mid-eighteenth century, when he witnessed several notarial acts and purchased an expensive house. In 1782 Natale Familari, though illiterate, was mayor of Pentidattilo, and later in the decade he was the public assessor in the village for the sale of church land, and he purchased some parcels himself. In 1794 Francesco Familari was the village notary.[10]

Domenica Orlando, then, could count, also through her mother, on a solid network of family connections in the village. This was even more true of her alleged lover, Pietro Crea, despite the fact that he was born outside Pentidattilo and did not own a house in the village. At the trial Pietro declared his age to be thirty-two and his occupation custodian of the Andilla forest. Most likely in an effort to exculpate himself from the case, Pietro claimed that he had very few acquaintances in Pentidattilo, that he resided in the forest, and that he stayed with his brother Marco whenever he needed to spend the night in the village. Though this strategy, if such it was, worked successfully for Pietro in this case, and though he may personally have been relatively extraneous to Pentidattilo's life, his family was among the most prominent in the village.

The Crea are one of the few clans to appear in sources relating to Pentidattilo from the sixteenth through the eighteenth century, and often in prominent positions within the village's society and economy. From the late sixteenth century onwards, members of the clan repeatedly rented baronial land and offices, testified in relevio investigations, occupied communal offices, and engaged in costly investments and activities, such as renting the Andilla forest. In the eighteenth century the Crea clan remained numerous in Pentidattilo, and other Crea households were to be found in nearby villages, especially Montebello, where the Crea owned several parcels of land in the middle of the century. In the 1745 Pentidattilo census three Crea households appear, headed by laborers and farmers. In the 1759 census there were four Crea households, making the clan the second largest in the village. The family was still present in Pentidattilo at the end of the eighteenth century.[11]

Less is known about the family of the last defendant, Anna de Amico. The fact that she did not belong to an established and large clan probably explains why she was the only one of the three defendants who received an actual punishment. Anna stated that she was thirty-six years old and had been born in Montebello, though she had long resided in Pentidattilo. Her personal situation placed her in the vulnerable position shared by many of the women who were suspected of witchcraft or magical practices throughout early modern rural Europe. She had been married to Francesco Albano, who was also from outside the village, and he had abandoned her, and Pentidattilo, long before the trial, leaving Anna in a difficult position in the village, one reflected in the bad reputation that nearly all witnesses assigned her. Her husband's departure, in fact, was ascribed by some witnesses to Anna's behavior, though, of course, these testimonials ought to be considered with more than usual skepticism, since Anna was also evidently well acquainted with many villagers, several of whom, by their own admission, appealed to her for help in various matters.[12]

Anna's family was of limited status in Pentidattilo. The only prominent man with this name appeared in Pentidattilo in the mid-seventeenth century. Cola Maria de Amico was owed money from the università in the 1650s, and he later sold 25 tomoli of land to the marquis, a large property. Maria Schirrica, who testified in the trial, was the widow of one Giuseppe de Amico. Cola de Amico was another witness, and he may have been Anna's half brother (though this is not mentioned in the trial), because his mother, Mattia Cuzzucli, is described as Anna's stepmother. In any case, though two de Amico rented land in Montebello in 1732, the family largely disappeared from Pentidattilo after the trial. No man of this name heads any household in the 1745 and 1759 censuses, though in 1752 the widow of a Nicola de Amico was a party to a land sale.[13]

The three defendants, therefore, like the murder victim and the plaintiff, had a clear place in the social and economic structure of Pentidattilo. Their standing in the village, and the image and status of their families, affected how the witnesses perceived and presented the defendants' actions, motives, and reputation and consequently how the latter were treated by the court during the trial. The identity of the trial's principals, their situation within the village community, and their relationships with their fellow villagers, which we can see through the depositions, also raise questions about family structures, gender relations, and community life in the village.

Antonino and Domenica were obviously not a happy couple, yet their marriage was not atypical: they belonged to established local clans, and they were probably related, and thus their union was part of the strategies employed by villagers to regulate the transmission of property and the continuation of families within their community. Domenica, in particular, despite her near abandonment by her husband and her dubious behavior, was integrated in a complex tangle of relations with other women, and also with a few men, which gave her access to exchanges of favors and provided her with practical help in routine matters and essential remedies when she was confronted with a crisis. Through censuses, church records, and trial records, we can place this unfortunate couple and this failed marriage in their broader demographic, residential, and communal contexts.

Demographic and Residential Patterns

> Abitano unitamente in casa della Camera Marchesale.

> They live together in a house belonging to the marquis.
> —Archivio di Stato di Napoli, Catasto Onciario 6091 (1745)

Fiscal records and censuses usually offer a frozen moment in the history of a living community. For this reason it is especially difficult to use them to analyze household structures, which are affected by the cyclical developments of each family's and community's history. Nonetheless, these documents taken together help illustrate the variety of settlements, and the connections between family structure and economic and social position, which affected the conditions of daily and family life for most villagers. Moreover, in the case of Pentidattilo and Melito, the fiscal surveys reveal the differences between the old and new community and hence the demographic transformations that occurred during the eighteenth century. The Catasto Onciario represents an invaluable source not only on the amount and distribution of wealth in the Kingdom of Naples but also on family structures, the internal hierarchies of each household, and demographic developments in the last decades of the old regime.

Most demographic studies of the Kingdom of Naples have relied on the Catasto Onciario and parish records. The kingdom's population structures, compared with western Europe in general, were characterized by somewhat earlier marriages and smaller households. Land management patterns affected demographic structures. In the areas of the kingdom in which extensive agriculture and grain cultivation predominated, peasant women tended to marry at a younger age (twenty to twenty-two on average) than in areas of mixed and intensive cultivation. As the eighteenth-century integration of the kingdom's economy into broad trade networks progressed, the percentage of nuclear families increased. Unlike the sharecropping peasant families of central Italy, southern households were relatively small (with an average below five members per household), and they very rarely included servants. Female domestic service or male apprenticeship with the purpose of acquiring a dowry or capital before marriage, which were frequent in many areas of western Europe, were unusual in the kingdom, where generally only about 1 percent of households included domestic servants, and these tended to remain servants throughout their lives. Pentidattilo generally follows this southern Italian model.[14]

In 1745 the average household size for the 108 lay resident citizen households in the università of Pentidattilo, which together included 479 inhabitants, was 4.43. Fourteen years later, the università had 156 such households for 635 inhabitants, or an average of 4.07.[15] A closer look at these figures shows different patterns of development and household structure in Melito. The coastal village accounted for only 30 households in 1745, as opposed to 73 for Pentidattilo proper and 5 scattered ones. Melito, however, accounted for more than 40 percent of the new households formed in the following years, and in 1759 there were 50 households there, as opposed to 106 in Pentidattilo. The 1759 census indeed includes two separate lists of households for the two villages, drawn by the respective parish priests, although the fiscal declarations still appear all together. In 1745 the università had been treated as a whole, and there had been no *status animarum,* or "list of souls," at all.[16]

There were several differences between the two settlements. In both years household size was higher in Melito. In 1745, 140 of the 479 inhabitants lived in Melito, for an average household size of 4.66, as opposed to 4.38 for the 320 people who lived in Pentidattilo proper (4.34 if the five isolated households are included). In 1759, 212 people lived in Melito, for an average household size of 4.24, while the 423 living in Pentidattilo proper were down to 4.17 In 1745, 7 of the 15 largest households in the università (those above 6 members) were in Melito, where they accounted for 1 household out of every 4, as opposed to about 1 in every 10 for the older village. More than half the households in Melito were either extended or multiple ones (16 out of 30), as opposed to about 40 percent in Pentidattilo (33 out of 78). The two villages were more similar in this respect by 1759, though Melito still had a larger percentage of large households, and indeed 7 of the 12 extended households in the later survey lived in Melito.

In addition to living in larger households, people in Melito were also poorer on average than their fellow citizens. In 1745 only 1 Melito household lived in its own house, and 20 of the 30 local households were living in housing built by the marquis for silk production. Forty-five households (out of 78, or almost 60%) in Pentidattilo proper, on the other hand, lived in their own houses. No "civil" households resided in Melito, and field laborers, the poorest occupational category, represented two-thirds of the local population (19 out of 30 households), as opposed to one-half in the università as a whole (55 out of 108), and four-ninths for Pentidattilo proper (36 out of 78). The remaining Melito households were made up by 5 massari, 2 fishermen, 2 greengrocers, an innkeeper, and an ironsmith.

Whereas 70 of the università's 101 taxpaying households (4 widows and the 3 other nontaxpaying ones were all in Pentidattilo) owned some taxable property, only 16 of Melito's 30 households did (or just over 50%), leaving 54 (out of 71, or almost 80%) for the older village. Apart from the massari, only 4 Melito households owned taxable animals, as opposed to 16 non-massaro households in Pentidattilo. The average taxable wealth of households for each village was slightly higher in Melito (23.15 *once* in Melito and 22.04 in Pentidattilo), but this still reflected less wealth in Melito, because there were in the latter no exempted, "civil" households; moreover, since Melito households had on average more members, the average *once d'industria* in the smaller village also were higher. Those in Melito who did own taxable assets beyond their labor were not very different in their level of wealth from those in Pentidattilo; indeed, they were slightly wealthier (the average *once di beni* were 8.06 for the università as a whole, 9.10 for Melito, and 7.87 for Pentidattilo), but they were, as we just saw, significantly less numerous in the village on the coast. This also shows that there were wider economic disparities within the new settlement than in the older one.

The Melito heads of households also were younger than those in Pentidattilo proper. The average age of heads of households in the entire università in 1745 was forty-three, but it was thirty-nine in Melito and forty-four in the older village.[18] The coastal settlement was also characterized, as would be expected, by the large presence of people new to the università. Most of the main old surnames of Pentidattilo (such as Battaglia, Vernagallo, Romeo, Tropea, Costarella, Orlando, Scrufari, Foti, or Crea) were not present in Melito in 1745, nor did the surnames of any of the "civil" households appear there.[19] Twenty-four surnames appeared in Melito's 30 households, as opposed to 51 in Pentidattilo's 78 households, which also shows the larger presence of clans in the old village.

The central decades of the eighteenth century witnessed the beginning of Melito's flourishing as a rival to the old settlement. By 1759 there were 36 surnames in Melito's 50 households and 59 in Pentidattilo's 106. Although the coastal village would continue to grow and attract immigrants, by the 1750s some members of the old families began to move towards Melito. In 1745 there were 8 surnames that appeared in both villages. By 1759 there were at least 12 and probably 14, and indeed by that year Paolino Malavendi, a member of the village elite and soon to be possibly the most prominent citizen in the università, lived in Melito. Melito became increasingly integrated into larger economic networks as its specialized agriculture developed later in the century and, like Corio, attracted outsiders. While in 1745 the only "foreigners" residing in Pentidattilo's territory were 8 households that had found refuge there from the plague epidemic in Reggio, by 1788 the università was home to 50 non-native households.[20]

While households were larger in Melito, the università as a whole was characterized by the frequency of extended households. Nuclear families in 1745 were less than 50 percent of the total, and extended households were more numerous in Pentidattilo than in other Calabrian villages and in the kingdom as a whole.[21] In 1745 there were in the whole università 37 extended and 12 multiple households out of 108 total households; 2 more extended households included domestic servants.[22] Sixteen of these 49 extended and multiple households were in Melito, where they represented one-half of the total; in Pentidattilo proper there were 33 such households out of 78. The prominence and importance of clan connections in the older village may have made extended households less necessary there, since households could count, in any case, on the support of the larger kinship group. The housing shortage in Melito also favored larger or extended households there. Indeed, all the individuals living alone in both censuses resided in Pentidattilo. Extended and multiple households were considerably less numerous in the 1759 survey, and it is likely that the recent epidemic led to the overrepresentation of these types of households in 1745.

There was a correlation between household size and complexity on the one

TABLE 4.1
Type of Household Structure in Pentidattilo, 1745 and 1759

From the 1745 Census

Type of Household	Number of Cases[a]		
	P	M	T
Individual living alone	3	0	3[b]
Married couple with children	30	7	37[c]
Widower with children	1	1	2
Childless married couple	6	5	11
Widow with children	0	0	0
Extended household	26	11	37[d]
Multiple household	7	5	12
Complex household	0	1	1[e]
Household including servants	5	0	5[f]
Total	78	30	108

From the 1759 Census

Type of Household	Number of Cases			
	P	M	C	T
Individual living alone	7	0	0	7[g]
Married couple with children	53	31	15	99[h]
Widower with children	1	0	0	1
Childless married couple	14	7	4	25
Widow with children	21	4	0	25[i]
Extended household	5	7	2	14[j]
Multiple household	0	0	0	0
Complex household	0	0	1	1
Household including servants	5	1	0	6[k]
Total	106	50	22	178

[a] "P" stands for Pentidattilo proper, "M" for Melito, and "T" for the total for the università; "C" stands for Corio.

[b] Two men and a widow.

[c] This and the next three categories amount to 50 nuclear families.

[d] These included 3 households headed by widows, one living with a daughter and a nephew, one with a nephew, and one with a son and a widowed sister.

[e] This was the household headed by the *bracciale* Antonino Furfari; see fig. 4.4.

[f] These were 2 married couples with children, 1 widower with children, and 2 extended households.

[g] Two men and 5 widows.

[h] One in Pentidattilo and 3 in Melito included stepchildren (the wife's children from a previous marriage—in one case perhaps the wife's illegitimate child); 1 in Melito included two children of the husband from a previous marriage. Adding this and the next three categories, therefore, results in 150 nuclear families (see, however, note i).

[i] One in Melito lived with both children and stepchildren (her deceased husband's children from a previous marriage). The 1759 survey considers widows as the heads of households even if they have one or more sons older than fourteen, whereas in 1745 these households were listed with the young man as the head and therefore appear in that part of the table as extended households. If one adopted the same criterion for 1759, 12 of the 25 households headed by widows would be counted as extended households (9 of the 21 in Pentidattilo and 3 of the 4 in Melito). Conversely, 7 of the 1745 extended households consisted of widowed mothers living with unmarried adult children and thus would have been counted as households headed by women in the 1759 survey.

[j] One in Pentidattilo consisted of a widow living with her young brother, and 1 in Melito of two elderly unmarried sisters.

[k] These were 2 married couples with children, 1 widower with children, 1 childless married couple, and 1 widow with children and an adopted child, all in Pentidattilo, and 1 childless married couple in Melito.

TABLE 4.2
Distribution of Household Size, Pentidattilo, 1745 and 1759

	1745		
	No. of Cases		
No. of Household Members	Pentidattilo	Melito	Total
1	3	0	3
2	9	6	15
3	15	2	17
4	16	8	24
5	18	3	21
6	9	4	13
7	4	5	9
8	1	2	3
9	1	0	1
10	2	0	2
Total	78	30	108

	1759			
	No. of Cases			
No. of Household Members	Pentidattilo	Melito	Corio	Total
1	7	0	0	7
2	19	12	4	35
3	26	9	4	39
4	17	7	1	25
5	13	7	2	22
6	12	9	3	24
7	5	4	5	14
8	5	2	1	8
9	1	0	2	3
10	0	0	0	0
11	1	0	0	1
Total	106	50	22	178

hand and the occupation and level of wealth of household heads on the other. As was common everywhere in western Europe, wealthier households were larger and more complex than poorer ones. In 1745 in Pentidattilo the households headed by *civili* or massari were larger than those headed by bracciali, with an average of 5 and 4.94 members, respectively, compared with 4.33 for the bracciali. In addition, 4 of the 10 civile households and 10 of the 18 massaro ones were extended or multiple ones, whereas only 21 of the 55 households headed by bracciali fell into those two categories. Although the civili still inhabited the largest households in 1759, these differences had decreased by then.[23]

Most extended households in Pentidattilo, in any case, remained very close to the nuclear family structure, which also explains their lower number in 1759. The size of the household depended, in fact, not only on occupation and wealth but also on the age of its members and therefore on the demographic cycle of each family. The young age of the head of household often resulted in the temporary cohabitation of generations or of several siblings. In 1745 almost half the extended and multiple households (22 out of 49) in the università included elderly mothers or mothers-in-law, presumably all widowed. In many households, also, a young head of household lived with his or his wife's siblings. Only in 4 cases did the extended household include more distant relatives (aunts, uncles, nephews, cousins, etc.), though to these we should add 2 of the households headed by widows.[24]

The tendency in Pentidattilo was towards virilocal households, as was common in areas of the Kingdom of Naples marked by fragmented landholdings

TABLE 4.3

Household Type by Occupational Category, Pentidattilo, 1745 and 1759

							No. of Households	Total Members	Avg. per Household
1745									
Occupation	S	N	E	M	C	D			
Civili	1	2	3	1	0	3	10	50	5
Massari	0	7	7	3	0	1	18	89	4.94
Foresi	0	3	2	0	0	0	5	25	5
Bracciali	1	31	17	4	1	1	55	241	4.33
Artisans	0	2	3	4	0	0	9	43	4.77
Others	0	2	1	0	0	0	3	11	3.62
Disabled	0	3	1	0	0	0	4	11	2.75
Widows	1	0	3	0	0	0	4	9	2.25
Total for village	3	50	37	12	1	5	108	479	4.43
1759									
Civili	2	14	1	0	0	4	21	98	4.67
Massari	0	23	1	0	0	1	25	97	3.88
Foresi	0	8	0	0	0	0	8	36	4.5
Bracciali	0	46	6	0	0	0	52	228	4.38
Artisans	0	8	0	0	0	0	8	29	3.62
Others	0	7	2	0	0	0	9	39	4.33
Widows	5	25	2	0	0	1	33	108	3.27
Total for village	7	131	12	0	0	6	156	635	4.07

NOTE: S stands for single individuals, N for nuclear household, E for extended, M for multiple, C for complex, and D for households including domestic servants. For 1745, the artisans include an innkeeper, 2 greengrocers, an ironsmith, a carter, 2 millers, and 2 fishermen; others include 2 cattle guardians and the captain of the tower; 4 households were headed by disabled men whose profession was not given, except for a hermit. For 1759, the artisans include 2 greengrocers, 2 millers, 2 barbers, a muleteer, and a tailor; others include 7 guardians of animals, a hermit, and a soldier; I am including among the widows 1 household in Melito consisting of two elderly unmarried sisters. I have not counted the 22 households in Corio.

TABLE 4.4

Household Size by Occupational Category, Pentidattilo, 1745 and 1759

| | 1745 | | | | | | | | | | |
Occupation	1	2	3	4	5	6	7	8	9	10	No. of Households
Civili	1	0	3	0	2	2	0	1	0	1	10
Massari	0	3	0	3	6	3	2	0	1	0	18
Foresi	0	0	0	2	1	2	0	0	0	0	5
Bracciali	1	6	10	15	11	5	5	1	0	1	55
Artisans	0	2	0	3	1	0	2	1	0	0	9
Others	0	1	1	0	0	1	0	0	0	0	3
Disabled	0	2	1	1	0	0	0	0	0	0	4
Widows	1	1	2	0	0	0	0	0	0	0	4
Total for village	3	15	17	24	21	13	9	3	1	2	108

| | 1759 | | | | | | | | | | | |
Occupation	1	2	3	4	5	6	7	8	9	10	11	No. of Households
Civili	2	2	3	5	1	3	3	1	0	0	1	21
Massari	0	9	5	2	2	4	2	1	0	0	0	25
Foresi	0	0	3	1	2	1	1	0	0	0	0	8
Bracciali	0	8	13	8	8	9	2	3	1	0	0	52
Artisans	0	2	2	2	1	1	0	0	0	0	0	8
Others	0	1	2	1	3	2	0	0	0	0	0	9
Widows	5	9	8	4	2	2	1	2	0	0	0	33
Total for village	7	31	36	23	19	22	9	7	1	0	1	156

NOTE: For 1759, I have not counted the 22 households in Corio.

and small-scale agricultural units. Domenica Orlando and Antonino Cuzzucli were unusual in this respect. They lived in the village in which her family was well established, while most of his lived in a neighboring community, as appears also from Antonino's frequent and prolonged stays in Montebello. These factors may well have influenced the support Domenica received from her community during her trial.

The prevalence of virilocal arrangements was, in any case, another way in which the new village of Melito differed significantly from the older settlement. Of the fifteen cases in 1745 when a son- or daughter-in-law joined the spouse's parental household, nine were of daughters-in-law who moved in with their husband's parents, and only two of these households lived in Melito.[25] Conversely, four of the six households in which a man went to live with his wife's parents were in Melito, and three of these sons-in-law bore names new to the village (the fourth case was the innkeeper's son-in-law, and the family in this case lived in the inn). One of the two remaining cases concerned a household in the countryside, in which the daughter was an only child and the son-in-law was also new to the village.[26]

Therefore, in 1745 there was only one case in Pentidattilo proper in which an adult man with connections in the village lived with his wife's parents in an apparently subordinate position. In Melito, on the other hand, these arrangements (four households out of thirty) served the purpose of facilitating immigration and the new village's growth, especially since most housing in the village at that time consisted of the houses built by the marquis for silk production. All these arrangements were most likely temporary, as their absence fourteen years later also shows. In only one of these fifteen households (that of one of the Melito greengrocers) did a younger couple with children cohabit with an older couple. In all other cases either the young couple was childless at the time of the survey, or the head of household was a widower.[27]

Similarly, there were seven households in 1745 which included a brother- or sister-in-law. Four of these presented specific circumstances that explain the arrangement, namely, the youth, disability, or widowhood of the sibling-in-law. Two of the other cases consisted of households in which the wife of the head of household's brother had joined the family. Finally, the "civil" Giuseppe Scrufari lived with his wife's adult brothers probably because they included a priest who offered the household its lodging free of rent. These households, too, probably were not lasting arrangements, and again in only one case we find siblings-in-law cohabiting when both couples have children.[28] By 1759, in at least one case the married brother had left the original household after having children of his own, and in another a married, though disabled, brother-in-law had done the same. These cases, then, also confirm the virilocal patterns in the old settlement of Pentidattilo.

In several cases the records of the two censuses make it possible to follow at least some members of a family over two decades and to explore further the cycles of family life. I have chosen a few examples to illustrate the living arrangements, types of households, and family links experienced by the people of Pentidattilo. Although the tendency was towards the formation of nuclear families, at some point in their life almost all villagers lived in extended or other complex households.

In 1745 the field laborer Diego Sergi, aged fifty and a widower, headed one of the village's extended households, which included his sons, Francesco (a servant at the notary's) and Antonio; Diego's brother Antonino and his wife, Francesca Corso; and Antonino and Francesca's son Saverio. With two adult

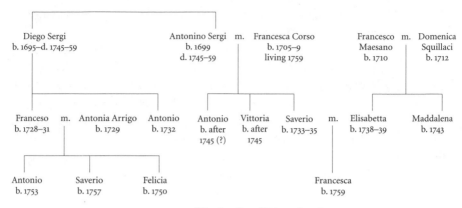

FIG. 4.2. The family of Diego Sergi

males and a boy over fourteen, the household was assessed for 30 *once di industria* but owned no taxable property. The living arrangement had probably been motivated by Diego's widowerhood and his lack of daughters, so that his sister-in-law, Francesca, presumably supervised the household's domestic life. By 1759, with Diego and his brother dead, the arrangement had broken down. Diego's elder son, Francesco, now lived with his wife and three children; young Saverio had married, too, and lived with his wife, Elisabetta Maesano, twenty and the daughter of another field laborer who had owned no taxable property in 1745, and an infant daughter; Francesca Corso, also widowed, lived with two children presumably born after the earlier census.[29]

A second example shows the mechanisms that brought two families together. In 1745 Vittorino Mercurio, aged fifty, was an invalid who owned property assessed at 4 *once* and lived with his wife, Giovanna Romeo, thirty, and their three-year-old son, Pasquale. In the same year Giuseppe Crea, a young farmer with property assessed at 1.15 *once,* headed a household including his brother, Antonino, his sister, Antonia, and their widowed mother, Maria Zuccalà. Vittorino's death led to the coming together of these two families. By 1759 Giuseppe had married the widowed Giovanna Romeo and lived with her and their three-year-old son, Giovanni, named after Giuseppe's father. Also living in the household were Giovanna's two children from her first marriage, Pasquale and Vittoria (whose name, the feminine version of her father's, indicates that she may have been born after his death), as well as Giuseppe's own brother, Antonino. Giuseppe's mother, Maria, who had still been alive in 1752, had presumably died, and his sister, Antonia, lived with her husband, Antonino Alati, son of a massaro, and their two sons.[30]

A final example illustrates the complicated living arrangements that poor families sometimes found it necessary to form. In 1745 the field laborer Antonino Furfari, aged twenty and owning no taxable property, lived with his young brother, Francesco, and their mother, Domenica Maldà. Also in the household were Anna Cammara, the widow of Antonio Todisco, and her three sons, Francesco, Antonino, and Antonio. This latter family group was apparently unrelated to the former one, and the cohabitation was presumably due to poverty and the shortage of housing in Melito. All members of the household worked in silk production for the marquis.

By 1759, as all household members had reached adulthood, the arrangement had been broken up. Antonino Furfari had married well; his wife was Lavinia Guerrera, the daughter of Marco Antonio Guerrera, a fairly wealthy massaro assessed in 1745 for 15.20 *once di beni*; the couple lived with their son, Domenico, named after Antonino's late father, and their two daughters. Antonino's mother, Domenica Maldà, lived with her second son, Francesco, now twenty-three. Anna Cammara had presumably died. Her eldest son, Francesco Todisco, had married an older widowed woman, Ursula Malara, and they lived with her son, Domenico Casili, fifteen, and one of Francesco's brothers.[31] These examples, even in the snapshots provided by the fiscal surveys, offer clear evidence of the frequent fluctuations of family cycles and household structures.

The order in which the members of each household are listed within each census entry and the occasional comments inserted after their names also confirm the general patriarchal nature of family structures in Pentidattilo.[32] In 1745 the head of household (whose name comes first and determines the household's place in the alphabetical list) is invariably a male, except for the

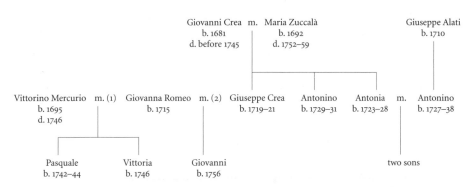

FIG. 4.3. The families of Vittorino Mercurio and Giuseppe Crea

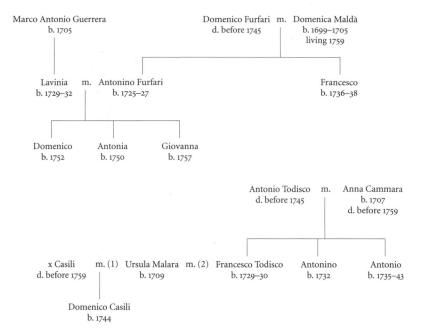

FIG. 4.4. The families of Antonino Furfari and Francesco Todisco
Note: The "x" indicates an unknown first name.

four households headed by widows. This was true even for boys over four-teen, the age at which they began to be taxable for *once d'industria*. All other household members were identified in terms of their relationship to the head of household. Wives followed their husbands immediately, though no mention was made of deceased wives (widows, however, were always identified by their name and by that of their late husbands).[33] Then came all children according to age, with the sons first and then the daughters (a boy, however young, took precedence over a sister, however old).[34] This pattern was altered when a child was married, and in general sons' wives immediately followed their husbands, but this rule was not without exceptions. On a couple of occasions, daughters-in-law were listed after all sons, or even after all children. Sons-in-law always took last place after all children had been listed.

After the children came the head of household's siblings, again brothers first, followed in general by their wives and then sisters, followed, in the few cases we have seen, by their husbands. The siblings of the head of household's wife were treated in the same way, but such cases were very rare. Most old men remained heads of their households into their late years, but this respect for the elderly was not manifested towards old mothers, who took last place in the list of family members in the fiscal survey. This was also the case with mothers-in-law and with the only elderly father not listed in 1745 as head of household (the notary's), whose name followed in the list those of his two granddaughters.[35] Though they were listed last, elderly mothers were rarely left alone in Pentidattilo. There was no instance in 1745 of a widow living alone when she had children living in separate households in the università; there were four such widows in 1759, all in Pentidattilo proper, but three lived in their own house and the last one was only thirty-six (and her son lived in his wife's house).[36] After all relatives came the few apprentices and servants who lived in Pentidattilo, with apprentices and men servants taking precedence over maids if both were present.

The lists are not generous with further descriptions. The most common other comment applies to all unmarried women of at least twelve years of age, who are described as *in capillis* ("with collected hair"), from the hairstyle standard for nubile women. The only other physical descriptions refer to disabilities, though not all the adult individuals so described received a tax exemption. Indications about boys at school or about clerical status, and a single case of twin girls, round out all other comments.

Pentidattilo's households thus had much in common with those found in many other mountainous and remote villages in the Kingdom of Naples and elsewhere in Italy. Extended and multiple households were more common than in regions characterized by high numbers of landless laborers and large-scale agricultural management. Although average household size was fairly small in Pentidattilo, especially for poorer villagers, most people, because of the vagaries of the family cycle, spent at least part of their lives in extended or multiple households. Family was organized, at least formally and in the understanding of the men of the village who drew up the survey documents, according to patriarchal traditions, and married couples largely followed virilocal settlement patterns. Melito, which by the mid-eighteenth century attracted residents from the older village as well as immigrants from the neighboring area, was home to younger, poorer, and usually larger households. Economic disparities were more pronounced within Melito than in the old village. The level of one's wealth was more important in the new village than in old Pentidattilo, where other factors contributed to each citizen's social status and where clan connections and vibrant forms of local sociability remained significant aspects of village life.

Village Ties and Local Sociability

> Per mezzo di communi familiari, amici, e congionti
>
> Through common acquaintances, friends, and relatives
> — From a 1754 Pentidattilo marriage contract

Clan and family connections helped shape the social status and role of Pentidattilo's citizens. Each villager was also linked to fellow villagers by social ties beyond those of blood and family alliance, primarily through godparenthood, neighborhood, and friendship. As historians have pointed out for other areas and communities, these links were crucial in early modern society to ensure stability, welfare, and protection, what David Vassberg has called "social solidarity."[37]

Godparenthood was an important religious and social relationship that helped form new ties within the community. According to canon law, the relationship created new links with the attendant marriage impediments, so that the ban on incest also prohibited marriage among godrelatives. In the social realm godparenthood established bonds of familiarity and support beyond the blood family and clan. This double importance is evident in the details provided in the baptismal records of Pentidattilo about each newborn's godparents. The parents of the baptized child, for instance, are identified in most cases simply by their own names, but the godparents are identified also by the names of their parents.[38]

With the likely intent of widening their social ties, most villagers in Pentidattilo chose for their children godparents to whom they were not related. In only 55 cases out of 611 (or 9%) did a godparent bear the same family name as one of the parents. In three-fifths of these cases (32 out of 55) it was the same name as the mother's. There is no case in which both godparents bear a family name in common with the newborn's parents. Only in 11 additional cases did the mother of a godparent bear the same family name as one of the newborn's parents (in 9 cases of the father, in 2 of the mother). In the remaining 545 cases the godparents had no apparent family link with either of the newborn's parents.[39]

The Catholic Church had long been fighting the practice of multiple godparents. The Council of Trent had allowed a maximum of two godparents, and in Pentidattilo by the end of the seventeenth century even this number was not very frequent. In fact, two godparents are listed in only 176 cases out of 611, or about 29 percent. The frequency of these double choices diminished over the years of this sample, from more than 40 percent in the first few years to less than 20 percent in the 1690s. When there were two godparents, they were almost invariably a man and a woman. There are only four exceptions (all with two godfathers, for three boys and a girl), one of which is explained by the fact that the child was a foundling and the dittereo served as the second godfather. Again, the tendency was to use the choice of godparents to widen one's social bonds: with one exception of a brother and sister, when there were two godparents, they were never related to each other. In only 1 of these 176 cases were the two godparents married to each other.[40]

Male children are somewhat more common in the sample of baptismal records under analysis (there are 320 boys, 290 girls, and 1 illegible name). The gender of the child did not affect the practice of choosing two godparents rather than only one. Of the 176 cases in which two godparents are listed, 92 concern newborn boys and 84 newborn girls, so that the percentage of boys and girls accompanied at the font by two godparents was about the same. The choice of two godparents was not linked to a family's social status in the village; the marquis's own children who were baptized in Pentidattilo had only one godparent, which was unusual for the kingdom's aristocracy. The children with two godparents did not come disproportionately from the ranks of the village's more established families, and even propertyless villagers gave these choices the same importance as their wealthier fellow citizens.[41]

There are 20 cases in which no godparent is mentioned in the records, but in 9 of these the child was actually baptized by the village's midwife, presumably because of poor health at birth, and so there probably was not enough time to arrange for godparents. There is no explanation for the other 11 cases.[42] Furthermore, there is 1 birth in which only the father's name is preserved, and 1 boy who died at the age of one month and was never baptized because of deformity. In the remaining 413 cases one godparent was recorded, although in 1 of these the godparent's first name is missing.[43]

For 412 baptisms performed between 1667 and 1695 in Pentidattilo we know the full name of one godparent. Men were preferred as godparents, and they represent 60.5 percent of the choices (or 250 cases), as opposed to 39.5 percent for women (or 162 cases). There was, however, no strict correlation between the sex of the newborn child and the sex of the godparent, and there was enough variety in the villagers' choices to show that the choice was influenced primarily by personal desires and connections. Both the 250 godfathers and the 162 godmothers were rather evenly split between newborns of each sex: 133 men acted as godfathers to newborn boys and 117 as godfathers to newborn girls, while 80 women acted as godmothers to newborn boys and 82 as godmothers to newborn girls. Unlike other areas of Europe, cases of godparents and godchildren with the same first name were extremely rare.[44]

The sources do not offer information on whether godparents were neighbors of, or shared an occupation with, the newborn's parents. I also have no evidence about the actual impact of godparenthood as a protective relationship in the lives of the citizens of Pentidattilo. Yet the fact that most godparents were not related to the child's parents, the choice of different godparents for each child of most couples, and the rarity of cases in which no godparent was chosen, even when the baptism was hurriedly administered by the midwife, show the importance of this link among the people of Pentidattilo and how they used it to build new ties between themselves and their fellow villagers, as happened in most early modern villages and communities.[45] Indeed, state and church authorities recognized the importance and power of the tie created by godparenthood. That priests were excluded from godparenthood unless specially authorized—as sanctioned also at Trent—points to the strength attributed by the church hierarchy to this social bond and to its desire to prevent priests from being perceived as too closely integrated into a community's social network. The royal government, as we saw, similarly prohibited justice officials from entering these relationships in the community in which they served.

The importance of godparenthood in Pentidattilo is evident also in the concern to find godparents for illegitimate children and foundlings. Five foundlings were baptized in Pentidattilo between 1667 and 1695, and their godparents were all established villagers. Only one of fifteen illegitimate children whose fathers were unknown had no godparent, and in all other cases men and women of solid village families acted as godparents, which indicates a higher acceptance of illegitimacy than historians have found in other communities.[46]

Members of the feudal lord's household not only contributed several of the village births in the years under study, but they were also fully involved in the network of ties formed by godparenthood, which frequently crossed social boundaries. While the godparents for the children of the marquis Domenico and his wife were not villagers, several members of the marquis's household and at times the marquis himself acted as godparents to village children. In addition, two women from the castle staff (both slaves of the marquis or of members of his family) bore children during these years. One of them, Ursula, bore two illegitimate children before marrying a village man of an old family and having more children, and she also frequently acted as godmother to other village newborns.[47]

Godparenthood served, then, to broaden the social network that bound each individual in the village to other citizens and residents beyond the ties of family and kin. Another strong link was offered by neighborhood, which was often tied to friendship. Neighbors represented, especially for village women, an important source of support and help, and women often developed a pattern of frequent exchanges and contacts with their neighbors. Neighbors usually constituted the inner core of a woman's friendship network, and men sometimes regarded neighborly ties among women with some degree of suspicion. Neighbors could also represent a source of unwanted control over one's behavior, owing to what one historian has called their "vigilant curiosity."[48]

In a small village like Pentidattilo it was likely that everyone knew everyone else, and indeed no witness in the 1710 trial denied knowing anyone. In fact, simply being "of the village" (*paesani*) was enough to explain how one knew everyone else, living or recently dead, while those who were "strangers to this village" were easily forgotten, as happened with Anna de Amico's husband. It was implausible for villagers to claim not to know one another; Pietro Crea's denial of any contact or acquaintance in the village was difficult for the court to believe, and he could only try to make it more acceptable by appealing to his occupation as a guardian who lived mostly in the neighboring woods rather than in the village itself. Even then, he sought further refuge behind his statement that "[he] never spoke to anyone." Domenica Orlando and Anna de Amico easily admitted knowing all the witnesses against them, if nothing else because they were "of this village," though Anna refused to state her opinion of their truthfulness and honesty.[49]

Neighbors were much more significant in one's daily life than other villagers. Most houses in Pentidattilo were—and their remains still are—small and huddled together, often sharing one or more walls with other houses. The villagers probably spent much time outside their homes, as is still the case throughout the Italian south, also in towns and especially for women, who go outdoors to cook, wash, or tend gardens or animals. Pentidattilo was too small to have separate neighborhoods in any administrative sense, but the rocky landscape created clusters of houses. Not only were the houses of Domenica Orlando and Anna de Amico contiguous, a fact most witnesses pointed out, but there was a hole in the wall uniting them, through which the two women exchanged objects and heard each other's conversations. Streets in the village are narrow and dark at night, so that villagers may often have been able to observe or hear their neighbors without the latter's awareness. The trial records refer to overheard conversations, observed movements and exchanges, and outright spying and eavesdropping on the part of neighbors. As discussed in Chapter 2, witnesses had to identify the source of the information they provided to the court, and neighborhood was frequently, and reliably, used to explain one's ability to witness otherwise private goings-on.[50]

Neighbors expected to be involved in one another's lives and were in constant contact. Two of the most informative witnesses in the trial were Vittoria Vernagallo and Domenico Malavendi, who both emphasized the fact that they were Domenica's neighbors to explain how they came to know as much as they did. Vittoria admitted to deliberate eavesdropping ("out of curiosity") at Anna's door when she had gone to ask for some fire. She expressed surprise at finding the door closed, and, since before knocking she heard voices from the inside, she set herself to listen carefully. After she satisfied her curiosity and knocked, "they changed their words."[51]

Domenico Malavendi carried his neighborly responsibilities even further. He first formed suspicions on frequently observing Pietro looking at Domenica's house. Then one night, on hearing music from Giovan Battista Corso's house, he went there and saw Pietro and Domenica dance together more than he thought appropriate, and his suspicions were strengthened. He therefore decided to go out and spy on them. After leaving the party, he stopped inside a niche opposite Domenica's house "on [his] own business." Such business kept him there two hours, until he saw, thanks to the "clear night"—and presumably to keen interest on his part, since they did not see him—Domenica letting Pietro into her house.[52]

Even these examples in which neighbors acted in a deliberately inquisitive, censorious way (or so, in any case, later in court they pretended to have done) show the fabric of daily contacts between them. Vittoria had gone to Anna's house when she needed fire, and she offered entertainment to her neighbors in her house at the ill-fated dance party, which was evidently an open-door affair. She herself, and several other witnesses who also lived nearby, felt perfectly free to go in and check on Antonino's health when the latter was close to death, and his passing was witnessed by several relatives and neighbors. Similarly, Domenica visited Anna when the latter was sick and called for help, the two often exchanged pots and other domestic objects, and obtaining the arsenic required Anna and Domenica to engage in a series of small exchanges of favors with neighboring women. Sicilia Zuccalà, who also lived near Anna, stated that "it was common that [she] always went" to visit and chat with Anna.

With the exception of Domenico's spying, all these exchanges took place between women and concern social contact that revolved around the domestic sphere. Such exchanges intensified whenever a neighbor experienced an important family event, like Antonino's illness and death or a birth or marriage.[53]

Neighborhood and neighborliness were therefore, both in the practice of daily life and in the perceptions and ideas expressed by the trial's protagonists, important links that created a series of mutual obligations among villagers, especially women. They also allowed for a high degree of knowledge of, and possible inquiry into, each neighbor's private life. Indeed, the very idea of a private domestic sphere outside the purview and potential control of one's neighbors would have seemed an unlikely one to the people of Pentidattilo, as can be detected in Vittoria Vernagallo's surprise when she found her neighbor's door closed. As we shall see, it was also up to the neighbors to observe and critique the degree of sorrow expressed by Domenica at her husband's death.[54]

A further source of contacts and sociability was the sphere of friendship and the rhetoric and practices the villagers recognized as pertaining to it. Like most elements of village life, friendship was essentially a functional concept. Friends represented an established circle of people to whom one could apply for help, support, and mediation. Friends helped arrange marriages, as we have seen in Margherita Battaglia's case. Men especially used their friends to help resolve disputes that opposed them to other men, as Giuseppe Crea and Antonio Marrari did to terminate their legal proceedings in the feudal court. The notary, and other witnesses, men as always, certified this amicable settlement.[55]

Men were supposed to inhabit a more public world in which one's existence was defined, at least in part, by one's relationships of friendship or enmity with other men. Jean-Michel Sallmann has argued that in Neapolitan culture only men had access to honor and to the world of friendships and enmities, whereas women were confined to a more passive role and to the sphere of godparenthood and family relationships. I believe, however, that women, too, both used the categories of friendship and enmity to express their understanding of their own status in their society and experienced the benefits and drawbacks of such relationships in their daily life.[56]

Undoubtedly, though, men played the more important, and more public, part in the sphere created by relationships of friendship. Even though all three defendants in the trial were asked by the judge for their opinion of the truthfulness and honesty of the witnesses—a standard legal procedure—only

Pietro Crea was asked if any of the witnesses against him were "his friends or enemies." Moreover, when Pietro was faced with the court's full charges against him, rather than simply denying them as Anna had done, he took refuge in the statement "they are out to get me." Although most likely other factors entered into the court's judgment of Pietro, this appeal to a generalized, fundamental enmity against him must have seemed at least plausible.[57]

Two expressions often used in the trial records to describe relationships of friendship were "frequenting" or "having dealings," both of which acknowledged more than casual acquaintance and mutual exchanges. Both of these could also cross into illicit or inappropriate relationships, as Pietro, Domenica, and Anna allegedly did when their "friendship" became too intense and visible. Friendship between women, in particular, represented an extension and intensification of the practices associated with neighborhood and neighborliness.

For instance, Anna de Amico, largely deprived of the strong links in the village which family and kin could create, engaged in a wide web of contacts and exchanges with other women of Pentidattilo in order to form a network of friendships. Apart from her ability to cause miscarriages through her knowledge of poisonous roots, of which she allegedly boasted to a couple of village women (perhaps in the hope of attracting business), Anna provided a variety of useful services. She helped her friend and neighbor Domenica Orlando, not only by giving her poison for her husband but also by cooking with and occasionally for her, and by offering her house for Domenica's rendezvous with her lover. She was friendly to neighbors such as Vittoria Vernagallo and Sicilia Zuccalà, and she acted as seamstress for Cata Vazzani, with whom she chatted about the abortions. Cata and other women testified about friendly conversations they had had with Anna. Despite these efforts, almost no witness defended Anna's actions during the trial, and in fact most of them—including some who had been on friendly terms with her, like Vittoria Vernagallo— attested to her bad reputation and disreputable life. Only Sicilia Zuccalà dared state that, when Anna was sick, "[she] went to see her, since she is my friend," and significantly Sicilia was not asked to give her opinion of Anna's reputation and character.[58]

That the dynamic of friendship and enmity applied also to women is shown in the trial records also when enmity is used to explain behavior and categorize a relationship. The arsenic allegedly used to kill Antonino Cuzzucli was lent to Domenica and Anna by Mattia Cuzzucli, sister-in-law of Domenica and possibly stepmother of Anna. The two women obtained it through a typical friendly exchange, by sending Mattia some bread and olives and claiming that the arsenic was needed to kill rats. However, they did not make this exchange in person but rather asked their friend Antonia Manti to send her young daughter, Gratia Costarella, on this errand. Antonia testified that Domenica had explained this "favor" by saying that she had just recently asked Mattia for arsenic. But Gratia, in her deposition, stated that Domenica had told her she could not go herself or send Anna "because they and Mattia [were] enemies." The enmity was such that the two women did not use the napkin in which they had originally wrapped the bread and olives, out of fear that Mattia would recognize it as one of Anna's and refuse the exchange. As would be expected in the small village society, enmity was closely tied not only to family connections but to familiarity and mutual knowledge, and, for these women, to the sphere of domestic favors.[59]

The vocabulary of friendship and enmity was regularly used by witnesses in the trial to describe this network of relationships, both among women and between men and women. In fact, it is in the friendship between the three defendants that the seven final witnesses in the trial, who were not eyewitnesses to any event under investigation but served rather as the spokesmen for and representatives of village public opinion, found the main force that had led to the murder of Antonino. All seven men testified that the "public rumor" in the village, universally and immediately after the murder, blamed Pietro and Anna for instigating and facilitating Domenica's action. The three were "great friends," and in particular Anna, because of the friendship that bound her to Pietro, allowed him to use her house to meet his mistress.[60]

Friendship between men and women was, however, rarely acknowledged, and in this case it was clearly regarded, both by the witnesses and by the court, as illicit and dangerous. One of the puzzling aspects of the events investigated during the trial in fact concerns the help Domenica Orlando received at the time of her abortion. The main help came from Anna, of course, who provided the poisonous root. Domenica's mother helped her dispose of the fetus, and Mariuzza Schirrica, who also stated that she knew Domenica "very well," housed her while the root took effect and was with her when the miscarriage occurred.[61]

However, Domenica's need was first reported to Anna by a man, Domenico Tropea, to whom Domenica had appealed for help and who also alerted Mariuzza of Domenica's need for refuge. Another man, Francesco Tropea, attended Domenica for a short while when she and her mother were about to dispose of the fetus. Although Domenico explained that he and Mariuzza were cousins, no other explanation is given of why Domenica and her mother had recourse to these two men. Indeed, no term at all is used to describe the links, whatever they might have been, between the two women and the two men, so that the interaction between them appears in the records to be entirely, though rather implausibly, accidental. Domenico was highly noncommittal about the motivations of his actions, and he simply said that "he had heard it said" that Anna had managed other abortions, and therefore he had described Domenica's predicament to her. Actions that would certainly have fallen within the sphere and discourse of friendship had they occurred between women could find no acceptable interpretation when performed by a man.

The marriage of Antonino Cuzzucli and Domenica Orlando obviously ended in a most atypical way: however different the stories of unhappy marriages may be from one another, it was the rare couple whose unhappiness resulted in a murder trial. Yet the union of Antonino and Domenica followed in several ways the model of marriages in small villages anywhere. The spouses were likely related, and their marriage created another of the many links that bound together established families and helped maintain stable communities. The respective roles of husband and wife were shaped by village traditions and culture and also by the position of each spouse's family within village society. Antonino's protracted sojourns in Montebello point not only to the early unhappiness of the couple but also to conflicting family strategies. His absences also placed Domenica in the peculiar position of a married woman living alone, and this must have intensified her friendship with her neighbor Anna de Amico, who also had been abandoned by her husband. At the same time, unlike Anna, Domenica could count on the support of her numerous and established family in dealing with the inevitable difficulties, and the threats to her reputation, to which lonesomeness exposed all women.

Honor, and the behavior that maintained or diminished it, was critical to each villager's status, and the community took a keen interest in the actions and reputation of all its members, especially in the area of family and domestic behavior. In the seventeenth and eighteenth centuries state and church increasingly attempted to regulate popular practices and to control the moral behavior of the masses. Village communities, however, preserved their own control and support mechanisms, and villagers found in their networks of neighbors, relatives, and friends a rich source of help in matters both mundane and serious. Villagers took rituals and traditions that were highly regulated by external forces, such as godparenthood, and adapted them to their own needs, customs, and values. Village culture was characterized by a practical attitude, and when villagers took a negative view of their neighbors, it happened less on the basis of abstract notions of morality than because someone's actions endangered the stability or well-being of the community. Judgment was thus much more severe with outsiders than with well-integrated members of the village.

Justice, Sexuality, and Women

In the early eighteenth century a profound crisis began in the operation and guiding principles of the justice system as it had been developed since the Renaissance. The inquisitorial procedure had been developed to respond to the perceived need, on the part of secular and ecclesiastic authorities, for a stricter control of crime and for an expansion of the repressive power of those authorities. The new procedure, and the growth in the judicial apparatus of the early modern states which accompanied its implementation, certainly centralized and strengthened judicial authority, but, owing to the available methods to gather evidence, it also forced the justice system to rely on the cooperation and involvement of the general population. This need for collaboration was particularly evident in the handling of crimes that left scarce or ambiguous physical evidence.

The increasing concern of state and religious powers, across the confessional divisions of Europe, not only for the prevention of violence but also for the proper and obedient behavior of subjects and the faithful placed special emphasis upon crimes that offended a moral code that had become, over the fifteenth and sixteenth centuries, much more clearly defined and rigorous. Also because of the interdependence of churches and secular governments, the notions of sin and crime often overlapped. Church leaders and sovereigns believed that the reform of church institutions and the building of more effective secular ones needed to be accompanied by a reform of popular beliefs and rituals and also of the moral and sexual behavior of the entire population. The rural masses appeared to be in particular need of such severe reform.

Sexual and moral crimes were especially troubling to authorities also because they posed remarkably difficult problems of proof. Jurists and judges throughout Europe devoted much time and effort, and much paper and ink, to the analysis of these crimes. More than any others, these crimes ensnared the justice system in complex negotiations with individuals and communities. The extreme difficulty of arriving at satisfactory proof in many of these cases also led to the development of increasingly complex and often contradictory procedures and to the violation of many of the principles on which the prevailing jurisprudence was founded. This slowed down and weakened justice and by the later eighteenth century resulted in the reconsideration of many legal ideas and judicial practices.

As we saw in Chapter 2, jurists often allowed for procedural exceptions when judges had to deal with crimes considered especially grave. All three of the crimes investigated in the Pentidattilo trial—poisoning, abortion, and adultery—were among those so regarded. All three were also classified by jurists as "hidden" crimes, of especially difficult proof, and two of them were of a sexual and moral nature, and as such they received special attention in laws and in theoretical discussions all over early modern Europe. All these crimes involved women. The position of women, in their roles as witnesses, defendants, or victims, vis-à-vis the law and the justice system thus also became the object of intense jurisprudential debates, which tell us much about general attitudes towards women and sexuality. These crimes were also central to the rethinking of the inquisitorial procedure and the attempts at legal and judicial reforms that took place during the course of the eighteenth century. The ideas and principles that inspired these attempts, in the Kingdom of Naples as elsewhere in Europe, came not only from Enlightenment concerns about the irrationality of justice and the arbitrariness of judges but also from the growing awareness among jurists and judges of the inner contradictions moral and sexual crimes, and their difficulty of proof, revealed in the existing procedures.

The Treatment of Defendants

> Corporis dolorem ad eruendam veritatem
>
> Bodily pain to elicit truth
> —ULPIAN, in the *Digest* describing torture

The first duty of the investigating judge in any trial was to gather physical evidence and the depositions of witnesses. This the Pentidattilo court did quickly and smoothly, and this task was completed on March 27, 1710. The investigative part of the trial was finished, and the scribe allowed himself the relief and luxury of leaving a blank page after the last deposition. Overall the governor and his dependents could be pleased with themselves and their work. Enough evidence had been gathered, and confirmed through different depositions, to move on to the next phase of the trial—the formal indictment and interrogation of the defendants. To this task the court proceeded without delay on the following day, March 28.

People suspected of major crimes could be arrested and detained with a minimum of evidence against them. In theory the evidence then gathered by the court was to remain concealed from the defendants, though in a small village like Pentidattilo it is hard to believe that Domenica, Pietro, and Anna were not somehow informed of the specifics of the investigation that had been taking place. The court had also followed the faster procedure of requiring the witnesses to take an oath in the presence of the defendants, so the latter certainly knew at least who had been questioned about the case.

The defendants were questioned separately, and some of the questions— such as whether they knew the reason for their imprisonment—were routinely asked of all defendants. The interrogations marked the entry in the proceedings of the coadiutore, the magnifico Domenico Romeo.[1] Unlike the governor and his counselor, Romeo belonged to a large clan in Pentidattilo, and he may be the same Domenico Romeo who served as assessor in the 1745 census. As coadiutore, he attended the interrogations and torture of the three defendants, and he later cooperated with Giovan Domenico Cuzzucli, the denouncer, in the attempt to speed up the proceedings and reach a sentence.

On March 28, the court questioned all three defendants, beginning with Anna and continuing with Pietro and Domenica. They had been kept for the previous ten days in the prison that was part of the feudal castle high above Pentidattilo. According to the 1648 agreement between the village and the marquis, women could only be jailed in the feudal criminal prison in capital cases, which both abortion and murder (as well as complicity therein), of course, were. Feudal lords were required to maintain separate prisons for male and female criminals, but in small villages such as Pentidattilo this was frequently not the case. It is therefore likely that the three defendants had been able to maintain some contact with one another during their imprisonment. In any case, their depositions under questioning by the court do not point to a common strategy.[2]

Anna took her oath and replied to the first routine questions that she had been jailed about ten days before and that after being jailed she had learned that the reasons for her imprisonment were the poisoning of Antonino Cuzzucli and the abortions of "some women." Pressed further on what she knew about the poisoning and abortions, Anna stated that she had indeed given arsenic to Domenica but declared herself ignorant of what Domenica had done with it, as well as of the abortions. Anna was then asked whether she knew Domenica Orlando, Antonia Crea, Lucretia Condello, and Antonina Flachi and whether she had had any "dealings" with them. Anna replied that she knew them "very well" because they were all in Pentidattilo, though Flachi was now dead, but she denied having had any "dealings" with them. She also replied in the negative when asked whether she had ever been pregnant. Asked then whether she knew fifteen people (all among the witnesses), and "what people they are, and whether they are people who speak the truth," Anna replied that she knew them all and wisely added, "Whether they are people who speak the truth or not is known to their own consciences."[3]

At this point the judge decided that the accused should be confronted with the evidence known to the court. Admonishing Anna to speak the truth under penalty for perjury, he went on to say that "the court knew" about the abortions induced by Anna by means of her root for Domenica, Antonia, Lucretia, and Antonina, as well as herself, adding all the details we have already seen. Then the judge turned to Antonino's murder and asked Anna "how she could deny" that she had plotted with Domenica to poison the latter's husband. The court presented its version of the events, distilled from all the depositions it had heard, which pointed to Anna's active role in pushing Domenica to the murder and in twice providing arsenic to be added to Antonino's food or drink. The two women, the judge alleged, had communicated easily and frequently through the hole between their houses and had persevered in their plan even after Antonino had remarkably survived their first attempt to poison him. The judge even showed Anna the small pitcher in which she allegedly had given Domenica poisoned water for her husband. The court's version of the events as presented to Anna assigned no role whatsoever to Pietro Crea, Domenica's alleged lover and, according to some witnesses, the murder's instigator.

Anna seemed undaunted by this long accusation. She simply replied: "Sirs, of what you have read to me I know nothing at all, only this small pitcher you have shown me is mine, since Domenica had borrowed it from me." After she had put her cross under her deposition, the scribe formulated the next steps. Her denials meant that Anna "contested" the indictment, and four days were granted her to prepare her defense. The court and the accuser would have the same time to strengthen their case against her. Since Anna, unsurprisingly, stated that she had neither a lawyer nor a procurator (legal counselor), Felice

Amodei, probably a relative of the governor, was assigned to her as her lawyer. With that, the court turned its attention to Pietro Crea.[4]

Pietro said he did not know the reason for his imprisonment. He denied knowing Domenica Orlando and stated that he had no home in Pentidattilo. He said that, as guardian of the forest, he rarely stayed in the village, and on those occasions he slept at his brother Marco's house. Pietro then denied having had sexual relations with anyone in Pentidattilo, having promised any woman to marry her, and knowing Antonino Cuzzucli (who Pietro seemed— or pretended—to think was alive). The judge then presented Pietro with the names of ten people and asked whether they spoke the truth and whether they were friends or enemies of his. The latter question, as we saw in Chapter 4, was only posed to Pietro, the lone male defendant, reflecting the gendered perception of enmity shared by the judge. Pietro denied knowing any of the people named. To the judge's indignant question as to how he could not know any of them, since he had lived for ten years previously in Pentidattilo, Pietro repeated that he did not know any of them, "since [he] never talked to anyone." In fact, about the only thing Pietro did not deny in his interrogation was knowledge of where the church and square of San Pietro were.[5]

The judge again turned to direct accusation and confronted Pietro with what "the court knew," namely, that two months earlier Pietro had gone to Domenica's house at night when her husband was away and told her that he would marry her if she poisoned Antonino, promising to provide her with the poison himself. With this, the court alleged, Pietro, "having undressed, got into bed and knew carnally the said Domenica," which he continued to do occasionally over the following months. Finally, the court said Pietro had again promised marriage to Domenica (and help with the poisoning) when they had met at Anna's house shortly before Antonino's murder. To all of this Pietro simply replied: "Sirs, they are out to get me." The same formalities followed Pietro's interrogation as in Anna's case.[6]

Whereas Anna acknowledged only marginal involvement in the case and Pietro stubbornly denied any awareness of it, the court met with a very different response from Domenica. Asked by the judge whether she knew the reason for her imprisonment, she said she "had to tell [him] the truth," and she quickly confessed her participation in the crimes of which she stood accused and offered her very lengthy version of the events. Everything had started two months before, when Pietro had first come to her late one night, when her husband was away; she had recognized him "because [she] knew him and also because the moon was shining." Pietro had come in, had "started to take [her] with good words," and had proceeded to undress by the bed. Domenica had "begun to get mad at him saying to him 'what manners are these,'" but Pietro had persuaded her "saying he wanted [her] for his wife as soon as [she] could poison [her] husband" and had promised to bring her poison from Reggio: "Thus we both undressed and went to bed and he knew me carnally."[7]

While the illicit relationship continued, Domenica went on, one day Antonino beat her. Her neighbor Anna heard this through the hole between their houses and came to talk and offer advice. Anna, according to Domenica, had said: "Oh Domenica, if you do not find the way to get rid of your husband you will not be happy," and, on Domenica's reply that she knew not how to do it, Anna had offered to provide her with some poison in exchange for 5 carlini she knew Domenica had recently earned. Since Pietro—despite Domenica's entreaties—had not come through on his own offer to provide the poison, Domenica agreed to this neighborly proposition. Domenica went on to relate how she and Anna had obtained the poison, her two attempts to poison her husband, and Antonino's death. Throughout her version of the events, Domenica presented herself as the meek and somewhat passive instrument of Pietro's and Anna's suggestions, though she could not deny that she had indeed twice given the poison to her husband herself. This passivity matched the role attributed to Domenica by the seven final male witnesses in the trial.[8]

The judge turned to the matter of Domenica's abortion. Here, too, she showed herself eager to talk. She confirmed everything the court knew about her pregnancy, the help provided by Domenico and Francesco Tropea, her stay at Mariuzza Schirrica's house, and Anna's effective roots. The only divergence from Mariuzza's testimony was that Domenica claimed not to have known whether her fetus was male or female and made no reference to its having been born alive. Domenica had left her mother to dispose of the little corpse, and the latter had told her that "she had buried it behind a shed." Domenica also confirmed what the court had already heard about Anna's own abortion, which had occurred only two months before the trial.[9]

Since Domenica had not only confessed her own crimes but also clearly implicated Anna and Pietro, it was now necessary for the court—faced with Anna's and Pietro's denials—to strengthen the accusatorial force of the one confession it had. To this purpose, on the next day, March 29, the court ordered and proceeded with the torture of Domenica, in order to "convalidate her confession in as much as it affects her accomplices." It was customary, when given a choice of defendants, to begin by torturing the one perceived as most likely to confess—for instance, women, younger or weaker people, or, as in this case, someone who had already confessed without torture. Torture was also (rather paradoxically) necessary to strengthen the confession of avowed criminals, whose testimony against others would otherwise have been tainted by their own confessed guilt. In this case the torture of Domenica in the presence of her alleged accomplices had the value of a confrontation between them and resulted in the incrimination of Pietro and Anna.[10]

The form of torture used in this case was the main one in use in the early modern Kingdom of Naples, as in most of Italy at the time, except for crimes of exceptional ferocity and gravity. The arms of the accused were tied behind her back, and she was then suspended by a rope attached to her arms and kept hanging for a period no longer than an hour. Domenica was taken to the "chamber of the secret rope," and the entire deposition she had given the previous day was read out to her. She was then undressed, tied, and raised by the rope, and, while she hanged thus, Pietro and Anna were introduced in the chamber. Under oath, Domenica identified them as those she had spoken of, and, "asked whether what she said and deposed in her deposition against these two was true, and if it were not true she should not say it nor should she endanger her soul, she said all was true and most true, and if it were not true she would not have said it." She was left hanging for "a short period of time," and, persisting in her declarations, she was eventually released and taken back to the prison.[11]

Following her session in the torture chamber, Domenica was also given the customary four days to prepare her defense "against her own spontaneous confession," and the same Felice Amodei was appointed as her defense lawyer. On March 31, the court messenger testified that he had notified the three defendants and their lawyer of the terms for their defense, and the lawyer had also been informed of two possible defense witnesses, Geronimo Marino and Francesco Manuscalco, about whom nothing else is known except that they were not from Pentidattilo.[12]

Up to this point, this case in Pentidattilo's feudal court had followed closely the practice and doctrine of early modern jurisprudence. The judge had done his job of investigator and questioner, and as solid a body of evidence from witnesses had been assembled as was likely in crimes of difficult proof, which adultery, abortion, and murder by poisoning all indubitably were. The defendants had been secured, the customary procedural guarantees had been granted them, and little seemed to stand in the way of a successful and speedy conclusion. Delay and inefficiency, however, and favoritism—all as typical of early modern judicial practice as anything that had hitherto happened in this trial—began to play their part.

The treatment of the defendants in the Pentidattilo trial points to some of the problems faced by early modern courts when dealing with difficult crimes, especially in rural contexts. However vigilant and suspicious anyone's neighbors may have been, adultery and abortion generally took place in private, so that eyewitnesses were unlikely. Poisoning was also difficult to prove beyond doubt, given the limits of medical expertise. The barber Giannetti probably would not have been able to perform an autopsy even if that might have resulted in firmer proof, which was in any case unlikely. Since courts could not pronounce verdicts on the basis of circumstantial evidence, the defendants' denials, however implausible, created the need for torture, with its own attendant theoretical and practical difficulties and its paradoxes. All these obstacles were grounded in the prevailing doctrine of proof, which became especially problematic with sexual and moral crimes.

Proof and Punishment

> Luce meridiana clariores
>
> Clearer than the light of midday
> —Early modern jurisprudential commonplace

Among the reasons for the replacement of the early medieval accusatorial procedure with the inquisitorial one was the church's dissatisfaction with traditional methods to verify accusations, which were seen as both inefficient and immoral. After ordeals and other nonjudicial methods of proof were discarded, new ways to ascertain the truth of matters under trial had to be developed, both in the doctrine of jurists and in the actual practice of courts. There was a concern to formulate a universal logical system that would prevent decisions based on the arbitrary opinion of the judge. This definition began with canon lawyers in the thirteenth century and by the early modern period had resulted in the construction of a coherent system of "legal proof," which continued to be debated and fine-tuned until the eighteenth-century reforms. Throughout these centuries, ever more limits were placed on defendants' rights and privileges, and ever more exceptions to the system's own guarantees of fairness were developed and allowed. This process took primarily the form of a learned debate, but it also reflected popular understandings of the law and of justice, since jurists knew that in practice no proof would be possible without the cooperation of the general population.

At the basis of the system was the idea of establishing unassailable full proof as the foundation for conviction and sentencing. The growing power of early modern states led to increased concern lest serious crime go unpunished, and to the legislation of ever more severe penalties. The very harshness of punishments, however, made jurists wish to find the most certain grounds to inflict them. This gave shape to a quantitative conception of proof, a detailed theory of clues, the frequent use of torture, and the development of separate types of punishments.[13]

The inheritance of Roman and medieval ideas led to the persisting doctrine that full proof was needed to convict and to inflict the harsh sentences required by the laws. Proof, as jurists repeated, had to be "clearer than the light of mid-day." It was, however, extremely difficult to establish what constituted full proof in the circumstances of early modern life and in the general lack of written evidence. Lawyers, many of whom were trained in both canon and civil law and deeply embedded in the culture of legal and moral casuistry, specialized in finding exceptions to even the seemingly clearest evidence.[14] It was generally agreed in the doctrine and in the laws about procedure that, barring a free and valid confession, full proof could only be found in the spontaneous and separate, but equal, testimony of two irreproachable witnesses who had been in the position of making undoubted observation of the facts under debate.

Given the near impossibility of such full proof, a theory of clues came into being. What value should be ascribed to the testimony of less than irreproachable witnesses? Could one piece of documentary evidence be added to one perfect witness to form full proof? When did the sum total of all available clues indeed constitute proof "clearer than the light of mid-day?"

Apart from the depositions of witnesses, object or documentary evidence, and the behavior of the defendant after his arrest, clues consisted of the reputation of both the defendant and the witnesses. In the Pentidattilo case, the court put much importance on the public opinion of the community where the crime had taken place, not only about the events but also about the character of the defendants. As we have seen, seven witnesses, who were otherwise entirely ignorant of the facts of the case, were called upon to express the community's opinion of what had happened and of the defendants, thereby legitimating the court's conclusions. The reputation, character, and past behavior of defendants became crucial issues in the theory of clues. A bad reputation, in fact, defined as the "opinion of good and honest men," was considered a "semi-full proof" for the purposes of torturing and convicting.[15]

When full proof was otherwise hard to come by, but when the need for repression was felt to be serious, confession became a logical alternative. Hence, from the concern to prevent the subjective decisions of judges came the widespread use of torture, not as a form of punishment but as a means to the end—held to be ultimately in the interest of defendants—of full proof. The problem of subjectivity was, however, far from solved. Torture could only be applied when there were enough clues to justify it, and further debate ensued on which clues could indeed be called "undoubted," legitimating the use of torture. Clues could be "proximate" or "remote," and the former were needed to justify torture. They might include reasonably concrete ones, such as escape attempts, threats, or old enmities, but also much vaguer ones, such as "trepidation, hesitation, vacillation, and trembling" when interrogated.[16]

Torture, moreover, created its own set of difficulties. As another remnant of older concerns for fairness, a defendant who resisted torture without confessing was held to have "purged" the clues against him, so that torture might end up being counterproductive for the prosecution's ends. More legal acrobatics were developed to prevent such "purgation of the clues" and to ensure that torture could be applied in an ever widening number of cases. Confessions given under torture had to be ratified the next day. Failure to do so, however, automatically triggered further torture, because, as Ambrosino brilliantly concluded, "the first confession given under torture creates a new clue."[17] Torture was, in fact, used less in cases of criminals acting alone than to incriminate accomplices, as happened in Pentidattilo. Since a defendant who confessed to a crime became tainted by infamy and therefore less valuable as a witness against others, torture was needed to strengthen his accusations against any accomplices.[18]

The difficulty of arriving at full proof often remained, however, an unsurmountable obstacle to full conviction. For particularly heinous crimes, such as lese majesty, the idea of "privileged proof" was formulated, whereby clues could be considered equivalent to full proof. But it was necessary to deal with the majority of crimes. Both doctrine and practice developed, therefore, a new theory of punishment, to ensure the primary interest of the repression of crime. The punishment set by law for any given crime was known as the "ordinary" punishment. In the absence of full proof but in the presence of clues variously defined as certain and undoubted, courts were allowed to sentence to "extraordinary" punishment, only slightly milder than the ferocious ordinary ones. Gradually, extraordinary punishments came to be inflicted in the great majority of cases. This could lead to a lesser use of torture, because, rather than torturing to gain full proof but risking the purgation of clues, a judge was better advised to sentence to extraordinary punishment on the basis of clues.[19]

The development of extraordinary punishments resulted in the renewed importance of the judge's discretion, and hence of his arbitrary opinion, which John Langbein has related to the growth of stronger states, less worried about the freedom of judges to act on their own beliefs. While this tendency to rely on the judge's opinion would later become one of the bases for Enlightenment reforms of judicial procedure, the logical consequences of this movement towards greater judicial discretion were enacted into law in the Kingdom of Naples as early as 1621. An edict in that year decreed that, even in the absence of confession and full proof, if there were "undoubted clues" and no doubt remained in the mind of the judge, ordinary punishments, including the death penalty, could be inflicted. The next year another edict restricted this provision to royal collegial magistracies.[20]

This law began a lively debate among Neapolitan jurists as to when exactly the magistracies could exercise this privilege. Some feared the ambiguity inherent in any attempt to define what the lack of doubt in the judges' mind was; others wrote of firm beliefs and inner quiet, or of absence of hesitations, and tried to set minimum conditions necessary for applying the law, such as a full examination of the corpus delicti yielding undoubted results. With blithe disregard for tautology, Scialoja described undoubted clues as "those that move the soul of the judge to believe that the crime was perpetrated by the defendant, so that he cannot be persuaded to believe the contrary." This law marked an important step in the development of European jurisprudence and judicial practice and was an essential moment in the intellectual movement towards the abolition of legal torture which would advance much further in the following century.[21]

Exceptions were, then, constantly being found whenever the need to prosecute and repress met with the obstacles inherent in the inquisitorial system. Entire categories of crimes were often exempted from even the few rights that the system accorded to defendants. Although a few jurists argued that the more heinous the crime, the fuller ought to be its proof, the majority opinion in the jurisprudence, and in the practice of most courts, was in favor of easing the prosecution of what were generally defined as grave and horrible crimes.[22] One major group of crimes subject to special, more relaxed rules of investigation and proof consisted of "hidden" crimes and crimes of a sexual and moral nature, which were considered of more difficult proof but the gravity of which called for special procedures.

"Hidden Crimes" and Sexual/Moral Crimes

> Multi sunt judices sitientes sanguinem humanum potius quam justitiam.
>
> There are many judges who thirst more for human blood than for justice.
>
> —NOVARIO, *De vassallorum*

Within the general growing concern with the repression of crime in the late medieval and early modern periods, hidden crimes and especially sexual and moral crimes were considered particularly subversive and dangerous, because of the difficulty of prosecuting them and because they struck at the core of the constituted order. Church and state worked together to protect religion, morality, authority, and the honor and safety of the family as the model for the stability of all institutions. The fundamental position of religion and the church in public life, the intertwining of theology and jurisprudence in the education of legal groups, and the increasing interest of the state in the behavior and views of its people allowed very little distinction between the notions of sin and crime. The centrality of sexual behavior to Christian morality further eroded that difference when it came to sexual crimes. Robert Muchembled, for instance, has seen the criminalization of popular behavior and attitudes especially in matters of sex and morality as central to what he has called "the invention of modern man."[23]

The lack of distinction between sin and crime, with the exception of men's adultery, was based on the common foundation of both law and moral theology on conceptions of natural and divine law. Thus, even though certain sexual practices, such as oral intercourse or masturbation, were rarely prohibited by specific secular laws, jurists argued that their undoubted condemnation in divine and natural law dictated their severe prosecution and punishment by secular courts. Illicit sexual practices, then, understood within this framework, were ranked according to their offense against nature and God, and therefore depending on how opposed they were to the procreative function, which alone was held to legitimate sexual activity—hence the relative toleration for prostitution and fornication and the harsh penalties reserved for sodomy. The prosecution of these crimes reflected the common interest of early modern states and post-Reformation churches in the reform and control of the moral behavior of the masses.[24]

In any case, because of the difficulty of prosecuting them and their likely substantial underreporting, sexual and moral crimes are generally rare in the annals of early modern crime. In the eighteenth century, for instance, sexual crimes represented between 1 percent and 7 percent of reported crimes in areas of Europe as diverse as rural and urban France, England, the Venetian Republic, Sardinia, and the Caracciolo Brienza fiefs.[25] It is all the more remarkable, then, that these crimes received enormous attention and concern in the pages (and perhaps the fantasies) of jurists, theologians, bishops, and judges. These crimes were handled with particular ferocity, at least in the laws and the doctrine (and in episcopal fulminations), in terms of both the procedures applied to their prosecution and the punishments inflicted on the convicted.[26]

This severity was, however, somewhat lessened in practice, because of the very difficulty of proof but also probably because of the commonness of these cases, especially in the rural world, which made both prosecution and harsh punishment harder to implement. As we have seen, prosecution of these crimes at the local level required a high degree of cooperation between judicial authorities and villagers, and thus only cases that had aroused concern or opposition within village communities had a real chance of coming to trial, let alone conviction. Much supposedly illicit behavior went unreported or unpunished because villagers regarded it as justified or simply did not find it offensive to their own ethical understanding.

By the late seventeenth and eighteenth centuries even the jurisprudence became more moderate in its discussion of these crimes, possibly also because of the degree of success achieved by both state and church in increasing their general control over the rural population in areas other than sexuality and morality. Prevailing attitudes towards women, who were typically heavily involved in these crimes, also may have led to the spread of this more moderate approach. While women were often seen as more prone to evil than men, they were also seen as weaker and frailer and therefore deserving of more mildness on the part of justice, especially when they might be shown to have acted in the defense of a sense of family honor.[27]

The category of hidden or special crimes included some forms of murder. Willful murder was the model capital crime. Although death was the ordinary punishment for many other crimes (in Naples, in theory, also for kissing women in public against their will),[28] the idea of a life for a life was a fundamental principle repeated unquestioningly by most jurists. There were, however, categories even within murder, depending on the circumstances, the "quality" (or social status) of the people involved, and the method of killing. Some circumstances, such as self-defense, could lessen the penalty for murder, indeed even eliminate it altogether: the husband or father finding his adulterous wife or daughter in "the venereal act" had the legal right to kill her and the lover, if he did so without hesitation, under the spur of anger and offended honor; the target of attempted sodomy had the right to kill the frustrated sodomite. But there were also many forms of murder which were worse than ordinary murder.[29]

Suicide was often seen as worse than homicide, because one killed not only a body but a soul. Other factors that could make murder a particularly horrible crime were possible relationships, of family, hospitality, or friendship, between the victim and the murderer; the circumstances of the actual killing, such as acting during the night or in a sudden manner (that would amount to a betrayal of the victim); and finally the murder weapon or method. Killing a parent, child, or spouse—termed *parricide* or *uxoricide*—was among the most heinous forms of murder and in the old days (and in Roman law) had been the ground for one of the most creative punishments: the parricide was tied in a sack with a viper, a rooster, a dog, and a monkey (slight variations were possible in this cast) and thrown into a river or the sea. Many jurists lamented the passing of this punishment and its replacement by the more humdrum quarterings and burnings that were considered sufficient by the sixteenth century even for especially horrific crimes.[30]

It was also a jurisprudential commonplace that to kill by poison was far worse than to kill by the sword, because of the elements of betrayal, premeditation, and hiding inherent in poisoning. Poisoning, moreover, was especially suited to the domestic setting and often involved family members, which made it doubly heinous. The traditional identification of women with the domestic sphere and with cooking made the possibility of poisoning especially troubling and horrifying. As Claro put it, "Women more than men are suspect of poisoning." Indeed, as a typically female form of murder, poisoning (particularly of husbands) became the ultimate symbol of betrayal and subversion. In England murdering one's husband was equivalent to petty treason and punished with gruesome executions.[31]

All nocturnal or hidden crimes (and poisoning obviously took place in secret) were classified as "of difficult proof" and therefore "privileged" in the procedure used to investigate them.[32] Because full proof was almost impossible to establish, the requirements for both torture and conviction were relaxed. For example, one good witness or public opinion was sufficient to justify torture, and the testimony of vitiated witnesses was allowed.[33] While poisoning was very difficult to prove unassailably, circumstances and the physical examination of the corpse could yield strong clues, which in such a grave crime would be more than sufficient to torture and often to convict, or at least to sentence to extraordinary penalties. Judges were therefore urged to consult experts, mostly physicians, and to examine the physical evidence carefully. In Pentidattilo the thorough examination of Antonino Cuzzucli's cadaver performed by the local barber was the first step in the court's investigation. The symptoms described by the barber closely match those listed in several treatises as indicative of arsenic poisoning.[34]

Crimes of a sexual and moral nature were also considered of especially difficult proof and therefore subject to relaxed rules of prosecution and severe penalties. In fact, possibly because of the harsh penalties themselves and of legal casuistry that found here a favorite field of action, the jurisprudence set ever higher standards of proof. This made the ordinary penalties ever more difficult to inflict, thereby justifying harsher extraordinary ones, in a vicious, and contradictory, circle of repression and legal guarantees.

These crimes were also situated at the juncture between secular and ecclesiastic jurisdiction, and their eager prosecution by secular courts shows the importance secular authorities attached to the protection and enforcement of official religion and morality, as well as their desire to curb the powers of ecclesiastic courts. Some of these crimes, such as sodomy, adultery, or concubinage, were deemed of mixed jurisdiction and could be prosecuted in both courts. Secular courts at times also claimed jurisdiction over sacrilege and over blasphemy of a nonheretical nature. Episcopal courts were the most active church courts in most of Catholic Europe in the prosecution of moral and sexual crimes, with the exception of Spain, where the Inquisition exercised careful jurisdiction over many of these crimes. Church courts also fought hard to maintain their exclusive purview over all crimes involving ecclesiastics.[35]

Sexual/moral crimes included a wide range of behavior deemed to be dangerous for society, either for the damage it wrought on individuals or for the threat it posed to the family as an institution and to the values church and state wished to uphold. They included abortion and infanticide (often, but not always, discussed by jurists within the homicide category), adultery, sodomy (the *crimen nefandum,* or unspeakable crime, for jurists who could not bring themselves to write the word), bestiality, the abduction of women, incest, rape, *stuprum* (sex, often consensual, with virgins, widows, or other "honest" women, since it was assumed to be the result of undue pressure from the man), and, occasionally, lesbianism, oral sex, and masturbation.[36] All these were made particularly horrendous if perpetrated with one's vassals or servants, clerics, Jews, or jailed prisoners.[37]

The ordinary penalty for almost all these crimes was death. But, since conviction required standards of proof which were hard to meet, especially in consensual cases,[38] the jurisprudence and the laws agreed that extraordinary penalties would be the norm. Because for some of these crimes the ordinary penalty was a particularly brutal form of death (such as burning for sodomites), even a simple hanging was seen as milder and was therefore allowed with less than full proof. In the case of rape, nonconsensual sodomy, or abduction, the testimony of the victim was available, though not always reliable or easy to assess. The other crimes were either victimless, consensual, or left no victim able to incriminate the perpetrator, as was the case with infanticide and bestiality.[39]

Judges were urged in these cases to use whatever clues might exist and above all to examine any physical evidence. Clues regarding rape and sodomy,[40] and to some extent abortion or infanticide, could be gained from expert analysis of the bodies of the accused and the victim. Handbooks and treatises detailed the signs of recent pregnancy, of loss of virginity, or of anal intercourse which could be detected by skilled physicians and especially, for the examination of women, by practiced midwives and elderly women. Legal writers debated evidence for the existence of the hymen in women and specified the clues to look for: blood or sperm in cases of sexual activity, and turgid, milk-filled breasts for suspected infanticides; since ejaculation had to be proved for full conviction, victims of rape were to be asked whether they had felt a "warm liquid" and so on. The texts bespeak the urgency of the search for clues.[41]

Such expert examination would not have yielded any result in the Pentidattilo case, since the alleged abortions had taken place long before the trial. Examples of how the suggestions of jurists were followed in practice, and of the contact between the doctrine and the working of local courts, can, however, be found in some of the trials from the Caracciolo Brienza fiefs discussed in Chapter 2. In the 1791 rape trial in Atena of Vincenzo Lopardo, for instance, the victim, Costanza Gaimari, knew which elements to stress in her deposition to give the court the clues it was looking for: she felt "the greatest pain," there was blood, and she felt in her vagina a stream of "warm water." The two midwives who examined her testified to the state of her genitals and nipples

(Costanza was pregnant), as well as to her good reputation, another essential element in proving rape. Vincenzo's defense touched on the same points in order to deny them. Similar procedures and factors, often expressed in very similar words, appear in the trials in Brienza of Rocco Lopardi in 1778–81 and Domenico Biondo in 1787.[42]

So, while the theory and the laws called for the severe repression of these crimes, in practice the difficulty of proof, acknowledged by legal writers, too, led eventually to milder penalties, once all avenues of examination and investigation had been explored. This was in no case truer than with abortion. While in antiquity its criminal status had been unclear, the laws and the jurisprudence of Christian Europe agreed on the extreme gravity of the crime, but it was not as easy to agree on its definition, let alone on how to prove it. Even if willful abortion could be proved (and this meant not only proving the use of some method but proving that the method had directly caused the abortion), consideration of the motive could lessen the penalty, particularly with a crime so closely tied to notions of honor and shame.[43]

The first contentious issue was the definition of the crime. It was agreed that a prosecutable abortion required that the fetus be animated, or endowed with the soul, but there was little agreement as to what this meant. Estimates, based on theological texts, ranged from the majority opinion of thirty to forty days (for male fetuses, usually double this figure for female ones, as even here God discriminated against females) to seven months (with the idea that before that the fetus could not survive a birth). In dubious cases jurists split as to what ought to be presumed, though quickening was also often used as the defining transition. Both the woman willfully obtaining an abortion and whoever aided her were guilty of a capital crime, but proving their actions caused further problems. The methods discussed in legal texts were blows (self-inflicted or otherwise), medicaments and potions, and poisonous roots or other vaginal suppositories. Again, the services of midwives and elderly women (who were often also suspected of offering aid to women seeking abortions) were called upon to examine the accused woman's body in search of any physical evidence, though proving that something had been used was not equivalent to proving it had been effective. Abortion was thus generally considered of difficult proof, although Moro argued that this was not the case in rural centers where everybody would know—he did not consider whether those who knew would also tell.[44]

Even if abortion was proved, several motives could provide extenuating circumstances. Many writers stated that early, pre-animation abortions should be punished mildly. If the woman had acted in hatred towards her husband, to protect her honor from shame if she was not married (or her husband was away, as was the case with Domenica Orlando), or out of fear for her own health, if she had been persuaded to it by her mother, or if the fetus was either deformed or a brute, she should also receive milder penalties (usually whipping or relegation); if a doctor had told her of dangers to her health, then she was altogether free of charge, "though not in the tribunal of conscience." In practice, said de Angelis, abortion was not actually seen as equivalent to murder, and even in willful late abortions the death penalty was almost never imposed. His 1783 commentator added that in his day most women were simply relegated to a convent for some time.[45]

The last major sexual crime was adultery, which belonged to a special category by virtue of the danger it posed to the institutions of marriage and the family. Only adultery and stuprum, in fact, could not be prosecuted by judges ex officio, except in notorious and public cases (in which the husband would be strongly suspected of pimping). With these crimes the state thus operated as the agent of family honor and private justice. Since "it is more important to protect the reputation of the offended [man] than to punish the offender," judges could investigate adultery only after the husband or father had made a denunciation.[46] Once a case had been investigated, no financial composition was possible, lest the court appear to engage in prostitution. The concern for family solidity was clear also in the provision that, should the husband take his adulterous wife back into his house, the trial would be ended.[47]

From the canonical point of view any break of the marriage bonds was adulterous, but secular courts only prosecuted adultery committed by married women (or by married men with women married to other men). This was the only explicit difference jurists noted between sin and crime. A married man having intercourse with a single free woman (who, that is, did not belong to protected categories such as virgins, widows, or nuns) certainly committed a sin and could be tried in church court, the jurists repeated, but he did not commit a crime. The adultery of wives was "greatly graver" than that of husbands, because of the concern for the paternity of children. Carpzov went so far as to say that a wife's adultery was worse for the husband than the death of his children. Jurists suspected wives of proneness to adultery, and perhaps such suspicions were not unjust in the case of Domenica Orlando. According to her own confession, she did not hesitate long when she began her adulterous relationship with Pietro Crea: a few sweet words from him (accompanied by his taking off his clothes) were apparently enough to win her over.[48]

With adultery, too, the "quality" of the people involved was crucial to an assessment of the crime. A servant having intercourse with his married mistress, for instance, deserved death.[49] Clerics who committed adultery, though particularly execrable, were not punishable by secular courts, and they were to be ordered by church courts to do penance in monasteries, although Claro noted, "If today clerics were locked up in monasteries because of adultery few of them would walk in the streets." Despite the fact that "God prefers the howling of a dog to the chant of a lustful cleric," adulterous priests were frequent enough that, when zealous bishops prosecuted them, de Luca warned, the effect was usually the murder of several wives by their husbands.[50]

Adultery combined the characteristics of sacrilege and theft, as it both took away another man's property and violated a sacrament, and death had originally been the ordinary penalty for all adulterers. However, here, too, the difficulty of proof and the problematic nature of honor and shame led to increased leniency. By the early modern period death was rarely, if ever, inflicted, and even the right of the husband or father to kill the adulteress found in flagrante was very carefully defined in legal texts to prevent its abuse. Even the fierce jurist Follerio was satisfied with whipping and cutting the nose of the adulteress.[51] Although de Sarno observed that "proof will be easy, because Love is blind, and men never think they will be found out," most writers emphasized the difficulty of arriving at full proof. Many clues and suspicions could be gleaned from the testimony of domestics, neighbors, and friends, as was done in Pentidattilo, and circumstantial evidence could be gathered, from displays of affection to correspondence, from frequent visits to simply the beauty of the two suspects compared with the ugliness of the husband, to the public opinion of the woman's reputation. But full proof was something else: "Adultery is among those crimes, of which no vestiges remain," and "it does not take place in the presence of many, but secretly and in hiding."[52]

Since even the limited physical evidence available in other sexual crimes was lacking in adultery, and given the grave risk an investigation represented for the husband's and the family's honor, judges were urged to exercise special care in the weighing of evidence and circumstances. De Angelis, perhaps with personal memories in mind, pointed out that, while a woman retiring to a secluded chamber with a man not her husband might easily be suspected, if "she is alone with her lawyer, even in some secret room, it should rather be presumed that she seeks his advice than that she fornicates with him." Even hugs or touches had to be assessed with consideration of the character of the people and the circumstances. A testimony of an eyewitness was best, though someone who testified to having clearly heard "happy sighs, loving kisses . . . and moans of pleasure" coming out of a window would create a strong presumption of guilt.[53]

The rarity of physical or other evidence in sexual and moral crimes, then, meant that the collaboration of local communities was especially necessary in prosecuting these crimes and forced judges to engage in negotiations with the attitudes and values of popular culture. The testimony of witnesses became crucial both for the reporting of crimes that left few traces and for the establishment of the reputation of defendants and plaintiffs, which was one of the few clues available to judges in many of these crimes.[54]

Moreover, while all authorities, intellectual and political, agreed that these crimes should be severely repressed, the very harshness of the penalties heightened a sensitivity to the difficulty of proof and resulted in doctrinal acrobatics, erratic prosecution and punishment, and increased reliance on that discretion of judges that the inquisitorial system had always regarded with concern. The judges' two thirsts—for human blood and for justice—nowhere came into greater tension with each other than in dealing with these crimes. By the early eighteenth century, awareness of the procedural problems caused especially by sexual and moral crimes provided a stimulus for a wholesale reassessment of the prosecutorial system. The fact that women were more heavily involved in this than in any other category of crimes also marked them as different and led to some of the problems of proof and punishment.

Women and the Law

> Celeres ad malum, pigrae ad bonum
>
> Quick to the evil, lazy to the good
> —R O T A, *Legalis androgynus*

As in all other aspects of life, in their dealings with the law women faced the contradictory attitudes of early modern society and culture: on the one hand, they were seen by legislators, jurists, and judges as peculiarly prone to evil and debauchery, on the other as frail and in need of the protection and guardianship of the law. Evidence of these contrasting views appears in both doctrine and practice whenever women encountered the legal and judicial system, as victims of crimes, as witnesses to them, or as their perpetrators.

Outside criminal law, there were strict traditional limits to the roles the law assigned to women. Carlo Rota divided his treatment of women and the law into various categories to which women may belong, all of which are expressed in terms of a woman's relation to men. We have, therefore, widows, wives, brides, fiancées, or—most troublesome of all—single free women (usually meaning prostitutes); mothers, stepmothers, or daughters; girls and virgins; and finally religious women. All of them suffered under similar limitations when it came to civil law: for instance, they had little control over money or property (including their dowries), they rarely could enter contractual agreements, they could only be witnesses to certain types of wills. The legal incompetence of women in civil law is confirmed in the papers of the Pentidattilo notary Francesco Celia, which show that women always needed the consent of their husbands or guardians to give validity to any contract they entered, even if it regarded the women's own property.[55]

Except for single free women, who were viewed with uniform suspicion, women's status depended on their relationship to a man. They also were rarely deemed to have an occupation. In trial depositions and other documents women were never asked—and if they told, it was not reported—about their occupation. The only recognized female occupation was that of midwife, a most useful one in village life and in judicial procedure but also the object of fear and attacks on the part of doctors, clerics, and jurists. In the Pentidattilo case, not only was the midwife the only woman witness whose occupation was given, but, while illiterate men were described as "not knowing how to write," women more simply were labeled "idiots."[56]

Women in general belonged to the legal category of "miserable people," which included the indigent, widows, orphans, ecclesiastics, and sometimes students, all of whom deserved the special protection and mercy of the law and the authorities because they were incapable of fully taking care of themselves. The situation of women with regard to the law depended heavily not only on their family status but on their "quality" and especially on their honor and reputation. Certain categories of women, such as those working in inns or domestic servants, were considered to have very little honor or reputation and, even if chaste, were known as "meretricious virgins" and could be molested with near impunity. From this focus on reputation, intended primarily as sexual reputation, resulted the emphasis on virginity and its proofs in many trials, as well as the insistence of jurists that women "deflowered by force," provided they had opposed the attack, remained virgins in the eyes of the law, entitled to the treatment and privileges the law accorded to "pure" women.[57]

This concern for reputation was the main element in determining the situation of women vis-à-vis the law. Honesty and modesty were used by jurists to justify excluding women from judicial offices, although they could, as feudal lords, exercise jurisdiction. This same preoccupation to shield the reputation and modesty of women from any potential danger, coupled with Mediterranean conceptions of male and family honor, shaped the approach to women in both legal doctrine and judicial practice, and both with crime in general and with crimes that particularly affected or involved women.

Women witnesses in investigations were regarded with intense suspicion. Again, a contradictory attitude prevailed. Often women could not be jailed for civil offenses, including debts. Women witnesses had to be treated with kid gloves. Their testimony in civil cases, especially if they were of high social status, had to be received at home, in order to spare them the indignity of openly participating in a trial. If married, they should be allowed to intervene in criminal cases through a procurator, "to protect their honesty."[58] But such troubles hardly seem worth taking when one considers the limited weight that jurists assigned to women's testimony.

The unreliability of women as witnesses and their tendency to perjury were commonplaces to which each jurist gave new formulation. Briganti claimed that "all women could be rejected [as witnesses] in criminal cases, for the great frailty of their sex and weakness of their wisdom." Even Rota, on the whole favorable to women's status in law, remarked that "if three women testify in a murder case without other depositions, they are not enough to condemn, for it would be akin to levity in a grave matter to have so many female depositions, to which full faith cannot be given in difficult cases, due to their frailty." In France until the Ordinance of 1670 women were also often suspected and rejected as witnesses in criminal cases. This unreliability was particularly problematic in sexual and moral crimes, in which the testimony of women was often indispensable. In fact, especially in such cases, women's access as witnesses to the justice system provided them with a means to negotiate the strictures of the prevailing moral system and to shape or retell contested events.[59]

Women who had committed crimes also received special treatment from the law, again mostly out of concern for their weakness and modesty. "However depraved a woman may be, she will always be naturally modest," claimed Rota, and penalties and procedures were adapted to her character. Certain types of punishment, such as deportation or the galleys, were deemed unsuited to women, because of the offense to their bashfulness. Some jurists argued that women were by definition to be exempted from ordinary penalties, even if guilty of lese majesty, according to Rota. When imprisoned, they were to be placed in separate prisons from men, to protect their honesty. A separate prison for women was, as we saw, among the requests the università of Penti-dattilo presented to its lord in 1648. In the royal court of the Vicaria in Naples a women's prison had been mandated by royal edict at least since 1558.[60]

This conception of the weakness of women also led to a disadvantage for them in the procedure pertaining to torture. Out of a desire to minimize the infliction of pain, the doctrine and the practice of torture decreed that, when there were more than one defendant, the one more likely to confess should be tortured first, in the hope of avoiding having to torture all defendants, as well as to diminish the risk of the "purgation" of the clues. Therefore jurists agreed that, if women and men were accomplices to a crime, the women should be tortured first because of the weakness of their constitution. The exception was pregnant women, who could not be tortured at all, until at least forty days after they had given birth. This principle, as we saw, was applied in Pentidat-tilo with the torture of Domenica Orlando before that of the other two defen-dants.[61]

Despite their protected status, women were particularly suspect in some crimes and especially punished in others. Women who took on male roles were to be severely punished. We saw this in the different penalties for lesbianism depending on whether one partner took on a male role. The same principle led to whipping and exile for women who dressed like men and severe penal-ties for women who dared practice medicine (apart from the activities allowed to midwives). Women, especially wives, were always the prime suspect in cases of poisoning, and their torture in such cases was readily decreed. Witchcraft, of course, was another major area in which the weakness and danger men saw in women came frighteningly together.[62] But it was with abortion and infan-ticide that women bore the brunt of the greatest suspicions.

Since the protection of her reputation, rather than destitution, was seen as the main reason a woman would seek an abortion or murder her newborn child, single women, or married women whose husbands were away, like Do-menica Orlando, were particularly suspect in these crimes. The Italian states did not pass laws as severe as the French edict of 1556 or the English one of 1624, which decreed the automatic suspicion of a capital crime for single women who hid their pregnancy or childbirth. Yet in Italy, too, single women who were known to be or have been pregnant were immediately suspect and liable to investigation and questioning. Their bodies, and the corpses of their newborn if available, were to be examined as thoroughly and promptly as possible. While parish priests were usually especially eager to denounce such cases to the courts, judges could also proceed ex officio in these matters. Carp-zov, after lamenting the frequency of infanticide "in this horrible and nefari-ous century," went on to invoke the heaviest penalties for the mother: "In this case the weakness of the female sex does not deserve any mercy or commiser-ation. . . . What indeed is more cruel than, in order to avoid the shame result-ing from the lesser crime of fornication, to commit the far graver crime of parricide! What more horrible than to turn one's pitiless hands on one's own children against affection, natural love, and the rights of blood!"[63]

Women were also especially suspect in cases of adultery and rape. A woman had to resist the adulterer "down to the most atrocious blows," and if her provocation could be proved, the man would receive a lesser punishment.[64] Rape had been severely condemned in the sixteenth and seventeenth centuries. As control over public order became more successful, however, concerns about excessive social mobility grew, leading to substantial changes in the treatment of rape and especially of stuprum. This crime, consisting of nonviolent inter-course with protected women, traditionally had been punished with the obli-gation for the man to marry or dower the plaintiff woman. This became harder to inflict or enforce with time.

All accusations of rape, in the absence of evidence of actual violence, be-came indeed highly suspect in the eyes of the law in the course of the eight-eenth century. A series of edicts in Naples and other Italian states made accu-sations of rape more and more difficult to prosecute, because of concern that these accusations were being used by "unworthy" women to force "poor and innocent" sons of good families to marriage. Concern for the stability of social status and families by the end of the century even led to the imprisonment of women who lodged accusations of rape, unless "true, real, effective violence" was proved (women "of better condition" could be placed in a convent). Bri-ganti lamented that "the arts of women of bad intentions [were] much finer and more frequent than could be thought by the most astute and clever man, let alone by an imprudent youth with his first beard." By the end of the cen-tury, stuprum had been basically decriminalized in Naples and other Italian states.[65]

The conception of female frailty and weakness therefore had both advan-tageous (such as reduced penalties) and negative consequences for women. The centrality of women and their behavior to the stability of the family had further contradictory effects. The full force of justice was supposed to protect order, morality, and family, and thus the penalties and procedures to punish malefactors were especially harsh in crimes against morality. Yet at the same time, protecting public order and the stability of the family often required leniency, or even neglect (as with adultery), on the part of the authorities. The focus on honor, reputation, and public opinion in crimes involving women further heightened the dependence of the judicial system on the general population and its willingness to participate in the operation of justice. The situation of women actually seems to have deteriorated in the eighteenth century, when reform ideas affected the legal system, as their traditional privileges were often reduced while the suspicions of which they were the victims remained. The ambiguities and contradictions in women's status in law and in judicial practice contributed to the increasing dissatisfaction felt by many eighteenth-century jurists with the existing prosecutorial system. The Pentidattilo trial offers thus a very good example of the types of crimes and issues on which the inquisitorial procedure was floundering. These cases brought to the surface the inherent contradictions of the traditional justice system and therefore became the focus of Enlightenment critiques and the starting point of many reform attempts in the eighteenth century.

Legal-Judicial Reform in the Eighteenth Century

> In nostro saeculo Philosopho sanguis humanus carius aestimatur.
>
> In our philosophic century human blood is esteemed dearer.
> —The 1783 commentator to de Angelis, *De delictis*

In the course of the eighteenth century a growing series of criticisms was leveled against the justice system, in Naples as elsewhere in western Europe, by philosophers and jurists alike. The inquisitorial procedure represented the main target in these attacks, because of its secrecy and cruelty as well as its contradictions. The main arguments for reform were the increasing confusion of legislation and jurisdiction; the irrationality and arbitrariness of the theory and practice of clues and proof; the cruelty and arbitrariness in the use of torture; the newly perceived unnaturalness of the emphasis on confession and self-incrimination; the exceeding severity of ordinary penalties and the unpredictability of extraordinary ones; the confusion between crime and sin and the attention given to magic and witchcraft; the use of the judicial oath; the excessive discretion left to judges in both procedure and sentencing; and, finally, the confusion between the functions of policing, prosecution, and adjudication.[66]

The solutions critics proposed varied, but they all favored more openness and certainty in procedure and laws, a clearer structure of royal justice which would eliminate or at least substantially reduce other jurisdictions, proportionality between crimes and punishments, and often the English model of jury trials. Rationally organized law codes and the jury trial were often considered the methods best suited to prevent abuses, corruption, and the arbitrary decisions of judges and to separate the prosecutorial and judicial roles wholly. These enlightened proposals were contained in treatises and suggested codes, which were then often the models for the actual legislation of the revolutionary and Napoleonic periods.[67]

In Naples the first target of reform, after ecclesiastic justice and privileges, was feudal jurisdiction. In 1738 the new Bourbon king, Charles VII (1734–59), attempted to curtail the power of the barons to dispense justice. An edict of that year restructured royal tribunals and sought to limit the duration and cost of lawsuits and trials, and another explicitly limited feudal jurisdiction over murder. In particular, barons were required to report to the provincial courts (*udienze*) all murder cases in their fiefs, although they could subsequently apply for return of these cases to their own courts, at the discretion of the udienze; the barons' composition and transaction of crimes had to be approved by the udienze; and certain forms of murder—for example, with firearms and those "scandalous and with aggravating circumstances"—were made the exclusive purview of the Vicaria. These reforms, however, were short lived. Because of the support the barons gave the king during the War of the Austrian Succession (and in response to a promise by Empress Maria Theresa to revoke these reforms should the baronage favor a Habsburg restoration), in 1744 the offending provisions were rescinded and feudal jurisdiction restored. Only in the later eighteenth century did the barons lose their jurisdiction over murder cases.[68]

The Bourbon monarchs achieved only limited reforms until the end of the old regime, in part, as was happening also in France, because of the strong opposition of the entrenched interests of the togati, the powerful elite of lawyers and magistrates which many historians see as the strongest social group in eighteenth-century Naples. Only in 1774 did Ferdinand IV (1759–1825) order judges to motivate their sentences, that is, to produce a written explanation of how they had arrived at their verdicts. Changes were implemented also in the police system. In 1789 torture was abolished in the Neapolitan military code, and public confrontation between the defendant and the court became part of criminal procedure. But more extensive reforms were suspended in the climate of fear and confusion of the 1790s and had to wait for the French domination of 1799 and 1806–15.[69]

Naples, however, partook very actively in the intellectual movement for enlightened reform at the end of the old regime. Gaetano Filangieri's *Scienza della legislazione* (1780–84) was, along with Beccaria's more famous book, the most influential legal work to come out of the Italian Enlightenment, and it remains a superb model of elegant and intelligent analysis. Filangieri aimed to present "a certain and ordered science, which joins means and rules, and theory and practice," to achieve "conservation and tranquillity." The purpose of law should be to assure the guilty of punishment and the innocent of justice, and therefore legislative confusion had to be clarified and the secret and despotic inquisitorial system dismantled. Filangieri favored the English model of open and public accusations and trials, with a judge who would not be also an accuser and prosecutor, in order to give citizens the "simplicity, clarity, and respect" they deserved.[70]

He argued further that penalties ought to be less severe and that the "fatal and despotic arbitrariness" of judges inherent in the system of clues and proof had to be replaced with a system based on both clear legal criteria for proof and what Filangieri called the "moral certitude" of the judge—hence the need for the double jury system (with the grand jury to indict and the petty jury to convict), which would separate the judgment of facts from the judgment of law and make the judge the neutral arbiter he was meant to be. While calling for the abolition of torture and the proportionality of crime and punishment, Filangieri accepted the need for the death penalty, if properly regulated. On the issue of sexual crimes, he urged the punishment of abortions and the protection of families, but he recognized the difficulty of proof and urged not only compassion but also a more active role of prevention on the part of the authorities, for instance, by offering aid to pregnant unwed women. Finally, albeit an aristocrat himself, Filangieri called for the suppression of feudal jurisdiction.[71]

Filangieri's ideas were echoed and refined by a number of other writers. Saverio Mattei published the new Tuscan code of 1786 and offered it as a model for Neapolitan reforms, urging the abolition of torture and the death penalty. The Tuscan code maintained the heaviest penalties for sexual crimes (specifically abortion, adultery, bigamy, sodomy, and bestiality, slightly less for incest), though it lessened them somewhat for women. A few years later Giuseppe Galanti attacked the despotism, confusion, and "bureaucratism" of Neapolitan tribunals and the horrors of torture and of the inquisitorial procedure, in which "two scoundrels sold to a calumniator [were] sufficient" to condemn an innocent. He, too, supported the jury system. Finally, Mario Pagano, who served in the Jacobin Republic of 1799 and was executed by the returning Bourbons, condemned the "forensic spirit, spirit of litigation, cheating, and cabal, [which] became the national spirit of the Kingdom of Naples." He attacked the theory of clues, the use of torture, and the arbitrary punishments and urged public trials, the jury system, and clear, proportionate penalties.[72]

The abolition of torture, the motivation of sentences, public debate in trials, and eventually the jury system were realized in revolutionary France during the 1790s, although soon the Napoleonic regime would again strengthen the prosecution and curtail the role of juries in trials. These developments heavily influenced reforms in Naples, where the failed 1799 republic and the first Bourbon restoration (1799–1806) had demonstrated the jurisdictional confusion and widespread abuses of the existing system. Under kings Joseph Bonaparte (1806–8) and Joachim Murat (1808–15) feudal jurisdiction was abolished, new tribunals with simpler procedures were instituted, and public debate, the motivation of sentences, and the separation of the policing and judging roles became the norm. The 1812 Neapolitan code transferred to the kingdom much of the Napoleonic code, though without a clear procedural code and without the jury system, which was held even by some reformers to be incompatible with the structure of Neapolitan society. The 1812 code punished murder, poisoning, and infanticide with death, abortion and rape with imprisonment, adultery (only the wife's) with up to two years of prison, while, like its French model, it had nothing to say about sodomy or bestiality.[73]

With the second Bourbon restoration many of these reforms remained in effect. A new code issued in 1819 maintained and indeed strengthened many of the procedural changes. Again the jury system was not instituted, because of concerns about the social structure of the kingdom. Nicola Nicolini argued that only the upper classes were worthy of the trust necessary in jury members, but he doubted that they could understand the lower people, who were "despised by and naturally inimical to their superiors." But public debate and the clear separation between the functions of public prosecutor and judge, legal writers hoped, would ensure fairness. Murder and poisoning remained capital crimes. In regard to sexual and moral crimes, the 1819 code abolished divorce (which the French code had allowed) and maintained stern penalties for abortion, infanticide, and rape. An adulterous wife could be condemned to seclusion for up to five years, though as usual she could be prosecuted only on the husband's denunciation; again, the husband was prosecuted only if he kept a concubine.[74]

With the exception of the abolition of the death penalty and the introduction of the jury system (neither of which had been unanimously supported by Neapolitan reformers), most of the Enlightenment proposals for legal and judicial reform were enacted and remained in effect even under the reactionary Bourbon restoration. Many of the procedures and principles at work in the Pentidattilo case (and feudal courts themselves) disappeared or were substantially altered within a century. But some of the fundamental attitudes and beliefs we have seen in that trial survived even these changes. The situation of women in adultery cases remained an inferior one, and the laws still protected the honor of husbands and families and acted in these matters primarily as the enforcer of private wishes. Even the Murat code of 1812 (art. 324) stated that the husband who caught his wife and her lover in flagrante and killed them was highly excusable. Wives were always highly suspect in cases of poisoning, still held to be worse than ordinary murder. Honor and reputation remained major concerns in the law and affected the treatment of women suspected of abortion or infanticide. In short, the reforms, which began largely because of problems posed by sexual crimes, were undoubtedly very extensive but probably changed the situation of women least of all.

The judicial methods and ideas at work in the trial of Domenica Orlando would, then, be substantially changed by the start of the nineteenth century. Her trial offers good examples of the inherent paradoxes and contradictions the inquisitorial procedure produced and confronted. The system of justice changed, in large part, because of the practical and intellectual problems caused by the difficulties of prosecuting and reforming the moral and sexual behavior of the general population. It is more doubtful that that behavior itself changed as much, especially in rural areas. Outward compliance with royal laws and episcopal edicts may have increased, but villagers continued to adhere to their own views of morality and sexuality, and they could easily shape the functioning of justice accordingly.

The Pentidattilo trial also illustrates the ambiguous position of women vis-à-vis the law—on the one hand helpless, frail creatures whose persons and especially reputations merited the protection of the authorities; on the other furtive, scheming poisoners, only too ready to murder their children and betray their husbands. This ambiguous view of women in the law and the jurisprudence would continue well past the procedural, legislative, and institutional reforms brought about as a result of the Enlightenment and the revolution, and crimes of sexuality would remain problematic and the object of special treatment.

Sexual/moral crimes always posed exceptional problems of proof for judicial authorities, and special procedures and penalties were developed to deal with them. The fact that these crimes were often victimless distinguished them also in other, more profound, ways: on the one hand, the prosecution of these crimes resulted in a more direct affirmation of the strength of the constituted powers (be they the feudal lord, the church, or the monarchy). Since the prestige and authority emanating from prosecution often did not have to be shared with victims or plaintiffs, the right and power of church, state, and lord to control popular behavior was most strongly asserted and demonstrated. On the other hand, successful prosecution would have been well-nigh impossible if the values upheld in punishing these crimes had been entirely alien to the communities—especially the rural communities—in which they took place. We witness in the Pentidattilo trial and in similar ones an intense interaction, in practice and in values, between authorities and subjects, which helps explain also why outsiders to the local community, or those who had made themselves such by persistent violation of community rules, were so often the target of these prosecutions. Thus it was also important in criminal procedure to take into account local factions, local hierarchies, and the virulent enmities of village life and to establish, as the basis of any proof, the reputation of those involved in crimes and the judgment of public opinion on the events at issue.

Community views were crucial to all operations of justice, given the prevailing theory of proof and the available types of evidence. As reputation was an even more essential factor in moral and sexual crimes, the wishes and values of villagers were reflected even more clearly in their prosecution. The practical, functional attitude of villagers towards ethical issues and the autonomous culture of rural communities would to a large extent resist the combined efforts of state and church to eradicate sin and punish crime.

SIX

Religion, the Church, and Popular Morality

Early modern secular authorities were attempting to control popular behavior in the spheres of family, sexuality, and morality, especially through the justice system. Owing to both the interdependence of church and state and the concurrence of the notions of crime and sin, this endeavor was a joint one involving judges, administrators, bishops, and priests. Religious institutions or agents played no part in the Pentidattilo trial; indeed, in the Kingdom of Naples, as in most of Italy, church courts were relatively inactive on matters of moral and sexual behavior and focused their energy on magic.[1] This did not preclude, however, ecclesiastic authorities from taking a keen interest in the moral and sexual life of their flocks. Episcopal visits and synods, missions organized by the new religious orders, and the policies enacted to improve the intellectual and spiritual quality of the parish clergy demonstrate the desire of the Counter Reformation church to better the beliefs and practices of the faithful. This engaged clerical authorities in the same process of negotiation with popular values and ideas faced by the justice system, and villagers proved adept at ignoring or thwarting, or at least substantially altering, all outside efforts to change their way of life and their established traditions.

The Pentidattilo trial reveals a peasant community nearly united in its opinions, its dealings with the feudal court, and its ostracism of the outsider, Anna de Amico. Through the trial records and other sources it is possible to analyze more generally the villagers' moral concerns and views and their shared values and assumptions. Despite the important transformations in rural economy and society which began in the mid-eighteenth century, village culture would long remain in many ways impervious to the changes represented and supported by outside authorities.

Historians have spoken of a prolonged battle from the late sixteenth through the eighteenth century between a traditional popular culture, characterized by community, orality, and a blend of sacred and profane elements, and the transforming impulses of early modern states and reforming churches. In this struggle, which has been called a process of acculturation, lay and ecclesiastic authorities used the weapons of the written word and of their own jurisdictional power in order to control the more turbulent elements of popular behavior and to instill the values of obedience to authority, moral self-control, and the internalization and individualization of emotions. The success of these attempts in urban and elite settings is well studied, but historians differ on how fast and how effectively rural culture and behavior were transformed and on the extent of the passivity of the peasant population in this process.[2]

Until recently these issues have not received much attention in the case of the Kingdom of Naples. The city of Naples itself was one of the cultural capitals of western Europe, and the Neapolitan authorities were fully integrated into the realm of European high culture. Spanish, and later Austrian and Bourbon, absolutism was the goal and the inspiration of the central government, Neapolitan jurists were actively involved in European jurisprudential debates, and the Neapolitan church leadership shared in the policies and ideas of Counter Reformation Catholicism. But the behavior and mentality of the kingdom's rural masses have been little studied, and the highly negative comments of clerics and Enlightenment reformers have been repeated with limited additions. The scarcity of sources renders investigation difficult, but enough information is available to attempt further study.

The Pentidattilo trial records and other judicial sources shed light especially on issues of morality and sexuality, which were central to the authorities' fight to regulate popular culture. Honor, reputation, and the adherence to a code of sexual behavior were important elements of village life, as they were of official values, but the views of villagers and outside authorities often differed as to the specific meaning of these values and how to implement them. Community control was strong in Pentidattilo, and it was difficult for the state and the church to impose their views without the cooperation and the agreement of the villagers themselves. Even the authorities' use of the written word brought limited advantages, as we saw in Chapter 1. Pentidattilo presented an additional difficulty in that it had long been characterized, like other areas of the kingdom, by a persistent Greek heritage in its religious life. By the early eighteenth century the Greek rite had been eliminated, at least on the surface, through the success of the Latin Counter Reformation church, but the ability of the reformed clergy to affect the villagers' moral behavior remained limited.

As we have seen with the creation of the trial records and with the production of virtually all other documents about village society, villagers were not passive recipients of the will, and objects of the actions, of external forces. The interaction of village values and state or church goals, of oral tradition and written culture, of local concerns and the aims of the authorities is also evident in the moral and spiritual world of the people of Pentidattilo.

The Church in the Village

> Queste montagne della Sicilia e Calabria sarebbero noviziati, dove provare coloro che desiderano di passare alle Indie.
>
> These mountains of Sicily and Calabria could be novitiates to test those who wish to go to the Indies.
>
> —A Messina Jesuit to his superior, 1575, cited in Tacchi Venturi, Storia

The church, at least in the aims of its leadership and in its inspiring values, was an active force in any village community's public life, and it aspired to shape the villagers' lives and way of thinking. The parish clergy was an important presence in the community—both economically, because of the role of church property, and in terms of the priests' diverse functions as public figures—but it was not a reliable tool of the church leadership's desires. Moreover, the religious life of Pentidattilo, like that of several areas of the kingdom, was characterized by its Greek heritage. In the early eighteenth century, at the time of the trial of Domenica Orlando, the passage to the Latin rite and language was still quite recent and fragile. This affected the attitude of the bishops towards the religious and moral behavior of the local population.

In Pentidattilo the ecclesiastic patrimony was organized according to the model of the *ricettizia* church, which by the eighteenth century prevailed in about 75 percent of the churches in the kingdom. This meant that the clergy of each parish collectively owned local church property and that the clerics (known as *porzionarii*) shared its revenues as well as the tithes, with the head priest enjoying a larger share. In addition, each cleric enjoyed whatever property was attached to his specific benefice. All local clerics shared the liturgical obligations. The bishop received a share of the tithes and maintained a vague spiritual jurisdiction over the clerics, but he had virtually no administrative power over them. The ricettizia clerics had to be native to the villages in which they served, and they were used to a high degree of autonomy. This system strengthened the links between the priests and their parishioners and made the church less unified as a structure than in other European countries affected by the Counter Reformation episcopate. The Greek heritage in Pentidattilo, and the crisis of leadership in the Archdiocese of Reggio in the early eighteenth century, complicated matters further.[3]

Pentidattilo was part of the Archdiocese of Reggio Calabria. The archbishops had jurisdiction over nine other bishops in southern Calabria, and their own diocese included, by the end of the sixteenth century, two cities and thirty-eight towns and villages. Along with a parish in the city of Reggio and four other villages (neighboring San Lorenzo, Montebello, and Motta San Giovanni and the village of Sant'Agata), Pentidattilo constituted the Greek area of the diocese, where the Greek language and Greek rites continued to be used in liturgical life. The presence of the Greek rite was well established in the Kingdom of Naples and in a few other areas of medieval Italy, and its existence was easily accepted by the papacy and the Latin episcopate until the mid-sixteenth century. The Greek areas were fully Catholic and accepted papal supremacy and Catholic theology on the issues that separated Rome from Orthodoxy. The Greek areas followed, however, their own liturgical calendar and observed their own feast days. The Greek clergy was allowed to marry. The head priest of each Greek parish was known as the *protopapa,* and the Greek language was used in church rites. As we have seen, the region of Pentidattilo also shared with other Calabrian villages a strong Greek linguistic heritage.[4]

At the end of the sixteenth century, Pentidattilo, with perhaps five hundred inhabitants, was served by ten Greek clerics, not an unusual ratio for the notoriously well staffed church of the kingdom. In the early seventeenth century the secular clergy alone probably accounted for 3 percent of the kingdom's population, and the percentage increased until the mid-eighteenth century. Only about half of the kingdom's clerics were priests charged with the care of souls. The rest included numerous clerics with minor orders and even many married clerics and the "wild deacons," or tonsured church servants, all of whom were entitled to clerical privileges. The Pentidattilo clerics managed the two main parish churches (the *protopapale* of San Pietro and the *dittereale* of San Costantino) and four of the five additional chapels and benefices existing in the village. The fifth chapel, the Candelora, was part of the only Latin ecclesiastic institution in the village, the homonymous Dominican monastery founded in 1518 by the feudal lords.[5]

The Counter Reformation made many church leaders weary of the tolerance hitherto granted to the Greek rite in Italy. The validity of the Greek rites had been confirmed by Paul III as late as 1540, but many post-Tridentine prelates nonetheless were suspicious of the Greek rites and clergy. The fact that contacts between the Greek clergy and the Orthodox Church continued and that the ordination of Greek priests was difficult for the papacy to control added to the tension. Reggio archbishop Gaspare del Fosso, for instance, remarked on the peculiarity of the Greek priests' married status and was suspicious of their ordination by possibly schismatic Eastern bishops. The Greek priests' alleged doctrinal ignorance also troubled del Fosso, but he was unsure what policy to follow towards them, given that the local population refused to accept the sacraments from Latin clerics. In 1595 Pope Clement VIII appointed an ordaining bishop for all Greek clergy in Italy, but this did not reassure all bishops.[6]

Eventually Reggio archbishop Annibale D'Afflitto attempted to suppress the Greek rite in his diocese. In his 1595 synod he discussed the theological issues on which those following the Greek rite were more likely to "err," such as papal primacy, transubstantiation, indulgences, and images. D'Afflitto saw the Greek rites as virtually equivalent to Orthodoxy, and he recommended a common creed based on the 1439 Florence council that had attempted the union of the two churches and on the Council of Trent. In his diocesan visit of the same year D'Afflitto questioned all Greek clerics and found many of them wanting in their knowledge both of the faith and of the Greek and Latin sacred texts. He suspended several clerics and transferred many of the others to the Latin rite. In Pentidattilo the protopapa, who was childless and apparently a widower, supposedly asked to be transferred to the Latin rite, as did the two youngest and unmarried local clerics. The dittereo and one other cleric, both with children, were suspended because of their ignorance, while for the remaining five, four of whom were married with children, no specific decision is reported.[7] The effectiveness of these measures is, in any case, open to question. Two years later D'Afflitto found that the baptismal font he had ordered the protopapa to build in San Pietro had indeed been built, but the two suspended clerics still occupied their previous positions, and the Greek rites were still performed.[8]

In 1634 Domenico Toscano was appointed as the first official Latin arciprete of Pentidattilo. The Greek rite continued to be allowed in the village, however, and D'Afflitto seems to have relented in his zeal. In 1634 the dittereo still kept several Greek sacred texts in his library. Although D'Afflitto tried to preserve the Dominican monastery in the village as a source of Latin influence, despite the scarcity of friars, its final suppression in 1652 further weakened the Latin presence in the village.[9] The later archbishops were less sedulous in their visits to the more outlying villages of their large diocese, and reports of visits become rarer. The archdiocese then went through a significant crisis at the turn of the eighteenth century, when Archbishop Giovan Andrea Monreal left the diocese following scandals and spent about thirty years in Rome and Naples. Only with the arrival of Archbishop Damiano Polou in 1727 did visits and synods resume. In these conditions it is not surprising that the Greek rite survived in the diocese to the end of the seventeenth century. In fact, it is likely that Greek traditions lingered on into the following century, as they did elsewhere in the kingdom, especially since both the papacy and the monarchy continued to accept the Catholic legitimacy of the Greek rite.[10]

In any event, the village had plenty of clergy. D'Afflitto reported the existence of more than twenty ruined chapels and churches in the territory of Pentidattilo—indicative of more populous past times—but the ten clerics he found in the village in the 1590s must have sufficed for the roughly five hundred local residents. At the turn of the seventeenth century the village had three confraternities with their own revenues, about ten churches and chapels, and a dozen clerics. In 1637, as the coastal settlement began to grow, a new church, Santa Maria di Portosalvo, was authorized in Melito. It was finished with help from the marquis in 1682. At the end of the seventeenth century Pentidattilo was home to between fifteen and twenty-five ecclesiastics, who served its nine churches.[11] At the time of the 1745 catasto, there were nine local priests residing in the village and one born in another village. There were eight in 1759.

The Pentidattilo clergy was not very wealthy, but ecclesiastic property represented a substantial presence in the village economy. Although Archbishop D'Afflitto in 1597 described the parish as "of small income and very poor," he listed revenues of at least 80 ducats a year for the various village churches and chapels. In 1745 there were two chapels and two churches owning property in addition to the two main parish churches, and twelve ecclesiastic institutions based in neighboring towns and villages (including the archdiocese) also owned property in Pentidattilo. Of the total 3,526.06 taxable *once* in the village, 408.07 (or about 12%) came from ecclesiastic income (including the small share owned personally by the priests). The role of the church in the village economy was in reality considerably larger, since church income was partly exempt and also taxed at only half the rate of all other income.[12] For the 1759 catasto, the diocesan office certified that the annual average income of priests in the diocese was between 30 and 40 ducats a year. In that year ecclesiastic taxable income represented 13 percent of the total for the entire village.[13]

The marquis and the università also contributed to the religious life of the village by supporting the clergy and religious activities. The marquis and various members of their family endowed altars and chapels throughout the early modern period. The Francoperta founded the Dominican monastery. The Alberti, especially after they began to reside regularly in Pentidattilo, provided money, often through bequests, for new chapels and benefices or left property and capital to various village religious institutions to pay for masses and alms. When he sold the fief in 1759, Litterio Caracciolo claimed that his income from it was burdened with 280 ducats a year in payments to various local chapels, churches, and benefices and with another 49 ducats a year in payments to ecclesiastic institutions in Reggio. The marquis were also keen on the symbolic affirmation of their role in the community through religious ceremonies, and they were embroiled in disputes with the archdiocese over their right to have a special seat, throne, and baldaquin in the parish church.[14] The università's contribution was much smaller, since the village had little money to spare. The main religious expense sustained by the community was for a preacher, who usually came during Lent. Alms were gathered to pay for this visit, but the università also contributed with 12 ducats in 1718 and again in 1745. In 1759 the preacher cost the village 17 ducats, and 20 more was spent on masses in honor of the local patron saints.[15]

At the end of the eighteenth century, especially with the rapid growth of the coastal settlement, the wealth of the church in Pentidattilo increased. The sale of church property in Calabria after the 1783 earthquake included substantial holdings in Pentidattilo. The various ecclesiastic institutions in the village owned houses, animals, parcels of land, and censi (rents) of various sorts due by many citizens. At the end of the century San Costantino, the dittereale, had an income of about 45 ducats a year. San Pietro, the main parish, had an income of more than 130 ducats a year from property and from tithes of 1 carlino per household, and a witness in 1785 stated that "it had always been esteemed a church of reasonably comfortable revenues." In 1796 its priest was endowed with the revenues of all remaining ecclesiastic foundations and charged with paying 60 ducats a year to the dittereo and 50 to the priest of the new church in the hamlet of Corio, which owned no property.[16]

Perhaps because of the villagers' slow acceptance of the Latin rite and clergy, the priests seem to have played a relatively minor role in the public life of the community during the seventeenth century. They are rarely, if ever, mentioned as witnesses or participants in the relevi inquiries, in the other documents and exchanges between the università and the central authorities, or in the documents relating to disputes between the community, its neighbors, and its lords. The few exceptions, all of which date from the late seventeenth century, involve either the priests' access to the parish documents to certify burials, or the arciprete's attendance when the marquis Domenico and his wife drew up their will.[17] This marginal role might partially explain why the village clergy played no formal role in the trial of Domenica Orlando, despite the religious connotations of the crimes of abortion and adultery.

Although the absence of notarial acts for the seventeenth century makes precise comparison impossible, the role of the priests, and especially of the arciprete and dittereo, in the life of the Pentidattilesi was much larger in the mid-eighteenth century, judging from the papers of notary Celia. There are few acts drawn up by the notary for which one or the other, or at times both, of the parish priests did not act as witness. This would be expected in acts dealing with the transfer of ecclesiastic property, which constitute the majority of the property transfers drawn up by the notary. But the priests also attended the drafting of public certificates of good conduct, wills, and especially most of the acts to which women were parties, signaling a protective role vis-à-vis women assigned to priests in the village's public life.[18]

The priests also had, of course, a more specifically religious role to play. Apart from keeping the parish records and performing the sacraments, they were to instruct their parishioners in the rudiments of the Catholic faith. In this task the priests' success is open to question. The religious ignorance of both the priests and the population is a recurrent complaint in the archbishops' reports, in the Reggio diocese as everywhere in the kingdom. The prelates fervently urged their priests to preach and instruct especially the young. The archbishops and new orders such as the Jesuits, and later the Redemptorists, sponsored missions in the countryside. The mountainous areas were perceived as particularly in need of religious instruction, and the Jesuits regularly referred to these areas of Calabria and Sicily as a mission land parallel to the Indies of the New World.[19]

The problem persisted in the Diocese of Reggio. In 1663 Archbishop Matteo de Gennaro wrote that many "peasants [did] not blush to be ignorant of the rudiments of the faith." In his synods Archbishop Polou repeatedly stressed the need for priests to attend the seminary and to instruct their parishioners, both in catechism for the young and through sermons delivered at mass. He even threatened, as other archbishops had done before, to deny marriage to those ignorant of the bases of the faith. One may doubt the effectiveness of these means in view of the difficulties encountered by the archdiocese in supporting a seminary. In any case, the archbishops, in the Tridentine tradition, stopped well short of endorsing any profound religious education for the laity. D'Afflitto, for example, insisted that the priests prevent lay people from discussing matters of faith or from reading religious books. The bishops were also keen on strengthening the primary role of the parish clergy, and, while at times welcoming rural missions, they were more often suspicious of the intrusion and activities of members of the regular clergy. A final persistent obstacle to religious instruction was the very inadequacy of many religious functions. D'Afflitto had to urge his priests to make sure that the masses they performed "last[ed] about half an hour." In other mountainous areas of the kingdom, as late as the early eighteenth century bishops complained about speedy and inadequate masses: in two villages near Benevento 80 percent of the local priests were deemed incapable of saying a proper mass.[20]

The church leadership faced here a paradoxical situation, especially in the rural world. The less the parish clergy was educated and the more distant it was from what the Counter Reformation bishops saw as the ideal, the more easily it was integrated into the life and culture of its flock. If rural priests became better educated and trained, if in brief they became more professional, they were increasingly alienated from the world and experience of the peasant population, in which they had fully shared for centuries. While the priests could thus become better suited to be moral teachers and models, they also lost much of their ability to communicate smoothly with their parishioners and to function as cultural mediators between peasant culture and the values of the official church. This dilemma confronted the church in much of Catholic Europe, and similar problems troubled Protestant reformers, as well.[21]

The concern to spread religious and moral instruction inexorably led the church to the attempt to control popular behavior and culture. The church, like the state, was motivated by a preoccupation with order, hierarchy, and respect for authority. It was also prompted by increasing anxiety about the mixture of sacred and profane elements which was typical of popular attitudes and which became greatly troubling for post-Reformation church leaders. Until the late sixteenth century, the sacred and the profane had formed a continuum expressed in a wide range of behaviors and ideas shared by both the literate elite and the illiterate masses. This was especially evident in the related spheres of medicine and magic, both of which were closely tied to people's search for protection against bodily and other harm and both of which traditionally were spheres in which intense exchanges and communication occurred between learned and popular culture.[22]

Those in need of healing or protection, be they ill or possessed, cursed or unlucky, had recourse to the remedies and help offered by a wide range of providers, from learned doctors to barbers, from wise women to hawkers of secret medicaments in public squares. There are countless examples well into the seventeenth century throughout western Europe of elite and poor individuals consulting any and all of these figures. In Salerno, for instance, learned eighteenth-century medical manuscripts included many popular concerns and remedies, such as how to restore the appearance of virginity or how to counter maleficent spells.[23]

Medicine and magic were also tightly linked to religious and ritual notions in traditional European thought. The Latin word *salus* joined the two meanings of salvation and health, and saints (both the official ones and the living, popularly venerated ones) were traditionally seen as protectors and healers. Many clerics of all sorts were deeply involved in both healing and magical activities, and religious items and practices (such as prayers, blessings, holy water) were frequently used in divinatory, healing, and other magical rituals. Even though the church had long been worried about the potential for diabolical intervention in these rituals, it had tolerated, indeed at times endorsed, most of them until the late sixteenth century. Many clerics, especially in the rural world, were thus ambiguous transitional figures, mediators between learned and popular culture. They belonged to local culture, but they also "owed allegiance" to an "orthodox hegemonic culture."[24]

With the need to confront the Protestant challenge to church authority, doctrine, and practices, and also with the flourishing of a new spiritualized conception of the Catholic faith, based on internalized moral conviction and discipline and on the rejection of worldly interests, the church began to strive for the clear separation of sacred and profane behavior. It also sought to assert its own monopoly on access to the sacred and the supernatural. This struggle entailed, on the one hand, religious instruction aimed at both the lower clergy and the laity and, on the other hand, repression. Through papal directives, episcopal synods and visits, and diocesan and inquisitorial courts, condemnation and repression were aimed especially at the entire area of medico-magical rituals and activities. Although the church in Italy was comparatively lenient and skeptical towards those accused of witchcraft, and although after the 1580s it did not face a significant heretical threat, from the late sixteenth throughout the eighteenth century it fought an intense battle against all the practices it viewed as superstitious or immoral. The program to instruct the rural masses in the proper religious and moral behavior was particularly directed at these practices.[25]

This struggle was part of a long and broad confrontation that gradually severed the links between learned and popular culture. Specifically in the medical field the learned practitioners were increasingly separated, in their activities and in the perceptions of the infirm, from the congeries of men and women healers who offered potions, incantations, and ritual methods. Learned magic and popular magic also grew apart, although both were regarded with suspicion by lay and clerical authorities. The fact that many superstitious practices dealt with the sphere of reproduction and sexuality also contributed to the focus on the part of the authorities on control of popular sexual and moral behavior. Church concerns here overlapped, as we have seen, with the increased severity with which early modern states prosecuted sexual and moral crimes.[26]

Finally, the attempt to curb and regulate popular culture and the emphasis on sexual behavior became closely connected with an attempt to control the actions of women. The church's fight against traditional healing and ritual practices led especially to the demonization of female medico-magical activities. Women, because of their domestic and family roles, were central to the transmission of popular culture, and their specific traditional involvement in healing and managing reproductive functions made them doubly suspicious. Midwives especially but also many women like Anna de Amico—women capable of providing healing remedies, knowledgeable in the ways of nature, and skilled at many other domestic tasks—found themselves targeted as particularly threatening to the new moral and religious values.[27]

In Pentidattilo, then, the church's wealth made it a significant presence in the local economy, as was true in most villages in the kingdom. By the mid-eighteenth century the new Latin clergy had finally earned the respect of the population, and the main parish priests played an important role in the public life of the community. Nonetheless, the effectiveness of the local clergy as religious or moral teachers and models was quite limited at least until the end of the old regime. Because of the limits of the priests' own education, the constraints imposed on episcopal reforms by the ricettizia system, and probably also the lingering of the Greek tradition in the Pentidattilo area, the church's impact on the traditional attitudes of the local peasantry and on the popular culture of the area was quite confined. The long struggle of the church and the state against many elements of popular culture and behavior yielded at best slow and mixed results.

Honor, Gender, and Reputation

> A fimmina a vint'anni o a mariti o a scanni.
>
> When a woman is twenty, you either marry her off or kill her.
>
> Cu non havi omu non havi nomi.
>
> Who has no husband has no name.
>
> —Calabrian proverbs

In Pentidattilo, as in other villages, the weight of one's word and the effectiveness of one's actions were closely tied to one's, and one's family's, reputation within the community. Each villager's reputation was closely linked to his or her observance of community codes of behavior. Honor and moral behavior were especially important to the status of women. While old age, as we have seen, could at times give women a higher status than that which they usually enjoyed, in general reputation and honor had different meanings and operated in different ways for men and women. Women's behavior was central not only to their individual reputation but also to that of their male relatives and the community in general. The morality of women, especially their sexual behavior, was crucial to villagers' conceptions of individual honor, family prestige, and personal respectability. Peasant culture was as deeply concerned as the church about women's honor and virtue, and community control was quite strong, but that concern at times manifested itself in behavior and values that the church and the state condemned and sought to suppress.

The conception and organization of the family in Pentidattilo were patriarchal. Women did not enjoy the full rights of citizens of the village, and they were placed in an inferior position in legal matters. Apart from their weaknesses as witnesses or defendants in criminal cases, they were faced with various obstacles in civil legal matters as well. Married women could not dispose of their personal property freely but had to receive the "express consent and will" of their husbands. Single or widowed women enjoyed fuller control over their assets, but they were especially vulnerable to financial crisis. The papers of notary Celia contain few deeds of outright sale of real estate, but many of them are entered by needy single women, or in one case by a married woman whose husband had abandoned her "burdened with children, without any support." The parish priests and other prominent village men served as witnesses to all deeds concerning women and their property, a recognition of women's weaker position in the village's economic life. The notary also twice reported declarations of pregnant unmarried women who were trying to obtain support.[28]

Whatever their marital status, the honor of women was primarily linked to their sexual reputation and status. The public sense of a woman's virtue, or her lack thereof, was based on her real or alleged sexual behavior. This affected her standing in the community, her chances for redress of grievances she might have against any other villager, and her ability to support herself should she be unmarried. Threats or assaults against the honor of women also affected the reputation of the men who were held responsible for the women's behavior, and by extension the dishonor of women also reflected poorly on the entire community. During the dispute with the village of San Lorenzo, the Pentidattilesi sought to undermine the standing both of the rival witnesses and of the latter's entire community by impugning the honor of their wives and daughters. Conversely, when in 1759 the università accused the marquis of usurping land and threatening the villagers' livelihood, the baronial agent Paolo Bosco was also accused of "contempt" for the community. Bosco's sin was the composition and performance, by one of his guards, of "a story in various songs . . . very tearful and causing the highest damage and dishonor to [the] villagers." The story had been sung at Carnival time and had greatly offended village women.[29]

Although threats to the sexual reputation of married women were rare, the honor of unmarried women was more at risk, and it was expected to be protected by their fathers, brothers, or other men placed in a position of responsibility over such women. When Antonina Tripodi, a servant in the home of her relative Antonino Asprea, was assaulted and made pregnant by a guard, rumors began that the father of her child was Asprea himself. She appeared before prominent witnesses, including Pentidattilo's governor and two priests, not only to dispel the rumors against her relative and employer but also to state that the assault had occurred when she had been forced by bad weather to spend a night outside his house and therefore away from the protection he was expected to offer her honor. In a later case in Atena a similar situation occurred, and a maid accused of having obtained an abortion defended herself by stating that "[she], and [her] masters . . . ha[d] well known how to guard [her] honor." When Anna Siciliano of Brienza, whose father had died, sued Rocco Lopardi for rape, it was her maternal uncle who joined the suit because of the "lost honor" of his family.[30]

In all such cases, what caused public scandal and the denunciation to judicial authorities was less the illicit sexual intercourse, which often was consensual and based on promises or hopes of marriage, than the pregnancy. To the villagers, honor was fundamentally a practical concept. A birth outside marriage would threaten the honor of the woman and her family but especially her (and the community's) economic welfare, in that no responsible male provider would be available to support the child and its mother. Hence the honor the women in these cases sought meant primarily support for their child. When that support was not problematic, the threat to honor was much diminished, as we shall see with the attitude towards illegitimate births in Pentidattilo. Honor could be restored by marriage, as happened in the case of the young Carmela di Stefano of Brienza and her seducer, or, in the case of a married seducer like Rocco Lopardi, by giving the seduced woman a dowry, as a sign of her suitability as a wife. In most cases, women thus dowered would be able to find a husband within the community, despite their well-known sexual misbehavior.[31]

These remedies became harder to achieve for women, and during the course of the eighteenth century the burden of proof in cases of sexual misconduct shifted more heavily to women, in particular single women. Women experienced increasing difficulties in defending their honor and also in attempting to regain it once it had been damaged, as reflected in the decriminalization of stuprum. Plaintiffs and defendants even in rural areas became adept at phrasing their complaints and defenses in terms that matched this new conception on the part of the judicial system. By the end of the century women needed to insist on their strenuous efforts to resist unwanted sexual intercourse in order to have a chance of redress in court. Conversely, the accused men all attempted to defend themselves by insisting on the consensual nature of the sexual act and by impugning the sexual reputation of their accusers. The father of one of the accused openly invoked the new laws that sought to "stop the malice of women" in search of husbands.[32]

The resolution of these sexual lawsuits hinged primarily on the reputation of the parties involved, especially of the women. In the Pentidattilo trial, more than any other factor it was probably the witnesses' consensus on the "bad fame" of Anna de Amico which sealed her fate. In later cases from the other fiefs of the Caracciolo Brienza, the reputations of plaintiffs and defendants were equally crucial. The plaintiffs all insisted on their sexual ignorance and virginity, which had made the sexual encounter so difficult, painful, and violent. While the prosecution witnesses stated that Costanza Gaimari "was held an honest virgin," Vincenzo Lupardi insisted that she was a "whore" and that "because of [a tradition of] very old tolerance, fornication with whores [was] not to be punished." The unusually bad reputation of Rocco Lopardi—whose bad example was deemed by one witness to have caused "innumerable vices" to be engaged in daily by boys and "even by infant girls"—certainly was the main reason for his condemnation, given the unwholesome reputation of his accusers (Rocco claimed that two of his accusers were "women of bad smell"). Carmela di Stefano, supposedly only eleven years of age, was described by a witness as honest and too young "to flirt with men," while the defendant's father was "of low condition."[33]

The community in these small villages took thus a keen interest in its members' reputations. Those who decided an individual's reputation, particularly a woman's, were first of all the neighbors. In all the trials mentioned here most of the witnesses who provided the court with specific information were neighbors of the plaintiffs, or sometimes of the defendants. It was assumed and indeed expected that they would be aware of the reputation and behavior of their neighbors. This was especially true of women defendants and women witnesses; in the case of a man, such as that of Pietro Crea, respected men in the community also reported on his behavior and standing.[34]

This role of the neighbors also functioned as a form of community control, as seen in the vigilance and the critical attitude of Domenica Orlando's neighbors towards her behavior. Again, the community was concerned less with absolute moral values than with conduct that caused public scandal. Witnesses in the trial against Vincenzo Lupardi, for instance, were especially troubled by the fact that Vincenzo and his alleged victim, Costanza Gaimari, were related. Indeed, after their father had married a woman who mistreated them, Costanza and her brother had gone to live near Vincenzo also because of their family connection, which made Vincenzo's behavior all the more offensive to communal values. The case of Rocco Lopardi began when Anna Siciliano and her mother threw stones at him and his new mistress and insulted them in public (calling Rocco a "pig" and the woman a "sow"). Rocco's conduct had allegedly been "of such scandal and awe to the people" that the marquis of Brienza himself had summoned him a few months earlier and urged him to change his ways. The accusations against him minced no words, including incest and having eaten sausages during Lent. We have seen how one witness expressed his concern for the bad example set by such conduct to the youth of the village.[35]

An even more scandalous case was reported by the head priest of Brienza to the baronial court in 1794. The priest denounced Giuseppe Luisi and the widow Caterina di Mare, who, not content with their concubinage, which had already brought many warnings by the priest, "swept by the impetuous fire of their criminal passion, having abandoned human shame," copulated in the barn of a farm while other people dined and slept there. Giuseppe and Caterina lay down together in a corner, and "they made those who saw them understand what point furious libido can reach, when it be not repressed with effective means." The priest, "in order to save his people from the infection which undoubtedly spreads vice when it is not stopped," had come to the governor with this "dreary, sordid, and filthy story." Three witnesses confirmed the scandalous event and the sense of excess felt by those who saw it. What particularly shocked the witnesses was the public context of the sexual behavior, and a young woman, for instance, testified that "even though [she was] a virgin" she could easily tell that Giuseppe and Caterina were "acting badly" that night.[36]

The public discourse about an individual's reputation or conduct was, then, a determining factor in all these trials. Very often in trial records and other documents witnesses stated that something was "true, public, and notorious," and they considered that to be sufficient justification for their knowledge and repetition of it.[37] The very fact that something was said among the people of the community became probatory in the eyes of many witnesses, as occurred in the trial of Domenica Orlando. In the case of Carmela di Stefano one witness affirmed his certainty that the rape had happened, because "if it had not been so it would not have been said and told with the same uniformity, as it [was] said and told by all in this village."[38]

This information and common knowledge was spread primarily through conversation and gossip. Witnesses occasionally reveal the popularity of these conversations and the function they served for men and women. A young day laborer in Brienza who testified in the 1794 case stated, "In groups of men, there always are talks about people's standing, and about who is good and who is bad." He had therefore long been aware of the ongoing relationship between Giuseppe Luisi and Caterina di Mare. The shocked young woman who testified in the same case also knew of the concubinage, since she "had heard it spoken about by other women, also of the village, on occasions when [they] had walked together."[39]

This type of gender-specific gossip circle also served women as a way to reduce the control exercised by men over their behavior. Although women were excluded from many public roles, their forms of sociability, especially among neighbors, gave them access to, and the ability to shape substantially, the powerful circuit of community gossip. Women chatted with other women, friends or neighbors, informally or at ritualized occasions such as births or wakes, and exchanged information about one another's health, family, and other affairs. Women could thus circulate information about their husbands or other men which would shape the community's perception and judgment of those men. Domenica Orlando certainly availed herself of this method to make her unhappiness with her husband widely known among the people of Pentidattilo.[40]

Public reputation and community gossip thus played a crucial role not only in the resolution of these trials but often also in the very fact that these instances of sexual misbehavior came to the attention of the authorities. This also confirms that, unlike the ecclesiastic or secular powers, the community was offended not so much by the sexual actions themselves but by their potential or actual disruption of public order and by the threat they posed to a community's economic welfare or peaceful relations with outside forces. Thus every witness in the Pentidattilo trial who was asked about them acknowledged that she (or in a few cases he) had known for a long time about the abortions managed by Anna de Amico. It was only when the abortions became an issue in a murder trial that the villagers expressed their criticism of Anna. Similar reactions can be found in many other cases.[41]

The concern about scandal was shared by the religious and secular authorities, as one can see in the interventions of the marquis of Brienza (and at other times of his officers) and the village priest in the cases mentioned above. That these cases all occurred later than the Pentidattilo case might also explain the relative frequency of these interventions on the part of the authorities, whose interest in controlling the rural population's behavior increased with time. The desire to regulate such behavior, particularly in the sexual sphere, had, of course, existed for a long time, and late medieval handbooks for confessors mentioned an array of sexual practices upon which the church frowned, such as coitus interruptus, masturbation, or intercourse with the woman on top.[42] Post-Tridentine bishops, in the Kingdom of Naples as in most Catholic lands, more aggressively tried to correct what they saw as scandalous and ungodly conduct current among their flocks. Means to this end were the establishment of seminaries and the attempt to improve the quality of the parish clergy, the regular visit of each diocese's outlying communities, and the holding of diocesan synods.[43] The records produced by these initiatives shed light on the behavior bishops sought to alter.

One of the instruments of moral control wielded through the synods were the "reserved sins." These were sins for which forgiveness and absolution could be granted only by the bishops themselves, not by parish priests. There was frequent agreement on what some of these sins were, as they typically included the "more atrocious and grave crimes." Each bishop could, however, establish additional categories—indications of what each bishop perceived as scandalous actions that represented a special problem within his diocese.[44]

The Reggio archbishops were particularly concerned about specific categories of sinful actions. Blasphemy was mentioned first in all their lists of reserved sins, and the archbishops identified various types of it, from blasphemy against God or the Virgin, to glorification of the devil, to heretical blasphemy. Murder, usury, and magical practices usually followed closely. Another important group of reserved sins concerned the safety of and respect for ecclesiastic property and goods. A variety of acts, then—such as arson on church land, refusal to pay tithes, obstructing or destroying proofs of pious bequests, or grazing one's livestock on cultivated land belonging to the church—constituted reserved sins, and some of them carried an automatic excommunication unless absolved by the bishop. Close in spirit to this category were a few acts that expressed lack of respect towards the clergy, for example, talking to nuns about obscene subjects.[45]

A final group of reserved sins that directly concerned the interaction between the church and popular views of morality consisted of sins of a moral and sexual nature, most of which did not carry an automatic excommunication. These sins, in the 1729 list, were sodomy among adult males, concubinage lasting longer than three months, intercourse with pagan women (which in the case of the Diocese of Reggio probably referred to the Muslim slaves present even in the remotest villages), causing abortions even before animation of the fetus, incest within two degrees of kinship, intercourse among couples engaged to be married, and "the defloration of a virgin through promise of marriage." An earlier list by Archbishop D'Afflitto had also included violent or sacrilegious rape and bestiality.[46]

The archbishops conceived of most of these acts as the responsibility of men, and they saw women as the victims of these crimes. Archbishop de Gennaro specified, for instance, that "in sins of the flesh one does not include women, nor males before puberty," and therefore those who needed his absolution were only the adult men guilty of these actions. The archbishops seem to have regarded the life of the lay population, especially in the villages, as rife with dangerous and almost irresistible opportunities to engage in these sinful activities.

Although peasant communities and bishops shared a dislike of public scandal, their views on what constituted it and on what to do about it often differed. The bishops' main suggestion to obviate most sexual sins was the avoidance of occasions for contact between men and women, especially but not only in the course of religious practices. Owing to the concern lest sacred and profane life be mingled, any sexual misdemeanor was made far graver, in the prelates' eyes, by being committed as the result of contacts established while engaging in religious activities. Especially in small isolated villages, however, close contact between men and women was frequent and inevitable, and religious events were welcome communal occasions. Moreover, the community could easily exercise its own control mechanisms. Villagers therefore resisted the attempt to limit occasions for men and women to interact in public and held fast to their own ways of defining morality.

The archbishops repeatedly called for the separation of the sexes. Archbishop D'Afflitto, inspired by Carlo Borromeo, urged that boys and girls be separated on the occasion of their confirmation and insisted that "as much as it [could] be done, males and females pray separately." He and later bishops also emphasized the need for proper behavior and separation of the sexes during mass and recommended caution when confessing women, so that the occasion not turn into an opportunity for contact with men. Archbishop Polou in 1729 still urged that during Lent men and women be unable even to see each other while in church. In the later synod he repeated the need for separation of the sexes during mass, and he stressed that women should never be allowed in the choir or sacristy. The sexes were also to be separated during the ceremonies accompanying missions.[47]

The biggest, and probably the least successful, fight of the bishops, and to a lesser extent of the state, against popular morality had to do with concubinage, especially with sexual intercourse before marriage. Concubinage was high on the list of reserved sins. All bishops thundered against it and urged all parish clergy to denounce and report it. D'Afflitto, for instance, ordered his priests to deny unmarried couples access to the Eucharist unless they repented.

Concubinage was seen by the clergy as the cause of great scandal and offense to God, but it left the villagers relatively untroubled, at least as long as it did not violate the community's sense of public scandal.

Rocco Lopardi lived in fairly open concubinage, despite the warnings of the marquis and the parish priest, until the fight between two of the women he had seduced led to public confrontations and caused disarray in the community. Similarly, the many warnings of the parish priest had been wholly ineffective in bringing about the reform or the ostracism of Giuseppe Luisi and Caterina di Mare, and their entire community, while it gossiped about their living arrangement, accepted it, at least until their public copulation finally caused scandal and triggered a judicial action, however short lived. Unmarried couples in Pentidattilo had no problem finding godparents for their children and were left alone by the parish priest. Despite the fact that after the 1741 concordat the state, too, had affirmed its serious preoccupation with and jurisdiction over concubinage, unless community standards were offended, unmarried couples enjoyed considerable acceptance in rural communities.[48]

A specific form of concubinage was even more troubling to the religious authorities—sexual intercourse, and often cohabitation, between couples engaged to be married (the *sponsi de futuro*). This was a very old problem against which the church fought vainly, particularly in rural areas, for centuries, as it undermined the very definition of marriage as a sacrament, and of the rituals that finalized it, upon which the church had insisted forcefully since at least the Council of Trent. The Reggio archbishops lamented these unsanctioned sexual relations repeatedly and sternly over almost two centuries, from D'Afflitto's council and synods through Polou's synods and reports to Rome. Polou, who overall found his flock's behavior not excessively scandalous and who in 1729 optimistically observed that "they [were advancing] a little bit in their piety," in a later report cited the cohabitation of sponsi de futuro as the single biggest problem of his diocese. The scarcity of parish records of marriages for Pentidattilo makes it impossible to establish the incidence of premarital conceptions, but the problem was widespread in all villages of the diocese, the kingdom, and western Europe.[49]

The central secular and religious authorities continued throughout the eighteenth century to find the moral and sexual behavior of the rural population wanting, and the philosophers and scholars of the Enlightenment were similarly disturbed by the perceived immorality of the peasantry. In his description of Calabria at the end of the old regime, Giuseppe Maria Galanti lamented the "infinite adulteries, most numerous abortions, and many illegitimate children" he found in the region. Other and also later observers were particularly troubled by the fact that village communities did not condemn or marginalize moral offenders. This impression of alienness and this image of the moral poverty of the rural population, reported by the Jesuit missionaries as early as the end of the sixteenth century, can still be found in the reactions of the writers who described the southern provinces after the end of the kingdom in 1860 and would continue until well into the twentieth century.[50]

Thus popular behavior and culture, especially in the areas of family, morality, and sexuality, continued to manifest their own values and conceptions over the centuries of the early modern period and beyond. The rural population had to interact with and respond to the changing values of state and church; it also had to respond to the increasing power of church and state to spread awareness of those values and attempt to impose them. Yet the villagers never abandoned their ways of doing things and of judging them. The people of Pentidattilo and similar villages had a clear sense of honor, and the individual reputation of each citizen—and in the case of women, particularly their sexual reputation—was a significant concern within a tightly knit and attentive community. But on important matters of moral and sexual behavior the villagers maintained a high degree of autonomy vis-à-vis the authority of church and state. Until a crisis brought on the village the attention of outside forces, questions of moral and sexual misbehavior were handled within the community, especially among village women. Thus Anna de Amico long enjoyed a solid place in Pentidattilo's society by offering a remedy to women with unwanted pregnancies, and the community, though it gossiped, paid little attention to Domenica Orlando's adultery, until Antonino's death raised the stakes too high.

Birth and Death in Village Culture

> Piangono, gridano, ululano, con le mani si strappano i capelli, batteno il petto, squarciano la faccia.
>
> They weep, cry, howl, with their own hands tear their hair, strike their breasts, rend their faces.
> —A Jesuit in Sicily, 1560, cited in Tacchi Venturi, *Storia*

During the seventeenth and eighteenth centuries, the increasing separation between the values encouraged by church and state and the views of the villagers was also apparent in the role of midwives and the treatment of illegitimate children, the villagers' conduct and attitudes in regard to abortion, and the rituals surrounding death in peasant culture. Outside observers and authorities tended to emphasize the obedience to general moral rules, the interiorization of emotions, a heightened sense of private shame and human sinfulness, and the avoidance of conduct that appeared disruptive of public quiet. Popular culture, on the other hand, remained direct, practical, and functional; it maintained a degree of blunt carnality in its understanding of—and attitude towards—the body and death; and it continued to uphold violent rituals, even stigmatizing those who did not participate in them when expected to do so.

Baptism was a very important community ritual and the locus of a struggle between church and village values. Like other life-cycle rituals, baptism was a crucial element of both social and religious life, and godparenthood was a central bond in village society. Judging from the baptismal records of Pentidattilo in the last third of the seventeenth century, the post-Tridentine bishops were reasonably successful in shaping how the villagers approached the choice of godparents for their children.[51] More problematic were other values and practices connected to baptism, namely, the role of midwives and the treatment of illegitimate children and foundlings. These issues remained areas of contention between popular and episcopal views.[52] Midwives played an essential function in women's health care and especially in the area of reproduction and sexuality. Their activities were central also to important community concerns and attracted increasing scrutiny and supervision from outside authorities.[53]

The midwives' crucial role in the life of the community was emphasized by the increasing care state and church authorities gave to their proper training and understanding of the laws and rules attending to their function. Midwives were, after all, the only women, and almost the only lay persons, who might frequently be called upon to perform a sacramental rite. Archbishop D'Afflitto, for instance, listed the three midwives of Pentidattilo in the records of his 1597 visit and checked their preparation, and in his 1602 council he required all priests in the archdiocese to ensure that all midwives be properly knowledgeable in the baptismal rites and formulas. Later bishops repeated these concerns.[54]

Midwives, at times accompanied by other elderly women, were also expert witnesses in all judicial cases concerning abortion or rape. The midwives who testified in the Brienza and Atena cases, all illiterate, were knowledgeable in the evidentiary theories of the time, as were the barber and the midwife in the Pentidattilo trial. Their testimony reported on all the factors required by jurisprudential literature, such as the conditions of the hymen, nipples, and breasts and the presence of traces of blood. Midwives, then, had to fulfill the functions assigned to them by both secular and church powers in order to have their abilities recognized by those powers and thereby maintain the traditional—and for women highly unusual—authority they enjoyed among their fellow villagers. Midwives had thus an especially ambiguous position: lay and clerical authorities had to trust them as experts in the handling of many crimes, but that expertise also made them liable to suspicions of complicity in the same crimes. The very suspicions awakened by the midwives' important functions in popular life led church and state to insist on their acquiring more knowledge and formal expertise, which in turn further empowered midwives within their communities.[55]

The status of midwives was increasingly threatened during the eighteenth century throughout Europe, especially in regard to their medical and judicial roles. While the church usually limited itself to insistence on midwives' proper training, state and medical authorities pressured for their replacement with professional doctors. The Neapolitan author of a treatise on legal medicine, for instance, denounced the help and herbs that midwives gave to women desiring abortions and thundered against "th[ese] awful pseudo-doctoress[es]," who brought "infamy to our Art." Midwives were excluded from testimony in some cases, and they attempted to present themselves in a manner more befitting the new scientific outlook. By 1803, when Giuditta Petrone was examined, the two midwives described themselves as "expert[s] in the obstetrical art."[56]

Midwives were responsible for almost all births in villages like Pentidattilo, where there was neither a medical doctor nor a pharmacist. As required by the church, midwives baptized newborns who appeared in danger of death. In the Pentidattilo sample I examined, these cases account for 27 out of 611 baptisms, or 4.5 percent, all but 2 baptized by Virginia Squillaci. In each case the priest noted that there was "imminent danger of death" and that the midwife was "approved" and had "correctly" performed the sacrament. In a few cases some of the baptismal rites were then repeated in the church.[57]

Illegitimate children and foundlings represented another area of tension between popular attitudes and the wishes of outside authorities. In my Pentidattilo sample there are a total of 24 baptisms of such children, or 4 percent. These include 6 children for whom no parents are identified (5 of these are marked as foundlings, and the last one was born within the marquis's household), 14 for whom the mother is identified but whose father is marked as "unknown," and 4 for whom both parents are identified and who received their father's surnames but who are marked as "illegitimate."[58] Pentidattilo in the late seventeenth century had a higher rate of illegitimate births than other areas of the rural south, where a rate of 4 percent was not usually reached until almost a century later. The Pentidattilo rate was also higher than those found in other European villages between 1600 and 1750.[59]

Church and state looked with some displeasure on illegitimate children and especially on foundlings, who were also increasingly assumed to be illegitimate. Priests and midwives were required to do their best to identify the parents, especially the fathers, if need be by questioning the mother while she lay in labor. As one jurist observed, finding out about abortions and illegitimate children could not have been too difficult "in the small villages of this Kingdom." Determining paternity should certainly have been fairly easy in a small community like Pentidattilo, yet the village priests seem on the whole to have been willing to let their parishioners deal with these situations as they pleased. In general, these children received a reasonably warm welcome in the village culture of Pentidattilo.[60]

The illegitimate children and the foundlings did not receive a different treatment in terms of godparenthood. All but 1 of the 24 had a godparent (a total of 20 out of the sample of 611 had no godparents), and 4 of them had two, which is not a much lower rate than that for the entire sample (176 out of 611). The 5 foundlings were attended at the font by prominent citizens. Two of them had as godparent Giacomo Minicuci, a man who, with thirty-nine god-children to his credit over twenty-eight years, was the busiest godparent in the village. This may mean that Minicuci was a friend or neighbor of the parish priest and simply available on short notice, but it still would have connected the foundlings to a broad network of spiritual kinship in the village. Giovan Filippo Romeo, also a popular godfather, attended another foundling at her baptism, and still another was accompanied by the woman who had found her, Maria Romeo, who would later be the village midwife. Finally, 1 foundling, who had been brought to the priest by the mayor's wife, received two godparents (one of very few cases with two godfathers), including the dittereo.[61]

The illegitimate children and their mothers also do not seem to have been stigmatized by the village community. All these children but one had a godparent from established village families, and three of them had two. No pattern can be observed which differentiates these cases from other baptisms. The mothers of the fourteen children of "unknown" fathers were, with a lone exception, women from the village, bearing old local surnames. In fact, nine of the fourteen children of "unknown" fathers were born to four women who, despite their multiple illegitimate pregnancies, were not shunned by their fellow villagers when it was necessary to find godparents for the women's offspring. Moreover, of the ten village women who gave births to illegitimate children in the years covered by my sample, five appear later in the parish records as married women, and two more were chosen at least twice by fellow villagers as godmothers. At least one of the illegitimate children himself appears late in the sample as a popular godfather. Although women who had illegitimate children were at risk of poverty and dishonor, then, the community was far from condemning them intransigently, especially if they belonged to established families. One of the trial witnesses, Sicilia Zuccalà, a single woman who had had two abortions, was also fully integrated into village society. The fact that the marquis's own son and heir, Lorenzo Alberti, fathered two illegitimate children and presumably lived in open concubinage with their mother also points to a general atmosphere within village society fairly accepting of what by external standards were illicit sexuality and parenthood.[62]

A similar discordance between the rules of outside powers on the one hand and peasant practice and the values of village culture on the other appears concerning miscarriage and abortion. One of the grounds for the increasing suspicion with which the authorities of state and church regarded midwives was their potential role in arranging abortions, especially for rural women. Midwives and other village women were seen as the holders of a knowledge of nature and natural remedies which came under concerned scrutiny during the early modern period in Europe and which, in its proximity to and likely identification with magic, was one of the main factors in many witchcraft accusations and trials. This closeness to nature, this knowledge of the powers of natural elements, of herbs and potions, also translated, especially among rural women, into a practical, natural, and direct approach to the human body and especially to its sexual and reproductive functions.[63]

Popular conceptions of the body and its workings were based on the idea of a balance of humors. The healthy body was a fluent body, in which humors and other substances circulated smoothly and freely. Disease was the result of a blockage in the free flowing that normally ensured the body's well-being. The "clogged" body, which lost the ability to purify itself regularly by ridding itself of humors, became corrupt and diseased. For this reason therapies and cures often took, in the popular and often in the learned view as well, the form of evacuatory remedies. The body was thus objectified, and as a result it was also possible for ill individuals mentally to distance themselves from their own diseased, and hence malfunctioning, body.[64]

This conception of the body was particularly problematic, especially in the eyes of the church, in regard to pregnancy. Learned medicine was quite mystified by pregnancy. Paolo Zacchia, in his popular treatise on forensic medicine, reviewed the physical signs of pregnancy and found all of them, at least until the fourth month, at best conjectural. After dismissing the presence of milk in the breasts as a clear sign, on the ground that it was known to occur in men, too, Zacchia noted that "moreover the lack of menses of all [signs] is the most deceptive. . . . Not only from the lack of menses one cannot affirm that a woman is pregnant, but also the presence of menses is not a sure sign that she is not; there are in fact women who have menstruations even when pregnant, and vice versa there are women who never or very rarely have menstruations, and yet they conceive."[65]

Notions such as these frequently led to conflict between learned or popular healing and church concerns. All forms of popular medicine, like magic, were high on the lists of reserved sins issued by the archbishops of Reggio. Women healers with their roots, potions, and herbs were certainly as common in the villages of the diocese as in most other parts of rural Europe. In a world in which bad or insufficient nutrition was the norm, amenorrhea must have been a frequent occurrence. Many rural women thus tended to see the absence of periods as an illness, an unwelcome alteration of the body, and they sought remedies that would cause menstruation. Their attitude towards abortion, or at any rate towards induced miscarriage, was blunt and functional, as were the remedies they obtained through their own efforts or by consulting the knowledgeable women of their community.[66]

Men were often not much help in these situations, even if they were around for the pregnancy. Costanza Gaimari testified, for instance, that Vincenzo Lupardi's idea of a remedy for her pregnancy consisted in asking her to lie on the ground, after which he "stood with his feet . . . on [her] back, and while [she] felt a bitter pain he kicked [her] in the back and on the shoulders." Women healers or midwives offered natural and somewhat less painful remedies such as potions or herbs to drink or the poisonous roots preferred by Anna de Amico. The expected result would be miscarriage and the restoration of regular menstruation. Women presented the abortion as a natural occurrence ("something came out," stated the Bavarian peasants studied by Regina Schulte), as a dirty discharge that restored the body's health, as the expulsion of "blood curls or leathery stuff or wrong growths." Similarly candid terms were used by Domenica Orlando and her friends when they spoke of the bloody corpse of Domenica's fetus and of the "piece of curdled blood" containing "two small pieces of flesh" with "two attached pieces of roots" which resulted from Anna de Amico's own induced miscarriage. Although their words may also exhibit a desire to distance themselves from the legal consequences of their act, these women's understanding of abortion indicates a view of both the body and the ethics of reproduction profoundly different from that of state and church.[67]

Knowledge of these methods was both valuable and dangerous, and if in eighteenth-century Italy witchcraft was no longer a likely accusation, the secular and ecclesiastic condemnation of abortion made any acknowledgment of such expertise to the authorities problematic. On the other hand, prosecution of crimes such as abortion or infanticide was impossible unless the community collaborated, and this was not usually the case. The women of Pentidattilo, for instance, prized Anna de Amico's ability to help them with unwanted pregnancies, and she managed at least eight abortions (including her own and Domenica Orlando's). Although during the trial most witnesses testified to Anna's bad reputation, village women sought her assistance, and information about her talents and methods was eagerly passed around in gossipy conversations.

For instance, Agostina Palomara testified that, while working in the fields with Antonia Crea, the latter had told her about her pregnancy. Two days later Antonia told Agostina that she was no longer pregnant, and she offered to show "it" to Agostina, although she supposedly would not tell Agostina exactly what remedy Anna had given her. Agostina claimed to have answered that she "did not anyway want to know it" and to have left "on [her] own business." Cata Vazzani admitted to more interest in the matter when she testified about a visit she had paid to Anna. Cata, who had already heard of Anna's abilities, asked her about her "power" to bring about abortions, and Anna allegedly claimed to have assisted three village women in their abortions. Cata then asked how Anna did this, and Anna replied, vaguely, "with a certain root." After this Cata, too, went away "on [her] own business."[68]

Sicilia Zuccalà, the only witness to refer to Anna as her "friend," also testified to her frequent visits to and conversations with Anna, who also lived near Sicilia's home, and to having talked to Anna about her abortion method and the village women who had had recourse to it. Domenico Tropea, one of the two men involved in Domenica Orlando's abortion, stated that Domenica had asked him "if [he] knew of any woman who had some remedy to obtain abortions" and that he referred the matter to Anna, who—he "had heard it said"—had managed other women's abortions. Domenica in her confession confirmed that she had asked Domenico Tropea for help and that he had put her in contact with Anna. Since Domenica's abortion had taken place four to six years before her trial for the murder of her husband, it is possible that she and Anna were at that time not yet neighbors and therefore Domenica, who would have been barely twenty, was not yet aware of Anna's activities.[69]

The women (and one of the men) of Pentidattilo thus exchanged information about Anna's skills, without alerting the authorities until the murder trial. That Anna lived alone, was not a native to the village, and had been abandoned by her husband, himself not a native Pentidattilese, probably led her to acquire these abilities in order to establish a position for herself in the village's small and rather closed society. Anna cut cloth, occasionally cooked for her neighbors, and managed abortions. As a result she was engaged in a network of visits, conversations, exchanges, and favors with other village women. Her status was, however, still fragile, and on the record and in front of the authorities (as represented by the lord's court) villagers, including women who had interacted frequently with Anna, took pains to distance themselves from her and her actions regarding abortion.[70]

Neither Anna's identity in the community nor this distancing of other villagers from her, when trouble occurred, was unusual. A case in Atena dating from the very end of the old regime reveals similar patterns. Giuditta Petrone, a servant in the home of the prominent Pessolano family (which included a priest), was accused of aborting the child she conceived during her relationship with the priest. Giuditta denied the accusation, but two midwives found "a most copious loss of blood from her pudenda, and milk in her right nipple, when pressed." The court then questioned two other witnesses. Felicia del Negro, an elderly widow who was a neighbor of the Pessolano, stated that Giuditta had come to her and told her "after many digressions" that she was pregnant and had asked her for a "remedy to repair her situation." Felicia told Giuditta that she knew not how to help her. When Giuditta came back saying that she had been given "an infusion of some herbs" by Maddalena Accetta and asking whether she could take it in Felicia's house to avoid scandal in her master's home, Felicia again refused to help her.

The only other witness was Maddalena Accetta, also a single woman. She stated that Giuditta had come to her "to seek advice on the lack of her benefits, that is menses," and to ask for some helpful herb. Maddalena gave Giuditta an herb the name of which she claimed not to remember, but after two weeks

Giuditta was back, "complaining that the infusion of that herb had not produced the expected effect." Maddalena testified that only at this point did she
become suspicious and she told Giuditta that "her condition was indicative of
pregnancy," which Giuditta admitted was, in fact, the case. Maddalena then
stated that "no more was needed to convince this witness not to get any more
involved and not to prescribe other medicaments." Some days later, on meet-
ing Giuditta, Maddalena asked her how things were, and Giuditta said that
"she was resigning herself to what destiny would send."[71]

The late date of this trial and its location in Atena, a large village on a major
trade route, may explain the greater reluctance of these witnesses to admit to
any deep involvement in the abortion. Popular awareness and fear of the condemnation of these practices on the part of secular and lay powers were presumably greater by this date and in a center like Atena than they had been in
Pentidattilo almost a century earlier. It is hard to believe that Maddalena, an
expert woman who prescribed "medicaments" and dispensed "advice," would
have been fooled by Giuditta about her condition. Maddalena's desire to deny
responsibility and her (likely pretended) naivete and ignorance are indicative
of the increasingly strict climate surrounding abortion and similar crimes as
both state and church became more adept at investigating them. At the same
time this example, like the case of Anna de Amico in Pentidattilo, points to
the functional and direct attitude of peasant culture towards pregnancy and
abortion and to the networks of solidarity developed within village society,
especially among village women, to deal with them away from the gaze of outside authorities. That all three women involved were single is also typical of
these situations.

The rituals and social behaviors surrounding death were also the focus of
struggle between outside forces and peasant culture and tradition. Bishops and
educated secular observers alike criticized and attempted to stop traditional
funeral rites and conduct, which appeared to them as primitive and brutal,
dangerously emotional and violent, and redolent of paganism. Bishops in particular were concerned about what to them were disruptions of public quiet,
and they instead wanted to compel obedience to the set rituals of the church
and the control and disciplining of emotions, as part of the long and varied
battle of the Tridentine church to move all aspects of religious, spiritual, and
ritual life away from the circle of kin and neighborhood activity and under the
supervision of the parish clergy.

As in many other areas of the Mediterranean, traditional funeral customs
in Calabria included the prolonged seclusion of female relatives of the de-

ceased to the extent of not attending religious services; their ritualized violent behavior, such as their pulling their hair and scratching their cheeks; and often the hiring of paid mourners (*prefiche*). These practices, once common in Italian cities, too, had by the Renaissance been mostly confined to rural areas and were repeatedly condemned by outsiders. In 1560 a Jesuit priest condemned as superstitious the women who "weep, cry, howl, with their own hands tear their hair, strike their breasts, rend their faces." Archbishop D'Afflitto in 1595 called women's absence from the services after family deaths a "depraved habit" because it gave the impression that they had no hope in the Resurrection. In the 1602 council he urged priests to "warn widows to go to church and not postpone attending mass without delay immediately after the funeral," and he required that all relatives attend services at the latest ten days after the burial. He "absolutely prohibited" the use of prefiche. These warnings had little effect. Archbishop de Gennaro "benignly exhorted all women . . . not to give themselves when they lose parents or blood relatives to extreme howlings and immoderate sighs, and even more to abstain from the laceration of cheeks and hair, and not to employ mourners to cry for the dead." He labeled these practices "pagan abuses." Archbishop Polou, however, still needed to repeat the prohibition against all these practices, and he ordered that men not stay secluded for longer than half a day and women for a day.[72]

Secular observers were equally disturbed and shocked by these practices, particularly visitors educated in the culture of the Enlightenment, and later foreign travelers echoed these reactions. Galanti, in his critical comments about Calabrian customs, habits, and morality, described at length the funeral rituals of self-inflicted wounds, hired mourners, and self-imposed and lengthy seclusion. Edward Lear in the 1840s continued in a long tradition of foreign visitors when he reported on these and other funeral practices (such as not shaving, not leaving the house, or not changing clothes).[73]

The popular practices remained strong, especially in the countryside. Indeed, the failure to act according to these popular codes of behavior led to stigmatizing on the part of the community and was even considered evidence of guilt in criminal proceedings. One of the most widely used Neapolitan judicial handbooks observed, "Not to shed tears and weep for the death of a wife is a sign of hatred, and brings suspicion against the husband. . . . Widows must cry, and dress according to the habit of their region. . . . Husband and wife are one flesh, and the one must bemoan the death of the other, according to the habit of the region." A later jurist also noted that suspicions are legitimate if the surviving spouse "fakes crying, if the expense for the funeral was tiny and improper, if [the spouse] does not wear mourning, although able to afford it, and such being the custom of the village."[74]

Suspicion was certainly aroused by Domenica Orlando's behavior at the death of her husband. For example, Vittoria Vernagallo noted that, while Antonino suffered and lamented various pains, Domenica "neither came close to her husband's bed, nor did she show any reaction to his suffering," which first aroused Vittoria's suspicions. Later, when Antonino received the last rites, Domenica "set herself to weaving." Even at the moment of Antonino's death, as his siblings cleaned his corpse, Domenica joined Vittoria and Anna de Amico in the next room "without ever crying or showing other signs of sorrow for the death of her husband." On the next day Vittoria, ever the solicitous neighbor, "seeing that Domenica did not go cry near where her husband had died, took her by the arm and led her near her [dead] husband, admonishing her that she did not do well not to cry his death, but notwithstanding [Vittoria's] admonition Domenica still shed no tears." Antonia Manti, another of the several neighbors and women who visited the house at the time of Antonino's death, also testified that Domenica "in seeing her husband dead showed no expression of affection [for him], nor did one tear escape her eyes."[75]

Village culture, then, expected a specific type of reaction, expressive of its values and beliefs, and villagers noticed and criticized Domenica for failing to follow their rules of behavior. Especially in the case of issues affecting the family and its events, such as births or deaths, it was primarily women who were expected to act according to the traditional codes, even if those codes were in direct contradiction with the will and the values of outside forces like the church. A crucial role in the enforcement of the values and expectations of popular culture in the field of family life was played by the neighbors, again primarily women, who had the opportunity to observe one another's conduct closely and used that opportunity to form the community's opinion of any individual's bearing and to pass judgment on it.

Peasant culture was, particularly in its conception of the body and its functions, blunt and practical in its carnality and matter-of-factness. The public expression of strong emotions was common, and indeed in some circumstances, like funeral customs, it was nearly required. This emerges from all the sources in which we hear, however mediated, the voices of villagers. Even accounting for the directness inherent in judicial records, the testimonies in the trials I have used in this chapter are remarkably candid. Very young witnesses speak with little hesitation of blood, violence, and pain, and they reveal a general discourse in which mutual violent insults were common.[76] As late as the 1930s, Carlo Levi noted the southern villagers' casual acceptance of violence, sex, and death. In Pentidattilo in particular, where the entire population had gone through the events of the massacre of 1686, violence must have been a regular facet of every villager's life.

Yet this bluntness and habit of violence occurred within a complex moral system, in which individual honor and reputation, as assessed by community observation, were crucial to each villager's standing. The reputation of women, which was central to that of their families and of the entire community, was founded on their sexual behavior, which neighbors and relatives carefully scrutinized and discussed. Judgment came not from universal standards that condemned certain actions categorically but from the specific circumstances and significance of each action and from the character and connections of each individual. Thus outsiders were in a fragile position, as their behavior could be severely condemned when that would benefit the community or established citizens.

In what has been called the age of confessionalization and discipline, the Tridentine church and the early modern state were deeply concerned with popular behavior and rituals, especially in matters affecting sexuality and family, and, in often complementary ways, they sought to impose new values and views. Counter Reformation ethics was focused on subjectivity and individual desire and stressed the need for moral and sexual self-control. Emotions were to be disciplined and internalized, and actions were to be judged according to absolute definitions of motives and intentions, with limited attention to the possible communal function and outcome of any behavior.[77] Popular culture, on the other hand, was factual and functional in its attitude towards— and judgment of—individual behavior. Emotions were best understood and assessed, and therefore safest for everybody, when expressed publicly and visibly, often in ritualized form. Actions were scandalous and dangerous if they threatened the community, not if they offended theoretical notions of sin. The well-being of the community, and not the abstract morality of individual intentions, was the paramount ethical consideration.

At the same time this peasant culture, still predominantly illiterate and suspicious of outside authorities, interacted frequently and effectively, and far from passively, with the representatives of state and church and had to respond to their various demands and to their attempts to impose different values and behaviors. It did so by mastering enough aspects of the written culture and of the outside values—and of judicial procedures and methods—to be able to engage in dialogue and negotiation with outside authorities, and occasionally to manipulate them. As Regina Schulte observed, "In court, this institution that belonged to another world, village society acted in contradiction with its own nature: it spoke on the record."[78] When this happened, the differences in values and outlook between the outside world and village society emerged sharply, but neither numerous trials nor certainly even more numerous episcopal admonitions succeeded in subordinating village culture to a new sense of shame, sin, and morality. The autonomy, dynamism, oral tradition, violently expressed emotions, and direct, practical outlook characteristic of rural culture continued to flourish throughout the early modern period.

The Trial's End

Until Domenica Orlando's confession, the case in Pentidattilo's feudal court had followed closely the practice and doctrine of early modern jurisprudence, in both the gathering of evidence and the treatment of defendants. Then the court, whose activities had so far been marked by considerable alacrity, stopped pursuing the case with any vigor. We do not know why the case was allowed to languish. Probably the defendants' friends in the village intervened in their behalf. Delays were also inherent in the procedure, as it was difficult to proceed speedily once people extraneous to the court were required to act. Moreover, Domenica's confession contrasted with Pietro's and Anna's denials to form a procedural impasse. In any case, nothing seems to have happened for more than a month, until May 2, when the defendants notified, or rather reminded, the court that Felice Amodei had immediately renounced their defense, "being indisposed," and that they therefore, "since they were indigent people," lacked legal aid. The governor took action on May 12, appointing Francesco Nostro as the defendants' lawyer and Giovan Filippo Romeo of Pentidattilo as their procurator and extending the terms of their defense for another four days. The defendants, their lawyer, the accuser Cuzzucli, and the coadiutore Romeo were notified of this decision.[1]

Again, nothing happened until June 14, when Cuzzucli and Domenico Romeo pleaded with the court to proceed, since no defense or other action was forthcoming from the defendants. Indeed, they argued, this lack of action "manifestly shows that [the accused] have no way to hide or avoid the penalties that the laws demand for their most enormous crimes." Thus prodded, the court issued a call to the three defendants to appear again and present their defense. This, too, led to no action, until the following January 9, 1711, when again the coadiutore demanded that the court act. This the court did not do, and on January 21 again Romeo and Cuzzucli noted that no sentence had been pronounced in the case, and they denounced that in the meantime "the said Domenica escaped from prison and it [was] to be feared that the same [might] happen with" the other two accused.[2]

This shook the court enough to issue another order to the defendants to appear, and to decide, on January 26, that Anna and Pietro be tortured. They were granted a medical visit—which Domenica, in violation of regular procedures, had not received before her own torture—and one doctor Franco Sambono found them both in good health and fit to be tortured: neither had any "wound in the arms, nor in the chest, nor in other parts of [their] bodies, so that [they] [might] freely and without danger be tortured." Their torture, on January 26 and 27, took the same form as Domenica's.[3]

Because Anna and Pietro had not previously confessed and the purpose of torturing them was to obtain evidence against them, not others, the procedure called for more formality than had been used with Domenica. Anna, under oath, was questioned about the murder and the abortions in the torture chamber before being tied to the rope and again after being tied, and she continued to deny any knowledge of the facts. Only then was she lifted and suspended, and again she was admonished to speak the truth and asked about the crimes. Twice she was asked and twice she denied, the second time replying simply: "Saint Catherine, help me." After a final denial, and having hanged for a full hour—usually the maximum time allowed for a daily session of torture—she was released and taken back to prison.[4]

Pietro was treated more leniently. He was asked about the murder and adultery, and like Anna he repeatedly denied all knowledge both before and after being suspended by the rope. He, too, invoked Saint Catherine ("Saint Catherine, you must free me, and I was an honest man") and later cried that he "did not do these things, but they [were] tales of ruffians." Possibly because of the different level of his alleged involvement in the crimes, the scantier evidence against him, or sympathy towards his well-connected family—or because the court regarded him, as a man, as both less criminal in these domestic crimes and less likely to confess—he was left hanging only for one-half hour before being taken back to prison.[5]

The court now faced a considerable problem. According to doctrine and tradition, a defendant's successful resistance to torture purged the evidence against her or him. While a tribunal could still condemn the accused to the so-called extraordinary punishments, full conviction, and the resulting ordinary, harsher punishment, necessitated a full confession or overwhelming evidence. This case lacked both, and now Anna's and Pietro's stubborn denials in theory weakened the court's case even further. Although the judge could have decided to repeat the torture, the court probably felt that enough had been accomplished, and again perhaps village pressure (both in favor of Pietro and against Anna) was brought to bear.

On January 30, 1711, therefore, more than ten months after the death of Antonino Cuzzucli, the feudal court of Pentidattilo issued its sentences. It ordered that Anna de Amico "be taken to the prison for women in Naples, in the palace of the Great Court of the Vicaria, [and that she stay there] for fifteen years, after which she [was to] be freed and not further molested for these crimes." Pietro Crea, on the other hand, was to be "released from prison, freed, and not further molested." No sentence was issued for the escaped Domenica. This decree was then given official standing by being read in front of the defendants, their procurator, the accuser, the coadiutore, and four prominent citizens acting as witnesses to the proper conclusion of the case. One final time the court sought the stamp of community approval by requesting the presence of prominent local men.[6]

The acquittal of one defendant, the flight of another, and the severe punishment of the third brought this trial to a close. Not many people—certainly very few poor unconnected women from the distant provinces—would easily survive fifteen years in the prisons of the Vicaria, so that Anna's sentence was indeed quite harsh. The family connections and integration into the society of Pentidattilo of Domenica Orlando and Pietro Crea probably explain what may seem an odd conclusion to a modern reader of the evidence. After all, Anna had mostly provided Domenica with the means to do what the latter wanted to do, and, as for Pietro, the court obviously placed much more weight on his denials than on Domenica's own accusations and those of others. His role in the murder remained, however, at most that of instigator, and, as a single man, he was from a legal point of view only marginally complicitous in Domenica's adultery. Nothing more is known about the later destinies of the three defendants.[7]

Conclusion

> Ma in questa terra oscura, senza peccato e senza redenzione, dove il male non è morale, ma è un dolore terrestre, che sta per sempre nelle cose, Cristo non è disceso. Cristo si è fermato a Eboli.
>
> But to this dark land, without sin and without redemption, where evil is not moral, but is an earthly pain, forever residing in things, Christ did not descend. Christ stopped at Eboli.
>
> —CARLO LEVI, *Cristo si è fermato a Eboli*

The end of the Pentidattilo trial raises the question of what the verdicts meant within village society and of how the court reached them. Even setting aside the likelihood that Domenica received local help in her escape, village opinion almost unanimously condemned Anna, defined a marginal role for Pietro, and presented Domenica as almost irrelevant to the alleged crimes. Indeed, in another sign that the court worked in agreement with the villagers, while the judge asked the witnesses for their opinion of Anna's character, Domenica's (or Pietro's) reputation was never investigated. Anna's marginality to village society, her status as a single woman, not native to Pentidattilo and with limited local family connections, made her an outsider who could be sacrificed at a time of crisis. Although the villagers tolerated, even probably in part welcomed, Anna's illicit abortion activities (as they tolerated Domenica's adultery), the death of Antonino and the ensuing murder trial opened up a dangerous situation, and at that point Anna became the most vulnerable and dispensable participant.

The trial thus illustrates the character and mechanisms of the village community. The villagers had their own social structures, value system, and concerns, and the protection of insiders, of settled, well-connected members of the community, was a paramount preoccupation when contact with outside forces and policies became problematic. Local connections and individual reputation and standing were crucial in all aspects of community life, as they were in the operation of the justice system, and the villagers used their power to assess and establish each individual's reputation to shape the developments of the trial.

The Pentidattilo case reveals not only the judicial system at work and the practical application of laws and jurisprudential doctrine in a local and feudal context but also the main structures of rural society, life, and culture. The trial records offer access, as much as it is possible with the early modern illiterate masses, to how the people of Pentidattilo viewed their world, their neighbors, their families, their community, and their traditions. The depositions show how men and women interacted with each other, what gave status to some in their midst, and what responsibilities came with it. The records also disclose how this rural world reacted to and dealt with the presence of external authorities, their rules, and one of their main instruments, the written word.

A productive process of cooperation, confrontation, and negotiation characterized the relationship between the population of Pentidattilo and the forces and institutions of the larger world outside the village, from the state administration to the Catholic episcopate, from the feudal lords to broad economic developments. In this process the villagers were never subordinate; they revealed, both as individuals and as members of a dynamic community, a consistent ability to mediate the impact of outside powers and also at times to manipulate them for the villagers' or the community's own ends. This mutual influence and interaction is also clear in the creation of all documents describing the community or in any way emanating from the village. In the persistently oral world of Pentidattilo, not only judicial records but also fiscal documents, notarial or administrative acts, and parish records could only be produced through a dialogue between written and illiterate cultures.

The trial of Domenica Orlando and her alleged accomplices, and the village community of Pentidattilo, have provided the starting point for the analysis of rural society and culture developed in this study. The trial presents peculiar traits yet is representative of issues and situations of much broader import. It offers a thorough example of the procedures discussed in early modern continental European jurisprudence and followed in all criminal courts. At the same time, the records of this trial offer the rare opportunity to observe how these procedures—and the principles on which they were based—operated not in central tribunals and important cities but rather in the reality of one of Europe's myriad small peasant communities and in the context of feudal jurisdiction. Moreover, the issues of evidence and proof and the type of crimes with which this obscure feudal court was dealing were central to the tensions and difficulties that would, by the late eighteenth century, push reformers across Europe to dismantle the traditional judicial system.

Pentidattilo itself also offers both peculiar and representative elements. The great strength and extent at the local level of feudal criminal jurisdiction was rather rare outside the Kingdom of Naples. From an economic point of view, the village belonged to what was, at least until the eighteenth century, a peripheral region of an increasingly marginal country. The surviving influence of Greek religious rites and linguistic tradition was particular to a few areas of the kingdom and affected the relationship between village beliefs and practices and the reforming impulses of the Counter Reformation church.

Nonetheless, Pentidattilo was far from atypical of western European villages. Its inhabitants had access to land in a variety of complex ways, and they labored at a traditional intensive subsistence agriculture, relying little on markets and producing locally virtually all they needed. The interplay of family and community shaped the lives of all villagers. Their community faced the increasing demands and power of an administrative state bent on raising its revenues and augmenting its central control. The villagers also confronted the zeal of post-Reformation prelates for the administrative and moral reform of the local clergy and of popular behavior and beliefs, especially in the area of family and sexual morality. Finally, the spread of the production of raw silk and, by the mid-eighteenth century, citrus fruits led Pentidattilo to share in the demographic growth and the integration into broad commercial networks which affected and began to change substantially much of western Europe's rural world.

The decades around the turn of the eighteenth century represented the start of important transformations in all aspects of the life of villages like Pentidattilo. The economic circumstances of the community improved and led to increased social stratification, new residential patterns, and the involvement of the village with broader market and migration networks. The gradual success of the bishops in reforming the education and character of the local clergy, and the decline of Greek traditions in the village's ritual and cultural life, affected traditional elements of popular behavior and belief. Finally, the judicial system, mostly in response to the problems caused by the prosecution of crimes such as those allegedly committed by Domenica Orlando and her accomplices, came under intense scrutiny and eventually was substantially reformed, in both its procedures and—in the Kingdom of Naples—its extensive feudal character. By the start of the new century the old village of Pentidattilo, and the social, economic, legal, and to some extent cultural order of its people, would be significantly altered.

Glossary

arciprete	head priest of a village, in charge of the main parish church (the *arcipretale*)
attuario	see *mastrodattia*
bagliva	office usually owned and rented out by the feudal lord, giving its holder (*baglivo*) jurisdiction over minor misdemeanors
bonatenenza	local tax on allodial (i.e., nonfeudal) property owed to the *università* by all property owners, including the baron
bracciali	field laborers
camera riservata	privilege exempting a fief from military billeting
cancelliere	village scribe, in charge of drafting and preserving the *università* documents
carlino	one-tenth of a ducat
casale	hamlet that did not enjoy administrative autonomy but was part of a *università*
casino	small villa
catasto	direct tax, or the survey drawn for fiscal reasons; the Catasto Onciario of the 1740s and 1750s was a fiscal survey of the entire kingdom
censi	rents on property or lodging
civil viventi or *civili*	those living "civilly," or without a formal occupation
coadiutor curiae or *coadiutore fiscale*	a prosecution lawyer usually representing the plaintiff or the state; literally, "helper of the court"
collettiva	final assessment in a *catasto*
conservatore	administrator of feudal revenues in kind
corpus delicti	physical evidence; literally, "body of the crime"

dittereo	the second priest in a village, usually in charge of the secondary parish (the *dittereale*)
dotario	the husband's gift upon marriage, to be paid at the husband's death
eletti	aldermen of a *università*, usually four or five
erario	administrator of feudal revenues, particularly in money, appointed by the feudal lord from among a fief's citizens
ex officio	procedure in which the judge may act without denunciation or complaint
fiscalari	creditors of the royal government who were assigned shares of the *fiscali*
fiscali	tax payments of each *università* to the royal government
fondaco	monopoly, often owned by the feudal lord, on fees levied on food sales
forese	tenant farmer
forestieri	residents not native to a village or town
fuoco	household
giudice a contratti	contract judge, officer needed to validate contracts
grano	one-hundredth of a ducat
in capillis	with collected hair, said of unmarried young women over twelve years of age
jus habitationis	fee paid by noncitizens to reside in a *università*
magnifico	honorific title bestowed on prominent citizens
massari	wealthier farmers; *massari di bovi* rented out animals
mastro	title given to artisans
mastrodattia	actuary office usually owned and rented out by the feudal lord, entitling the holder (*mastrodatti* or *attuario*) to produce written documents with legal value
oncia	unit of account used in fiscal surveys, equivalent to six ducats; the catasto of the 1740s and 1750s used also *once d'industria* to assess earning capacity and *once di beni* to assess property
pescato	monopoly right over the salting of fish
platea	inventory list of revenues or tenants or parcels of land
prammatiche	royal laws, edicts
prefiche	paid female mourners employed in popular funeral customs

preside   provincial governor, in charge of administrative, judicial, and military affairs

processus informativus   the investigative part of a trial

procurator fisci   lawyer in royal courts guarding the interests of the royal treasury

protopapa   Greek title of the head priest in the parish, same as *arciprete*; his church is the *protopapale*

relationes ad limina   reports to Rome of episcopal visits

relevio   feudal succession tax; also the name of the inquiry to ascertain its amount

ricettizia   type of parish church organization common in the kingdom: each parish owned land and revenues that were shared by the participant clergy (*porzionarii*)

rivele   individual declarations of each household in a fiscal survey

sindacato   evaluation period for former officers, during which grievances against them could be brought

sindaco   mayor

Sommaria   highest financial and fiscal tribunal of the kingdom

sponsi de futuro   couples engaged to be married

status animarum   "list of souls," drawn by parish priests, often for the *catasti*

stuprum   crime consisting of nonviolent, often consensual intercourse with women belonging to protected categories

tarì   one-twentieth of a ducat

terraggio   feudal lord's share of the harvest of feudal land

togati   the robe elite of the kingdom, lawyers and judges

udienze   provincial royal tribunals

università   the legal entity representing the citizens of a village or town

Vicaria   central civil and criminal court in Naples

Notes

ACB	Archivio Caracciolo di Brienza, in ASN
ADRC	Archivio Diocesano di Reggio Calabria
AHR	*American Historical Review*
ASCC	Archivio della Sacra Congregazione del Clero (formerly del Concilio, a detached section of ASV)
ASCL	*Archivio Storico per la Calabria e la Lucania*
ASCZ	Archivio di Stato di Catanzaro
ASN	Archivio di Stato di Napoli
ASPN	*Archivio Storico per le Province Napoletane*
ASRC	Archivio di Stato di Reggio Calabria
ASV	Archivio Segreto Vaticano
MEFRM	*Mélanges de l'École Française de Rome: Moyen Age et Temps Moderne*
QS	*Quaderni Storici*
RSC	*Rivista Storica Calabrese*
RSI	*Rivista Storica Italiana*
TR	Trial records for the trial of Domenica Orlando (ACB, 21.5)

INTRODUCTION

1. For examples of the debate, see Stone, "Revival"; Hobsbawm, "Revival"; Strauss, "Dilemma"; Beik, "Debate" (with Strauss's "Reply"); and Maza, "Stories." On Italy and the use of judicial sources, see Sbriccoli, "Fonti"; Grendi, "Sulla 'storia criminale'"; and Zorzi, "Tradizioni." On microhistory, see note 10 below.

2. I have searched the inventories of several aristocratic archives in ASN, namely, of the Sanseverino di Bisignano, Giudice Caracciolo (which includes the papers of four families), Caracciolo di Santo Bono, Masola di Trentola, Caracciolo di Torella, Tocco di Montemiletto, Ruffo di Scilla, Ruffo di Bagnara, Doria d'Angri, Carafa di Castel San Lorenzo, and Serra di Gerace. The last two are the only ones that include

papers relating to the feudal courts' activities, and the Serra di Gerace's inventory is the only one that mentions the records of two actual trials, held in 1622 and 1723. ACB contains the records of the Pentidattilo trial (21.5), as well as those of several trials dating from the final decades of the old regime, for which see ch. 2.

3. Astarita, *Continuity.*

4. See, e.g., Caridi, *Uno "stato," Il latifondo,* and *Dal feudatario;* Delille, *Croissance;* Ebner, *Storia;* Trasselli, *Lo stato;* Merzario, *Signori;* and Massafra, *Problemi.* A more anthropological study of a small town is Minervino, *La città.*

5. For similar approaches to the study of popular culture and rural society, see, e.g., Vardi, "Peasants"; Sabean, *Power;* Levi, *Inheriting Power;* Robisheaux, *Rural Society;* Schulte, *Village in Court;* Wegert, *Popular Culture;* and Vassberg, *Village.*

6. Recent discussions in Prodi and Penuti, *Disciplina;* see also Chapter 6.

7. Hanley, "Engendering" and "Social Sites."

8. Ginzburg, "Inquisitor." On these issues, see also idem, *Cheese* and *Night Battles;* Levi, *Inheriting Power;* Davis, *Return;* Kuehn, "Reading Microhistory"; introduction and afterword to Muir and Ruggiero, *History from Crime;* Allegra, "Limiti." On women and on courtroom narratives, see Gowing, *Domestic Dangers,* 41–58 and 232–62.

9. Ginzburg, "Clues," "Checking the Evidence," *Il giudice,* "Ekphrasis," and "Aristotele"; see also "Paradigma indiziario."

10. Apart from the works already cited, examples of these studies (with highly varying amounts of methodological discussion) are Brown, *Immodest Acts;* Brucker, *Giovanni and Lusanna;* Cabibbo and Modica, *La Santa dei Tomasi;* Kagan, *Lucrecia's Dreams;* Fiume, *Vecchia;* Merzario, *Anastasia;* Muir, *Mad Blood Stirring;* Hsia, *Trent 1475;* Contreras, *Sotos contra Riquelmes;* Garnot, *Un crime conjugal;* Guarnieri, *Case of Child Murder;* Rosoni, *Criminalità;* and Cook, *Trials.* Methodological discussions are Muir, "Introduction: Observing Trifles"; Levi, "On Microhistory"; Ginzburg, "Microstoria"; Grendi, "Ripensare la microstoria?" Revel, "Microanalisi"; the "Dibattito" between Raggio, Lombardini, and Muir on Muir's *Mad Blood Stirring;* and Egmond and Mason, *Mammoth and the Mouse.* For critiques, see Firpo and Ferrone, "From Inquisitors to Microhistorians"; Cohn, *Women in the Streets,* ch. 1 and passim; and the particularly venomous (though not wholly undeserved) Bertelli, "Review of R. Merzario's *Anastasia.*"

11. Examples are Sheppard, *Lourmarin;* McArdle, *Altopascio;* Dewald, *Pont-St-Pierre;* Brown, *In the Shadow of Florence;* and, for Naples, the works cited above in note 4.

12. A similar approach is in Levi, *Inheriting Power;* see also Raggio, *Faide;* Grendi, *Il Cervo;* and Sabean, *Property* and *Kinship.* Other models of community studies based primarily on judicial sources are Le Roy Ladurie, *Montaillou* and *Carnival in Romans,* and Boyer and Nissenbaum, *La città;* see also a discussion of the connections between social and legal history in Grossi, *Storia sociale,* and Grendi, "Microanalisi."

13. Recent examples of these discussions are in Davis, *Fiction*; the essays in "Porter plainte"; Maza, *Private Lives*; and Gentilcore, "Contesting Illness."

14. Examples of the second approach are the works by Brown, Brucker, and Kagan cited above in note 10, and Kertzer, *Kidnapping*. The last method is employed in Cohen and Cohen, *Words and Deeds*, and in the works, primarily based on letters, of Steven Ozment: *Magdalena and Balthasar, Three Behaim Boys*, and *Bürgermeister's Daughter*; the subtitle of the first book defines Ozment's role as that of "illuminating" the letters. For an example in which the accumulation of narrative detail overwhelms any analysis, see Le Roy Ladurie, *Beggar and the Professor*.

15. Examples in ACB, 19.35, 19.43, 20.4–10; see Chapter 2.

16. See discussions of these issues in Davis, *Fiction*, 16–24; Wegert, *Popular Culture*, 16–18; Greenshields, *Economy*, 182–83; "Porter plainte," 16–19; and Castan, *Honnêteté*, ch. 2.

17. In his inventory of 1663, for instance, the local administrator of feudal revenues still used the letter *X* to reproduce some of the sounds of local names and toponyms, but he also at times replaced the *X* with the more Italian *Ch*, or even *Sc*. Similar examples appear in other documents from that period, while the *X* is no longer used by the eighteenth century, reflecting, if not necessarily a change in local parlance, more awareness of official Italian orthography. ACB, 21.11, 1663 document; other examples in ASN, Relevi 356.17, fols. 298r–301r (1627), and 358.16, fols. 383r–384v (1654).

18. Castan, *Honnêteté*, 115, mentions the same phenomenon with snippets of Occitan dialogue reported in quotation marks.

19. I have used Rohlfs, *Dizionario dialettale*, to help with the vocabulary of the documents.

20. "Tu voi autru che mi ti fazzu muriri a toi maritu," TR, fol. 28r. This is the only occasion in which the typical Calabrian spellings with a predominance of *i*, *u*, and *z* appear, along with the "toi" for "your" (instead of the Italian "tuo"), and the "a" construction for the direct object.

21. See, e.g., the near absence of the Kingdom of Naples in Zorzi, "Tradizioni," and Dean and Lowe, *Crime*.

O N E   *The Village of Pentidattilo, Its Lords, and the State*

1. Lear, *Journals*, 122; Lear spells the village's name Pentedatilo. The name, from the Greek word for five fingers, is inspired by the shape of the rock situated above the village and is one of the many signs of the area's Greek heritage. On place names in this area, see Rohlfs, *Dizionario toponomastico*. On Lear's Italian journals, see D'Angelo, "Viaggiatori."

2. Giustiniani, *Dizionario geografico, sub voce*; Minicucci, "Il feudo"; and De Lorenzo, *Un terzo manipolo*, 225–40. The assessment (reported in Minicucci) dates from 1688; there are no equivalent data for Pentidattilo, but feudal succession tax figures

indicate annual feudal income of about 850 ducats at that time. ASN, Relevi 390.2, fols. 104r–127r (1689).

3. ASN, Collaterale Provvisioni 248, fols. 160r–161v (1682); ACB, 21.1; and the following published sources: Confuorto, *Giornali,* 1:146–47 and 2:38; Spanò-Bolani, *Storia,* 2:67–76 (who declares his version "a tragic domestic story which will horrify my readers"); and Mandalari, *Note,* 3–33. Less useful accounts are in Salazar, "La strage" and De Lorenzo, *Monografie,* 56–58. All these versions depend on the same original brief chronicle, which I have been unable to locate. Costantino, *La tragedia,* and Ficara de Palma, *Storia,* are fictionalized accounts, testimonies to the enduring dramatic appeal of the story. The only tourist postcard of Pentidattilo I have found also mentions the massacre in its description of the village, as does Laruffa, *Pentidattilo.* Bernardino had been born around 1650; his homonymous grandfather had been threatened by his vassals in 1648. Spadaro, *Società in rivolta,* 82–83 and 224–28 (Spadaro conflates the two Bernardino into one); see also *Dizionario biografico, sub voce,* and ASN, Carte Gerace, 3:916.

4. It was the Tuesday after Easter, hence the name "Easter massacre" for the events. Some sources report 40 armed men with Bernardino, others 150. Confuorto, *Giornali,* 1:146.

5. Most sources only mention one slain brother, Simone, and Francesco had likely died previously; in any case, it is clear that Bernardino intended to leave no male Alberti alive and to make Antonia heir to the fief. The children's uncle Francesco avoided death, probably by hiding. Anna was sixteen years old. The slain Lorenzo was later buried in one of the village chapels; as he was killed before one year had elapsed since his father's death, the family was exempted from paying a second relevio, which is why the date of his death became of interest to the fiscal tribunal. ASN, Relevi 390.2bis, fol. 91r (1690). For the marriage, see also Russo, *Storia,* 2:76–77.

6. Minicucci, "Il feudo"; ASN, Collaterale Provvisioni 284, Assensi Feudali, fols. 99r–103v; and ACB, 19.53 and 54. The fact that Bernardino escaped judgment and that summary justice was applied to his men means that there is no judicial record of the events narrated here. The scarcity of sources, apart from the brief narrative ones I have just reviewed, makes it impossible to give this episode the detailed analysis it would deserve.

7. ACB, 19.49 and 50, and 21.1.

8. One would think that this story is violent enough. However, an even more shocking, though totally false, version was in circulation when Lear visited the area, and he reported it in his *Journals,* 123–25. In this thoroughly gothic tale it is Antonia herself who opens the castle to Bernardino, thinking that he wishes simply to elope with her. Bernardino, once in the castle, takes his atrocious vengeance on the Alberti family. He first attacks Lorenzo while he sleeps, and the latter, awakening after the first blow, suspects his own wife—sleeping at his side—of the act and quickly stabs and kills her before succumbing to Bernardino's repeated blows. The dying Lorenzo falls

on a wall and stains it with a bloody five-fingered print that echoes the village's name. Antonia soon after her forced marriage becomes mute and insane and poisons herself within a month. Bernardino, unpunished, lords it over the two villages, but the quarrel between the two families continues as an Alberti grandson survives the slaughter and later murders Bernardino's family and blinds and imprisons Bernardino. This "Calabrian horror" ends when the castle, struck by an earthquake, buries both Bernardino and the last Alberti!

9. Reggio Calabria is the current name of the city, to distinguish it from Reggio Emilia in the North; in the early modern period the city was called simply Reggio.

10. Giustiniani, *Dizionario, sub vocibus.* See also Mazzella, *Descrittione,* 149–72.

11. Labrot, *Quand l'histoire murmure,* esp. pt. 1; on population and mountainous settlements in the Mediterranean, see McNeill, *Mountains,* 176–189, for southern Italian examples.

12. Grimaldi, *Saggio,* 180. Many descriptions of the kingdom were written at the end of the eighteenth century, such as Alfano, *Istorica descrizione,* 92–117, for Calabria Ultra; idem, *Compendio,* 81–100, for Calabria Ultra; Sacco, *Dizionario,* 2:204–5 for Melito and 3:55 for Pentidattilo; and Giustiniani, *Dizionario.* On the image of Calabria in travelers and other writers, see Placanica, *Storia della Calabria,* 255–86.

13. For the geography, climate, and morphology of Calabria, see Gambi, *La Calabria,* quote on 65; Placanica, *La Calabria,* vol. 1, ch. 1; idem, "I caratteri originali"; and Filangieri, *Territorio,* pt. 2; on roads, see De Rosa, "Land and Sea Transport."

14. Gambi, *La Calabria,* 292 and 462–67. Calabria had 93 titled feudal lords and 123 simple barons, whose fiefs, along with the region's 124 uninhabited fiefs, covered 83% of its territory, a higher percentage than the kingdom's average. Placanica, "I caratteri originali," 93–95.

15. Milone, *Memoria;* Lupo, *Il giardino degli aranci,* ch. 1; Matacena, *Architettura,* 92–94. Similar market forces and production structures applied to licorice, another celebrated Calabrian product. Matacena, *Architettura,* 77–83.

16. Filangieri, *Territorio,* 125–53.

17. Placanica, *La Calabria,* vol. 1, ch. 2; idem, *Uomini,* chs. 1 and 2 (with slightly different figures for the expansion); Galasso, *Economia e società,* 99–114; Da Molin, *Popolazione e società,* 7–81. See table 1.1. On other regions, see Visceglia, *Territorio,* 52–92, and Volpe, *Il Cilento,* chs. 1 and 5.

18. Filangieri, *Territorio,* 154–55 and 239–42; Placanica, "I Caratteri originali," 16–17, 40–41.

19. See, for instance, ADRC, the manuscript report of the 1597 visit by Archbishop Annibale D'Afflitto, fols. 76r–104r.

20. The disputes in ACB, 19.3 (1578, with San Lorenzo), and ASN, Sommaria Partium 1226 (1592, with Montebello). There are also four other references to such disputes in one of the old inventories of the Sommaria Partium series, though the state of the collection is such that I was unable to find the actual documents; the references,

all from inventory 6, are to Sommaria Partium 855 (1580–81, with Reggio), 1169 (1590, with Reggio), and 1246-II and 1256-II (both 1592–93, with Montebello). Notary Nicola Maria Pannuti appears in ASN, Torri e Castelli 37, fols. 661r–663r (1589). For comparisons with a much larger Calabrian village, see the demographic information in Merzario, *Signori*; population trends in Pentidattilo were similar to those in nearby, and larger, Motta. Caridi, *Dal feudatario,* 43–47.

21. The early census data are from Giustiniani, *Dizionario, sub voce*; the bishops' information is in ADRC, the 1597 report, which counted 100 households and 400 souls, and in ASV, Sacra Congregazione del Concilio, Rheginen, 685-A, the 1603 report, fols. 155r ff., counting 400 souls; the 1683 report, fol. 141r, counting 622 souls; the 1686 report, fols. 147r–v, counting 174 households and 590 souls; the 1690 report, unnumbered fol., counting 150 households and 500 souls; the 1693 report, unnumbered fol., counting 160 households and 536 souls; and the 1729 report, unnumbered fol., counting 766 souls. The bishops' figures represent an indication of trends rather than absolute figures. The official tax figure for the village stayed at 99 households from 1595 to 1669—e.g., ASN, Diversi Sommaria, I serie, 72, unnumbered fol.; it then stayed for a long time at 116 households, as seen also in ASN, Tesorieri e Percettori 4292/684, 4293/685, 4294/686, 4315/707, 4316/708, 4318/710, fol. 27r, 4319/711, fol. 26r (all dating between 1694 and 1712); Conti Comunali 214.2, Calabria Ultra, fols. 84r–v (1718); Frammenti di Fuochi, 192bis, fol. 179v (1701–2). The 1732 figure is in ASN, Attuari diversi Sommaria, fascio 523, processo 34, fols. 74r–76r. Zilli, *Imposta diretta,* 159 and 203, reports 153 households calculated for fiscal purposes in 1732, reduced to 125 in 1737. The 1745 and 1759 censuses are in ASN, Catasto Onciario 6090 and 6091. See table 1.2.

22. ASCZ, Cassa Sacra, Segreteria Ecclesiastica, busta 39, fascicolo 907 (1788 on), fol. 8r. Melito's growth is evident in the papers of notary Francesco Celia in ASRC, notai, busta 420, fascicoli 2217–24 (1740–54), and in ACB, 19, e.g., 19.94 and 95.

23. The 1795 figure is in Galanti, *Giornale,* 371 and 481–84; Giustiniani, *Dizionario,* for 1804; Valente, *Dizionario,* 2:609–11 and 731–32. See also table 1.2.

24. Filangieri, *Territorio,* 237–38; Rodotà, *Dell'origine,* 1:410; Petropoulou, "Lingua"; Ferrari, "Greci e albanesi"; Zangari, *Le colonie.* On the Greek and Albanian presence in southern Puglia, the other major area of settlement, see Visceglia, *Territorio,* 93–104. See Chapter 6 for a discussion of the religious history of the area.

25. Much of the information in this section is taken from the works of local erudites; see Russo, *Storia,* 1:40, 304, 314–15, 325–26, 329, 336, 362, 376; Mandalari, *Note,* notes; "Registri di Cancelleria"; a survey of Calabria's history is in Mafrici, "Calabria Ulteriore."

26. On these issues, see Astarita, *Continuity.*

27. ASN, Relevi 347.7, fols. 111r–115v (1546); the 1477 grant to Giacomo de Letizia is in ASN, Cedolari Nuovi 81, fols. 316r–317v (which, with fols. 365r–366r, 611r–v, and 710v, recapitulates some of the feudal history of the village); Valente, *Dizionario,* 2:731–32, gives the date as 1447, probably a copying mistake. The Francoperta grants

are also in ASRC, Statuti Capitoli Grazie Apprezzi e Privilegi (hereafter cited as "Statuti Capitoli"), busta 2, fascicoli 133–34; and the full 1509 grant is in ASN, Relevi 390.2bis, fols. 144r ff. A list of the Francoperta lords is in ACB, 19.46. See also table 1.3.

28. In 1594, for instance, the coastal area of Pentidattilo was sacked, women and children killed or captured, and the local tower stormed; Valente, *Le torri*, 61; idem, *Calabria*, 195 and 240. On piracy in Calabria, see also idem, "L'incursione"; Aromolo, "Notizie"; Riggio, "Corsari"; and Crispo, "Incursioni." On the tower, see ASN, Torri e Castelli 36, fols. 262r–263r (1589); 37, fols. 661r–663r (1589); 39, fols. 159r–160r (1594); 42, fols. 642r–643r (1606); 44, fols. 227r–228r (1626); 46, fols. 211r–218v (1707); and 120, old fols. 1283r–1300r (1569–70). On Ottoman and Berber raids in other regions, see Visceglia, *Territorio*, 109–114; Volpe, *Il Cilento*, ch. 2; Bono, *Corsari*.

29. ASN, Relevi 347.7, fols. 111r–115v (1546); 351.16, fols. 588r–600v (1587); 380.6, fols. 117r–120v, and 380.18, fols. 414r–415v (1585); and 382.2, fols. 37r–39v (1591).

30. The genealogy of the Alberti is in ACB, 3.2.19, and in ASN, Carte Gerace, 3:893. The full formal investiture is in ACB, 19.5 (the revenues from fiefs were usually calculated at 4% of the capital value); examples of Simonello's businesses are in ACB, 19.7–8; his will is in ACB, 19.9; see also all of ACB, 19, 20, and 21. Pentidattilo came rather cheap, if one compares its price, for instance, with the 316,000 ducats paid in 1616 by the Saluzzo to purchase Corigliano. Merzario, *Signori*, 101. On the fief's history, see also ASN, Relevi 354.3, fols. 29r–57r (1602); 356.17, fols. 288r–314r (1627); 384.1 (1648); 358.16, fols. 334r–385r (1648–54); 390.2 (1686); 390.2bis (1690, which includes on fols. 104r–106v the 1589 purchase receipt); 367.6 (1691); Significatorie dei Relevi 66, fols. 129r–131r (1658); 83, fols. 37r–59v and 488r–493r (1690s); 85, fol. 120r (1690s); Cedolari Nuovi 80, fol. 20v.

31. On the Ottoman raids, see ACB, 21.11, esp. the 1663 document, fol. 25v; on economic developments in general, see Astarita, *Continuity*, ch. 2, and Lepre, *Storia*.

32. ASN, Relevi 354.3, fols. 29r–v; 356.17, fols. 292r and 288r–290v; ACB, 19.13–14.

33. ACB, 19.12 and 15; ASRC, Statuti Capitoli, busta 1, fascicolo 22, agreement of March 21, 1648; ASN, Collaterale Partium 430, fols. 87r–v, and 432, fols. 55r–v (both old numbering); ASN, Sommaria Partium 2080, fols. 186v–187r and 253v–254v (1621), 2094, fols. 131r–137r and 237v–238r (1621), and 2220, fols. 187v–188r (1631); ASN, Relevi 358.16, fols. 341r and 382r–v. On the revolt, see the classic Villari, *La rivolta*.

34. Spadaro, *Società*, 64 and 192–95; see also Rovito, *La rivolta*.

35. See ACB, 19, esp. documents 11, 18, 20, 23, and 30.

36. ACB, 19.19, 24, 25, and 19.26–27 for the ceremonies, for which see also Mariotti, *Problemi*, 322, and Russo, *Storia*, 2:85. ACB, 19.45, for Lorenzo's birth; ADRC, the baptismal records of Pentidattilo, for the baptisms of members of the family: the four children born in the village were Francesco (baptized February 10, 1675), Simone (baptized August 19, 1676), Teodora (baptized January 1, 1678), and Giovanna (baptized June 1, 1681).

37. ACB, 19.35 and 42; ASN, Relevi 390.2, fols. 2r–8r, for economic developments.

On the revolt, see Di Bella, *La rivolta,* particularly the essay by Di Bella and Marzotti, "Nella spirale."

38. ACB, 19.40, 43, 44, and 49; Pietro Cortes was later also governor of Capua and died in 1702.

39. ACB, 19.51, 55, 59, 62, and 68; ACB, 20.1 and 21.2; ASN, Relevi 367.6, fols. 413r–508v; Teodora's marriage contract in ACB, 140.42, fols. 23r–39r; her dowry consisted, as usual with an heiress, of all her assets, including the fief and its title; on the Ruffo, see Caridi, *La spada.*

40. Astarita, *Continuity,* on the Caracciolo di Brienza; ACB, 19.73–75 and 78; ACB, 18.80; ACB, 4.1.57, a 1758 inventory of Teodora's property, describes the contents of the family's new *casino* (villa) in Melito, which had nine rooms plus storage spaces, a stable, and a small fort; another inventory for 1759 in ACB, 21.11, describes the *casino,* which also included a chapel, a belvedere, and an oven; the fort included a prison. On the Austrian period, see Villari, "La Calabria."

41. The notary is Francesco Celia, whose surviving papers are in ASRC, cited in note 22 above; fascicolo 2220, fols. 6r–v (1747), notes the presence of a medical doctor in Melito; see also ACB, 4.1.56a, 4.1.52b, 19.88, and Russo, *Storia,* 2:30. For the general economic development of the kingdom in the early eighteenth century, see Di Vittorio, *Gli Austriaci,* and Calabria, "Per la storia."

42. ACB, 19.91, and ASRC, Demani, inventario 33, busta 241, fascicolo 1; ACB, 8.53, fol. 9v; Litterio's succession is in ASN, Intestazioni feudali 17, no. 300, and ASN, Cedolari Nuovi 85, fols. 490v–491v; no relevio was due at Teodora's death because of the extraordinary one paid in 1708 by all feudal lords to help royal war expenses.

43. The sale is in ACB, 8.51–53; ASN, Refute dei Quinternioni 226, fols. 528–35, and ASN, Cedolari Nuovi 85, fols. 554r–560r (Cedolari Nuovi 87, fols. 445v–451v, records the succession in 1790 of Alessandro Clemente to his father, Lorenzo). The disputes are in ASRC, Demani, inventario 33, busta 241, fascicolo 2 (pt. 2, fol. 1r, for the quote), and ASN, Bollettino delle Sentenze della Commissione Feudale, vol. 12 (1809), pp. 289–92, no. 38, and vol. 4 (1810), pp. 179–81, no. 28.

44. For the shifts in parish titles and residence, see Russo, *Storia,* 2:159–60, and Mandalari, *Note,* notes; see also ASCZ, Cassa Sacra, Vendite e censuazioni, busta 31, fascicolo 1510 (1786), and ASCZ, Cassa Sacra, Segreteria ecclesiastica, busta 39, fascicolo 908, fols. 4r–5v and 6r–7v. Many new names appear in the documents relating to the sale of church property in the 1780s and 1790s.

45. See Placanica, L'*"Iliade Funesta,"* with documents. Among contemporary reports of the earthquake is one by Sir William Hamilton, the English ambassador to Naples and husband of the notorious Emma, who toured the area shortly after the catastrophe. Hamilton, *Relazione.*

46. Vivenzio, *Istoria;* Carbone-Grio, *I terremoti,* 143–52; the quotes in Placanica, L'*"Iliade Funesta,"* 79–80, both from the report by the royal representative Pignatelli.

47. Mandalari, "La terra," quotes on 112, 122, and 137.

48. Astarita, *Continuity*, 108–19; Spagnoletti, *"L'incostanza delle umane cose"*; Galasso, *Economia e società*, 293–324; Spadaro, *Società*, ch. 1; Cancila, *Baroni e popolo*, 193–95; Muto, "Istituzioni." The phenomenon occurred also elsewhere; Gutton, *La sociabilité*, ch. 3, and Vassberg, *Village*, ch. 1.

49. See Chapter 3; given the rare use of written documents in village life, the absence of records for the parliaments, which rarely survive for any community, is not surprising.

50. Cervellino, *Direttione*; Pecori, *Del privato governo*, 1:106–7, for the requirements. See also the *prammatiche de administratione universitatum* (on the administration of università) in Giustiniani, *Nuova collezione*, 1:251–306.

51. Fiscal sources detail the different treatment of citizens and foreigners (*forestieri*); see Chapter 3. Sources always specify the università of origin and citizenship of all individuals; see the trial records for the public perception of Pietro and Anna (quote in TR, fol. 16r). On outsiders in Spanish villages, see Vassberg, *Village*, ch. 1.

52. The main treatise on feudal abuses and disputes between università and their lords is Novario, *De vassallorum*.

53. Astarita, *Continuity*, esp. ch. 2, and also the prammatiche *de baronibus et eorum officio* (on barons and their office) in Giustiniani, *Nuova collezione*, 3:95–115. In Pentidattilo there was an erario but no conservatore.

54. See Chapter 2.

55. On the contacts between state and village elsewhere in Europe, see Vassberg, *Village*, and Schneider, "Village" (I thank Zoë Schneider for letting me cite her work).

56. Examples of all these communications are in ASN, Diversi Sommaria, I serie, 72, unnumbered fols. on Calabria Ultra, *sub voce*; Voci di Vettovaglie 56.6 (1721), fol. 109r; Tesorieri e Percettori 4292/684, 4293/685, 4294/686, 4315/707, 4316/708, 4318/710, 4319/711, all *sub voce*; Attuarî diversi Sommaria 523.34, fols. 74r–76r; Fiscali e Adoe 5bis, fol. 65v, 6, no. 413, fol. 21r, and 13, *sub voce*; and esp. Torri e Castelli 36 (1589), fols. 262r–263r, 37 (1589), fols. 661r–663r, 39 (1594), fols. 159r–160r, 42 (1606), fols. 642r–643r, 44 (1626), fols. 227r–228r, 46 (1707), fols. 211r–218v, 120 (1569–70), fols. 1283r–1300r (old numbering). Several of these last documents include the seal of the università, which depicts a hand in the foreground with five rocks resembling fingers in the back, and a large leaf.

57. The formal recognition of the new lord was accompanied by a ceremony known as the taking of possession, which was echoed sometimes also in private transactions to mark the new ownership of land or buildings. A description from Pentidattilo, for a sale of land and two houses, is in ASRC, notai, busta 420, fascicolo 2220, fols. 16v–17v (1747): the new owner walked and sat on the land, gathered stones, and dug up soil; he then entered the two houses and opened and closed their doors and windows. See also Astarita, *Continuity*, 129–30, and ACB, 19.43, 45, 55, and 56.

58. Examples in ASN, Relevi 347.7 (1536), 380.6 and 380.18 (1584), 351.16 (1587), 382.2 (1591), 354.3 (1602), 382.64 (1604), 356.17 (1627), 358.16 (1651), 384.I (1655), 390.2

(1686), 390.2bis (1690), and 367.6 (1691); Significatorie dei Relevi 66, fols. 129r–131r (1658), 83, fols. 37r–59v and 488r–493r (1691), and 85, fol. 120r (1696).

59. ASN, Torri e Castelli, cited in note 56 above; the Latin expression is "persona idiota et scribere nesciens," in which "idiota" still had the original meaning of illiterate, though it was flanked by the already less offensive-sounding "scribere nesciens." The scribe verified the crosses. See also ASN, Relevi 382.2, fols. 37r–39v (1591). On literacy and the implications of the ability to sign one's name, see Pellizzari, *Sulle vie*.

60. ACB, 19.17; ASN, Relevi 390.2bis, fol. 31r; ASN, Catasto Onciario 6091, fol. 2r, and 6090; ASCZ, Cassa Sacra, Miscellanea B-7, fascicolo 161; other examples in the Relevi cited in note 58 above. See also Di Vittorio, *Gli Austriaci*, 2:429.

61. ASN, Torri e Castelli 37, fols. 661r–v (1589), and 120, fol. 1283r ff. (1569; old numbering), for Pannuti (none of Pannuti's records survive); ASRC, notai, busta 420, fascicoli 2217–24 for Celia; ASCZ, Cassa Sacra, Segreteria Ecclesiastica, busta 39, fascicolo 908 (1794), fols. 4r–7v, for Familari.

62. See, e.g., ASRC, notai, busta 420, fascicolo 2217, fols. 6v–7r (1740).

63. ASN, Relevi 358.16, fol. 385r; the 1648 erario stated that in the few cases in which he had had written documentation prepared for feudal rents he had asked the mastrodatti to provide it. ASN, Relevi 384.I, fol. 5v.

64. ASRC, Statuti Capitoli, busta 1, fascicolo 22, pp. 7–8 (this is a nineteenth-century copy of the original agreement). The chancellor was paid 12 ducats a year according to a 1718 budget for the università, and 6 or 8 ducats a year at the time of the 1745 and 1759 catasti. ASN, Conti Comunali 214, Calabria Ultra, fascicolo 2, fols. 84r–v, and Catasto Onciario 6091, fol. 52v, and 6090, fols. 24r–v and 835r.

65. ASN, Relevi 367.6, fols. 429r–430r, 436r, 446r–v, 472r–v, and 484v.

66. ASN, Catasto Onciario 6091, fol. 2r; ACB, 19.93.

67. ASN, Relevi 358.16, fol. 378r; see also the marquis's report to the central government about the destroyed papers, ASN, Collaterale Partium 430, fols. 87r–v (old numbering), also cited in Spadaro, *Società*, 64 (with wrong reference).

68. Sallmann, "Alphabétisation," argues, on the other hand, for the exclusion of the illiterate masses from all power; see also Burke, *Historical Anthropology*, ch. 9; Collomp, *La maison du père*, ch. 8; Cressy, *Literacy*; Raggio, "Costruzione."

69. ASN, Relevi 384.I, fols. 5v and 8r–9r (1655); 390.2, fols. 2r–8r (1686); 367.6, fol. 484v (1694).

70. ASN, Relevi 358.16, fols. 373r–v; see also fols. 374r–378r. Of course, age indications in these documents are likely to be approximate and probably exaggerated, but that too is indicative of the respect expected to be granted to old age. Similar examples in Grendi, "La pratica dei confini," and Vardi, "Peasants and the Law"; see also Vassberg, *Village*, 20–23 and 119–22.

71. ASN, Sommaria Partium 1226, fol. 232r (1592); ACB, 20.4 (1662); ACB, 21.8 (1669–72; the quotes on fols. 73r–v). Needless to say, the San Lorenzo witnesses themselves had few gracious things to say about the Pentidattilesi.

72. ADRC, baptismal records for Pentidattilo, book covering the years 1667–1703; when I saw them, the inquiries and the testimonies appeared in unnumbered pages inserted in the pages covering the years between 1673 and 1680, and they were dated between 1686 and 1730. Other examples in Frascadore, "Livelli," 178–79, and Merzario, *Il paese stretto*, 7 and 35–36.

73. ASN, Catasto Onciario 6090 and 6091; ASCZ, Cassa Sacra, Vendite e censuazioni, busta 31, fascicoli 1499–1512, and busta 37, fascicoli 1742–1759, all dating from 1786.

74. E.g., TR, fols. 7v, 12r, and 15v; similar examples in Garnot, *Un crime*, 40–49; on these issues, see also Merzario, "La buona memoria."

75. ASRC, Statuti Capitoli, busta 1, fascicolo 36; in 1682 the università of Pentidattilo had accused Montebello of innovations in their sharing of border waters. ASN, Collaterale Provvisioni 248, fols. 160r–161v. Raggio, "Costruzione," reports similar uses of memorable events to establish borders within a system of mainly oral proof.

76. ASRC, Demani, inventario 33, busta 241, fascicolo 1, fols. 9r–55r.

77. Similar considerations in Crouzet-Pavan, "Testimonianze."

T W O   *Jurisprudence and Local Judicial Practice*

1. Similar considerations in Reinhardt, *Justice*, 183–84, and Greenshields, *Economy*, 58–59.

2. The archive of the Caracciolo di Brienza contains partial records of a few other trials from Pentidattilo's feudal court, but these all pertain to the defense of feudal privileges and the prosecution of their violators. ACB, 20.4–10. All information on the trial comes from the trial records, so I indicate the folio numbers only for direct quotations.

3. The records consistently refer to the house as Domenica's, not Antonino's; though Antonino was dead and Domenica still living in it, this seems to indicate that she had been the original owner. There is no evidence about Antonino's estate, and no marriage contracts from Pentidattilo survive for this period, so it is impossible to know what each spouse had brought to the marriage. Because of the ruinous state of the old village today, it is impossible to determine which houses Domenica and Anna inhabited, though witnesses stated that they were near the parish church of San Pietro, in the center of the village.

4. TR, fols. 2r–v; the records have two sets of numbers, an older one and a more recent one in pencil which is higher by one because it also counts the front page of the bundle; I refer always to this second number.

5. This is reflected also in the large number of treatises from this time entitled simply *Praxis* or *Practica*.

6. I discuss some of these issues in more detail in Chapter 5.

7. Giulio Guerrera was the università's chancellor in 1718. ASN, Conti Comunali

214, Calabria Ultra, fascicolo 2, fols. 84r–v. Members of the family appear frequently in the acts of notary Francesco Celia in the 1740s (ASRC, notai, busta 420, fascicoli 2217–24) and in many other eighteenth-century village documents, e.g., ASN, Catasto Onciario 6090, fol. 6r; ASRC, Demani, inventario 33, busta 241, fascicolo 1, fols. 9r–13v and 45r–50v; and ASRC, Carte e Miscellanea Blasco, 4b E, fols. 593r–598v.

8. Ajello, *Giuristi*; Rovito, *Respublica*; Cernigliaro, *Sovranità*.

9. See Astarita, *Continuity*, 202–6; Povolo, "Considerazioni"; Gasparini, "Signori"; Zamperetti, *I piccoli principi*; Dewald, *Pont-St-Pierre*, ch. 4 and 251–63; Chittolini et al., *Origini*; Musi, *Mezzogiorno spagnolo*; Tocci, introduction to Tocci, *Le comunità*; Benadusi, *Provincial Elite*.

10. Astarita, *Continuity*, 71–81 and 108–131, and Spagnoletti, "Il governo." The lords' jurisdiction was not nearly as extensive in Spain or France—see, e.g., Tomás y Valiente, *El derecho*, 192; Schneider, "Village"; Castan, *Justice*, 103–21 and 149–55 (in Languedoc, though, 54% of rural litigation still took place in seignorial courts in 1779–90); and the survey by Ago, *La feudalità*.

11. See the prammatiche *de baronibus et eorum officio* (on barons and their office) in Giustiniani, *Nuova collezione*, 3:95–115; for other edicts affecting jurisdiction, see especially the titles *de carcerariis* (on prison wardens) and *de compositionibus et commutationibus poenarum* (on compositions and commutations of penalties) in vol. 3; *de officialibus et his, quae eis prohibeantur* (on officials and the things forbidden to them) in vol. 8; *de officio iudicum et aliorum officialium* (on the office of judges and other officials) in vol. 9; *de ordine et forma iudiciorum* (on the order and form of trials) and *de quaestionibus* (on torture) in vol. 12; and all those on specific crimes and magistracies.

12. Among these treatises, which form the basis for these pages, are de Leonardis, *Prattica*; de Angelis, *Tractatus*; Novario, *De vassallorum*; Capobianco, *Tractatus*; Cervellino, *Direttione*; Tassone, *Observationes*, 141–74 and 354–72; and Briganti, *Pratica*; a survey of jurisdictions is Miceli, "La giurisdizione."

13. De Angelis, *Tractatus*, 5 and 184.

14. "Composition" was the power of courts to settle cases with defendants; it consisted not of reduced sentences or acceptances of guilt but of payments (in cash or property) by the defendant to the court in exchange for dropping the case. Compositions took place when there was proof or a confession; if there were only clues, the process was called a transaction. Ajello, *Il problema*, 88.

15. De Leonardis, *Prattica*, 45–53.

16. For a description of the activities and concerns of episcopal courts from the Pentidattilo area, see ASCC, Fondo Concilî 21 Calabria, the volume covering the 1602 provincial council, pt. 3, fols. 25r ff.; see also Mancino, "Ecclesiastical Justice."

17. These fiefs are studied in depth in Astarita, *Continuity*.

18. ACB, 94–107; ACB, 108, contains the "inventory" of cases between 1742 and 1792. Total cases for each fief are 109 for Atena, 180 for Brienza, 91 for Pietrafesa, 128 for

Sasso. Since there are no other records with which to compare them, I do not know whether these records, even those for 1780–1806, are exhaustive.

19. Cases of disputed jurisdiction also include, besides many thus called in the records, a few others such as violations of the lord's rights or edicts and escapes from or damage to the feudal prison.

20. Often these cases originated from a denunciation by the parish priest, so that the feudal court served as an instrument for the enforcement of church-sanctioned morality.

21. This resulted from the sale of a pig to an unemancipated minor, whose father sued to rescind the sale.

22. For other examples, see the essays in "Porter plainte."

23. These two examples, among many, appear in the records of notary Celia, fascicolo 2217 (1740), fols. 3v–6v.

24. Examples in ACB, 19.35 and 43.

25. ASN, Relevi 358.16, fols. 348r–352r (1649).

26. On conflict, see ASRC, Demani, inventario 33, busta 241, fascicoli 1 and 2; see also Astarita, *Continuity,* 146–57, and Chapter 1 of the present volume. For the pescato, see ACB, 20.5–10 (early eighteenth century), and ASN, Sommaria Partium 2075, fols. 158r–159r (1620). Another example of the governor as the Sommaria's delegate is in ASN, Sommaria Partium 2220, fols. 187v–188r (1631). On the beneficial role of baronial jurisdiction, see also D'Amelia, *Orgoglio.*

27. The first quote is in Capobianco, *Tractatus* (1614 ed.), 445, the second one in de Jorio, *Feracissimus tractatus,* 389; Novario, *De vassallorum,* discusses twenty possible cases of baronial abuse relating to feudal prisons. The università was supposed to contribute to the expense for a civil prison; see de Angelis, *Tractatus,* 314. Examples of the expense and problems a prolonged stay in prison could cause for the vassals are found in the trials of Rocco Lopardi (ACB, 99, in 1778–81), Domenico Biondo (ACB, 98, in 1787), and Angelo del Nigro (ACB, 96, in 1802).

28. ASRC, Statuti Capitoli, busta 1, fascicolo 22, pp. 8–9; ACB, 21.11, particularly the 1759 description. In 1809 one of the items in a dispute between the marquis and Pentidattilo was the fact that the marquis, because there was no prison, forced delinquent villagers to be jailed in other, distant fiefs; ASN, Bollettino delle Sentenze della Commissione Feudale, vol. 12 (1809), pp. 289–92, no. 38. There were also prisons in the castles of the Caracciolo Brienza in their other fiefs; Astarita, *Continuity,* 122–23.

29. One way in which jurisdiction could add to feudal revenues, besides the fines and fees of justice, was in the power to compose disputes, of both a civil (often cases of debt) and criminal nature, by releasing delinquents in exchange for the cession of land to the baron; examples of land received in this way appear in the 1663 list of baronial holdings in Pentidattilo, ACB, 21.11. On feudal jurisdiction specifically in Calabria, see also Cozzetto, *Territorio,* ch. 8.

30. See prammatica V *de baronibus* (1536) in Giustiniani, *Nuova collezione,* vol. 3.

31. See esp. prammatiche IV (1536), XXI (1567), and XXIII (1613) *de baronibus*; de Angelis, *Tractatus*, 6.

32. Capobianco, *Tractatus* (1622 ed.), 115; prammatica IX *de officialibus et his, quae eis prohibeantur* (1579) in Giustiniani, *Nuova collezione*, vol. 8. This is another sign of the importance attached to godparenthood; see Chapter 4.

33. De Angelis, *Tractatus*, 25–27. On illiteracy in other officials, see Pecori, *Del privato governo*, 1:106–7.

34. Rovito, "Le riforme" (the quote, from Briganti's treatise, is on 560); Del Bagno, *Legum doctores*; D'Amelia, *Orgoglio*, 54–60.

35. ASN, Sommaria Partium 2080, fols. 186v–187r and 253v–254v.

36. Capobianco, *Tractatus* (1614 ed.), 256, and Novario, *De vassallorum*, pt. 1, nos. 161–62, and pt. 3, nos. 91–92 and 94; Novario, *De vassallorum*, pt. 3, no. 103, on the indigents' defense lawyer. Only the prince of Bisignano, by special privilege, could keep a procurator fisci. Cervellino, *Direttione*, 156–57.

37. At least in the secular sense, heresy was, of course, a victimless crime, as the offense to God left no physical traces. Brundage, "Proof," argues that banning the sexual activity of clerics was as important as heresy in causing changes in procedure. On medieval backgrounds, see also Berman, *Law*.

38. Among the texts I have used are Levy, "Accusatorial and Inquisitorial Systems"; Lenman and Parker, "The State"; Soman, "Deviance"; Tedeschi, *Prosecution of Heresy*, esp. ch. 5; Langbein, *Prosecuting Crime*; Esmein, *Histoire*; Andrews, *Law*; Cameron, *Crime*; Muchembled, *Le temps des supplices*; van Dülmen, *Theatre of Horror*; Strauss, *Law*; Scholz, *Fallstudien*; Reviglio della Veneria, *L'inquisizione*; Weisser, *Crime*; Fasano Guarini, "Produzione"; and Levack, *Witch-Hunt*, 69–84; see also Elmsley and Knafla, *Crime History*.

39. On jurisprudence, see Calisse, *Svolgimento* and *Storia*; Mereu, *Storia*; Maclean, *Interpretation*; on the Italian states, Brackett, *Criminal Justice*; Stern, *Criminal Law System*; Berlinguer and Colao, *Le politiche criminali*; Cattini and Romani, *Il potere di giudicare*; Dean and Lowe, *Crime*, esp. the introduction by Dean and Lowe; Povolo, "Aspetti e problemi"; Marchetti, *Testis contra se*; Ambrosini, "Diritto e società"; Ascheri, *Tribunali*, chs. 3 and 4; on Southern Italy, Trifone, "Diritto"; Pescione, *Corti*; Vallone, "Il pensiero."

40. On executions, see Farge, *Fragile Lives*, 177–204; Spierenburg, *Spectacle of Suffering*; Evans, *Rituals of Retribution*; Paglia, *La morte confortata*; Prosperi, "Esecuzioni"; Zorzi, "Rituali"; Panico, *Il carnefice*; Notari, "La Compagnia"; Romeo, *Aspettando il boia*.

41. I have consulted a number of treatises on judicial procedure, for both Naples and other areas of Europe: Ambrosino, *Processus* (this was a very popular handbook, published five times between 1597 and 1620, and is the clearest of those here cited); Follerio, *Practica*; Claro, *Opera* (Claro was one of the most famous jurists of the sixteenth century; see Massetto, *Un magistrato*); Carpzov, *Practica* (this was the main work of

early modern German jurisprudence); Masini, *Sacro arsenale*; de Liguoro, *Guida*; Fulgoni, *Summa*; de Sarno, *Novissima*; Fighera, *Institutiones*; Sanfelice, *Decisionum*; Moro, *Pratica*; Sorge, *Iurisprudentia*, vol. 9, *Praxis criminalis*; de Luca, *Il Dottor volgare* (this is the translation of de Luca's *Theatrum veritatis et justitiae*), esp. vol. 10; Rapolla, *Commentariorum*; Scialoja, *Praxis*. Many were published many times, and I have cited the edition I read, usually the one available in the Biblioteca Nazionale of Naples. See also the thirty-five prammatiche *de ordine et forma iudiciorum* in Giustiniani, *Nuova collezione*, 12:91–143.

42. The differences between the Continental and the English system went beyond the role of the jury; see Cockburn and Green, *Twelve Good Men*; Baker, "Criminal Courts"; McLynn, *Crime*; Sharpe, *Crime*; Hay et al., *Albion's Fatal Tree*.

43. Clark and Crawford, *Legal Medicine*, esp. the introduction and Crawford, "Legalizing Medicine"; the main Italian treatise on forensic medicine was Zacchia, *Quaestiones*. In England, because of the different procedure, legal medicine developed later, often in the context of inquests into infanticide cases. Jackson, *New-Born Child Murder*, ch. 4, and idem, "Suspicious Infant Deaths."

44. For the specific issues concerning women witnesses, see Chapter 5; in this chapter I use mostly the masculine pronoun.

45. These procedures are described with little variation in most treatises, often in the same formulation. Moro, *Pratica*, 1:173–78, for the *causa scientiae*.

46. By guards I mean the urban (or occasional rural) police of the time, who were universally despised for their lowly origins and dubious character; an even greater stigma afflicted jailers and executioners.

47. Briganti, *Pratica*, 188–201. There were always exceptions in cases of grave crimes which could speed up the process or give added weight to the testimony of less than perfect witnesses. See also Schnapper, "Testes inhabiles" (on children, see 579 and 609: before 1670 in France children under fourteen years of age were not admitted at all as witnesses); idem, *Voies nouvelles*; Maire Vigueur and Paravicini Bagliani, *La parola all'accusato*; Niccoli, *Il seme della violenza*, ch. 1.

48. Tellingly, the defendant was referred to in laws and in the doctrine as *reus*, the main meaning of which was "guilty."

49. Ambrosino, *Processus*, 122–35.

50. Moro, *Pratica*, 4:241.

51. De Sarno, *Novissima*, 320–339. The repetition was not necessary if the witnesses had already testified after an oath taken in the presence of the defendant, a step recommended by jurists to save time and which was applied in the Pentidattilo case; see Scialoja, *Praxis*, 53.

52. Moro, *Pratica*, 4:246–47.

53. Scialoja, *Praxis*, 114.

54. This and other forms of torture are described in gory detail in most judicial treatises. Other forms still in use, though increasingly rare, included water (forcing the

victim, in variously unpleasant ways, to imbibe huge quantities of water), the wake (preventing sleep), the wheel (stretching the victim's body), hunger and thirst, fire (covering the victim's feet with lard and placing them near a fire that would burn the lard), and the goat (covering the victim's wet feet with salt and letting goats eat the salt). The quote is in Follerio, *Practica,* 401. Briganti, *Pratica,* 211–12, reviews the various methods.

55. De Luca, *Il dottor volgare,* 10:88; Tomás y Valiente, *La tortura,* 56–77; Soman, "Criminal Jurisprudence" (the quote is on 59; the preferred form of torture here was "stretching the victim and bloating him with lukewarm water" [57]); idem, "La giustizia criminale"; idem, "Les procès de sorcellerie." See also Fiorelli, *La tortura*; Lea, *Torture*; Peters, *Torture.*

56. Follerio, *Practica,* 233, observed that "prison is not given for punishment, but for custody" except in canon law; on the transition, see Langbein, "Historical Origins"; Sarti, "Appunti"; Spierenburg, *Prison Experience*; Pike, *Penal Servitude*; Fornili, *Delinquenti*; Scarabello, *Carcerati.*

57. Calà, *Tractatus,* 6 and 21; Claro, *Opera,* 553; de Leonardis, *Prattica,* 53–74; Moro, *Pratica,* 4:281–82; Pescione, *Corti,* 77–117 and 359; Rapolla, *Commentariorum,* 1:180–90; Novario, *De vassallorum,* pt. 2, nos. 122–25; Briganti, *Pratica,* 205.

58. See, e.g., Dean, "Criminal Justice"; Ago, *Un feudo,* 111–12; Raggio, *Faide e parentele,* chs. 1 and 6; Soman, "Deviance," 10–11; Hufton, "Le paysan"; Sharpe, *Crime,* 39 and 80–82; Garnot, *Un crime,* 47–49 and 88–98; idem, "Une illusion"; Dayton, "Taking the Trade"; Gaskill, "Reporting Murder."

59. The lists of witnesses are in TR, fols. 2v–3r; the depositions are in TR, fols. 4r–22r. There is no indication of why Lucretia Condella and Mattia Cuzzucli, who were among those called, did not testify (it is unlikely that they did and their depositions were not reported, given the completeness of the trial records); the witness not originally listed is Domenico Tropea. The witnesses bore twenty-one different surnames.

60. The scribe began the record of each question with "asked what he knows . . . " and of each answer with "he said . . . ," but the depositions often switch to first-person narrative. I do not know what form the oath took. The formula used most of the time for the question as to the *causa scientiae* was simply *dixit ut supra* ("he said as above," that is, he referred to the statement already given). Latin, of the macaronic variety favored by most juridical texts of the period, was used in the trial records mostly in formulaic passages.

61. Giannetti had been the barber for the marquis Domenico Alberti, who left him 4 *once* at his death in 1685, and he was remembered by the marquis Francesco Ruffo in his 1708 will for serving the marquis in his infirmities. ACB, 19.42 and 18.80.

62. TR, fols. 4r–v; mastro is the usual title for artisans.

63. See the next chapter for a discussion of these witnesses.

64. A few witnesses took their oath in the presence of only one or two defendants,

whenever their testimony only concerned the actions of those defendants. The formula is: "having taken the oath in the presence and in front of [names], jailed defendants, she was questioned and examined in their absence under the same oath." See above, note 51.

65. My assessment of the status and size of the witnesses' families comes primarily from the censuses and the baptismal records: ASN, Catasto Onciario 6090 and 6091, and ADRC, baptismal records for Pentidattilo, book covering the years 1667–1703. Vittoria's deposition in TR, fols. 6r–7v; she was actually thirty-two, as she had been baptized on January 15, 1678. See Chapter 4 for neighbors and neighborliness in village life and culture.

66. See Chapter 6.

67. Arsenic (*zargara*) was common in village life, as it was used to kill rats; an area of Pentidattilo was known as La Zargara.

68. Only one of these four women would testify in this trial: Vittoria alleged that Sicilia Zuccalà (who testified) and Antonia Crea had each had two abortions and Lucretia Condella and Francesca Cateforo one each; if these allegations were true, Anna's activities would stretch at least some years into the past, since Lucretia Condella, wife of Domenico Crea, had had a child as early as 1691.

69. TR, fols. 8r–v. "Of bad life and repute" (*di mala vita e fama*) was clearly a formula, and it is, of course, possible that as such it was implicitly or otherwise suggested to the witnesses by the questioner. It is not clear what these women meant by concubine—Agostina actually says *concubinata*—since there is no evidence that Anna was a prostitute or of any stable relation she might have been maintaining with any village man.

70. TR, fols. 9r–10v; in the next testimony, Domenica was reported to have given her own enmity with her sister-in-law as the reason why she could not ask for the arsenic in person.

71. TR, fols. 11r–v.

72. Cola was also probably Anna de Amico's half brother, since his mother, Mattia, is referred to as Anna's stepmother.

73. On the prominence of the Malavenda (or Malavendi), see e.g., ASN, Relevi 367.6, fols. 429r–430r, 432r–435r, 436r, 446r–v, 472r–v, 475r–v, and 484v; ACB, 19.55; ACB, 19.35; and Chapter 3.

74. ADRC, baptismal records; her testimony is in TR, fols. 12r–13r.

75. The term used by Mariuzza for Domenica's giving birth is *disertare*, which means to abort, but in this case it seems to have been rather a very premature induced birth, since the child was not stillborn, though it died almost immediately (assuming that Mariuzza was not lying about the child's being alive and her having baptized it, in order to avoid any personal blame for her involvement in the matter); the six or seven months obviously refers to Mariuzza's estimate of Domenica's gestation, and I have therefore used the word *fetus* in that context.

76. TR, fols. 15r–16r; though I do not know for sure that the signatures in the rec-ords were in fact written by the witnesses themselves, Tropea's is the only one written in a wobbly and hesitant hand. I do not know whether Francesco was a close relative of Antonia Tropea's, who had already testified.

77. Why Domenica left her dead child on the ground to get a flask, or why indeed she and her mother felt the need to be accompanied by this man, remains unexplained and unaddressed in the records.

78. TR, fol. 16v; on gossip and favors among women, see Chapter 4.

79. For married women or widows the names (and sometimes the occupation) of husbands are reported in the deposition.

80. Sicilia's deposition is in TR, fols. 17r–v.

81. Maria's deposition is in TR, fols. 17v–18r; *prattica* ("expert") is the same term the barber had used to describe his expertise in surgery.

82. TR, fols. 18r–v. This would be a substantial sum for a peasant woman. Again, it is not explained why Domenica had recourse to Domenico's help. I do not know whether Francesco and Domenico Tropea, the two men involved in the abortion epi-sode, were related to each other, or to Domenica.

T H R E E   *Economic Structures and Social Hierarchies*

1. Examples in ACB, 18.80, 19.35, 55–56, 84, 89, 91, 94–95, and 21.1; ASN, Torri e Castelli 37, fols. 661r–v; ASN, Conti Comunali 214, fascicolo 2, fols. 84r–v; ASN, Voci di Vettovaglie 56, fascicolo 6, vol. 2, fol. 109r; ASRC, Demani, inventario 33, busta 241, fascicolo 1.

2. The seven were Carlo Molé (aged thirty-three, and the only one who signed his name), Filippo Palumbo (aged thirty-four), Michele Maropato (aged fifty), Giacomo Costarella (aged twenty-five, whose wife and daughter had earlier given much more intriguing depositions), Francesco Viglianisi (aged twenty-five), Giovan Domenico Ficara (aged thirty-five), and Giovan Battista Corso (aged thirty, husband of earlier witness Vittoria Vernagallo, and the only laborer); their depositions are in TR, fols. 19r–22r.

3. Public rumor was among the recognized standards of evidence, and these men were probably questioned for the specific purpose of demonstrating what that rumor had been even among people who had not witnessed any of the events of the trial. They all remarked that the rumor had started immediately, which matches Giovan Domenico Cuzzucli's accusations and the arrest of the three defendants on the day fol-lowing Antonino's death.

4. In addition to previously cited works, among other studies of villages in the kingdom and in early modern Europe, see *Storia del Vallo di Diano,* vol. 3; Delille, *Croissance*; Galt, *Church Bells*; Bouchard, *Le village immobile*; and Sabean, *Property*. See also Leone, "Agricoltura e contadini."

5. See, e.g., ASRC, Demani, inventario 33, busta 241, fascicolo 1, esp. fols. 3r–4v. These conflicts were common in the kingdom's villages; see Villari, *Mezzogiorno,* and Minervino, "Un comune."

6. See, e.g., Merzario, *Signori;* Cozzetto, *Territorio,* ch. 7; Caridi, *Il latifondo;* Petrusewicz, *Latifondo;* Lepre, *Feudi;* idem, *Terra di Lavoro;* Villani, *Economia;* Massafra, *Problemi;* Marino, *Pastoral Economics;* Galt, *Church Bells;* Brasacchio, *Storia,* vol. 3; Arlacchi, *Mafia;* De Clementi, *Vivere nel latifondo;* Musgrave, *Land;* Astarita, *Continuity,* ch. 3.

7. It was 10% in the Caracciolo Brienza fiefs in Basilicata and Principato Citra; Astarita, *Continuity,* 82–89. Both in those fiefs and in Pentidattilo, however, the terraggio was based on the harvest and not on the area cultivated (as was the case elsewhere in the kingdom, especially in wealthier plain areas), and therefore it allowed the peasants to share the risks of bad years with the feudal lord. In the mid-sixteenth century the Francoperta lords of Pentidattilo had managed much of their land directly, according to a witness in ASN, Relevi 382.2, fols. 37r–39v (1591), but that had changed by the time the Alberti acquired the fief; given the heavy debts incurred by the Francoperta, direct management was probably never the most profitable approach in Pentidattilo.

8. ASN, Relevi 356.17, fols. 288r–290v, and 358.16, fols. 382r–v; silk had played a very small role in feudal revenues in the late sixteenth century (e.g., ASN, Relevi 354.3, fols. 49r–52r), while the shift is often mentioned in the later Relevi, e.g. ASN, Relevi 390.2, fols. 2r–8r (1686), and 367.6, fols. 432r–435r and 48orff. (1691). The change seems to have started after the 1647–48 upheavals (see ASN, Relevi 384.I, fols. 2r–42r), at least on the marquis's lands; some villagers were already trading silk, as well as grains and other foodstuffs, by 1648. ASRC, Statuti Capitoli, busta 1, fascicolo 22, p. 7. For the division of the product, see ASN, Relevi 367.6, fol. 482v. The inventory of the castle in 1686 mentions large provisions in oil, wine, and wheat; ACB, 19.47. On silk production in the Reggio area, see Arillotta, *Reggio,* 53–67, 137–43.

9. For comparisons see Bouchard, *Le village immobile,* and Vassberg, *Village.*

10. Swinburne, *Travels,* 1:354–55; see also Abbé de Saint-Non, *Voyage pittoresque,* 3:124; ACB, 19.68, unnumbered fol. (1704), ASN, Catasto Onciario 6091, fol. 47v (1745), and ACB, 8.53, fols. 4r–9v (1759). On citrus trees, see the observations of Grimaldi, *Saggio;* on silk production in Calabria, [Spiriti], *Riflessioni,* 135–38. See also Chorley, *Oil;* Lupo, *Il giardino;* Milone, *Memoria,* 79–95; and Gambi, *La Calabria,* 462–67 (on the more recent poverty of the area) and passim.

11. The data from the relevi are, of course, not reliable as absolute figures, because of the fraud and evasion that certainly occurred, but they offer an indicative trend; see also Caridi, *Dal feudatario,* 31–42. The relevio consisted of about half the net feudal revenues; see ASN, Relevi, 347.7, fol. 114r (1536); 354.3, fols. 49r–52r (1585); 382.64, fols. 1206r–1209ter (1602); 356.17, fols. 288r–290v (1627) and 298r–301r (1602); 384.I, fols. 11r–13r (1648) and 30r–31r (1655); 358.16, fols. 355r–361r (1651); 390.2, fols. 2r–8r (1686);

367.6, fols. 432r–435r and 484v–505v (1691); ASN, Significatorie dei Relevi 83, fols. 488r–493r (1691); ASN, Cedolari Nuovi 85, fols. 554r–560r, and Cedolari Nuovi 81, fols. 611r–v, summarize the data of most relevi for Pentidattilo; ACB, 19.68, unnumbered fol. (1704); see also ASN, Refute Quinternioni 226, fols. 528–535, and ASN, Intestazioni Feudali 17.300, fols. 2r–5v. For prices, see ASN, Relevi 347.7, fols. 115r–v (1536); 382.2, fols. 37r–39v (1591); 354.3, fols. 32r–v (1602); 356.17, fols. 311r–v (1627); 358.16, fol. 353r (1649); 367.6, fol. 436r (1691); ASN, Significatorie dei Relevi 66, fols. 129r–131r (1649); ASN, Voci di Vettovaglie 56.6, vol. 2, fol. 109r (1721); ASN, Catasto Onciario 6090, fols. 22r–23r (1759).

12. See the relevi just cited; ACB, 19.57; and ASN, Catasto Onciario 6091, fol. 47v. A definition of the fondaco and pescato in Melito is in ASN, Relevi 367.6, fols. 480r and 499v; their growth, of course, was also tied to the demographic growth of Melito.

13. ACB, 19.17, 19.42, fol. 18v, and 19.91; other data on village finances are in ASN, Diversi Sommaria I serie, fascicolo 72, unnumbered fols. (1630s); ASN, Tesorieri e Percettori 4292/684 (1694), 4294/686 (1697), 4315/707 (1709), and 4316/708 (1712); ASN, Frammenti dei Fuochi 192 bis, fol. 179v (1701–2); ASN, Conti Comunali 214.2, fols. 84r–v (1718); ASN, Fiscali e Adoe 5 bis, fol. 65v (1612), 6, fol. 21r (1709), and 13, unnumbered fol. (1737–39); ASN, Attuarî Diversi Sommaria 523.34, fols. 74r–76r (1737); ASN, Catasto Onciario 6090, fols. 24r–v (1759); and ASCZ, Cassa Sacra Miscellanea B. 7, fascicoli 160 and 161 (1780s). Pentidattilo's finances were in much better shape than nearby Motta's; Caridi, *Dal feudatario*, 60–64. On village finances in the kingdom, see Muto, "Strutture."

14. ASN, Conti Comunali 214.2, fols. 84r–v; see table 3.1.

15. ASN, Catasto Onciario 6091, fol. 52v, and 6090, fol. 835r; Merzario, *Signori*, 29; see table 3.1.

16. ACB, 8.51–53, and ASN, Refute Quinternioni 226, fols. 528–35 (the rate of 4% was the norm in estimates of the value of fiefs; Astarita, *Continuity*, 44–46).

17. ASRC, Carte e Miscellanea Blasco, 4a B, pp. 338–40, and 4b E, fols. 593r–598v; ASCZ, Cassa Sacra, Vendite e Censuazioni, busta 31, fascicoli 1499–1512, and busta 37, fascicoli 1742–59; ASCZ, Segreteria Ecclesiastica, busta 39, fascicoli 907–8, and busta 20, fascicolo 413; and ASN, Processi Cassa Sacra, Suprema Giunta di Corrispondenza, busta 120, fascicolo 2072.

18. The documents cited in the previous note include numerous references to citizens qualified as magnifico or with the title Don. The occupations are included in the fiscal surveys; ASN, Catasto Onciario 6091 and 6090. Melito's growth was also faster than that in the coastal areas of nearby Motta; Caridi, *Dal feudatario*, 65–73. Similar trends occurred elsewhere in the late eighteenth century; see, e.g., *La Calabria*; McArdle, *Altopascio*; and Dewald, *Pont-St-Pierre*.

19. In addition to the examples cited in Chapters 1 and 2, see the disputes in ASN, Collaterale Provvisioni 148, fols. 277r–279r (1634, with the marquis over local taxes),

and ASN, Sommaria Partium 2101, fol. 149r (1621, with the archbishop of Reggio Calabria over land).

20. The Catasto Onciario produced more than nine thousand volumes of documents for the entire kingdom; the volumes for Pentidattilo are ASN, Catasto Onciario
6090 (1759) and 6091 (1745). They cover the whole territory of the università and therefore Pentidattilo proper, Melito, and scattered households. Villani, *Mezzogiorno,* ch. 3;
Placanica and Mafrici, *Il Mezzogiorno;* Valente, "I Catasti"; on censuses, see Burke, *Historical Anthropology,* ch. 3. Similar categories were used in censuses in Spain; Vassberg,
Village, 15–17 and 163–65. On the Bourbon monarchy, see Spagnoletti, *Storia.*

21. See Pellizzari, "Alfabeto e fisco," 134–35.

22. The deputies in 1745 were Bartolo Battaglia and Nuntio Palermo from the first
estate, Giuseppe Scrufari and Giuseppe Tropea from the middle one, and Domenico
Ficara and Francesco Petrulli from the third; Antonino Celia (the notary's father) and
Domenico Romeo were the local evaluators, Giorgio Donato and Giuseppe Giudice
the outside evaluators. Battaglia, Palermo, Scrufari, Petrulli, and Romeo were able to
sign their name. The literate among the 1759 cast were actually only five, since one of
them served as both alderman and deputy (for another alderman the information is
lacking).

23. The *oncia* was the unit of account used to assess the capital value of labor and
property; it was worth 6 ducats, and thus the labor of a field laborer was held to have
the capital value of 72 ducats, that of a massaro of 84 ducats.

24. Royal orders mandated also the taxing of capital invested in business or trade,
but nobody in Pentidattilo was taxed for any such capital. It is, of course, possible that
fraud occurred to favor wealthier citizens.

25. Villari, *Mezzogiorno,* 105–11 and 132–45; see also Caracciolo, *Sud* (on which see
Astarita, *Continuity,* 116), and Bulgarelli Lukacs, *L'imposta diretta.*

26. Villani, *Mezzogiorno,* 121–36. An *oncia* equaled 6 ducats in capital value, which
would result in 30 grana of income (at 5%).

27. Pentidattilo is one of several università for which two different Catasti Onciari
exist. The following differences between the two documents at times make direct comparison difficult: (a) the 1759 document includes twenty-two households residing in
the hamlet of Corio, in the università's territory, which is not mentioned at all in the
1745 survey; since most of those households are headed by non-native citizens and
more than a third of them live in haystacks rather than houses, it is possible that Corio
was a new settlement in 1759, but the sources provide no details about it; (b) the two
documents differ substantially in the reporting of households that included widowed
mothers; see Chapter 4; (c) the later document contains a considerably higher estimate for the marquis's patrimony, and the low early estimate may have been one reason why a second survey was drafted; (d) the later survey reports a substantially larger
population than the earlier one; a plague epidemic had affected the area in 1744, so the
1745 survey probably reflects a low point in the village's population, and this may be

another reason why the later survey was prepared; (e) the 1759 document is longer than the 1745 one but also contains more internal contradictions.

28. All data here are from ASN, Catasto Onciario 6091. The *oncia* was divided into thirty *tarì*, so, for instance, 16.15 *once* means 16 and one-half *once*.

29. Villani, *Mezzogiorno*, 121–26; Caridi, *Dal feudatario*, 53–60; see table 3.2. In the 1759 survey the percentage for resident citizens was 50.1% (or 3,254.10 *once* out of 6,508.05), while the marquis and other nonresident lay owners went from the 19.9% of 1745 to 31.4%. This reflects the higher estimate in the later survey for the marquis's assets, the value of which grew by almost six times (from 277.22 to 1,622 *once*); the fact that in 1759 Litterio Caracciolo sold the fief to Lorenzo Clemente may have led the appraisers to revise their previous estimate of the lord's patrimony; see table 3.2.

30. The tenth "civil" man, as I mentioned above, was not taxed at all, because he owned no taxable goods. The four disabled men counted here do not include the two other ones mentioned above whose households were not taxed at all. In another case a disabled member of a household was actually charged for *once d'industria*; he was not, however, the household head.

31. See, e.g., Galt, *Church Bells*, 78; Merzario, *Signori*, 113; Caridi, *Latifondo*, 71–73; and idem, *Dal feudatario*, 53–60; for a French example, see Dewald, *Pont-St-Pierre*, 53.

32. Astarita, *Continuity*, 65–66; Merzario, *Signori*, 81–89; Brasacchio, *Storia*, 3:308.

33. Wheat was priced at 1 ducat per tomolo, rye at 0.80 ducats, barley at 0.50 ducats, wine at 1.60 ducats per *salma*, and oil at 1.80 per *cafiso* of eighteen *rotoli*; ASN, Catasto Onciario 6091, fols. 3r–v. These prices are close to those indicated for the Calabrian market in Di Bella, *Grano*, ch. 2. On landownership, see also Vassberg, *Land*, ch. 5, and Cozzetto, *Territorio*, ch. 7.

34. The slight disparity between these figures and the total in the collettiva for *once di beni* is due to minor arithmetic mistakes in the document. Six of the thirty-five landowning field laborers drew no taxable net revenue from their land. In nearby Motta most bracciali owned nothing; Caridi, *Dal feudatario*, 58.

35. *Proprio uso* meant personal transportation, since plowing and carting were taxable uses. Only four mules were used for carting and one mare for reproduction.

36. He is identified as a forese, which I translate as tenant farmer; the term indicated a category between the wealthier massari and the poorer bracciali; see also Da Molin, *La famiglia*, 163.

37. Most parcels are described as including various fruit and mulberry trees. Galt also found no great differences in the wealth of various social categories in the Puglia village he studied, though the village was larger and had a more complex social structure than Pentidattilo; *Church Bells*, ch. 5. Economic disparities were much more pronounced in French villages; see Sheppard, *Lourmarin*, and Schneider, "Village."

38. Two more households paid no rent because of their work in silk production, but in the countryside and not in Melito. The percentage of renters was low (21%) also

in Aiello in Calabria Citra; Cozzetto, *Territorio,* 186. Another study on Calabria (Mafrici, "La Calabria") indicates about 60% of homeowners.

39. In none of these cases did the cleric live with his family.

40. ASN, Catasto Onciario 6090; most of Melito's homeowners paid a fee (censo) to the marquis for their houses. In 1759 twenty-five of the houses owned by their residents were described as *dotale,* that is, part of a dowry. This was the case with only one house in 1745; the records offer no explanation.

41. One of the sons is not defined as magnifico in the list but is elected as one of the deputies for the "better" estate. ASN, Catasto Onciario 6090, fol. 28r.

42. Both widows have sons over fourteen who are not taxed for *industria,* which would indicate "civil" status, but the document does not include any title or definition for the sons or for the deceased fathers. The 1759 survey includes two types of lists of households: "lists of souls" drafted by the two parish priests for Pentidattilo and Melito, respectively, fols. 30r–39r and 42r–46v, and then the rivele, usually in two copies, and the collettiva. In collating these lists I counted thirteen magnifici in 1759, all but one in Pentidattilo; there are, moreover, five additional households in Pentidattilo, two in Melito, and one in Corio which are identified as "civil" and the heads of which are not taxed for *industria,* and one more in Pentidattilo (the mayor's) which is called "civil" but taxed for *industria.* The records are not consistent in the use of these terms. I have assumed that "living civilly" (or, in 1759, being called magnifico) was equivalent to enjoying elite status (the terms *better, middle,* and *low* are never used except in reporting the elected deputies for the three estates).

43. In 1745 only three more boys in Pentidattilo went to school, one of them the nephew of Giuseppe Vernagallo, who lived with his other uncle, a priest, and who was one of the magnifici in 1759. On village education, see Barionovi, "Scolari."

44. The notary's rivela is the only case in 1745 in which an adult son is listed as head of household while his father is alive and living with him.

45. Astarita, *Continuity,* 139–46, and Caridi, *Dal feudatario,* 65–73. A good example of new notions emerging at the end of the century is a 1786 official note attached to the 1759 catasto at the page on which the bracciale Martino Familari's assets were appraised: Martino was illiterate, he was assessed only for his own *industria,* and he owned no taxable assets; yet in 1786 his son Francesco, soon to be Pentidattilo's notary, petitioned to have the records altered to show that his father, and thus all his family, had indeed been civil. ASN, Catasto Onciario 6090, fols. 749r–827v, *sub nomine.*

46. ASRC, notai, busta 420, fascicoli 2217–24, for the years 1740–42, 1747–48, 1751–52, and 1754. Five of the thirty-six acts drawn up in the università of Pentidattilo were prepared in Melito; a majority of the forty-one others were drawn up in nearby Montebello, with a few in Motta, San Lorenzo, Bagaladi, and Reggio Calabria. There is no indication of whether the remaining bundles were lost or whether the notary simply suspended his business during the missing years. The surviving papers appear complete for each year (each year has its own notebook), but ACB 19.89 and 90 consist of

two acts drawn up by Celia in 1741 and not included in his notebook for that year in ASRC, so it is evident that at least some papers are missing.

47. ASRC, notai, busta 420, fascicolo 2221 (1748), fols. 8r–9v.

48. Ibid., fascicolo 2220 (1747), fols. 6r–v, and fascicolo 2222 (1751), fols. 14v–18v.

49. The same prevalence of a few individuals as witnesses in each generation can be found in the Relevi and in other documents of village life.

50. The definitions are ambiguous. As we have seen, many bracciali and foresi owned land and animals on their own, as well. See tables 3.5, 3.6, and 3.7. For these issues, see also Caridi, *Latifondo,* which studies the area of Crotone, characterized by large-scale management: he observes much more poverty among the bracciali, two-thirds of whom owned nothing. See also Cozzetto, *Territorio,* ch. 5, and Merzario, *Signori.*

51. It is not fruitful to compare this figure of 34.15 total *once* with the much lower one (18.05 *once*) for the ten "civil" people, because the *once d'industria* (i.e., labor) represent a large part of the massari's taxable assets. Even when only *once di beni* are considered, the average for massari is still 12.15 *once,* 50% above the village average of 8.06 *once di beni* (for the seventy households who had any) and higher than the 11.24 *once di beni* of the ten "civil" heads of household. The four secondary household members identified as massari also all belonged to households owning taxable animals. See tables 3.8 and 3.9.

52. Presumably somebody herded the sheep and goats present in the village, but these animals were few, and long-range pastoralism was absent in the Pentidattilo area. For Motta, see Caridi, *Dal feudatario,* 53–60; for Spain, see Vassberg, *Village,* 12, 37–38, 129–34, and ch. 3.

53. ASRC, notai, busta 420, fascicolo 2217 (1740), fols. 1v–3v.

54. Ibid., fascicolo 2224 (the folio numbers are illegible); for this and the next example, see figures 3.1 and 3.2.

55. See Malanima, *Il lusso dei contadini,* ch. 1; Muchembled, *L'invention,* ch. 6. On dowries and wills in the kingdom, see Delille, "L'ordine," 526; idem, "Dots"; Pappalardo, "Scelte"; Villone, "Contratti"; Luise, "Solofra"; and Belli, "Famiglia." Forms of partible inheritance based on Roman law prevailed in the kingdom; see also Tentori, "Social Classes," and Davis, "Account of Changes." On the transmission of property in other parts of Europe, see also Medick and Sabean, *Interest and Emotion,* and Sabean, *Property,* ch. 10.

56. Giuseppe's 1759 rivela in ASN, Catasto Onciario 6090, fols. 233r–234v; he also owned two houses (including the one Margherita had brought with her dowry), but they gave no income because Giuseppe's mother and mother-in-law inhabited them without paying rent. The rivela states that Giuseppe lived in Reggio, but the list of households gives him as a resident of the village.

57. Giuseppe's father had also been called Giovan Battista, though the age difference makes it unlikely that it was the same person as the 1710 witness. Only two chil-

dren with the surname of Corso were baptized in Pentidattilo between 1667 and 1695; Giovanni's mother was a Caterina Crea.

58. ASRC, notai, busta 420, fascicolo 2222 (1751), fols. 21v–24r.

59. ASN, Catasto Onciario 6090, fols. 73r–74v. I cannot be positive that the mayor is Lucretia's widower because his age in 1759 is given as sixty-two, but the difference in age is not such as to cast too much doubt on the identification.

60. The identification is very likely, although Lucretia is listed as twenty-four in 1745 and only as thirty in 1759.

61. I have here, therefore, eliminated all villagers who had relations and connections in the village either during the 1740s and 1750s (also through the notary's documents) or in earlier decades (as seen, for instance, through the trial records or the Relevi). On the poverty of abandoned women, see, e.g., ASRC, notai, busta 420, fascicolo 2224 (1754), illegible fols. (the last act recorded). On the marginality of rootless people and the mistrust they encountered, see also Muchembled, *La violence*, 70 ff; Gutton, *La sociabilité*, ch. 2; and Vassberg, *Village*.

F O U R   *Family, Household, and Community*

1. Rohlfs, *Dizionario toponomastico* and *Dizionario dei cognomi, sub vocibus* (as Cuzzucli or Cuzzucoli); Lofaci does not appear among the nicknames listed by Rohlfs.

2. ADRC, Pentidattilo, baptismal records. Antonia and Francesca Familari (the latter was Domenica Orlando's mother) were both having children in the 1680s and were therefore presumably close in age, though I have no evidence that they were sisters. I have not found Antonino Cuzzucli's baptismal record. For the pattern of marriages within the same clans, see Delille, *Famille*, and Sabean, *Kinship*, ch. 5. There were many homonyms within village society, and I have not assumed family connections on the basis only of names.

3. Examples in ASN, Relevi 356.17, fols. 298r–301r (1602); Relevi 390.2, fols. 52r–56v, Relevi 358.16, fols. 348r–352r and 378r, and Relevi 384.I, fols. 11r–13r (1646–49); Relevi 384.I, fols. 30r–31r (1655); ACB, 21.11, the 1663 *platea*; Relevi 390.2bis, fols. Ir and 83r (1685); Relevi 367.6, fols. 472r–v (1694); ACB, 19.68 (1704).

4. ACB, 18.80 (1708); ASN, Catasto Onciario 6091, fol. 26r, and 6090, fols. 42r–46v, for the censuses; in 1759 a man by the last name of Lofaci was listed in Pentidattilo, so perhaps the nickname had by then become a new surname. See also ASRC, notai, busta 420, fascicolo 2220, fol. 18v, and ACB, 21.11, the 1759 list of revenues; ASCZ, Cassa Sacra, Segreteria Ecclesiastica, busta 39, fascicolo 907, fols. 3r–10v (1788).

5. See Denisi, *L'opera*, 75; Spadaro, *Società in rivolta*, 224–48; ASRC, Statuti Capitoli, busta 1, fascicolo 36 (1708); ACB, 19.84 (1732); ASRC, notaio Celia, busta 420, fascicolo 2218, fols. 10r–13r (1741).

6. Rohlfs, *Dizionario toponomastico* and *Dizionario dei cognomi, sub vocibus*. De Amico does not appear in Rohlfs's dictionaries.

7. ADRC, baptismal records.

8. ASN, Relevi 390.2, fols. 52r–56v, Relevi 384.I, fols. 11r–13v, Relevi 358.16, fols. 348r–352r, and Significatorie 66, fols. 129r–131r; ASRC, Capitoli Statuti, busta 1, fascicolo 22; ACB, 19.17 and 21.8.

9. ACB, 21.11, the 1663 platea; ASN, Relevi 390.2bis, fols. IIIr–v, 9v, and 68r, and Relevi 367.6, fols. 464r ff. and 475r–v; Catasto Onciario 6091, fols. 10r and 27v, and 6090, fol. 6r; ASRC, notaio Celia, fascicolo 2217, fols. 3v–5r; ASRC, Carte e Miscellanea Blasco 4b E, fols. 593r–598v, and ASCZ, Cassa Sacra, Vendite e censuazioni, busta 37, fascicolo 1750.

10. ASN, Relevi 356.17, fols. 298r–301r, Relevi 390.2, fols. 52r–56v, Relevi 384.I, fols. 11r–13v, and Relevi 358.16, fols. 348r–352r; ACB, 21.11, the 1663 platea; ASN, Relevi 390.2bis, fol. 9v; Catasto Onciario 6091, fol. 19r, and 6090; ACB, 19.84; ASRC, Demani inventario 33, busta 241, fascicolo 1; ASRC, notaio Celia, fascicolo 2220, fols. 6v–7r, and fascicolo 2222, fols. 13r–14v; ASCZ, Cassa Sacra, Miscellanea, busta 7, fascicolo 161; ASCZ, Cassa Sacra, Vendite e censuazioni, busta 31, fascicoli 1499–1512, and busta 37, fascicoli 1742–59; ASRC, Carte e Miscellanea Blasco, 4b E, fols. 593r–598v; ASCZ, Cassa Sacra, Segreteria Ecclesiastica, busta 39, fascicolo 908.

11. ASN, Relevi 382.2, fols. 37r–39v; Torri e Castelli 44, fol. 228r; Relevi 356.17, fols. 288r–290v; ACB, 19.17; ASN, Relevi 384.I, fols. 4v and 30r–31r; ASN, Relevi 358.16, fols. 377r–v and 382r–v; ACB, 21.11, the 1663 platea; ASN, Relevi 390.2, fol. 74v; Relevi 390.2bis, fols. IIr, IIIr–v, VIr, 9v, 69v, and 72r; Relevi 367.6, fols. 464r ff. and 475r–v; ACB, 19.68 and 18.80; ASN Torri e Castelli 46, fols. 211r–218v; ACB 19.84 and 21.11; ASRC, notaio Celia, fascicolo 2223 (passim for several Crea in Montebello who included two clerics); ASN, Catasto Onciario 6091, fols. 17v–18r, 20r–v, and 27v, and 6090; ASRC, notaio Celia, fascicolo 2217, fols. 3v–5r, and fascicolo 2220, fols. 28r–29v; ACB, 4.1.56a; ASRC, Demani, inventario 33, busta 241, fascicolo 2, fols. 86r–87r.

12. For an example from another village of an outsider woman who offered cures and help to villagers and was later accused of witchcraft, see Volpe, *Il Cilento*, ch. 3.

13. ASN, Relevi 390.2bis, fol. 158r; Relevi 367.6, fols. 432r–435r; ACB, 19.84; ASRC, notaio Celia, fascicolo 2223, fols. 8r–10v. Mattia (a female name here) Cuzzucli is described as Anna's *parrostra* (TR, fol. 11v), which Rohlfs, *Dizionario dialettale, sub voce,* translates as stepmother ("parrastra" in Rohlfs) and ascribes to the Reggio area, which includes Pentidattilo. Mattia Cuzzucli was also Antonino's sister and hence Domenica's sister-in-law; see figure 4.1.

14. Da Molin, *La famiglia* and *Popolazione,* 7–81, particularly 72–77, on family types; de Matteis, *L'Aquila;* Delille, *Agricoltura, Famille,* and "L'ordine," 554–55; Merzario, *Il paese stretto;* McArdle, *Altopascio,* ch. 6; Flandrin, *Familles;* Flinn, *European Demographic System.* Benigno, "Southern Italian Family," argues for the prominence of nuclear families in the "Mediterranean model" of household, as well as early marriage for women and neolocality.

15. Adding the 22 households and 113 residents of Corio, the total is 178 households

and 748 people, or an average of 4.2; I have concentrated in this section on the two larger villages (Pentidattilo and Melito), also because the Corio households were all but one non-native.

16. ASN, Catasto Onciario 6090 (1759) and 6091 (1745); the status animarum do not include households that held no taxable assets. The five scattered households of 1745 were all in the countryside near Pentidattilo, except for a hermit and his sister who lived near the sea.

17. The figures for Pentidattilo proper in 1745 would decrease further if the six households of resident local priests (accounting for 15 people) were included; Corio in 1759 had an average household size of 5.1.

18. This difference was negligible in the 1759 survey, with an average age of forty for Pentidattilo and thirty-nine for Melito.

19. The only old clan present in Melito in 1745 was the Foti, with one of their four households. The wives of the Melito heads of household also included only a Domenica Romeo but otherwise did not belong to the large or "civil" Pentidattilo clans. In 1759 two Battaglia, an Orlando, and a Romeo men headed households in Melito, and there were a Romeo, a Battaglia, and a Crea wife.

20. Two of the 1759 surnames are almost the same, and the difference might be due to inconsistent spellings. Melito also developed a continuity of its own: members of 26 of the 30 households that resided there in 1745 can be identified in households still residing there in 1759, and members of 37 of the 50 households of 1759 can be traced back to the previous census, all but four of them already in Melito. For 1788 see ASCZ, Cassa Sacra, Miscellanea, busta 7, fascicolo 160. Similar trends of commercialization, social stratification, and changes in demographic patterns occurred in eighteenth-century French and German villages; see Sheppard, *Lourmarin*; Dewald, *Pont-St-Pierre*; and Sabean, *Property*.

21. Mafrici, "La Calabria"; Galt, *Church Bells*, 103–5; Da Molin, *La famiglia*, ch. 2. See tables 4.1 and 4.2.

22. I am using here the definitions employed by Da Molin, *La famiglia* and *Popolazione*, and Flandrin, *Familles*: nuclear families include a married couple (or a widowed parent) with or without children; extended households include other relatives (parents or siblings of either spouse, nephews or nieces); multiple households include more than one married couple; households with servants or households including unrelated individuals are not included in these categories.

23. See tables 4.3 and 4.4. In 1745 the nine households headed by artisans, while not especially large (their average size was 4.77), were mostly non-nuclear (seven out of nine); this also helps explain the prevalence of non-nuclear households in Melito, which was home to six of these seven non-nuclear households.

24. See table 4.1. In 1759 there were also four households that included such distant relatives.

25. In five of these cases the head of household was elderly and presumably a widower, since his wife was not listed.

26. In 1759 there was no household in which a son- or daughter-in-law cohabited with the spouse's family, except for one case in which a married couple lived with the husband's father, but the older man was not listed as the head of household.

27. On these issues, see, e.g., Giacomini, *Sposi*; Ago, *Un feudo*, ch. 3; Collomp, *La maison du père*; Vassberg, *Village*, 97–102.

28. Again, there were no such households in 1759, when there were only three households in which a married head of household cohabited with a sibling (all brothers), and the motivations were similar (one brother was a priest, one a minor); there was also a widow cohabiting with her young brother. One household in Corio consisted of two brothers, one married and one widowed, both with children.

29. The ages reported in the documents sometimes differ; it is thus not entirely clear when Francesca's two children of 1759 were born; see figure 4.2.

30. Maria Zuccalà appears in two 1752 notarial acts, ASRC, notaio Celia, fascicolo 2223, fols. 2v–3r and 15v–18r; see figure 4.3.

31. Which brother it is not clear, as his name is given as Antonino but his age as sixteen; see figure 4.4. The Guerrera's unusual, classicizing first names also probably indicate higher status.

32. Again, here we have probably an interplay between general standards and local views. Villani, *Mezzogiorno*, ch. 3, does not mention any directives from the central government about the order to be followed in the lists.

33. Women kept their surname for legal identification, but their husbands, dead or alive, were also always mentioned in the women's identification. Only one wife in the 1745 census is not given her surname (and she is not the wife of the head of household but of his brother-in-law).

34. There is only one unexplained exception to this rule; the same rule applies to the 1759 lists with very few exceptions.

35. The same fate befell the one elderly father not listed as head of his household in the 1759 lists.

36. The listing of widows is the biggest difference between the two fiscal surveys. In the 1759 documents for Pentidattilo there are 28 households headed by widows (out of 106 households in the old village); 9 of these, however, lived with sons over the age of fourteen (and a tenth one lived with a brother above that age); one widow, in fact, had been placed last in the 1745 survey only to be given the first place fourteen years later, although her son was now an adult. The documents for Melito include 4 households headed by widows (out of 50), and in 3 of these the widows lived with sons (in one case a stepson) of at least fourteen years of age. In none of these cases did a widow head a household that included a married child. I have not been able to find any explanation for the discrepancy, though possibly, given the favorable fiscal regime pertain-

ing to widows' assets, the compilers of the 1759 document may have been trying to help these households by listing them as headed by widows.

37. See, e.g., Klapisch-Zuber, *Women;* Ago, *Un feudo,* ch. 3; Haas, "Il mio buono compare"; Fine, *Parrains;* Vassberg, *Village,* ch. 1. See also Davis, *Land;* du Boulay, *Portrait;* Pitt-Rivers, "Kith and the Kin"; idem, *Fate of Shechem,* ch. 3; idem, "Ritual Kinship"; Bossy, "Godparenthood"; Cressy, *Birth,* 149–61; Sabean, *Kinship,* 23–26 and chs. 7 and 13.

38. ADRC, baptismal records for Pentidattilo ("libro dei battesimi di San Pietro"). This volume covers the years 1667–1703, but given the conditions of research in the ADRC, I have only been able to read the years 1667–95, for a total of 611 baptismal acts (there is a gap between April 1668 and July 1670); other books spottily cover earlier decades. I have focused on the 1667–95 records because these were the years when many of the protagonists of the 1710 trial were born. Each entry typically gives the date, the full name and surname of the child, the father's name, the mother's name and surname, and the godparents' full names and surnames, with their own parents' names (and surnames for their mothers); the entries do not indicate whether a godparent was married or not.

39. Twenty-five of the 55 cases in which a godparent bore the same family name as one of the newborn's parents concern the Battaglia clan, the largest in the village. It is possible that members of this kinship group would operate with different intent than other villagers, since they already had a network of support within their own clan, and choosing relatives as godparents might have reinforced their prominence. In particular the Battaglia account for 19 of the 32 cases in which godparents bear the same family name as the newborn's mother and for 6 of the 23 cases in which godparents bear the same family name as the newborn's father. Bearing the same family name did not, of course, necessarily mean a close family relation. The frequency of godparents from outside the family was higher in Pentidattilo than elsewhere; see, e.g., Sabean, *Kinship,* ch. 7.

40. This last case concerns a boy born with a twin brother, and therefore the parents were already establishing multiple godparenthood relationships. There are also one case in which the two godparents might be mother and son, one in which the mothers of the two godparents bore the same family name, and one in which the godparents bore the same family name but had different parents. In all but one of the cases of double godparents the man is listed first (in the one exception the godmother and the mother come from the Battaglia clan). The presence of a priest as godfather was rare and required the special license of the bishop (there are only 2 other cases among the 611 here discussed). The archbishops of Reggio Calabria had long prohibited the choice of more than two godparents, prescribing that, should there be two, they be a man and a woman. See ASCC, Fondo Concilî 21, Calabria, report of the 1602 council of Archbishop D'Afflitto, fol. 14r.

41. David Sabean has argued that landless peasants (which were rare in Pentidat-

tilo) were unconcerned about the choice of godparents for their children; "Aspects," 97–98. The marquis's children usually had prominent godparents from outside the village, who, however, rarely traveled to Pentidattilo for the occasion and were instead represented by another member of the feudal household (most often by the marquis's eldest son, Lorenzo); see also Astarita, *Continuity,* 130.

42. In twenty-seven cases overall was the child baptized by the midwife, but in the other eighteen there was also at least one godparent mentioned. In the years when a new parish priest takes office, the records are sometimes sketchy. The twenty cases with no godparent concern thirteen boys and seven girls.

43. The case with no specifics is on a torn page; the birth of Domenico Manda is regularly reported with the names of his parents, but no godparent is mentioned, and the entry is accompanied by the sign of the cross and the notation that the child was "buried without rites at the age of one month, unable to [receive] the sacraments." The baptism of "monstrous" births was forbidden by the church; see, e.g., the synod of Reggio archbishop Damiano Polou, *Secunda synodus,* 209. On "monsters," see also Gélis, *History,* ch. 20, and Cressy, *Birth,* 117.

44. A few times the records show the same person acting as godparent on a few occasions very close in time to one another (at most three or four), and in these cases it is possible that the godparent might have been suggested by the priest rather than chosen by the parents, but these cases represent only a small number of the total (and often they concern foundlings, as might be expected). Many newborns are named after their grandparents, as is still common in southern Italy, and frequently children born on Sunday (*domenica*) received the name of Domenico or Domenica; Domenico/a and Antonio/a (or Antonino/a) were by far the most common names in the village. In France the great majority of children were named after their godparents. Fine, *Parrains,* 265 ff. See also Delille, "Le système," and Sabean, *Kinship,* 26–29 and ch. 8.

45. In Neckarhausen the same godparent often served for all the children of one household. Sabean, *Kinship,* 152–58; see also 23–26, and idem, *Property,* ch. 16.

46. One of the fifteen illegitimate children (as we saw for one of the foundlings) had two godparents. In these fifteen cases the father is either marked "unknown" or left unmentioned. Four additional births are marked "*spurio/a*" (illegitimate), but in these cases both parents are reported and the child bears the father's family name; these were probably cases of concubinage, a practice much lamented by Calabrian bishops (see Chapter 6). Finally, there are a few cases in which the child is given the mother's family name, although not only is a father reported but the parents are reported as married; I believe these were slips on the part of the priest, and in at least one case there is a correction to erase the mother's family name and write in the father's. The bishops insisted on the baptism of foundlings. Polou, *Prima synodus,* 38; see also Pelaja, *Matrimonio,* ch. 3, and Chapter 6 in the present volume.

47. Ursula was a slave of Francesco Alberti, brother of Domenico, who may have

been the father of her first two children. She later married Leonardo Squillaci. Chiara Alberti, also a slave of the marquis's family, appears, too, as both a mother and a god-mother in the baptismal records. They were probably North African women taken slave during pirate raids and purchased by the Alberti; they must have been baptized, and they were probably emancipated before long (certainly Ursula before her marriage). Two black women slaves (bearing Christian names and therefore likely also baptized) were mentioned in the will of Simonello Alberti in 1601; ACB, 19.9. Slaves were frequently bought and sold in seventeenth-century Reggio; Arillotta, *Reggio,* 211–18. On slaves, see also Visceglia, *Territorio,* 112–13; Ligresti, *Sicilia moderna,* ch. 4; Vitale, "Servi." On Calabrians taken slaves, see Riggio, "Schiavi calabresi in Tunisia," "Schiavi calabresi nell'ospedale," and "Un censimento." On slaves and illegitimate births, see Mazzi, *Prostitute,* 52–53; Vincent, "Affective Life."

48. Castan, "Mentalité rurale," 172; Flandrin, *Familles,* 40–42.

49. TR, fols. 23r (for Anna), 25v (for Pietro; the judge expressed his incredulity that someone who had lived in Pentidattilo for ten years could pretend not to know any of the local witnesses, even if Pietro spent most of his time as guardian of the forest). Bartolo Battaglia explained that he easily recognized Antonino's corpse "because he was my *paesano*" (fol. 5v), and the same expression recurs in the trial records.

50. Cozzetto, *Territorio,* ch. 7, describes similar houses in Aiello; see also Fiume, *Vecchia,* 153–56. When Gratia Costarella asked Cola de Amico for some arsenic to kill rats, for instance, the latter had been staying outside his house (in early March); TR, fol. 13v. Both Domenica and Anna refer to the "hole" through which each could hear the other talk.

51. TR, fols. 6v–7r. She must also have peeped, since she said that the fire was on and that she recognized Pietro and the two women, who were conspiring to murder Domenica's husband.

52. TR, fol. 14v. The otherwise loquacious Vittoria Vernagallo, wife of Giovan Battista Corso, did not mention this dance party at her own house, perhaps to protect herself from possible blame for facilitating the illicit relationship (her husband said nothing about it when he testified as one of the seven final witnesses in the trial). Dances were often delicate affairs; see Chapter 6 and Muchembled, *La violence au village,* 310 ff.

53. The witnesses referred to the exchanges necessary to obtain the arsenic as "doing [each other] a favor"; TR, fols. 10r and 11v; for Sicilia's visit, TR, fol. 17r. This link between the domestic sphere and space and affective or friendly relationships among women appears in other judicial records; see Crouzet-Pavan, "Testimonianze." See also Davis, *Pisticci,* ch. 4, and Gélis, *History,* chs. 7 and 14.

54. See Chapter 6. As another example of the amount of information easily available to neighbors, when Anna first suggested that Domenica poison her husband, she knew that her neighbor had five carlini saved up; no explanation was given, nor any demanded, of how Anna knew this.

55. ASRC, notai, busta 420, fascicolo 2217 (1740), fols. 3v–5r, where the settlement is described as taking place "through friends." On friendship, see also Castan, *Honnêteté*, ch. 3.

56. Sallmann, *Chercheurs*, 119–40; also Fiume, *Vecchia*, 158–67, and Friese, "La prassi."

57. TR, fols. 25r–v; see also Chapter 5.

58. TR, fol. 17r. Anna herself, during her interrogation, admitted knowing all the witnesses, but she denied any particular relationship with any of them: "With these women I never had any dealings"; TR, fol. 23r.

59. TR, fols. 9r–10r and 11r–v.

60. TR, fols. 19r–22r. Vittoria Vernagallo had put the same emphasis on what she saw as the "great friendship" between Pietro and Anna (fol. 7r).

61. TR, fol. 12r.

F I V E   *Justice, Sexuality, and Women*

1. The coadiutore represented the interests of the court in its prosecutorial aspect, that is, in theory, the public interest; he was basically the public prosecutor and therefore formally entered the trial at the moment when indictments were brought against the defendants. See Chapter 2.

2. ASRC, Statuti Capitoli, busta 1, fascicolo 22 for the 1648 agreement, p. 8.

3. TR, fols. 23r–24r. Like the following two, Anna's deposition was attended by Governor Amodei, Nesci, Romeo, and the scribe. It was standard to ask defendants for their opinion of the witnesses' veracity; see Chapter 2.

4. "Contesting" the suit meant that the accused did not confess and therefore further action was necessary.

5. TR, fols. 25r–v.

6. I am somewhat liberally translating Pietro's reply ("Signori, à me mi vonno male"), typical in its vagueness as to who "they" are and in its vision of a world of fundamental enmities that need no explanation. The same Felice Amodei was appointed as Pietro's defense lawyer.

7. TR, fols. 27r–29v.

8. Domenica revisited in detail what the court already knew from previous depositions. She might actually have been questioned informally before the other two defendants, as details of her confession appear in the judge's accusations to Pietro and Anna.

9. According to Domenica's deposition, her mother, Francesca, at the time of the trial was living in Melito, which may explain why she was not questioned by the court.

10. TR, fols. 29v–30r; see Chapter 2.

11. TR, fols. 30r–v.

12. TR, fols. 30v–31r.

13. In addition to the literature cited in Chapter 2, see Alessi Palazzolo, *Prova legale*; Langbein, *Torture*; Schnapper, "Les peines arbitraires"; Gilissen, "La preuve."

14. A favorite example cited in many treatises was that of someone seen with a bloody sword in his hands exiting a house in which a slain corpse was then found; jurists topped one another's creativity in elaborating reasons why this could not be held to constitute full proof.

15. Novario, *De vassallorum*, pt. 3, no. 209. For another example of the importance of reputation, see Ago, "Conflitti."

16. De Sarno, *Novissima*, 183. Other jurists were rarely more concrete in their discussion of the value of clues; Novario, for instance, stated that "light" clues were enough to arrest, "grave" ones to question, and "undoubted" ones to torture the defendant; *De vassallorum*, pt. 3, no. 209. Scialoja, *Praxis*, also struggled with these definitions. See also Nani, *Degl'indizi*. On the centrality of confession, see Marchetti, *Testis*.

17. Ambrosino, *Processus*, 221.

18. Marchetti, *Testis*, 86–87.

19. Langbein, *Torture*, and Alessi Palazzolo, *Prova legale*, discuss these developments at length. Cardinal de Luca specifically advised judges to avoid torture on this ground at "their prudent discretion." *Il dottor volgare*, 10:83–84.

20. Giustiniani, *Nuova collezione*, vol. 9, prammatiche XIV (1621) and XV (1622) *de officio iudicum* (in this edition they appear as nos. XIV and XV, although in most discussions they are referred to as nos. XII and XIII); Alessi Palazzolo, *Prova legale*, ch. 4; Panico, *Il carnefice*, 38–39; Marchetti, *Testis*, 183–84.

21. Alessi Palazzolo, *Prova legale*, discusses several moments of the debate in Naples. Scialoja, *Praxis*, 24. See also Sorge, *Iurisprudentia*, 9:196–200, and Briganti, *Pratica*, 91.

22. A moderate voice is Sorge, *Iurisprudentia*, 9:157: "The graver the crime the fuller must be its proof, and the more vehemently have all presumptions to concur in it."

23. Muchembled, *L'invention*, ch. 3; idem, *Le temps des supplices*, 202. See also Tomás y Valiente, *El derecho*, ch. 4; Bonacchi, *Legge e peccato*; Davidson, "Theology"; Prodi and Penuti, *Disciplina*; Turrini, *La coscienza e le leggi*.

24. See also Chapter 6. Because women by themselves lacked the seed necessary for procreation, some jurists extended relative toleration even to lesbianism; see Clavero, "Delito y pecado"; Brown, *Immodest Acts*, 12; Sánchez Ortega, *La mujer*, 32–33. Prostitution was, of course, quite common, but, although increasingly regulated, it was rarely, if ever, criminalized; see, e.g., Mazzi, *Prostitute*; Brackett, "Florentine Onestà"; Perry, *Crime*, ch. 10.

25. Champin, "Un cas"; Margot, "La criminalité"; Ruff, *Crime*, 167–72; Petrovitch, "Recherches"; Sharpe, *Crime*, 55; Zorzi, "Sull'amministrazione"; Doneddu, "Crimine"; Carli Sardi, "Analisi," finds for Siena in 1762–86 a rate of about 3%, but with an additional almost 10% in rape cases alone (413–14).

26. For the bishops' condemnations, see Chapter 6. The following treatises deal closely with specific crimes: Rovito, *Luculenta commentaria* (this is a collection of writings from other jurists; see esp. Follerio's *De sodomia* [1553]); de Angelis, *De delictis* (the author is a seventeenth-century jurist; the edition I used includes commentaries from a later editor); Muscatello, *Practica,* esp. 549–686. See also, besides Giustiniani, *Nuova collezione,* these collections of laws: *Constitutiones*; Cirillo, *Codicis*; *Dizionario*; de Sariis, *Codice.*

27. See, e.g., Fasano Guarini, "The Prince"; Petrovitch, "Recherches"; Deleito y Piñuela, *La mala vida,* pt. 1; Brackett, *Criminal Justice,* ch. 6.

28. See the prammatica *de osculantibus mulieres* (1563) in Giustiniani, *Nuova collezione,* 12:175–76.

29. De Leonardis, *Prattica,* 79; on sodomy, de Angelis, *De delictis,* 1:323, and Claro, *Opera,* 103. See also Andrews, *Law,* ch. 18.

30. De Angelis, *De delictis,* 1:224; Claro, *Opera,* 397; see also Egmond and Mason, *Mammoth and the Mouse,* ch. 6; on suicides, Clavero, "Delito y pecado"; although no penalty was to be inflicted on the corpses of successful suicides other than the denial of church burial, Fighera, contemptuous of irony, recommended the death penalty for attempts. *Institutiones,* 2:319.

31. Claro, *Opera,* 728. See McLynn, *Crime,* ch. 7; Doody, "'Those Eyes'"; Dolan, *Dangerous Familiars*; Garnot, *Un Crime*; Juratic, "Meurtrière"; Fiume, *Vecchia*; Wegert, *Popular Culture,* 137–42.

32. There were many such. Novario (*De vassallorum,* 3:121) lists fraud, simulation, fake birth, incest, adultery, sodomy, simony, conspiracy, false coinage, usury, all domestic and nocturnal crimes, clandestine marriage, and destruction of documents. On nocturnal crimes, see Follerio, *Practica,* 270.

33. Sanfelice, *Decisionum,* 1:81, for instance, allowed for torture in hidden and difficult crimes even in the absence of corpus delicti and on the basis of simple clues.

34. Lists of symptoms in Muscatello, *Practica,* 590–92; Follerio, *Practica,* 30; de Angelis, *De delictis,* 1:490; de Liguoro, *Guida,* 7–13; de Sarno, *Novissima,* 402–3; Moro, *Pratica,* 1:341–65; Zacchia, *Quaestiones,* 1:127–50; and esp. Greco, *Il medico fiscale,* in de Sarno, *Novissima,* 466–556 (this is a handbook for physicians involved in criminal investigations, and it discusses all symptoms and physical evidence to be analyzed for various crimes; for the symptoms of poisons, see 466–77). In a Sicilian poisoning case the court fed the suspect substance to two dogs, which quickly died. Fiume, *Vecchia,* 101–8 and 202–12.

35. Claro, *Opera,* 512–15, on "mixed" crimes; Sallmann, *Chercheurs,* 56–57; de Angelis, *Tractatus,* 209–12, on blasphemy; on church courts, Diaz de Luco, *Practica.* See also Flynn, "Blasphemy"; Burke, *Historical Anthropology,* ch. 8; Gacto, "El delito"; Monter and Tedeschi, "Toward a Statistical Profile." On the Spanish Inquisition and sexual crimes, see Haliczer, *Inquisition*; Monter, *Frontiers*; Perry, *Crime,* 71–72.

36. The last three were rarely, if ever, explicitly condemned in the laws, so they are

discussed only in the writings of jurists with more vivid imaginations. De Angelis, *De delictis*, 1:315, argued that oral intercourse was even worse than anal intercourse "because the mouth is a more precious, more handsome, and more noble receptacle, given to men by God for a more excellent goal." Moro, *Pratica*, 3:13, specifies that, as the laws do not explicitly punish lesbianism (a "desperate, incredible lasciviousness"), the judge can inflict any penalty he sees fit. In a revealingly phallocentric conception of intercourse, the penalty suggested by jurists for lesbianism was death if an instrument was used, corporal punishments or relegation if not (Claro, *Opera*, 359–61; de Angelis, *De delictis*, 1:326); see also Crompton, "Myth"; van der Meer, "Tribades"; and Brown, *Immodest Acts*. The discussion of these crimes is always more detailed in Latin than in vernacular texts; Cardinal de Luca, in the Italian version of his great work, explicitly says that he will tread lightly upon sodomy in order not to offend his readers, the more learned among whom he refers to the Latin version for details; *Il dottor volgare*, 10:320–22. On stuprum, see the next section of this chapter. See also Di Simplicio, "Sulla sessualità," and Scarabello, "Devianza sessuale"; on the concept of "unspeakable" crimes, see Chiffoleau, "Dire l'indicibile," and Szabo and Pietralunga, "Ruptures."

37. Muscatello, *Practica*, 664; brutes and demons were also especially forbidden categories of partners, but they cannot have been very easy to come by; Moro, *Pratica*, 3:1–111, is entirely devoted to crimes "of sensuality."

38. Masturbation was the ultimate solitary crime and was therefore considered the most difficult to prove. The offense to God, however, made any crime a public concern and made it necessary to punish this one, too. Fighera recommended exile, prison, or whipping; *Institutiones*, 2:289–90. De Angelis emphasized that any "pollution outside the [natural] vase" had to be punished if at all possible, despite the silence of Roman and Neapolitan laws on this matter; *De delictis*, 1:314–16. In 1727 a man in Modena was hanged by the local Inquisition for maintaining that, while anal sex was indeed sinful, thinking about it for the purpose of masturbating was but a venial sin; Canosa, *Storia*, 107–16.

39. Since laws and doctrine strictly decreed that, to erase any memory of the offense, both the perpetrator and his partner ought to be burned alive, it would, in any case, hardly have been in the interest of the animal to lodge accusations. Bestiality, though in theory considered even worse than sodomy, in practice was prosecuted with much less vehemence, since it was primarily a rural crime and "not a matter of negative consequences to the common weal"; de Luca, *Il dottor volgare*, 10:160–61. See also de Angelis, *De delictis*, 1:76–77; while as a reminder of the act the animal partner to bestiality was to be burned, animals were not considered to have a will and therefore should not be put to death if they killed someone, Claro, *Opera*, 866 and 361. An exception to the usual neglect of bestiality by the courts took place in Sweden, where one-third of all executions were aimed at its perpetrators; Liliequist, "Peasants." See also

Parker, "Is the Duck an Animal?"; Wegert, *Popular Culture,* ch. 6; Salisbury, *Beast Within,* ch. 3; Gilbert, "Conceptions."

40. "A fetid, vile, horrendous, detestable, and nefarious subject"; de Sarno, *Novissima,* 231. The condemnation was unanimous: all sodomites had died the day Christ had been born—including Virgil (Diaz de Luco, *Practica,* 365); the devil himself, after luring the sinner to it, "immediately flees, for not even he can observe such a horrendous crime" (ibid., 365); sodomy caused "famines, earthquakes, pestilences" (Fulgoni, *Summa,* fol. 111v); it was worse than sleeping with one's mother (Claro, *Opera,* 102); it had been invented either by Orpheus or by women (Sorge, *Iurisprudentia,* 9:406); though common in Italy, it was much rarer among the Germans (Carpzov, *Practica,* 2:209). Casalicchio, *Gli stimoli,* reports that two young sodomites burned "in a stinking, black fire" while fornicating in church (pt. 1, pp. 27–28).

Sodomy could not be composed; in Naples sodomites could not be pardoned even by the viceroy (see the three prammatiche *de sodomia* in Giustiniani, *Nuova collezione,* 14:146–48), and not only could a judge proceed ex officio, but he must do so (Cirillo, *Codicis,* 2:126–28). The penalty was death by burning (mitigated often by hanging before burning) entirely to remove the offending bodies from the community. Being accused by a boy (or even having slept in the same bed with a boy) was enough to torture the accused (Muscatello, *Practica,* 669; Sanfelice, *Decisionum,* 2:151). Mercy could only be shown to a wife who had given in to the husband's urging; both partners were to be burned, though the worst offender was a mature man who took the passive role, "too great a filthiness" (de Luca, *Dottor volgare,* 10:322). However, as full conviction required that completion of the act be proved (something virtually impossible in consensual cases), extraordinary penalties were often imposed, frequently short of death. See also Follerio, *De sodomia,* fols. 110r–112v, and *Practica,* 589–90; de Angelis, *De delictis,* 314–16 and 320–28; de Sarno, *Novissima,* 221–32. Modern studies are Labalme, "Sodomy"; Martini, *Il "vitio nefando"*; Carrasco, *Inquisición* and "Lazarillo"; Gerard and Hekma, *Pursuit of Sodomy*; Rocke, "Il controllo" and *Forbidden Friendships.*

41. De Angelis, *Tractatus,* 250–53; idem, *De delictis,* 1:453–64; de Liguoro, *Guida,* 14–21; Muscatello, *Practica,* 663–73; de Sarno, *Novissima,* 400–402 (even without a hymen "the first coition for women is most laborious" [400]); Greco, *Medico,* 478–91 and 510–56; Moro, *Pratica,* 2:365–89; Zacchia, *Quaestiones,* 1:262–69.

42. These cases, not otherwise numbered, appear in ACB, 95 (1791), 99 (1778–81), and 98 (1787); the trial of Angelo del Nigro for the rape of a boy (ACB, 96 [1802]) includes a clear echo of jurisprudential language in the complaint that the defendant is being held despite the lack of "proof as clear as the light of mid-day" (no fol.); see also Chapter 6 for an 1803 abortion trial in Atena with the depositions of the midwives. Moro, *Pratica,* 2:370, recommended consulting two midwives or, if only one was available, adding an elderly woman. See also a 1738 trial in Giacomini, *Sposi,* 61–69. Women were used as experts in these and other cases also in English law. Oldham, "On Pleading the Belly," and Sharpe, "Women."

43. The laws in Naples were relatively silent on the matter, leaving the field open to jurisprudential debates; the *Dizionario* mentions only a royal dispatch of 1758 on abortion (1:1). See also Schnapper, "La justice"; McLaren, *History of Contraception,* chs. 1 and 2.

44. Fulgoni, *Summa,* fol. 118v; Follerio, *Practica,* 488 and 498–99; Sorge, *Iurisprudentia,* 9:365–66; de Angelis, *De delictis,* 1:9–12; Claro, *Opera,* 717; de Sarno, *Novissima,* 377, 463–64; Greco, *Medico,* 502–5; Moro, *Pratica,* 1:369–73; Carpzov, *Practica,* 1:49; Zacchia, *Quaestiones,* 1:27 and 2:194–211. On the methods, see Claverie and Lamaison, *L'impossible mariage,* ch. 11; Dolan, *Dangerous Familiars,* ch. 4. In England quickening was usually the moment when abortion became criminal; Cressy, *Birth,* 47–50. For a specific case, see Povolo, "Aspetti sociali." A survey of contraceptive and abortion methods is in Riddle, *Contraception.* See also Chapter 6.

45. De Angelis, *De delictis,* 1:11–12; Follerio, *Practica,* 498, on deformed or brutish fetuses.

46. Cirillo, *Codicis,* 2:106; see also the prammatiche *de adulterio* in Giustiniani, *Nuova collezione,* 1:308–12: the prammatica I (1731) specifically prohibited proceeding ex officio with adultery and stuprum, "from which would result the dishonor of families, and hence murders and other crimes, which relatives, from the publicity given to their shame, are as if forced to commit." Similar concerns applied in England; Ingram, *Church Courts,* ch. 8.

47. Sorge, *Iurisprudentia,* 9:371–86; see also Trasselli, "Du fait divers."

48. De Angelis, *Tractatus,* 215–21; idem, *De delictis,* 1:13–25; Claro, *Opera,* 343–47; Carpzov, *Practica,* 2:3; the quote in Sorge, *Iurisprudentia,* 9:375; TR, fols. 27r–29v.

49. Claro, *Opera,* 727; Follerio, *De sodomia,* fols. 110v–111r.

50. Claro, *Opera,* 344 (the phrase originates with Alciatus, an earlier jurist, and is repeated by de Luca, *Il dottor volgare,* 10:114; on 117–18, his comment on the effect of prosecution); the second quote is in Rota, *Legalis androgynus,* 265.

51. Follerio, *Practica,* 575.

52. De Sarno, *Novissima,* 404; de Angelis, *De delictis,* 1:16; Moro, *Pratica,* 3:3.

53. De Angelis, *De delictis,* 1:17–18.

54. See also Panico, "Criminali e peccatori."

55. Rota, *Legalis androgynus,* 327–73 for contracts and economic rights, 52–54 for wills; Rota also categorized types of illicit relationships: *concubinae* live with a man to whom they are not married; *amasiae* are the mistresses of only one man, but they do not live with him; *meretrices* are prostitutes (257–61). See also Maclean, *Renaissance Notion of Woman,* ch. 5; Kuehn, *Law; Las mujeres;* Kermode and Walker, *Women;* Wiesner, *Women,* 30–35 and 46–56; Beattie, "Criminality"; Sponsler, "Status"; Jütte, "Geschlechtspezifische Kriminalität"; Cohn, *Women in the Streets;* Dayton, *Women before the Bar.*

56. These notations come after the cross marks at the end of each deposition in the trial records: "This is the sign of the cross of X, who does not know how to write" or

"idiot"; "idiot" here has its old meaning of rustic and illiterate, but by the eighteenth century it had certainly acquired the new, more derogatory connotation, and thus it is telling that it should have been reserved for women; as we saw in Chapter 1, in the late sixteenth century "idiot" had been used also for men.

57. De Angelis, *Tractatus,* 219–20; idem, *De delictis,* 2:154; Follerio, *De sodomia,* fol. 111r; Rota, *Legalis Androgynus,* no. 152, p. 8. Another sign that virginity was not a physical but a legal condition is in Rota's example of the town of Palinuro, where girls at age twelve supposedly lost their virginity because of the hot air but kept its legal privileges (124).

58. Rota, *Legalis Androgynus,* no. 140, p. 8; Moro, *Pratica,* 1:119; de Leonardis, *Prattica,* 138; Perry, *Crime,* 92.

59. Briganti, *Pratica,* 194 (see also 77); Rota, *Legalis Androgynus,* 52; Follerio, *Practica,* 29; Schnapper, "Testes inhabiles"; Gowing, *Domestic Dangers.*

60. Rota, *Legalis Androgynus,* 124 (the quote) and 266; on the penalties, see Capobianco, *Tractatus* (1614 ed.), 182; Novario, *De vassallorum,* 2:165; Fulgoni, *Summa,* fols. 133v–134r; de Angelis, *De delictis,* 2:158; on prisons Rota, *Legalis Androgynus,* 65 (he argued also that noble women should be imprisoned in their own castles); the prammatica XXXI (1558) *de officio magistri iudiciarii seu M.C. Vicariae* in Giustiniani, *Nuova collezione,* vol. 10, and the twenty-four edicts *de carcerariis,* ibid., 3:141–71; on the Vicaria prison, see Scaduto, "Le carceri"; Canosa and Colonnello, *Storia,* 77–89; Calà-Ulloa, *Dell'amministrazione,* 215–26.

61. Claro, *Opera,* 695; Rota, *Legalis Androgynus,* no. 140, p. 8; Scialoja, *Praxis,* 80–81 and 112–13.

62. De Angelis, *De delictis,* 2:155–56; Follerio, *Practica,* 358. Witchcraft is too large a subject to discuss here in detail; examples of trials of women are in Bondì, *Strix*; Francia, *Storia minima*; Vissière, *Procès de femmes.*

63. Carpzov, *Practica,* 1:39–45 (quotes on 42; he refers to infanticide under the rubric of parricide); Moro, *Pratica,* 1:339–41 and 371–72. See also Povolo, "Aspetti sociali"; idem, "Dal versante"; Ingram, *Church Courts,* 158–60; Malcomson, "Infanticide"; Wessling, "Infanticide Trials"; Jackson, "Suspicious Infant Deaths" and *New-Born Child Murder*; Hoffer and Hull, *Murdering Mothers*; Schulte, *Village in Court,* ch. 4; Flandrin, *Les amours paysannes,* 203–4; Sharpe, *Crime,* 60–62; Trexler, "Infanticide"; Wrightson, "Infanticide"; Wegert, *Popular Culture,* ch. 5.

64. De Angelis, *Tractatus,* 221; Follerio, *De sodomia,* fol. 111v.

65. Briganti, *Pratica,* 106; the other quotes are in the four prammatiche *de adulterio* in Giustiniani, *Nuova collezione,* 1:308–12, issued between 1731 and 1799, and in the prammatica XIX *de ordine et forma iudiciorum* (1738), 12:121. Stuprum was a form of illicit seduction and fornication; Coluccia, "Indagine"; Peccianti, "Gli inconvenienti"; Farr, *Authority,* ch. 4; Alessi, "L'onore riparato" and "Il gioco degli scambi"; Raffaele, "'Essendo Real volontà'"; Ruggiero, *Violence,* ch. 10; Gambier, "La donna"; Cavallo

and Cerruti, "Onore femminile"; Di Simplicio, "Violenza." On the background for stuprum, see Moses, "Livy's Lucretia," and Laiou, "Sex," 114 ff.

66. See, e.g., Grevi, *"Nemo tenetur"*; Buganza, "Il teste"; Marchetti, *Testis,* pt. 2; Fiume, *Vecchia,* 212–26; Schnapper, "Les Peines arbitraires"; Maza, *Private Lives,* ch. 4.

67. See the codes proposed by Cirillo and de Sariis; see also Grimaldi and Grimaldi, *Istoria,* and Calisse, *Storia,* pt. 3.

68. The prammatiche are XIX (1738) *de ordine et forma iudiciorum* in Giustiniani, *Nuova collezione,* 12:98–129; III (1738) and V (1744) *de homicidiis puniendis,* ibid., 5:95–106; and XXV (1744) *de baronibus,* ibid., 3:111–12. See Miceli, "La giurisdizione"; Ajello, *Il problema,* ch. 3; and Rao, *Il Regno.* According to de Angelis, *Tractatus,* 401–7, the barons had always had to consult the udienze before executing criminals, but they had no obligation to defer murder cases to them.

69. Ajello, *Il problema,* for the togati; Manna, *Della giurisprudenza,* proudly observed that, after those of Rome, the Neapolitan magistrates and lawyers were "the most numerous, the most powerful, the wealthiest, the most celebrated" in Europe (51). On the reforms, see Nicolini, *Della procedura,* 2:234, 251, and 275–78; Alessi, *Giustizia,* 62–68, on moral crimes. Ferdinand IV of Naples (and III of Sicily) became Ferdinand I of the Two Sicilies after the 1815 restoration. On legal reforms elsewhere in Italy, see Scarabello, "Progetti."

70. Filangieri, *Scienza,* esp. 1:14 and 17; 2:2 and 87.

71. Ibid., esp. 2:117, 191–208, 250–61, and 297; 3:24–37 and 412–16. On the question of the certitude of the judge, see Andrews, *Law,* 580–82; this issue had already appeared, as we saw, in the Neapolitan edict of 1621.

72. Mattei, *Che la dolcezza*; Galanti, *Testamento forense,* 57 and 87; Pagano, *Considerazioni,* 137, *Principii,* and *La logica* (which includes [53–64] the two laws of the Jacobin Republic, authored by Pagano, which abolished torture and arbitrary penalties and guaranteed free justice to all citizens). See also Masci, *Esame.* On these thinkers, see Galasso, "La legge" and "L'ultimo feudalesimo"; Massafra, "Un problème"; Rao, *L'"amaro".*

73. On French developments, see Esmein, *Histoire,* pt. 3; Muller, "Magistrats"; on Naples, de Martino, *Antico regime,* chs. 4 and 5. See also the *Codice penale del 1812,* esp. 78–79, 82–83, and 86–88: a husband who kept a concubine (i.e., a mistress living in the home) could not denounce his adulterous wife and could himself be fined.

74. Nicolini, *Della procedura,* 4:12–17 (quote on 13), 37–39, and 274–333, and on adultery 3:188–89; the 1819 codes in *Leggi penali* and *Leggi della procedura*; see also Vacca, *Indice*; Calà-Ulloa, *Dell'amministrazione,* which favored the English model; and Marini, *Del diritto,* which also argued for the jury system, "the only means to achieve the triple goal of criminal justice, namely to take away the criminal's hope for impunity, the innocent's fear of oppression, the judge's license for arbitrariness" (notes, p. 105); Marini also urged lesser penalties for abortion and infanticide when commit-

ted in the defense of honor (207). Modern studies are in Landi, *Istituzioni,* and Greco, "Istituzioni."

s i x   *Religion, the Church, and Popular Morality*

1. Romeo, *Inquisitori.* In Spain, on the other hand, the Inquisition was active in the repression of sexual crimes.

2. See, e.g., the works of Muchembled, *Popular Culture, L'invention, La violence au village,* and *Le temps des supplices;* Muchembled minimizes the resilience of rural popular culture. For critiques, see Wegert, *Popular Culture,* and Briggs, *Communities,* conclusion. See also Burke, "From Pioneers to Settlers" and *Varieties,* ch. 11; Scribner, "Is a History of Popular Culture Possible?"; Muir, *Ritual.*

3. The ricettizie declined under French rule at the start of the nineteenth century but were only abolished in 1867; see Russo, *Chiesa e comunità;* idem, *Chiesa, assistenza e società;* De Vitiis, "Chiese ricettizie"; De Rosa, *Chiesa;* De Rosa and Malgeri, *Società;* Rosa, *Religione;* idem, *Clero;* De Maio, *Società;* Pellegrino and Spedicato, *Società;* Carroll, *Madonnas That Maim,* ch. 5; idem, "Religion"; idem, *Veiled Threats,* 200–206; Gentilcore, *From Bishop to Witch;* Martucci, "'De vita'"; Brancaccio, *Il trono;* Astarita, *Continuity,* 131–32.

4. See Chapter 1; Gentilcore, *From Bishop to Witch,* 53–55; Rodotà, *Dell'origine;* Peri, "Chiesa."

5. Russo, *Storia,* 2:199; on the clergy's numbers, see Martucci, "'De vita'"; Caridi, *Chiesa,* 41–45 and 158; Tondo, "Proprietà."

6. Gentilcore, *From Bishop to Witch,* 55; Rodotà, *Dell'origine,* vol. 1, ch. 10, and vol. 3, chs. 3–4 and 6; the acts of del Fosso's 1565 council are in ASCC, Fondo Concilî 21, Calabria, fol. 3r.

7. The most extensive treatment of D'Afflitto is Denisi, *L'opera,* which includes several documents, including the 1595 synod and the report of the 1595 visit; for the synod's discussion of the Greek beliefs, see 343–45, and for the visit to the Greek area, see 252–316 (Pentidattilo at 283–88). One of the sons of the dittereo was himself one of the other married clerics; *protopapa* was simply the Greek version of *arciprete.* On the Counter Reformation in the Reggio diocese, see also Denisi, "Consistenza"; Sposato, "Note," and *Aspetti;* Mariotti, "Le costituzioni," "Studi," and *Problemi,* which points out the limited success of seminaries in the Diocese of Reggio and the continuing ignorance of the priests well into the seventeenth century (171–79). On Tridentine reforms elsewhere in the kingdom, see De Rosa and Cestaro, *Il Concilio;* Di Leo, *I sinodi;* Miele, *Provinzialkonzilien.*

8. ADRC, Visite pastorali D'Afflitto (1597), fols. 76r–104r for Pentidattilo.

9. Ferrante, "Manoscritti" (I thank Padre Ferrante for giving me a copy of his article); Minicucci, "Notizie"; Longo, "Presenze." The monastery was suppressed as part of the general suppression of small monasteries in the kingdom ordered by Pope

Innocent X in 1652 (see also the acts of D'Afflitto's 1595 visit, cited in note 7 above); the monastery's revenues and property were transferred to the secular churches of the village.

10. A list of the bishops is in Spanò-Bolani, *Storia,* appendix. See also Russo, *Storia,* vol. 3 for the bishops and vols. 1 and 2 for information about Pentidattilo. On the Greek clergy, see also De Lorenzo, *Un secondo manipolo,* 31–40. The Greek rite continued until the early eighteenth century in areas of Abruzzi and Puglia; see Donvito and Pellegrino, *L'organizzazione,* 31–34; Carnevale Caprice, "Chiesa"; Giura, *Storie,* 119–73. Rodotà, *Dell'origine,* vol. 1, ch. 10, and vol. 2, ch. 10, details the Greek areas and monasteries (most of the latter were in the region of Reggio and Messina). Mariotti, "Concili," lists (149–69) all synods and councils held by the archbishops: there were four provincial councils between 1565 and 1602 and then no more; D'Afflitto held seventeen diocesan synods between 1595 and 1635, while his successors held only five between 1647 and 1691, and then no more were held until the two held by Archbishop Polou in 1729 and 1751 (for which see below), which were to be the last synods until 1823. The same pattern can be observed in the *relationes ad limina*; see the next note.

11. Denisi, *L'opera,* 38–42, for the confraternities; for clerical numbers, see also Manduca, "Clero," 148–56. See also the reports of the bishops to papal authorities in ASV, Relationes ad limina, Rheginen, 685-A, dating from 1589 to 1770. Because of the size of the diocese, the reports are often repetitive and not very specific. Their frequency also reflects the diligence of the bishops, so that there are at least thirteen under D'Afflitto, only a few (and concentrated on the city of Reggio itself) for the mid-seventeenth century, four between 1683 and 1693, and then three under Polou. On the Melito church, see Russo, *Storia,* 2:159–60.

12. The 1597 visit by D'Afflitto in ADRC, Visite pastorali D'Afflitto (1597), fol. 78v, and passim for the total revenues. ASN, Catasto Onciario 6091, the collettiva at the end of the document. Much of the income of chapels and churches was not taxed because of deductions due to obligations (mostly liturgical) attached to it; see Chapter 3. On the property of the archdiocese in Pentidattilo, see also ASN, Sommaria Partium 2101, fol. 149r (1621).

13. ASN, Catasto Onciario 6090, fols. 12r and 834v.

14. ACB, 19.26–27; Mariotti, *Problemi,* 322; ACB, 19.24 and 71; ACB, 8.53, fols. 19r–20r; ACB, 4.52b and 4.56a.

15. ASN, Conti Comunali 214, Calabria Ultra, fascicolo 2, fols. 84r–v; Catasto Onciario 6091, fol. 52v, and 6090, fol. 835r; ACB, 19.28.

16. ASRC, Carte e Miscellanea Blasco 4aB (1796), pp. 338–40, 4bC, 4bE, fols. 593r–598v; ASCZ, Cassa Sacra, Vendite e Censuazioni, busta 31, fascicoli 1499–1512, and busta 37, fascicoli 1742–59; ASCZ, Cassa Sacra, Segreteria Ecclesiastica, busta 39, fascicolo 907, fols. 3r–10v, 22r, 32r–35v, and 72r–v, and fascicolo 908, fols. 4r–7v, and busta 20, fascicolo 413, fols. 1r–2r, 15r–40v, 42r–43v (with the quote); ASN, Suprema Giunta di Corrispondenza, Processi di Cassa Sacra, busta 120, fascicolo 2072. On church prop-

erty and the 1783 earthquake, see also Placanica, *La Calabria*, vol. 2, chs. 1 and 4, and *Il patrimonio*.

17. Arciprete Francesco Fiati was asked to certify the date of death of the marquis; ASN, Relevi 390.2, fol. 11r (1686). The two wills are in ACB, 19.35 and 19.42 (the dittereo also witnessed the marquis's will); in another document Fiati again attests to Domenico's burial (ACB, 19.41). In 1649 a man with a name similar to the then arciprete's is among the witnesses to the agreement between the università and the marquis, but he is not identified as a priest (ACB, 19.17).

18. ASRC, notai, busta 420, fascicoli 2217–24.

19. The "Indies of this side" became something of a cliché and was applied also to parts of Spain; see Tacchi Venturi, *Storia*, vol. 1, ch. 16, esp. 269–70; Kamen, *Phoenix*, 84–85; Ginzburg, "Folklore"; Prosperi, "'Otras Indias.'" On missions, see Prosperi, "Missioni" and *Tribunali*, pt. 3; Châtellier, *Religion*; Gentilcore, "'Adapt Yourselves'"; De Rosa, *Vescovi*, ch. 5; Faralli, "Le missioni"; Sampers, "Primi contatti" and "Missioni"; Orlandi, "I redentoristi"; Rienzo, "Il processo"; Novi Chavarria, "L'attività" and "Le missioni"; Paolucci, *Missioni*. None mentions missions near Pentidattilo.

20. De Gennaro's quote in Mariotti, *Problemi*, 124; see also the records of the two synods of Archbishop Polou: Polou, *Prima synodus* and *Secunda synodus*. Polou's threat to the ignorant is in his 1729 relatio ad limina. D'Afflitto's urgings against lay reading and about the mass appear in his 1602 provincial council, ASCC, Fondo Concilî 21, Calabria, fols. 12r–v and 5r, respectively. On bishops and regulars, see Mariotti, "Rapporti"; for the Benevento example, Campanelli, "Clero," 103–4. See also Martucci, "'De vita,'" and Miele, *Provinzialkonzilien*, ch. 8.

21. See, e.g., Allegra, "Il Parroco"; Gentilcore, "Methods"; Turchini, "La nascita"; Dewald, *Pont-St-Pierre*, 145–46; Farr, *Authority*, ch. 3; Greenshields, *Economy*, 139–46; Luria, *Territories*; Gutton, *La sociabilité*, ch. 6; Briggs, *Communities*, chs. 6–7 and conclusion; Nalle, *God in la Mancha*; Forster, *Counter-Reformation*; and Hoffman, *Church*. On rural community and religious life, see also Torre, *Il consumo di devozioni*; more generally on the Counter Reformation church and popular culture, see Kamen, *Phoenix*, and the survey by Hsia, *World*. Recent studies of Protestant areas are Dixon, *Reformation*, and Tolley, *Parishes*.

22. For an introduction to these issues, on which there is a rich bibliography, see, e.g., the works cited in note 2 of this chapter; Burke, *Popular Culture*; Ginzburg, *Cheese and the Worms* and "Folklore"; Delumeau, *Catholicism*; Bossy, *Christianity*; Monter, *Ritual*; Sabean, *Power*; Levi, *Inheriting Power*; Saint-Saëns, *Permanence*. In the following notes I cite primarily works of specific relevance to Italy or Naples.

23. Marino, *Medicina e magia*. See also O'Neil, "Magical Healing" and "*Sacerdote*"; Gentilcore, "'All That Pertains to Medicine,'" "'Charlatans,'" and "Contesting Illness"; Brancaccio, *Il Trono*, 207–10; Delogu, *L'erba*; Burke, *Historical Anthropology*, ch. 15; Henry, "Doctors."

24. Gentilcore, *From Bishop to Witch*, 106; idem, "The Church."

25. Romeo, *Inquisitori*; Monter and Tedeschi, "Toward a Statistical Profile"; Volpe, *Il Cilento*, ch. 3; Ficco and D'Ambrosio, *Trasgressione*, 5–53.

26. See Chapter 5; Sallmann, *Chercheurs*; Pomata, *La promessa*; Fiume, *Vecchia*.

27. Zanelli, *Streghe*; Viscardi, "Magia." Like Anna, many suspect women joined medical skills with expertise in cloth making.

28. See Celia's papers in ASRC, busta 420, fascicolo 2217, fols. 5r–6v (1740); 2220, fols. 6v–7r (1747); 2218, fols. 13r–14v (1741); 2221, fols. 10v–15r (1748); 2224, unnumbered fol. (1754); 2219, fols. 3r–4v and 4v–7r (1742). At their death married women could dispose of their property fairly freely if they had no children; see 2221, fols. 15r–17v (1748, a woman with a child), and 2222, fols. 21v–24r (1751, a childless woman). For dowries, see Caridi, "Capitoli"; Goody, "Inheritance"; Sabean, *Property*, chs. 7–9; and Groppi, *Il lavoro delle donne*.

29. ACB, 21.8, fols. 73r–v; ASRC, Demani inventario 33, busta 241, fascicolo 1, fols. 12r–v. Similarly, when Giuseppe Caracciolo Brienza wanted to show his contempt towards his vassals after the 1647 revolt, he allegedly forced local women to dance with his servants; see Astarita, *Continuity*, 149–50. On honor and women, see Sallmann, *Chercheurs*, 119–23; Fiume, *Onore*; Castan, *Honnêteté*, ch. 3; Peristiany, *Honour*; Pitt-Rivers, *Fate of Shechem*, ch. 4; Gowing, *Domestic Dangers*.

30. ASRC, Celia papers, 2220, fols. 6v–7r (1747); the Atena case in ACB, 96, unnumbered file starting August 5, 1803, no fol.; the Brienza case in ACB, 99, unnumbered file starting August 25, 1778, fol. 14r. In a case of rape of a boy, it was similarly the father who brought the suit to defend the family's honor; ACB, 96, unnumbered file starting July 17, 1802, no fol.

31. Anna Siciliano asked in her trial that Rocco Lopardi restore, with a dowry, her lost honor. The case of Carmela di Stefano is in ACB, 98, unnumbered file starting February 8, 1787. Similarly, the cleric who in 1738 had fathered a child with Barbara de Luca in the Calabrian town of Belmonte was condemned to pay 45 ducats for her dowry, and Barbara was thus able within two years to find a husband; Giacomini, *Sposi*, 61–69. Later examples are in Pelaja, *Matrimonio*; non-Italian examples are in Barahona, "Courtship," and Jackson, *New-Born Child Murder*, ch. 2.

32. Examples are Costanza Gaimari of Atena against Vincenzo Lupardi (ACB, 95, unnumbered file starting September 6, 1791, no fol.); Anna Siciliano of Brienza against Rocco Lopardi (ACB, 99, unnumbered file starting August 25, 1778, fols. 41r–v for Anna's description of the violence); and Carmela di Stefano of Brienza against Domenico Biondo (ACB, 98, unnumbered file starting February 8, 1787, fols. 3r–v for Carmela's testimony and 18r for the father's appeal). It is clear, especially in the testimony of the defendants and their supporters, that people familiar with legal language and concepts helped shape their words, although there is no explicit mention in the records of the intervention of lawyers for either party; see Chapter 5.

33. Records cited in note 32, no fol. for Costanza Gaimari, fols. 36r and 91v for

Rocco Lopardi, and fol. 13r for Carmela di Stefano. See also Merzario, *Il paese stretto*, 27–36; Ditte, "La mise en scène"; and Sabean, *Property*, 329–334.

34. See also Povolo, "Aspetti sociali."

35. Records cited in note 32; in Rocco's trial the quotes are on fols. 11r and 1v, respectively. Some of the accusations were rhetorical devices (the cleric in the Belmonte trial was similarly accused of sex during Lent; Giacomini, *Sposi*, 67), but they nonetheless indicate the sense of public scandal.

36. ACB, 100, unnumbered file starting April 18, 1794, fols. 1r–v for the accusation and fol. 6r for the witness's comment; another witness declared himself "scandalized and awed" (fols. 3v–4r).

37. Examples abound in TR and in many other documents; see, e.g., the witnesses' depositions about the 1686 massacre in ACB, 21.1.

38. ACB, 98, unnumbered file starting February 8, 1787, fol. 16r.

39. ACB, 100, unnumbered file starting April 18, 1794, fols. 3r and 5r.

40. See Cavallo and Cerruti, "Onore"; Fiume, *Vecchia*, 20–22 and 160–63; Stanton, "Recuperating Women"; Ferraro, "Power to Decide"; Ruggiero, *Binding Passions*, ch. 2; Cashmere, "Sisters Together"; Medick, "Village Spinning Bees"; Sabean, *Property*, ch. 4; Castan, "Condition féminine"; Norton, "Gender and Defamation"; Flandrin, *Familles*, 104–9; du Boulay, "Lies"; Gutton, *La Sociabilité*, 244–47; Gélis, *History*, 96–100; Garnot, *Un crime*, 108–24; Duden, *Woman*, 85–86; Gowing, "Language"; Cressy, *Birth*, pt. 1.

41. E.g., Gentilcore, *From Bishop to Witch*, 43–45; Farr, "Crimine."

42. See Branciforti, *Regole*, 132–78 (examples on 136, 158–59, 169, 175).

43. On visits, see Burke, *Historical Anthropology*, ch. 4.

44. For instance, Archbishop D'Afflitto in his 1602 provincial council specified that each bishop within his archdiocese could announce in his own synod which sins were reserved to him; ASCC, Fondo Concilî 21, Calabria, fol. 18r. The quote is in Polou, *Prima synodus*, 41. The bishops used the terms *sins* and *crimes* interchangeably.

45. I am using here four lists of reserved sins, the two included in the Polou synods (*Prima synodus*, 41–42, and *Secunda synodus*, 271–72); de Gennaro, *Constitutiones*, 341–42; and the 1595 D'Afflitto list, in Denisi, *L'opera*, 354–55. They are similar but not identical. Some, but not all, of the reserved sins carried automatic excommunication. Blasphemy also features prominently among the problems of the diocese in the Relationes ad limina; see, e.g., Polou's 1729 report, no fol.

46. The 1751 and 1672 lists do not include all these sexual sins, but they do not add any other ones; D'Afflitto's 1595 list also does not include all the 1729 sins. For premarital intercourse, see also below.

47. For D'Afflitto, see ASCC, Fondo Concilî 21, Calabria, fols. 15r and 17r, and the 1595 synod, in Denisi, *L'opera*, 355; Polou, *Prima synodus*, 21, and *Secunda synodus*, 137–38 and 145. See also Mariotti, *Problemi*, 77–79; Faralli, "Le missioni"; Rienzo, "Il

Processo," 477; Novi Chavarria, "L'attività," 172–73; Headley and Tomaro, *San Carlo Borromeo*; Allegra, "Il parroco"; Viscardi, "La religiosità popolare."

48. D'Afflitto's prohibition in his 1602 council, cited in note 47, fol. 16v (he also recommended excommunication for adulterers and concubines [fol. 20v]). The two trials are cited in notes 32 and 36 of this chapter: the case of Rocco Lopardi, which included physical violence, led to his condemnation, but in the case of Luisi and di Mare there is no evidence that the court took any measure beyond gathering the denunciation and the testimonies. See also the 1742 prammatica *de matrimoniis contrahendis* (on the forming of marriages) in Giustiniani, *Nuova collezione*, 7:191–216. The same struggle was engaged by bishops and missionaries all over the kingdom and Europe; see Sannino Cuomo, "Il matrimonio"; Di Leo, *I sinodi*, 177; Ficco and D'Ambrosio, *Trasgressione*, 55–78; Novi Chavarria, "Le missioni"; Farr, *Authority*, 133–36; Pelaja, *Matrimonio*, ch. 4. A similar popular tolerance applied to the sexual activity of clerics; see Giacomini, *Sposi*, 65–66.

49. Polou's 1729 and 1747 *Relationes ad limina* are unfoliated like most of the others. See also Cozzetto, *Territorio*, 139, and Caridi, *Uno "stato,"* 111–12. Giacomini, *Sposi*, 54, notes the bishop's concerns, but she places the rate of premarital conceptions at only 4%. See also Gentilcore, *From Bishop to Witch*, 217; Torre, "Il consumo"; Flandrin, *Les amours paysannes*, 180–81; idem, *Sex*; Gutton, *La Sociabilité*, chs. 2 and 7; Haliczer, *Sexuality*, 150–53; Kamen, *Phoenix*, ch. 6; Barahona, "Courtship"; and Prosperi, *Tribunali*, 650–59. The issue was not limited to Catholic Europe; see Ingram, *Church Courts*, ch. 7, which reports that at least one out of five brides in England was pregnant (219–20); Quaife, *Wanton Wenches*, 179–81; Adair, *Courtship*, chs. 3 and 5–6; Cressy, *Birth*, 277–81; Robisheaux, *Rural Society*, 107–14; Dixon, *Reformation*, 118–24.

50. Galanti, *Della descrizione*, 1:240; other observers are cited in Di Bella, "La pozzanghera." On postunification writers, see Moe, "'Altro che Italia!'" and "Representing the South" (I thank Nelson Moe for letting me cite his work). The most famous example of this impression in twentieth-century writing is, of course, Carlo Levi's *Cristo si è fermato a Eboli* (Turin, 1945). See also Galasso, *L'altra Europa*, and Gribaudi, "Images of the South."

51. In Catalonia, too, success on this point did not lead to broad conformity with church wishes; Kamen, *Phoenix*, 305–6. On life-cycle rituals, see Cressy, *Birth*.

52. Another area of tension was the fate reserved by theology for children who died before baptism; Cavazza, "Double Death." I use "foundling" for children usually described as "exposed"; exposed children were left at church doors or other places where they would readily be found. A mother who exposed her newborn child had a reasonable expectation that the child would be cared for.

53. The role of midwives was debated throughout Europe; see, e.g., Harley, "Scope"; Green, "Women's Medical Practice"; Laget, "La naissance"; Cressy, *Birth*, 59–73.

54. ADRC, Visite pastorali D'Afflitto (1597), fols. 85r–v; the 1602 council in ASCC, Fondo Concilî 21, Calabria, fol. 14r; also Polou, *Prima synodus*, 37–38.

55. Costanza Gaimari's trial, no fols.; Carmela di Stefano's trial, fols. 4r–6v; Giuditta Petrone's trial is in ACB, 96, unnumbered file starting August 5, 1803, no fols. No midwife was questioned in the case of Anna Siciliano presumably because the alleged rape had occurred too long before. See also Giacomini, *Sposi,* 65–67.

56. Giuditta's trial, no fols. Nobody examined the raped boy Francesco Caggiano; ACB, 96, unnumbered file starting July 17, 1802, no fol. (a pharmacist testified that he had given Francesco herbs to treat the venereal disease that had resulted from his rape). The treatise is Greco, *Il medico fiscale,* 503. See also Gélis, *La sage-femme* and *History,* 103–11; Coluccia, "Indagine"; Filippini, "The Church"; Pancino, *Il bambino;* Gentilcore, *From Bishop to Witch,* 144–49; Wilson, *Making of Man-Midwifery;* and Schnorrenberg, "Is Childbirth Any Place for a Woman?" The fight between doctors and midwives continues to this day; see, e.g., Chandrasekaran, "Midwife Charged."

57. See Chapter 4; the two exceptions were baptized by another village midwife (probably Virginia's predecessor) and by a woman not identified as the midwife (this might have been an unexpected early birth not attended by Virginia). There were twelve cases of twins in the sample, and the midwife baptized one of the twins in five of these cases, presumably because of the higher danger posed by twin births; see also Volpe, "Struttura."

58. The sixth child whose parents are not identified (baptized on March 1, 1671) is described as a "slave of the marquis," she is given the surname Alberti, and her godfather is the marquis's son Lorenzo, so she was probably born to one of the palace slaves. Lorenzo is later identified as the father of two illegitimate children, both born to Caterina Squillaci and both receiving the numerous names customary for children of the lord's family.

59. See Placanica, *La Calabria,* ch. 2, who notes an illegitimacy rate in the eighteenth century of 0.8% in the towns and 2.1% in the countryside; idem, *Uomini,* chs. 4 and 5. Giacomini, *Sposi,* 55, finds a rate of less than 2% for illegitimate children and foundlings. Cozzetto, *Territorio,* 190; Volpe, *Cilento,* 236. De Rosa, "L'emarginazione," notes the quick rise in the number of foundlings at the end of the old regime. Da Molin, *L'infanzia,* finds rates of less than 2% throughout Italy until about 1750; idem, "Les enfants" and *Popolazione,* 195–245. Rates of 2–3% have been observed for seventeenth-century England; Ingram, *Church Courts,* 158; Adair, *Courtship,* ch. 2. See also D'Ario, "Gli esposti"; Pelaja, *Matrimonio,* 77–80; Merzario, *Signori,* 42–43; Kertzer, *Sacrificed for Honor;* McArdle, *Altopascio,* 63–65; Bigi et al., "Demografia"; Sheppard, *Lourmarin,* 40–42. In much of western Europe the rates declined after the sixteenth and did not rise again until the late eighteenth century; see also Quaife, *Wanton Wenches,* 56–57; Flandrin, *Familles,* 179–82; Flinn, *European Demographic System.*

60. In the eighteenth century, for example, foundlings were excluded from the priesthood on presumption of illegitimacy; Povolo, "Dal versante," 116; Moro, *Pratica,* 1:370.

61. Minicuci's activity intensified with time, and nineteen of his appearances

occurred between 1691 and 1695. The finder is mentioned only in two cases, and in only one case there is a notation that the baby was found "without the note" indicating that the child had already been baptized; the diocesan rule was, in any case, to baptize all foundlings, even in the presence of such a note; Polou, *Prima synodus*, 38.

62. The one exception is a woman from Messina. Ursula Alberti, Luisa Attinà, and Marianna Foti each had two illegitimate children, while Francesca Vazzani had three, after she had already had a child with an identified man to whom she was not married. Ursula married and served repeatedly as a godmother in later years, and Marianna was twice chosen as godmother. One of Ursula's illegitimate children served as godfather in later years. Caterina Squillaci and Lorenzo Alberti had illegitimate children in 1681 and 1684; she later married, had legitimate children, and served as godmother. This relatively welcoming atmosphere may have become less evident by the end of the old regime, so, for example, Anna Siciliano had sent two of the three children she had had with Rocco Lopardi to a foundlings' home; ACB, 99, unnumbered file starting August 25, 1778, fol. 41v.

63. On traditional methods, see Riddle, *Contraception* and *Eve's Herbs*; Riddle's work is criticized by van de Walle, "Flowers and Fruits." On women healers, see, e.g., Sannita, "Induzione," and Sánchez Ortega, "Sorcery." On midwives, see also Briggs, *Witches and Neighbors*, ch. 7.

64. Pomata, *La Promessa*, ch. 5; Gélis, *History*, ch. 2; Rublack, "Pregnancy"; Gentilcore, "Contesting Illness"; Duden, *Woman*; Crawford, "Attitudes."

65. Zacchia, *Quaestiones*, 1:44–45; see also Schleiner, *Medical Ethics*, chs. 5–6; Cressy, *Birth*, 41–44.

66. See, e.g., Ruggiero, *Binding Passions*, chs. 2 and 4 and pp. 61–62. Wiesner, "Midwives," observes in note 49 that until the fourth or fifth month women spoke not of abortion but of "restoring menses." See also Merzario, "La donna"; McLaren, *History of Contraception*, 124–26; Leboutte, "Offense"; Casarini, "Maternità"; Fiume, *Vecchia*, 133–39; Wegert, *Popular Culture*, 178–79; Jackson, *New-Born Child Murder*, ch. 3; Gowing, "Secret Births." On perceptions of the female body, see Duden, *Woman*, esp. 112–19 and 157–70; idem, *Disembodying Women*; and Riddle, *Eve's Herbs*, chs. 4 and 5. For contemporary echoes, see Hoffman, "An Infant's Death," and Seelye, "Concealing a Pregnancy."

67. Costanza Gaimari in ACB, 95, unnumbered file starting on September 6, 1791, no fol.; Anna de Amico's miscarriage in TR, fols. 17v, 18r, and 29v; Schulte, *Village*, 104–5. The other quote is in Wiesner, "Midwives," 94 n. 49. See also Wiesner, *Women and Gender*, 63–64; Ingram, *Church Courts*, 159; Claverie and Lemaison, *L'impossible mariage*, 225–27. Some men were aware of these natural remedies, too: in the Belmonte case it was the cleric who gave Barbara de Luca various potions; Giacomini, *Sposi*, 65–66. Other examples of priests providing remedies are in Haliczer, *Sexuality*, 124–31.

68. TR, fols. 8r and 16v; here is the passage from Agostina's deposition: "She

[Antonia Crea] told me that she was pregnant, and two days later I brought her a barrel of water and she told me 'O Agostina, I just had an abortion, do you want to see it,' and I, having answered that I thanked her, asked her who had done it for her, and Antonia told me herself that 'Anna de Amico gave me something that made me have the abortion, but I do not tell you what it was,' and I, having answered that anyway I did not want to know it, left on my own business." It is not clear exactly what Antonia planned to show Agostina, and the thanking is ambiguous enough that we do not know if indeed Agostina saw "it."

69. TR, fols. 17r, 18v, and 29r.

70. Similarly, it was only when a trial began that the network of exchanges and aid among women was broken in a Sicilian poisoning case; Fiume, *Vecchia,* 163–64.

71. ACB, 96, unnumbered file starting August 5, 1803, no fols.

72. Tacchi Venturi, *Storia,* 1:274. D'Afflitto's synod is in Denisi, *L'opera,* 347; the 1602 council is in ASCC, Fondo Concilî 21, Calabria, fols. 11v and 23v. De Gennaro, *Constitutiones,* 65–66 and 75; Polou, *Prima synodus,* 26–27, and *Secunda synodus,* 133–34. On these rituals in other areas of the kingdom, see also Gentilcore, *From Bishop to Witch,* 55–56; Viscardi, "Magia"; Di Leo, *I Sinodi,* 155 and 196; De Rosa, *Vescovi,* 68–69; Carroll, *Veiled Threats,* 96–98; and Miele, *Provinzialkonzilien,* 510–14. On medieval cities, see Hughes, "Mourning Rites."

73. Galanti, *Della descrizione,* 2:577–78. Various eighteenth-century visitors are analyzed in Cavalcanti, "Fonti," (on 194 a long quote from another work by Galanti). See also Minervino, "Un comune," 390, and von Lobstein, *Settecento calabrese,* passim, and 2:186 for Lear. Elements of this very public and ritualized mourning behavior survived among the popular classes of the Italian south at least until the 1970s and can still be found today in small villages.

74. Follerio, *Practica,* 276–77; Moro, *Pratica,* 1:362; see also Garnot, *Un crime,* 157–59.

75. TR, fols. 6v and 9v; on visible gestures and the expected exteriority of emotions, see also Merzario, "La buona memoria."

76. See, e.g., the trials for the rapes of Carmela di Stefano and Francesco Caggiano cited in notes 32 and 30 of this chapter; see also Niccoli, *Il seme della violenza,* chs. 7–9.

77. On these themes, see the essays in Prodi and Penuti, *Disciplina,* in particular Prosperi, "L'inquisitore"; Prosperi, *Tribunali*; Hurteau, "Catholic Moral Discourse"; Myers, *"Poor Sinning Folk."*

78. Schulte, *Village,* 199; similar reflections in Ago, *Un feudo.*

EPILOGUE

1. TR, fols. 32r–v. Nostro, like Felice Amodei before him, was a law graduate, which was necessary for any lawyer in any court; the procurator acted as the defendant's representative and did not need to be a law graduate.

2. TR, fols. 33r and 35r. Domenica had escaped between June 14, 1710, and January

9, 1711, when she was no longer mentioned alongside her alleged accomplices in the trial papers.

3. TR, fols. 35v–37v. Again, as custom suggested, Anna was tortured first. The doctor (who came from outside the village) examined them separately in the torture chamber immediately before their torture.

4. TR, fol. 36v. Saint Catherine, martyred on the wheel, made for a fitting invocation when under torture.

5. TR, fol. 37v.

6. TR, fols. 38r–v. The four witnesses were magnifici Giuseppe Battaglia, Domenico Pannuti, Antonio Foti, and Bartolo Battaglia; the last two had already served as witnesses in the trial, confirming the barber's examination of Antonino's corpse.

7. No prison records survive for the Vicaria, and none of the defendants appears again in the Pentidattilo records I have seen.

Note: On feudal jurisdiction, see also M. Benaiteau, *Vassalli e cittadini* (Bari, 1997), which I came across too late for full consideration.

Bibliography

PRIMARY SOURCES

Afan de Rivera, C. *Tavole di riduzione dei pesi e delle misure delle Due Sicilie.* Naples, 1841; 1st ed., 1840.

Alfano, G. M. *Istorica descrizione del Regno di Napoli diviso in 12 province.* Naples, 1795.

———. *Compendio portatile di tutte le 12 province che compongono il Regno di Napoli.* Naples, 1798.

Ambrosino, T. *Processus informativus, sive de modo formandi processum informativum.* Venice, 1620.

Branciforti, F., ed. *Regole, costituzioni, confessionali e rituali.* Palermo, 1953.

Briganti, T. *Pratica criminale delle corti regie e baronali del Regno di Napoli.* Naples, 1755.

Calà, G. *Tractatus de praeeminentia Magnae Curiae Vicariae Regni Neapolis.* Naples, 1680.

Calà-Ulloa, P. *Dell'amministrazione della giustizia criminale nel Regno di Napoli.* Naples, 1835.

Capobianco, G. F. *Tractatus de iure et officio baronum erga vasallos burgenses.* Naples, 1622; 1st ed., 1614.

Carpzov, B. *Practica nova imperialis saxonica.* 4th ed. 2 vols. Wittenberg, 1652.

Casalicchio, C., S.J. *Gli stimoli al timor di Dio.* Naples, 1686.

Cervellino, L. *Direttione overo guida dell'Università per la retta amministrazione.* Naples, 1686.

Cirillo, G. P., ed. *Codicis legum neapolitanarum libri xii.* 2 vols. Naples, 1789.

Claro, G. *Opera omnia, sive practica civilis atque criminalis.* Lyon, 1661.

Codice penale del 1812. Naples, 1812.

Confuorto, D. *Giornali di Napoli dal MDCLXXIX al MDCIC.* 2 vols. Naples, 1930–31.

Constitutiones Regni Neapolitani cum glossis. Lyon, 1537.

de Angelis, F. *Tractatus de officialibus baronum.* Naples, 1689.

———. *De delictis et poenis opera omnia.* 3 vols. Naples, 1783.

de Gennaro, M. *Constitutiones et decreta edita in secunda dioecesana synodo.* Reggio Calabria, 1673. Celebrated in 1672.

de Jorio, C. *Feracissimus tractatus de privilegiis universitatuum.* Naples, 1713.

de Leonardis, G. F. *Prattica degli officiali regii e baronali del Regno di Napoli.* Naples, 1619; 1st ed., 1599.

de Liguoro, O. *Guida per lo stile o sia pratica criminale.* Venice, 1725.

de Luca, G. B. *Il dottor volgare.* 10 vols. Rome, 1673.

de Sariis, A. *Codice delle leggi del Regno di Napoli.* 6 vols. Naples, 1792–97.

de Sarno, A. *Novissima praxis civilis et criminalis.* 5th ed. Naples, 1717.

Diaz de Luco, J. B. *Practica criminalis canonica.* Venice, 1614.

Dizionario delle leggi del Regno di Napoli. 2 vols. Naples, 1788.

Fighera, O. *Institutiones juris Regni Neapolitani.* 6th ed. 2 vols. Naples, 1802.

Filangieri, G. *La scienza della legislazione.* 3d ed. 8 tomes bound in 5 vols. Naples, 1784–91.

Follerio, P. *De sodomia.* 1553. In Rovito, *Luculenta commentaria.*

———. *Practica criminalis.* Naples, 1644.

Fulgoni, C. *Summa criminalis.* Venice, 1568.

Galanti, G. M. *Della descrizione geografica e politica delle Sicilie.* 2 vols. Naples, 1969; 1st ed., 1786–94.

———. *Testamento forense.* Venice, 1806.

———. *Giornale di viaggio in Calabria.* Naples, 1981.

Giustiniani, L. *Dizionario geografico ragionato del Regno di Napoli.* 12 vols. Naples, 1797–1805.

———, ed. *Nuova collezione delle prammatiche del Regno di Napoli.* 15 vols. Naples, 1803–8.

Greco, H. *Il medico fiscale.* In de Sarno, *Novissima,* 466–556.

Grimaldi, D. *Saggio di economia campestre per la Calabria Ultra.* Naples, 1770.

Grimaldi, G., and G. Grimaldi. *Istoria delle leggi e magistrati del Regno di Napoli.* 12 vols. Naples, 1767–86.

Hamilton, G. [William]. *Relazione dell'ultimo terremoto delle Calabrie e della Sicilia.* Florence, 1783.

Lear, E. *Journals of a Landscape Painter in Southern Calabria.* 1852. In *Edward Lear's Journals: A Selection,* edited by H. Van Thal. London, 1952.

Leggi della procedura ne' giudizi penali contenute nella quarta parte del codice per lo Regno delle Due Sicilie. 1819. 2d ed., Naples, 1835.

Leggi penali contenute nella seconda parte del codice per lo Regno delle Due Sicilie. 1819. 2d ed., Naples, 1835.

Manna, G. *Della giurisprudenza e del foro napoletano dalla sua origine fino alla pubblicazione delle nuove leggi.* Naples, 1839.

Marini, C. *Del diritto pubblico e privato del Regno delle Due Sicilie.* Naples, 1853.

Marino, R., ed. *Medicina e magia: Segreti e rimedi in due manoscritti salernitani del '700.* Rome, 1991.

Masci, A. *Esame politico-legale de' dritti e delle prerogative de' baroni del Regno di Napoli.* Naples, 1792.

Masini, E. *Sacro arsenale, overo prattica dell'officio della Santa Inquisitione.* Genoa, 1625.

Mattei, S. *Che la dolcezza delle pene sia giovevole al fisco più che l'asprezza.* Naples, 1787.

Mazzella, S. *Descrittione del Regno di Napoli.* Naples, 1601. Reprint, Bologna, 1981.

Moro, D. *Pratica criminale.* 4 vols. Naples, 1768.

Muscatello, G. B. *Practica tum civilis . . . tum criminalis.* Naples, 1713.

Nani, T. *Degl'indizi ed uso dei medesimi per conoscere i delitti.* Published with his *Principii di giurisprudenza criminale.* Naples, 1856. Latin ed., 1783.

Nicolini, N. *Della procedura penale nel Regno delle Due Sicilie.* 5 vols. Naples, 1828–31.

Novario, G. M. *De vassallorum gravaminibus tractatus.* Naples, 1774; 1st ed., 1634.

Pagano, F. M. *Considerazioni sul processo criminale.* Milan, 1801.

———. *Principii del codice penale.* Milan, 1803.

———. *La logica dei probabili.* Salerno, 1924.

Paolucci, S., S.J. *Missioni dei Padri della Compagnia di Giesu nel Regno di Napoli.* Naples, 1651.

Pecori, R. *Del privato governo delle Università.* 2 vols. Naples, 1770–73.

Polou, D. *Prima synodus dioecesana.* Naples, 1730. Celebrated in 1729.

———. *Secunda synodus dioecesana.* Naples, 1755. Celebrated in 1751.

Rapolla, F. *Commentariorum de jure Regni Neapolitani.* 2 vols. Naples, 1770.

Rodotà, P. P. *Dell'origine, progresso e stato presente del rito greco in Italia.* 3 vols. Rome, 1758–63. Reprint, Cosenza, 1986.

Rota, C. *Legalis androgynus, sive tractatus de privilegiis mulierum.* Naples, 1665.

Rovito, S., ed. *Luculenta commentaria.* 6th ed. Naples, 1649.

Sacco, F. *Dizionario geografico-istorico-fisico del Regno di Napoli.* 4 vols. Naples, 1795–96.

Saint-Non, Abbé de. *Voyage pittoresque ou descriptions des royaumes de Naples et de Sicile.* 4 vols. Paris, 1781–86.

Sanfelice, G. F. *Decisionum supremorum tribunalium Regni Neapolitani.* 2 vols. Naples, 1642.

Scialoja, A. *Praxis torquendi reos.* 2d ed. Naples, 1711.

Sorge, G. *Iurisprudentia forensis.* 11 vols. Naples, 1740–44. Vol. 9, *Praxis criminalis.* 1743.

[Spiriti, G.]. *Riflessioni economico-politiche d'un cittadino relative alle due province di Calabria.* Naples, 1793.

Swinburne, H. *Travels in the Two Sicilies.* 2 vols. London, 1783–85.

Tassone, G. D. *Observationes jurisdictionales.* Naples, 1716; 1st ed., 1626.

Tavole di ragguaglio dei pesi e delle misure già in uso nelle varie province del Regno col sistema metrico decimale. Rome, 1877.

Vacca, D. *Indice generale-alfabetico della collezione delle leggi e dei decreti per il Regno delle Due Sicilie.* Naples, 1837.

Vivenzio, G. *Istoria de' tremuoti avvenuti nella provincia di Calabria Ulteriore e nella città di Messina nell'anno 1783.* 2 vols. Naples, 1788.

Zacchia, P. *Quaestiones medico-legales.* 3 vols. bound in one. Venice, 1751; 1st ed., 1655.

SECONDARY LITERATURE

Abbiateci, A., et al. *Crimes et criminalité en France sous l'Ancien Régime (17e–18e siècles).* Paris, 1971.

Adair, R. *Courtship, Illegitimacy, and Marriage in Early Modern England.* Manchester, 1996.

Ago, R. "Conflitti e politica nel feudo: Le campagne romane del Settecento." *QS* 21 (1986), no. 63: 847–74.

———. *Un feudo esemplare: Immobilismo padronale e astuzia contadina nel Lazio del '700.* Fasano, 1988.

———. *La feudalità in età moderna.* Bari, 1994.

Ajello, R. *Il problema della riforma giudiziaria e legislativa nel Regno di Napoli durante la prima metà del secolo XVIII.* Naples, 1968; 1st ed., 1961.

———, ed. *Giuristi e società al tempo di Pietro Giannone.* Naples, 1980.

Alessi, G. "L'onore riparato: Il riformismo del Settecento e le 'ridicole leggi' contro lo stupro." In Fiume, *Onore,* 129–42.

———. "Il gioco degli scambi: Seduzione e risarcimento nella casistica cattolica del XVI e XVII secolo." *QS* 25 (1990), no. 75: 805–31.

———. *Giustizia e polizia: Il controllo di una capitale, Napoli 1779–1803.* Naples, 1992.

Alessi Palazzolo, G. *Prova legale e pena, la crisi del sistema tra Evo Medio e Moderno.* Naples, 1979.

Allegra, L. "Il parroco: Un mediatore fra alta e bassa cultura." In *Storia d'Italia Annali,* vol. 4, *Intellettuali e potere,* 895–947. Turin, 1978.

———. "I limiti della plausibilità." *QS* 30 (1995), no. 90: 843–55.

Ambrosini, G. "Diritto e società." In *Storia d'Italia,* vol. 1, *I caratteri originali,* 305–97. Turin, 1972.

Andrews, R. M. *Law, Magistracy, and Crime in Old Regime Paris, 1735–1789.* Vol. 1, *The System of Criminal Justice.* Cambridge, 1994.

Arillotta, F. *Reggio nella Calabria spagnola, storia di una città scomparsa (1600–1650).* Rome, 1981.

Arlacchi, P. *Mafia, Peasants, and Great Estates: Society in Traditional Calabria.* Cambridge, 1983. Italian ed., 1980.

Aromolo, G. "Notizie sulle incursioni barbaresche nel territorio di Cirò." In acts of the *Terzo Congresso Storico Calabrese,* 769–89. Naples, 1964.

Ascheri, M. *Tribunali, giuristi e istituzioni dal Medio Evo all'età moderna.* Bologna, 1989.

Astarita, T. *The Continuity of Feudal Power: The Caracciolo di Brienza in Spanish Naples*. Cambridge, 1992.

Baker, J. H. "Criminal Courts and Procedure at Common Law, 1550–1800." In Cockburn, *Crime*, 15–48.

Barahona, R. "Courtship, Seduction, and Abandonment in Early Modern Spain: The Example of Vizcaya 1500–1700." In Saint-Saëns, *Sex and Love*, 43–55.

Barionovi, L. "Scolari e studenti nella Valle Caudina a metà Settecento." In Pellizzari, *Sulle vie*, 227–57.

Beattie, J. M. "The Criminality of Women in Eighteenth-Century England." *Journal of Social History* 8 (1975): 80–116.

Beik, W. "Debate: The Dilemma of Popular History." *Past and Present*, no. 141 (November 1993): 207–15.

Belli, C. "Famiglia, proprietà e classi sociali a Montefusco nella prima metà del secolo XVII." *MEFRM* 95 (1983): 339–92.

Benadusi, G. *A Provincial Elite in Early Modern Tuscany: Family and Power in the Creation of the State*. Baltimore, 1996.

Benigno, F. "The Southern Italian Family in the Early Modern Period: A Discussion of Co-Residential Patterns." *Continuity and Change* 4 (1989): 165–94.

Berlinguer, L., and F. Colao, eds. *Crimine, giustizia e società veneta in età moderna*. Milan, 1989.

———, eds. *Le politiche criminali nel XVIII secolo*. Milan, 1990.

———, eds. *Criminalità e società in età moderna*. Milan, 1991.

Berman, H. J. *Law and Revolution: The Formation of the Western Legal Tradition*. Cambridge, Mass., 1983.

Bertelli, S. "Review of R. Merzario's *Anastasia*." *Archivio Storico Italiano* 151 (1993): 560–64.

Bigi, P., et al. "Demografia differenziale di un villaggio alessandrino: Dall'analisi quantitativa alle storie di famiglia." *QS* 16 (1981), no. 46: 11–59.

Bonacchi, G. *Legge e peccato: Anime, corpi, giustizia alla corte dei papi*. Bari, 1995.

Bondì, C. *Strix: Medichesse, streghe e fattucchiere nell'Italia del Rinascimento*. Rome, 1989.

Bono, S. *Corsari nel Mediterraneo: Cristiani e musulmani fra guerra, schiavitù e commercio*. Milan, 1993.

Bossy, J. "Godparenthood: The Fortunes of a Social Institution in Early Modern Christianity." In *Religion and Society in Early Modern Europe, 1500–1800*, edited by K. v. Greyerz, 194–201. London, 1984.

———. *Christianity in the West, 1400–1700*. Oxford, 1985.

Bouchard, G. *Le village immobile: Sennely-en-Sologne au XVIIIe siècle*. Paris, 1972.

Boyer, P., and S. Nissenbaum. *La città indemoniata: Salem e le origini sociali di una caccia alle streghe*. Turin, 1986. American ed., *Salem Possessed: The Social Origins of Witchcraft*. Cambridge, Mass., 1974.

Brackett, J. *Criminal Justice and Crime in Late Renaissance Florence.* Cambridge, 1992.

———. "The Florentine Onestà and the Control of Prostitution, 1403–1680." *Sixteenth-Century Journal* 24 (1993): 273–300.

Brancaccio, G. *Il trono, la fede e l'altare: Istituzioni ecclesiastiche e vita religiosa nel Mezzogiorno moderno.* Naples, 1996.

Brasacchio, G. *Storia economica della Calabria.* 4 vols. Chiaravalle Centrale, 1977.

Briggs, R. *Communities of Belief: Cultural and Social Tension in Early Modern France.* Oxford, 1989.

———. *Witches and Neighbors: The Social and Cultural Context of European Witchcraft.* New York, 1996.

Brown, J. *In the Shadow of Florence: Provincial Society in Renaissance Pescia.* Oxford, 1982.

———. *Immodest Acts: The Life of a Lesbian Nun in Renaissance Italy.* Oxford, 1986.

Brucker, G. *Giovanni and Lusanna: Love and Marriage in Renaissance Florence.* Berkeley, 1986.

Brundage, J. A. "Proof in Canonical Law." *Continuity and Change* 11 (1996): 329–39.

Buganza, G. "Il teste e la testimonianza tra magistratura secolare e magistratura ecclesiastica." *Atti dell'Istituto Veneto di Scienze, Lettere e Arti,* Classe di Scienze Morali, Lettere e Arti, 145 (1986–87): 257–80.

Bulgarelli Lukacs, A. *L'imposta diretta nel Regno di Napoli in età moderna.* Milan, 1993.

Burke, P. *Popular Culture in Early Modern Europe.* New York, 1978.

———. "From Pioneers to Settlers: Recent Studies of the History of Popular Culture." *Comparative Studies in Society and History* 25 (1983): 181–87.

———. *The Historical Anthropology of Early Modern Italy: Essays on Perception and Communication.* Cambridge, 1987.

———. *Varieties of Cultural History.* Ithaca, N.Y., 1997.

Cabibbo, S., and M. Modica. *La Santa dei Tomasi: Storia di Suor Maria Crocefissa (1645–1699).* Turin, 1989.

Calabria, A. "Per la storia della dominazione austriaca a Napoli, 1707–1734." *Archivio Storico Italiano* 139 (1981): 459–77.

Calisse, C. *Storia del diritto penale italiano.* Florence, 1895.

———. *Svolgimento del diritto penale in Italia dalle invasioni barbariche alle riforme del secolo XVIII.* In *Enciclopedia del diritto penale italiano: Raccolta di monografie,* edited by E. Pessina, 2:1–538. Milan, 1906.

Cameron, I. A. *Crime and Repression in the Auvergne and the Guyenne, 1720–1790.* Cambridge, 1981.

Campanelli, M. "Clero e cultura ecclesiale a Sant'Agata dei Goti agli inizi del Settecento." *ASPN* 110 (1992): 95–152.

Cancila, O. *Baroni e popolo nella Sicilia del grano.* Palermo, 1983.

Canosa, R. *Storia dell'Inquisizione in Italia dalla metà del '500 alla fine del '700.* Vol. 1, *Modena.* Rome, 1986.

Canosa, R., and I. Colonnello. *Storia del carcere in Italia dalla fine del '500 all'Unità.* Rome, 1984.

Caracciolo, F. *Sud, debiti e gabelle: Gravami, potere e società nel Mezzogiorno in età moderna.* Naples, 1983.

Carbone-Grio, D. *I terremoti di Calabria e di Sicilia nel secolo XVIII.* Naples, 1884.

Caridi, G. "Capitoli matrimoniali, dote e dotario in Calabria (XVI–XVIII secolo)." *ASCL* 54 (1987): 11–44.

———. *Uno "stato" feudale nel Mezzogiorno spagnolo.* Rome, 1988.

———. *Il latifondo calabrese nel Settecento.* Rome, 1990.

———. *La spada, la seta, la croce: I Ruffo di Calabria dal XIII al XIX secolo.* Turin, 1995.

———. *Dal feudatario ai notabili: Il principato di Motta San Giovanni dal Seicento agli inizi dell'Ottocento.* Reggio Calabria, 1996.

———. *Chiesa e società in una diocesi meridionale: Santa Severina dal Cinque al Seicento.* Reggio Calabria, 1997.

Carli Sardi, L. "Analisi statistica sulla criminalità nel Settecento (reati e pene) con riguardo allo stato senese." In Berlinguer and Colao, *Criminalità*, 327–475.

Carnevale Caprice, L. "Chiesa e società a Laurino tra XVI e XVIII secolo." In Russo, *Chiesa, assistenza e società*, 39–96.

Carrasco, R. *Inquisición y represión sexual en Valencia: Historia de los sodomitas (1565–1785).* Barcelona, 1985.

———. "Lazarillo on a Street Corner: What the Picaresque Novel Did Not Say about Fallen Boys." In Saint-Saëns, *Sex and Love*, 57–69.

Carroll, M. *Madonnas That Maim: Popular Catholicism in Italy since the Fifteenth Century.* Baltimore, 1992.

———. "Religion, *Ricettizie,* and the Immunity of Southern Italy to the Reformation." *Journal for the Scientific Study of Religion* 31 (1992): 247–60.

———. *Veiled Threats: The Logic of Popular Catholicism in Italy.* Baltimore, 1996.

Casarini, M. P. "Maternità e infanticidio a Bologna: Fonti e linee di ricerca." *QS* 17 (1982), no. 49: 275–84.

Cashmere, J. "Sisters Together: Women without Men in Seventeenth-Century French Village Culture." *Journal of Family History* 21 (1996): 44–62.

Castan, N. *Justice et répression en Languedoc à l'époque des Lumières.* Paris, 1980.

———. "Condition féminine et violence conjugale dans la société méridionale française au XVIIIe siècle." In *Le modèle familial européen: Normes, déviances, contrôle du pouvoir,* edited by G. Delille and F. Rizzi, 175–84. Rome, 1986.

Castan, Y. "Mentalité rurale et urbaine à la fin de l'Ancien Régime dans le ressort du Parlement de Toulouse d'après les sacs à procès criminels (1730–1790)." In Abbiateci et al., *Crimes*, 109–86.

———. *Honnêteté et relations sociales en Languedoc (1715–1780).* Paris, 1974.

Cattini, M., and M. A. Romani, eds. *Il potere di giudicare: Giustizia, pena e controllo sociale negli stati d'Antico Regime.* Brescia, 1983.

Cavalcanti, O. "Fonti settecentesche per una conoscenza demo-antropologica della regione." In De Bonis et al., *Settecento calabrese*, 184–201.

Cavallo, S., and S. Cerruti. "Onore femminile e controllo sociale della riproduzione in Piemonte tra Sei e Settecento." *QS* 15 (1980), no. 44: 346–83. Also in Muir and Ruggiero, *Sex and Gender*, 73–109.

Cavazza, S. "Double Death: Resurrection and Baptism in a Seventeenth-Century Rite." In Muir and Ruggiero, *History from Crime*, 1–31. Originally in *QS* 17 (1982), no. 50: 551–82.

Cernigliaro, A. *Sovranità e feudo nel Regno di Napoli, 1505–1557.* 2 vols. Naples, 1983.

Champin, M.-M. "Un cas typique de justice bailliagère: La criminalité dans le bailliage d'Alençon de 1715 à 1745." *Annales de Normandie* 22 (1972): 47–84.

Chandrasekaran, R. "Midwife Charged in Death of Newborn Baby." *Washington Post*, May 18, 1996, A-1, A-11.

Châtellier, L. *The Religion of the Poor: Rural Missions in Europe and the Formation of Modern Catholicism, c. 1500–c. 1800.* Cambridge, 1997. French ed., 1993.

Chiffoleau, J. "Dire l'indicibile: Osservazioni sulla categoria del 'nefandum' dal XII al XV secolo." In Maire Vigueur and Paravicini Bagliani, *La parola*, 42–73.

Chiffoleau, J., et al., eds. *Riti e rituali nelle civiltà medievali.* Spoleto, 1994.

Chittolini, G., et al., eds. *Origini dello stato: Processi di formazione statale in Italia fra medioevo ed età moderna.* Bologna, 1994.

Chorley, P. *Oil, Silk, and the Enlightenment: Economic Problems in Eighteenth-Century Naples.* Naples, 1965.

Clark, M., and C. Crawford, eds. *Legal Medicine in History.* Cambridge, 1994.

Claverie, E., and P. Lamaison. *L'impossible mariage, violence et parenté en Gévaudan, 17e, 18e, et 19e siècle.* Paris, 1982.

Clavero, B. "Delito y pecado: Noción y escala de transgresiones." In Tomás y Valiente, *Sexo barroco*, 57–89.

Cockburn, J. S., ed. *Crime in England, 1550–1800.* Princeton, N.J., 1977.

Cockburn, J. S., and T. A. Green, eds. *Twelve Good Men and True: The Criminal Trial Jury in England, 1200–1800.* Princeton, N.J., 1988.

Cohen, T. V., and E. S. Cohen. *Words and Deeds in Renaissance Rome: Trials before the Papal Magistrates.* Toronto, 1993.

Cohn, S., Jr. *Women in the Streets: Essays on Sex and Power in Renaissance Italy.* Baltimore, 1996.

Collomp, A. *La maison du père: Famille et village en Haute Provence aux XVIIe et XVIIIe siècles.* Paris, 1983.

Coluccia, A. "Indagine tecnico-scientifica e valenza etica nell'attività peritale sul reato di stupro nella trattatistica settecentesca." In Berlinguer and Colao, *Criminalità*, 147–66.

Contreras, J. *Sotos contra Riquelmes: Regidores, inquisidores, criptojudíos.* Madrid, 1992.

Cook, H. J. *Trials of an Ordinary Doctor: Joannes Groenevelt in Seventeenth-Century London.* Baltimore, 1994.

Costantino, A. *La tragedia degli Alberti di Pentidattilo tra la storia e il romanzo.* Reggio Calabria, 1977.

Cozzetto, F. *Territorio, istituzioni e società nella Calabria moderna.* Naples, 1987.

Cozzi, G., ed. *Stato, società e giustizia nella Repubblica veneta (secoli XV–XVIII).* 2 vols. Rome, 1980–85.

Crawford, C. "Legalizing Medicine: Early Modern Legal Systems and the Growth of Medico-Legal Knowledge." In Clark and Crawford, *Legal Medicine,* 89–116.

Crawford, P. "Attitudes to Menstruation in Seventeenth-Century England." *Past and Present,* no. 91 (May 1981): 47–73.

Cressy, D. *Literacy and the Social Order: Reading and Writing in Tudor and Stuart England.* Cambridge, 1980.

———. *Birth, Marriage, and Death: Ritual, Religion, and the Life-Cycle in Tudor and Stuart England.* Oxford, 1997.

Crispo, C. F. "Incursioni barbaresche in Calabria alla fine del secolo XVIII." *ASCL* 8 (1938): 187–90.

Crompton, L. "The Myth of Lesbian Impunity: Capital Laws from 1270 to 1791." *Journal of Homosexuality* 6 (1980–81): 11–25.

Crouzet-Pavan, E. "Testimonianze ed esperienza dello spazio: L'esempio di Venezia alla fine del Medio Evo." in Maire Vigueur and Paravicini Bagliani, *La parola,* 190–212.

D'Amelia, M. *Orgoglio baronale e giustizia: Castel Viscardo alla fine del Cinquecento.* Rome, 1996.

Da Molin, G. *L'infanzia abbandonata in Italia nell'età moderna: Aspetti demografici di un problema sociale.* Bari, 1981.

———. "Les enfants abandonnés dans les villes italiennes aux XVIIIe et XIXe siècles." *Annales de démographie historique* (1983): 103–24.

———. *La famiglia nel passato: Strutture familiari nel Regno di Napoli in età moderna.* Bari, 1990.

———. *Popolazione e società: Sistemi demografici nel Regno di Napoli in età moderna.* Bari, 1995.

D'Angelo, M. "Viaggiatori e mercanti inglesi nel Sud: Edward Lear tra Sicilia e Calabria nel 1847." *ASCL* 57 (1990): 139–84.

D'Ario, C. "Gli esposti a Napoli nel XVIII secolo." In Russo, *Chiesa, assistenza e società,* 515–68.

Davidson, N. "Theology, Nature, and the Law: Sexual Sin and Sexual Crime in Italy from the Fourteenth to the Seventeenth Century." In Dean and Lowe, *Crime,* 74–98.

Davis, J. *Land and Family in Pisticci.* London, 1973.

———. "An Account of Changes in the Rules for Transmission of Property in Pisticci, 1814–1961." In Peristiany, *Mediterranean Family Structures,* 287–303.

Davis, N. Z. *The Return of Martin Guerre.* Cambridge, Mass., 1983.

———. *Fiction in the Archives: Pardon Tales and Their Tellers in Sixteenth-Century France*. Palo Alto, Calif., 1987.

Dayton, C. H. "Taking the Trade: Abortion and Gender Relations in an Eighteenth-Century New England Village." *William and Mary Quarterly* 48 (1991): 19–49.

———. *Women before the Bar: Gender, Law, and Society in Connecticut, 1639–1789*. Chapel Hill, N.C., 1995.

Dean, T. "Criminal Justice in Fifteenth-Century Bologna." In Dean and Lowe, *Crime*, 16–39.

Dean, T., and K. J. P. Lowe, eds. *Crime, Society, and the Law in Renaissance Italy*. Cambridge, 1994.

De Bonis, M., et al., eds. *Settecento calabrese*. Cosenza, 1985.

De Clementi, A. *Vivere nel latifondo: Le comunità della campagna laziale fra '700 e '800*. Milan, 1989.

Del Bagno, I. *Legum doctores: La formazione del ceto giuridico a Napoli tra Cinque e Seicento*. Naples, 1993.

Deleito y Piñuela, J. *La mala vida en la España de Felipe IV*. Madrid, 1987; 1st ed., 1950.

Delille, G. *Croissance d'une société rurale: Montesarchio et la Vallée Caudine aux XVIIe et XVIIIe siècles*. Naples, 1973.

———. *Agricoltura e demografia nel Regno di Napoli nei secoli XVIII e XIX*. Naples, 1977.

———. "L'ordine dei villaggi e l'ordine dei campi: Per uno studio antropologico del paesaggio agrario nel Regno di Napoli (secoli XV–XVIII)." In *Storia d'Italia Annali*, vol. 8, *Insediamenti e territorio*, 499–560. Turin, 1978.

———. "Dots des filles et circulation des biens dans les Pouilles aux XVIe et XVIIe siècles." *MEFRM* 95 (1983): 195–224.

———. "Le système de transmission des prénoms en Italie du Sud aux XVI–XVII siècles." *L'uomo* 7 (1983): 65–91.

———. *Famille et propriété dans le royaume de Naples*. Rome, 1985.

Delogu, S., ed. *L'erba delle donne: Maghe, streghe, guaritrici: La riscoperta di un'altra medicina*. Rome, 1978.

De Lorenzo, A. *Monografie di storia reggina e calabrese*. Reggio Calabria, 1888.

———. *Un secondo manipolo di monografie e memorie reggine e calabresi*. Siena, 1895.

———. *Un terzo manipolo di monografie e memorie reggine e calabresi*. Siena, 1899.

Delumeau, J. *Catholicism between Luther and Voltaire: A New View of the Counter-Reformation*. London, 1977. French ed., 1971.

De Maio, R. *Società e vita religiosa a Napoli nell'età moderna (1656–1799)*. Naples, 1971.

de Martino, A. *Antico regime e rivoluzione nel Regno di Napoli: Crisi e trasformazione dell'ordinamento giuridico*. Naples, 1972.

de Matteis, A. *L'Aquila e il contado: Demografia e fiscalità (secoli XV–XVIII)*. Naples, 1973.

Denisi, A. "Consistenza numerica e formazione intellettuale del clero nella diocesi di

Reggio Calabria nella prima metà del Seicento." In acts of the *Terzo Congresso Storico Calabrese*, 353–89. Naples, 1964.

———. *L'opera pastorale di Annibale D'Afflitto, arcivescovo di Reggio Calabria (1594–1638)*. Rome, 1983.

De Rosa, G. "L'emarginazione sociale in Calabria nel XVIII secolo: Il problema degli esposti." in *La Calabria*, 1:117–40.

———. *Chiesa e religione popolare nel Mezzogiorno*. Naples, 1979; 1st ed., 1978.

———. *Vescovi popolo e magia nel Sud: Ricerche di storia socio-religiosa dal XVII al XIX secolo*. Naples, 1983; 1st ed., 1971.

De Rosa, G., and A. Cestaro, eds. *Il concilio di Trento nella vita spirituale e culturale del Mezzogiorno tra XVI e XVII secolo*. 2 vols. Venosa, 1988.

De Rosa, G., and F. Malgeri, eds. *Società e religione in Basilicata*. 2 vols. Rome, 1978.

De Rosa, L. "Land and Sea Transport and Economic Depression in the Kingdom of Naples from the Fourteenth to the Eighteenth Century." *Journal of European Economic History* 25 (1996): 339–68.

De Vitiis, V. "Chiese ricettizie e organizzazione ecclesiastica nel Regno delle Due Sicilie dal Concordato del 1818 all'Unità." In Galasso and Russo, *Per la storia*, 2:349–481.

Dewald, J. *Pont-St-Pierre 1398–1789: Lordship, Community, and Capitalism in Early Modern France*. Berkeley, 1987.

Di Bella, S. *Grano, mulini, baroni nella Calabria moderna e contemporanea*. Cosenza, 1979.

———. *Eros e Priapo nelle classi subalterne italiane: La Calabria: Materiali per una analisi*. Soveria Mannelli, 1980.

———. "La pozzanghera di Narciso: I ceti popolari nel Settecento in Calabria tra storia e miti storiografici." In De Bonis et al., *Settecento calabrese*, 129–54.

———, ed. *La rivolta di Messina (1674–78) e il mondo mediterraneo nella seconda metà del Seicento*. Cosenza, 1979.

Di Bella, S., and A. Marzotti. "Nella spirale del sottosviluppo: Problemi di storia della Calabria nel XVII secolo." In Di Bella, *La rivolta*, 81–111.

Di Leo, A. *I sinodi cilentani nei secoli XVI–XIX*. Naples, 1993; 1st ed., 1981.

Di Simplicio, O. "Violenza maritale e violenza sessuale nello stato senese di Antico Regime." In *Emarginazione, criminalità e devianza in Italia fra '600 e '900: Problemi e indicazioni di ricerca*, edited by A. Pastore and P. Sorcinelli, 33–50. Milan, 1990.

———. "Sulla sessualità illecita in Antico Regime (secoli XVII–XVIII)." In Berlinguer and Colao, *Criminalità*, 633–75.

Ditte, C. "La mise en scène dans la plainte: Sa stratégie sociale: L'example de l'honneur populaire." *Droit et culture* 19 (1990): 23–48.

Di Vittorio, A. *Gli Austriaci e il Regno di Napoli, 1707–1734*. 2 vols. Naples, 1969–73.

Dixon, C. S. *The Reformation and Rural Society: The Parishes of Brandenburg-Ansbach-Kulmbach, 1528–1603*. Cambridge, 1996.

Dizionario biografico degli Italiani. Rome, 1960–.

Dolan, F. *Dangerous Familiars: Representations of Domestic Crime in England, 1550–1700.* Ithaca, N.Y., 1994.

Doneddu, G. "Crimine e società nella Sardegna del secondo Settecento." In Berlinguer and Colao, *Criminalità,* 581–632.

Donvito, L., and B. Pellegrino. *L'organizzazione ecclesiastica degli Abruzzi e Molise e della Basilicata nell'età post-tridentina.* Florence, 1973.

Doody, M. A. "'Those Eyes Are Made So Killing': Eighteenth-Century Murderesses and the Law." *Princeton University Library Chronicle* 46 (1984): 49–80.

du Boulay, J. *Portrait of a Greek Mountain Village.* Oxford, 1974.

———. "Lies, Mockery, and Family Integrity." In Peristiany, *Mediterranean Family Structures,* 389–406.

Duden, B. *The Woman beneath the Skin: A Doctor's Patients in Eighteenth-Century Germany.* Cambridge, Mass., 1991. German ed., 1987.

———. *Disembodying Woman: Perspectives on Pregnancy and the Unborn.* Cambridge, Mass., 1993. German ed., 1991.

Ebner, P. *Storia di un feudo del Mezzogiorno: La baronia di Novi.* Rome, 1973.

Egmond, F., and P. Mason. *The Mammoth and the Mouse: Microhistory and Morphology.* Baltimore, 1997.

Elmsley, C., and L. A. Knafla, eds. *Crime History and Histories of Crime: Studies in the Historiography of Crime and Criminal Justice in Modern History.* Westport, Conn., 1996.

Esmein, A. *Histoire de la procédure criminelle en France.* Paris, 1882.

Evans, R. J. *Rituals of Retribution: Capital Punishment in Germany, 1600–1987.* Oxford, 1996.

Faralli, C. "Le missioni dei gesuiti in Italia (sec. XVI–XVII): Problemi di una ricerca in corso." *Bollettino della Società di Studi Valdesi* 138 (1975): 97–116.

Farge, A. *Fragile Lives: Violence, Power, and Solidarity in Eighteenth-Century Paris.* Cambridge, Mass., 1993. French ed., 1986.

Farr, J. R. "Crimine nel vicinato: Ingiurie, matrimonio e onore nella Digione del XVI e XVII secolo." *QS* 22 (1987), no. 66: 839–54.

———. *Authority and Sexuality in Early Modern Burgundy (1550–1730).* Oxford, 1995.

Fasano Guarini, E. "The Prince, the Judges, and the Law: Cosimo I and Sexual Violence, 1558." in Dean and Lowe, *Crime,* 121–41.

———. "Produzione di leggi e disciplinamento nella Toscana tra Cinquecento e Seicento: Spunti di ricerca." In Prodi and Penuti, *Disciplina,* 659–90.

Ferrante, N. "Manoscritti e libri greci nel reggino (1594–1638)." *Bollettino della Balìa Greca di Grottaferrata,* n.s. 36 (1982): 137–45.

Ferrari, G. "Greci e albanesi in Calabria nei secoli XVI–XVII." In acts of the *Terzo Congresso Storico Calabrese,* 391–99. Naples, 1964.

Ferraro, J. "The Power to Decide: Battered Wives in Early Modern Venice." *Renaissance Quarterly* 48 (1995): 492–512.

Ficara de Palma, A. *Storia di Pentidattilo e strage degli Alberti (Pasqua 1686).* Reggio Calabria, 1979.

Ficco, A., and A. D'Ambrosio. *Trasgressione e criminalità in Terra di Bari.* Lecce, 1991.

Filangieri, A. *Territorio e popolazione nell'Italia meridionale: Evoluzione storica.* Milan, 1980.

Filippini, N. "The Church, the State, and Childbirth: The Midwife in Italy during the Eighteenth Century." In Marland, *Art of Midwifery,* 152–75.

Fine, A. *Parrains, marraines: La parenté spirituelle en Europe.* Paris, 1994.

Fiorelli, P. *La tortura giudiziaria nel diritto comune.* 2 vols. Milan, 1953.

Firpo, M., and V. Ferrone. "From Inquisitors to Microhistorians: A Critique of Pietro Redondi's *Galileo Eretico.*" *Journal of Modern History* 58 (1986): 485–524.

Fiume, G., ed. *Onore e storia nelle società mediterranee.* Palermo, 1989.

———. *La vecchia dell'aceto: Un processo per veneficio nella Palermo di fine '700.* Palermo, 1990.

Flandrin, J.-L. *Les amours paysannes: Amour et sexualité dans les campagnes de l'ancienne France (XVIe–XIXe siècles).* Paris, 1975.

———. *Familles: Parenté, maison, sexualité dans l'ancienne société.* Paris, 1976.

———. *Sex in the Western World: The Development of Attitudes and Behaviours.* Chur, Switzerland, 1991. French ed., 1981.

Flinn, M. W. *The European Demographic System, 1500–1820.* Baltimore, 1981.

Flynn, M. "Blasphemy and the Play of Anger in Sixteenth-Century Spain." *Past and Present,* no. 149 (November 1995): 29–56.

Fornili, C., OFMC. *Delinquenti e carcerati a Roma alla metà del '600: L'opera dei papi nella riforma carceraria.* Milan, 1991.

Forster, M. *The Counter-Reformation in the Villages: Religion and Reform in the Bishopric of Speyer, 1560–1720.* Ithaca, N.Y., 1992.

Fout, J. C., ed. *Forbidden History: The State, Society, and the Regulation of Sexuality in Modern Europe.* Chicago, 1992.

Francia, A. *Storia minima: Streghe, inquisitori, peste e guerra in un episodio di violenza collettiva del XVII secolo.* Genoa, 1990.

Frascadore, A. "Livelli di alfabetizzazione e cultura grafica a Lecce intorno alla metà del XVII secolo (1640–1659)." In Pellizzari, *Sulle vie,* 177–226.

Friese, H. "La prassi dell'onore femminile: La politica delle liti tra donne in un paese della Sicilia." In Fiume, *Onore,* 315–48.

Gacto, E. "El delito de bigamía y la Inquisición española." In Tomás y Valiente, *Sexo barroco,* 127–52.

Galasso, G. "La legge feudale napoletana del 1799." *RSI* 76 (1964): 507–29.

———. *Economia e società nella Calabria del Cinquecento.* Milan, 1975; 1st ed., 1967.

———. *L'altra Europa: Per un'antropologia storica del Mezzogiorno d'Italia.* Milan, 1982.

———. "L'ultimo feudalesimo meridionale nell'analisi di Giuseppe Maria Galanti." *RSI* 95 (1983): 262–81.

Galasso, G., and R. Romeo, eds. *Storia del Mezzogiorno.* 15 vols. Naples, 1986–94.

Galasso, G., and C. Russo, eds. *Per la storia sociale e religiosa del Mezzogiorno d'Italia.* 2 vols. Naples, 1980–82.

Galt, A. *Far from the Church Bells: Settlement and Society in an Apulian Town.* Cambridge, 1991.

Gambi, L. *La Calabria.* Vol. 16 of *Le regioni d'Italia.* Turin, 1965.

Gambier, M. "La donna e la giustizia penale veneta nel XVIII secolo." In Cozzi, *Stato,* 1:531–75.

Garnot, B. "Une illusion historiographique: Justice et criminalité au XVIIIe siècle." *Revue historique* 113 (1981), no. 281: 361–79.

———. *Un crime conjugal au 18e siècle.* Paris, 1993.

Gaskill, M. "Reporting Murder: Fiction in the Archives in Early Modern England." *Social History* 23 (1998): 1–30.

Gasparini, D. "Signori e contadini nella contea di Valmareno, secoli XVI–XVII." In Cozzi, *Stato,* 2:133–90.

Gélis, J. *La sage-femme ou le médecin: Une nouvelle conception de la vie.* Paris, 1988.

———. *History of Childbirth: Fertility, Pregnancy, and Birth in Early Modern Europe.* Boston, 1991 French ed., 1984.

Gentilcore, D. *From Bishop to Witch: The System of the Sacred in Early Modern Terra d'Otranto.* Manchester, 1992.

———. "Methods and Approaches in the Social History of the Counter-Reformation in Italy." *Social History* 17 (1992): 73–98.

———. "The Church, the Devil, and the Healing Activities of Living Saints in the Kingdom of Naples after the Council of Trent." In *Medicine and the Reformation,* edited by O. P. Grell and A. Cunningham, 134–55. London, 1993.

———. "'Adapt Yourselves to the People's Capabilities': Missionary Strategies, Methods, and Impact in the Kingdom of Naples, 1600–1800." *Journal of Ecclesiastic History* 45 (1994): 269–96.

———. "'All That Pertains to Medicine': *Protomedici* and *Protomedicati* in Early Modern Italy." *Medical History* 38 (1994): 121–42.

———. "'Charlatans, Mountebanks, and Other Similar People': The Regulation and Role of Itinerant Practitioners in Early Modern Italy." *Social History* 20 (1995): 297–314.

———. "Contesting Illness in Early Modern Naples: *Miracolati,* Physicians, and the Congregation of Rites." *Past and Present,* no. 148 (August 1995): 117–48.

Gerard, K., and G. Hekma, eds. *The Pursuit of Sodomy: Male Homosexuality in Renaissance and Enlightenment Europe.* New York, 1989.

Giacomini, M. *Sposi a Belmonte nel Settecento: Famiglia e matrimonio in un borgo rurale calabrese.* Milan, 1981.

Gilbert, A. "Conceptions of Homosexuality and Sodomy in Western History." *Journal of Homosexuality* 6 (1980–81): 57–68.

Gilissen, J. "La preuve en Europe du XVIe au début du XIXe siècle." In *La preuve*, pt. 2, 755–833. Brussels, 1965.

Ginzburg, C. "Folklore, magia, religione." In *Storia d'Italia*, vol. 1, *I caratteri originali*, 601–76. Turin, 1972.

———. *The Cheese and the Worms: The Cosmos of a Sixteenth-Century Miller.* New York, 1982. Italian ed., 1976.

———. *The Night Battles: Witchcraft and Agrarian Cults in the Sixteenth and Seventeenth Centuries.* New York, 1983. Italian ed., 1966.

———. "Ekphrasis and Quotation." *Tijdschrift voor filosofie* 20 (1988): 3–19.

———. *Clues, Myths, and the Historical Method.* Baltimore, 1989. Italian ed., 1986.

———. "Clues: Roots of an Evidential Paradigm." In Ginzburg, *Clues*, 96–125.

———. "The Inquisitor as Anthropologist." In Ginzburg, *Clues*, 156–64.

———. *Il giudice e lo storico: Considerazioni in margine al processo Sofri.* Turin, 1991.

———. "Aristotele, la storia, la prova." *QS* 29 (1994), no. 85: 5–17.

———. "Checking the Evidence: The Judge and the Historian." In *Questions of Evidence: Proof, Practice, and Persuasion across the Disciplines*, edited by J. Chandler, 290–303. Chicago, 1994.

———. "Microstoria: Due o tre cose che so di lei." *QS* 29 (1994), no. 86: 511–39.

Giura, V. *Storie di minoranze: Ebrei, greci, albanesi nel Regno di Napoli.* Naples, 1984.

Goody, J. "Inheritance, Property, and Women: Some Comparative Considerations." In Goody et al., *Family and Inheritance*, 10–36.

Goody, J., et al., eds. *Family and Inheritance: Rural Society in Western Europe, 1200–1800.* Cambridge, 1976.

Gowing, L. "Language, Power, and the Law: Women's Slander Litigation in Early Modern London." In Kermode and Walker, *Women*, 26–47.

———. *Domestic Dangers: Women, Words, and Sex in Early Modern London.* Oxford, 1996.

———. "Secret Births and Infanticide in Seventeenth-Century England." *Past and Present*, no. 156 (August 1997): 87–115.

Greco, G. "Istituzioni e procedure delle Gran Corti Criminali." In *Il Mezzogiorno preunitario: Economia, società e istituzioni*, edited by A. Massafra, 533–47. Bari, 1988.

Green, M. "Women's Medical Practice and Health Care in Medieval Europe." *Signs: Journal of Women in Culture and Society* 14 (1989): 434–73.

Greenshields, M. *An Economy of Violence in Early Modern France: Crime and Justice in the Haute Auvergne, 1587–1664.* University Park, Pa., 1994.

Grendi, E. "Microanalisi e storia sociale." *QS* 12 (1977), no. 35 (1977): 506–20.

———. "La pratica dei confini: Mioglia contro Sassello, 1715–1745." In Tocci, *Le comunità*, 261–75.

————. "Sulla 'storia criminale': Risposta a Mario Sbriccoli." *QS* 25 (1990), no. 73: 269–75.

————. *Il Cervo e la Repubblica: Il modello ligure di Antico Regime.* Turin, 1993.

————. "Ripensare la microstoria?" *QS* 29 (1994), no. 86: 539–49.

Grevi, V. *"Nemo tenetur se detegere": Interrogatorio dell'imputato e diritto al silenzio nel processo penale italiano.* Milan, 1972.

Gribaudi, G. "Images of the South: The Mezzogiorno as Seen by Insiders and Out-siders." In *The New History of the South: The Mezzogiorno Revisited,* edited by R. Lumley and J. Morris, 83–113. Exeter, 1997.

Groppi, A., ed. *Il lavoro delle donne.* Bari, 1996.

Grossi, P., ed. *Storia sociale e dimensione giuridica: Strumenti d'indagine e ipotesi di lavoro.* Milan, 1986.

Guarnieri, P. *A Case of Child Murder: Law and Science in Nineteenth-Century Tuscany.* Cambridge, 1993. Italian ed., 1988.

Gutton, J.-P. *La sociabilité villageoise dans l'ancienne France: Solidarités et voisinages du XVIe au XVIIIe siècle.* Paris, 1979.

Haas, L. "Il Mio Buono Compare: Choosing Godparents and the Uses of Baptismal Kinship in Renaissance Florence." *Journal of Social History* 29, no. 2 (Winter 1995): 341–56.

Haliczer, S. *Inquisition and Society in the Kingdom of Valencia, 1478–1834.* Berkeley, 1990.

————. *Sexuality in the Confessional: A Sacrament Profaned.* Oxford, 1996.

Hanley, S. "Engendering the State: Family Formation and State Building in Early Modern France." *French Historical Studies* 16 (1989): 4–27.

————. "Social Sites of Political Practice in France: Lawsuits, Civil Rights, and the Separation of Powers in Domestic and State Governments, 1500–1800." *AHR* 102 (1997): 27–52.

Harley, D. "The Scope of Legal Medicine in Lancashire and Cheshire, 1660–1760." in Clark and Crawford, *Legal Medicine,* 45–63.

Hay, D., et al. *Albion's Fatal Tree: Crime and Society in Eighteenth-Century England.* New York, 1975.

Headley, J. M., and J. B. Tomaro, eds. *San Carlo Borromeo: Catholic Reformation and Ecclesiastic Policy in the Second Half of the Sixteenth Century.* Washington, 1988.

Henry, J. "Doctors and Healers: Popular Culture and the Medical Profession." In *Science, Culture, and Popular Belief in Renaissance Europe,* edited by S. Pumfrey et al., 191–221. Manchester, 1991.

Hobsbawm, E. J. "The Revival of Narrative: Some Comments." *Past and Present,* no. 86 (February 1980): 3–8.

Hoffer, P. C., and N. E. H. Hull. *Murdering Mothers: Infanticide in England and New England, 1558–1803.* New York, 1981.

Hoffman, J. "An Infant's Death, an Ancient 'Why?'" *New York Times,* December 22, 1996, E-4.

Hoffman, P. *Church and Community in the Diocese of Lyon, 1500–1789.* New Haven, 1984.

Hsia, R. P. *Trent 1475: Stories of a Ritual Murder Trial.* New Haven, 1992.

———. *The World of Catholic Renewal, 1540–1770.* Cambridge, 1998.

Hufton, O. "Le paysan et la loi en France au XVIIIe siècle." *Annales ESC* 38 (1983): 679–701.

Hughes, D. O. "Mourning Rites, Memory, and Civilization in Premodern Italy." In Chiffoleau et al., *Riti,* 23–38.

Hurteau, P. "Catholic Moral Discourse on Male Sodomy and Masturbation in the Seventeenth and Eighteenth Centuries." *Journal of the History of Sexuality* 4 (1993): 1–26.

Ingram, M. *Church Courts, Sex, and Marriage in England, 1570–1640.* Cambridge, 1987.

Jackson, M. "Suspicious Infant Deaths: The Statute of 1624 and Medical Evidence at Coroners' Inquests." In Clark and Crawford, *Legal Medicine,* 64–86.

———. *New-Born Child Murder: Women, Illegitimacy, and the Courts in Eighteenth-Century England.* Manchester, 1996.

Juratic, S. "Meurtrière de son mari: Un 'destin' criminel au XVIII siècle? L'affaire Lescombat." *Revue d'histoire moderne et contemporaine* 34 (1987): 123–37.

Jütte, R. "Geschlechtspezifische Kriminalität im späten Mittelalter und in der Frühen Neuzeit." *Zeitschrift der Savigny-Stiftung für Rechtsgeschichte* 108 (1991): 86–116.

Kagan, R. L. *Lucrecia's Dreams: Politics and Prophecy in Sixteenth-Century Spain.* Berkeley, 1990.

Kamen, H. *The Phoenix and the Flame: Catalonia and the Counter-Reformation.* New Haven, 1993.

Kermode, J., and G. Walker, eds. *Women, Crime, and the Courts in Early Modern England.* Chapel Hill, N.C., 1994.

Kertzer, D. *Sacrificed for Honor: Italian Infant Abandonment and the Politics of Reproductive Control.* Boston, 1993.

———. *The Kidnapping of Edgardo Mortara.* New York, 1997.

Klapisch-Zuber, C. *Women, Family, and Ritual.* Chicago, 1985.

Knafla, L. A., ed. *Crime and Criminal Justice in Europe and Canada.* Waterloo, Ontario, 1981.

Kuehn, T. "Reading Microhistory: The Example of *Giovanni and Lusanna.*" *Journal of Modern History* 61 (1989): 512–34.

———. *Law, Family, and Women: Toward a Legal Anthropology of Renaissance Italy.* Chicago, 1991.

Labalme, P. "Sodomy and Venetian Justice in the Renaissance." *Tijdschrift voor rechtsgeschiedenis* 52 (1984): 217–54.

Labrot, G. *Quand l'histoire murmure: Villages et campagnes du royaume de Naples (XVIe–XVIIIe siècle)*. Rome, 1995.

La Calabria dalle riforme alla Restaurazione. Acts of the *Sesto Congresso Storico Calabrese* (1977). 2 vols. Naples, 1981.

Laget, M. "La naissance aux siècles classiques: Pratique des accouchements et attitude collectives en France aux XVIIe et XVIIIe siècles." *Annales ESC* 32 (1977): 958–92.

Laiou, A. "Sex, Consent, and Coercion in Byzantium." In Laiou, *Consent*, 109–221.

———, ed. *Consent and Coercion to Sex and Marriage in Ancient and Medieval Societies*. Washington, 1993.

Landi, G. *Istituzioni di diritto pubblico del Regno delle Due Sicilie (1815–1861)*. 2 vols. Milan, 1977.

Langbein, J. *Prosecuting Crime in the Renaissance*. Cambridge, Mass., 1974.

———. "The Historical Origins of the Sanction of Imprisonment for Serious Crime." *Journal of Legal Studies* 5 (1976): 35–60.

———. *Torture and the Law of Proof*. Chicago, 1977.

Laruffa, R. *Pentidattilo: Guida Turistica*. Reggio Calabria, 1997.

Las mujeres medievales y su ámbito jurídico. Madrid, 1983.

Lea, H. C. *Torture*. Philadelphia, 1973.

Leboutte, R. "Offense against Family Order: Infanticide in Belgium from the Fifteenth to the Early Twentieth Century." In Fout, *Forbidden History*, 29–55.

Lenman, B., and G. Parker. "The State, the Community, and the Criminal Law in Early Modern Europe." In *Crime and the Law: The Social History of Crime in Western Europe since 1500*, edited by V. A. C. Gatrell et al., 11–48. London, 1980.

Leone, A. "Agricoltura e contadini nella Calabria del '700." In De Bonis et al., *Settecento calabrese*, 202–8.

Lepre, A. *Feudi e masserie: Problemi della società meridionale nel '600 e '700*. Naples, 1973.

———. *Terra di Lavoro nell'età moderna*. Naples, 1978.

———. *Storia del Mezzogiorno d'Italia*. 2 vols. Naples, 1986.

Le Roy Ladurie, E. *Montaillou, the Promised Land of Error*. New York, 1978. French ed., 1975.

———. *Carnival in Romans*. New York, 1979. French ed., 1979.

———. *The Beggar and the Professor: A Sixteenth-Century Family Saga*. Chicago, 1997. French ed., 1995.

Levack, B. *The Witch-Hunt in Early Modern Europe*. 2d ed. London, 1995.

Levi, G. *Inheriting Power: The Story of an Exorcist*. Chicago, 1988. Italian ed., 1985.

———. "On Microhistory." In *New Perspectives on Historical Writing*, edited by P. Burke, 93–113. University Park, Pa., 1992.

Levy, L. W. "Accusatorial and Inquisitorial Systems of Criminal Procedure: The Beginnings." In *Freedom and Reform: Essays in Honor of Henry Steele Commager*, edited by H. M. Hyman and L. W. Levy, 16–54. New York, 1967.

Ligresti, D. *Sicilia moderna: La città e gli uomini.* Naples, 1984.

Liliequist, J. "Peasants against Nature: Crossing the Boundaries between Man and Animal in Seventeenth- and Eighteenth-Century Sweden." In Fout, *Forbidden History,* 57–87.

Longo, C. "Presenze domenicane nella Calabria reggina: Il convento di Santa Maria della Candelora in Pentidattilo." *RSC,* n.s., 4 (1983): 315–47.

Luise, F. "Solofra fra il 1640 e il 1676 nei capitoli matrimoniali e nei testamenti." *MEFRM* 95 (1983): 299–338.

Lupo, S. *Il giardino degli aranci: Il mondo degli agrumi nella storia del Mezzogiorno.* Venice, 1990.

Luria, K. *Territories of Grace: Cultural Change in the Seventeenth-Century Diocese of Grenoble.* Berkeley, 1991.

Maclean, I. *The Renaissance Notion of Woman: A Study in the Fortunes of Scholasticism and Medical Science in European Intellectual Life.* Cambridge, 1980.

———. *Interpretation and Meaning in the Renaissance: The Case of Law.* Cambridge, 1992.

Mafrici, M. "La Calabria e le sue strutture socio-demografiche." In Placanica and Mafrici, *Il Mezzogiorno,* 2:131–60.

———. "Calabria Ulteriore (1266–1806)." In Galasso and Romeo, *Storia,* 7:95–232.

Maire Vigueur, J.-C., and A. Paravicini Bagliani, eds. *La parola all'accusato.* Palermo, 1991.

Malanima, P. *Il lusso dei contadini: Consumi e industrie nelle campagne toscane del Seicento e Settecento.* Bologna, 1990.

Malcomson, R. W. "Infanticide in the Eighteenth Century." In Cockburn, *Crime,* 187–209.

Mancino, M. "Ecclesiastical Justice and the Counter-Reformation: Notes on the Diocesan Criminal Court of Naples." In *The Civilization of Crime: Violence in Town and Country since the Middle Ages,* edited by E. A. Johnson and E. H. Monkkonen, 125–37. Chicago, 1996.

Mandalari, M. *Note e documenti di storia calabrese.* Caserta, 1886.

———. "La terra di Pentidattilo in Calabria dopo il terremoto dell'anno 1783." *RSC* 14 (1906): 112–52, 201–39.

Manduca, R. "Clero e benefici nella diocesi di Catania fra Seicento e Settecento." In *Chiesa e società in Sicilia: I secoli XVII–XIX,* edited by G. Zito, 135–94. Turin, 1995.

Marchetti, P. *Testis contra se: L'imputato come fonte di prova nel processo penale dell'età moderna.* Milan, 1994.

Margot, A. "La criminalité dans le bailliage de Mamers, 1695–1750." *Annales de Normandie* 22 (1972): 185–224.

Marino, J. *Pastoral Economics in the Kingdom of Naples.* Baltimore, 1988.

Mariotti, M. "Concili provinciali e sinodi diocesani post-tridentini in Calabria." *Ri-*

vista di storia della Chiesa in Italia 21 (1967): 461–81; 27 (1973): 130–69; 41 (1987): 111–27.

——. "Le costituzioni dei sinodi diocesani e dei concili provinciali e le relazioni delle visite pastorali e per le visite *ad limina* come fonti per la storia religiosa e sociale della Calabria." In *La società religiosa nell'età moderna,* edited by F. Malgeri, 893–922. Naples, 1973.

——. *Problemi di lingua e di cultura nell'azione pastorale dei vescovi calabresi in età moderna.* Rome, 1980.

——. "Rapporti tra vescovi e religiosi in Calabria (attraverso i sinodi diocesani 1574–1795)." In *Ordini religiosi e società nel Mezzogiorno moderno,* 3 vols., edited by F. Gaudioso and B. Pellegrino, 1:269–324. Galatina, 1987.

——. "Studi su riforma cattolica tridentina e Calabria (secoli XVI–XVIII): Stato attuale e prospettive di sviluppo." In De Rosa and Cestaro, *Il concilio,* 2:707–47.

Marland, H., ed. *The Art of Midwifery: Early Modern Midwives in Europe.* London, 1993.

Martini, G. *Il 'vitio nefando' nella Venezia del Seicento: Aspetti sociali e repressione di giustizia.* Rome, 1988.

Martucci, R. "'De vita et honestate clericorum': La formazione del clero meridionale tra Sei e Settecento." *Archivio Storico Italiano* 144 (1986): 423–67.

Matacena, G. *Architettura del lavoro in Calabria tra i secoli XV e XIX.* Naples, 1983.

Massafra, A. "Un problème ouvert à la recherche: La 'crise' du baronnage napolitain à la fin du XVIIIe siècle." In *L'abolition de la féodalité dans le monde occidental,* 2 vols., 1:245–62. Toulouse, 1968.

——, ed. *Problemi di storia delle campagne meridionali nell'età moderna e contemporanea.* Bari, 1981.

Massetto, G. P. *Un magistrato e una città nella Lombardia spagnola: Giulio Claro pretore a Cremona.* Milan, 1985.

Maza, S. *Private Lives and Public Affairs: The Causes Célèbres of Prerevolutionary France.* Berkeley, 1993.

——. "Stories in History: Cultural Narratives in Recent Works in European History." *AHR* 101 (1996): 1493–515.

Mazzi, M. S. *Prostitute e lenoni nella Firenze del Quattrocento.* Milan, 1991.

McArdle, F. *Altopascio: A Study in Tuscan Rural Society, 1587–1784.* Cambridge, 1978.

McLaren, A. *A History of Contraception from Antiquity to the Present Day.* Oxford, 1990.

McLynn, F. *Crime and Punishment in Eighteenth-Century England.* Oxford, 1991.

McNeill, J. R. *The Mountains of the Mediterranean World: An Environmental History.* Cambridge, 1992.

Medick, H. "Village Spinning Bees: Sexual Culture and Free Time among Rural Youth in Early Modern Germany." In Medick and Sabean, *Interest and Emotion,* 317–39.

Medick, H., and D. Sabean, eds. *Interest and Emotion: Essays on the Study of Family and Kinship.* Cambridge, 1984.

Mereu, I. *Storia del diritto penale nel '500: Studi e ricerche.* Naples, 1964.

Merzario, R. *Signori e contadini di Calabria: Corigliano Calabro dal XVI al XIX secolo.* Milan, 1975.

———. "La donna e il suo corpo: Un tentativo di analisi (diocesi di Como, 1550–1650)." In Delogu, *L'erba,* 57–74.

———. "La buona memoria: Il ricordo familiare attraverso la parola e il gesto." *QS* 17 (1982), no. 51: 1001–26.

———. *Il paese stretto: Strategie matrimoniali nella diocesi di Como, secoli XVI–XVIII.* Turin, 1989.

———. *Anastasia, ovvero la malizia degli uomini: Relazioni sociali e controllo delle nascite in un villaggio ticinese, 1650–1750.* Bari, 1992.

Miceli, M. "La giurisdizione civile e criminale nel Regno di Napoli." *Rivista araldica* 65 (1967): 159–65, 300–309; 66 (1968): 62–66, 87–96, 159–62, 257–61; 67 (1969): 142–45, 306–9; 68 (1970): 55–58.

Miele, M. *Die Provinzialkonzilien Süditaliens in der Neuzeit.* Paderborn, Germany, 1996.

Milone, F. *Memoria illustrativa della carta della utilizzazione del suolo della Calabria.* Naples, 1956.

Minervino, M. F. "Un comune calabrese del '700: Paola—Società, mondo subalterno e patologia della vita quotidiana." In De Bonis et al., *Settecento calabrese,* 361–94.

———. *La città, gli uomini e le cose: Società, vita materiale e civilizzazione urbana a Paola (secoli XIV–XVIII).* Cosenza, 1989.

Minicucci, C. "Il feudo di Montebello dei baroni Abbenavoli [*sic*] del Franco al secolo XVII." *RSC* 15 (1907): 129–39.

———. "Notizie storiche sul monastero della Candelora in Pentidattilo." *RSC* 16 (1908): 52–74.

Moe, N. "'Altro che Italia!': Il Sud dei piemontesi." *Meridiana* 15 (1992): 53–89.

———. "Representing the South in Post-Unification Italy, c. 1860–1880." Ph.D. diss., Johns Hopkins University, 1994.

Monter, E. W. *Ritual, Myth, and Magic in Early Modern Europe.* Athens, Ohio, 1984.

———. *Frontiers of Heresy: The Spanish Inquisition from the Basque Lands to Sicily.* Cambridge, 1990.

Monter, E. W., and J. Tedeschi. "Toward a Statistical Profile of the Italian Inquisitions, Sixteenth to Eighteenth Century." In *The Inquisition in Early Modern Europe: Studies on Sources and Methods,* edited by J. Tedeschi and G. Henningsen, 130–57. DeKalb, Ill., 1986.

Moses, D. C. "Livy's Lucretia and the Validity of Coerced Consent in Roman Law." In Laiou, *Consent,* 39–81.

Muchembled, R. *Popular Culture and Elite Culture in France, 1400–1750.* Baton Rouge, 1985. French ed., 1978.

———. *L'invention de l'homme moderne: Sensibilités, moeurs et comportements collectifs sous l'Ancien Régime.* Paris, 1988.

———. *La violence au village: Sociabilité et comportements populaires en Artois du XVe au XVIIe siècle.* Brussels, 1989.

———. *Le temps des supplices: De l'obéissance sous les rois absolus, XVe–XVIIIe siècles.* Paris, 1992.

Muir, E. "Introduction: Observing Trifles." In Muir and Ruggiero, *Microhistory*, vii–xxviii.

———. *Mad Blood Stirring: Vendetta and Factions in Friuli during the Renaissance.* Baltimore, 1993.

———. *Ritual in Early Modern Europe.* Cambridge, 1997.

Muir, E., and G. Ruggiero, eds. *Sex and Gender in Historical Perspective: Selections from Quaderni Storici.* Baltimore, 1990.

———, eds. *Microhistory and the Lost Peoples of Europe: Selections from Quaderni Storici.* Baltimore, 1991.

———, eds. *History from Crime: Selections from Quaderni Storici.* Baltimore, 1994.

Muller, D. "Magistrats français et peine de mort au 18e siècle." *Dix-huitième siècle* 4 (1972): 79–107.

Musgrave, P. *Land and Economy in Baroque Italy: Valpolicella, 1630–1797.* Leicester, 1992.

Musi, A. *Mezzogiorno spagnolo: La via napoletana allo stato moderno.* Naples, 1991.

Muto, G. "Strutture e funzioni finanziarie delle 'università' del Mezzogiorno tra '500 e '600." *Quaderni sardi di storia* 1 (1980): 101–22.

———. "Istituzioni dell'Universitas e ceti dirigenti locali." In Galasso and Romeo, *Storia*, 9:17–67.

Myers, W. D. *"Poor Sinning Folk": Confession and Conscience in Counter-Reformation Germany.* Ithaca, N.Y., 1996.

Nalle, S. *God in La Mancha: Religious Reform and the People of Cuenca, 1500–1650.* Baltimore, 1992.

Niccoli, O. *Il seme della violenza: Putti, fanciulli e mammoli nell'Italia tra Cinquecento e Seicento.* Bari, 1995.

Norton, M. B. "Gender and Defamation in Seventeenth-Century Maryland." *William and Mary Quarterly* 44 (1987): 3–39.

Notari, F. "La Compagnia dei Bianchi di Giustizia: L'assistenza ai condannati a morte nella Napoli moderna." In Russo, *Chiesa, assistenza e società*, 281–371.

Novi Chavarria, E. "L'attività missionaria dei Gesuiti nel Mezzogiorno d'Italia tra XVI e XVIII secolo." In Galasso and Russo, *Per la storia*, 2:159–85.

———. "Le missioni dei gesuiti in Calabria in età moderna." In *I Gesuiti e la Calabria*, edited by V. Sibilio, S.J., 103–25. Reggio Calabria, 1992.

Oldham, J. C. "On Pleading the Belly: A History of the Jury of Matrons." In Knafla, *Crime*, 1–64.

O'Neil, M. "*Sacerdote ovvero strione*: Ecclesiastic and Superstitious Remedies in Sixteenth-Century Italy." In *Understanding Popular Culture: Europe from the Middle Ages to the Nineteenth Century*, edited by S. Kaplan, 53–84. Berlin, 1984.

———. "Magical Healing, Love Magic, and the Inquisition in Late Sixteenth-Century Modena." In *Inquisition and Society in Early Modern Europe*, edited by S. Haliczer, 88–114. London, 1987.

Orlandi, G. "I redentoristi napoletani tra rivoluzione e restaurazione." *Spicilegium Historicum* 42 (1994): 179–229.

Ozment, S. *Magdalena and Balthasar*. New York, 1986.

———. *Three Behaim Boys: Growing Up in Early Modern Germany*. New Haven, 1990.

———. *The Bürgermeister's Daughter: Scandal in a Sixteenth-Century German Town*. New York, 1996.

Paglia, V. *La morte confortata: Riti della paura e mentalità religiosa a Roma nell'età moderna*. Rome, 1982.

Pancino, C. *Il bambino e l'acqua sporca: Storia dell'assistenza al parto dalle mammane alle ostetriche (secoli XVI–XIX)*. Milan, 1984.

Panico, G. *Il carnefice e la piazza: Crudeltà di stato e violenza popolare a Napoli in età moderna*. Naples, 1985.

———. "Criminali e peccatori in Principato Citra alla fine del Settecento (1770–1780)." In Berlinguer and Colao, *Criminalità*, 549–80.

Pappalardo, A. "Scelte testamentarie e pratica matrimoniale a Bitonto tra XVI e XVII secolo." *MEFRM* 95 (1983): 161–94.

"Paradigma indiziario e conoscenza storica: Dibattito su *Spie* di Carlo Ginzburg." *Quaderni di storia* 12 (1980): 3–54.

Parker, G. "Is the Duck an Animal?: An Exploration of Bestiality as a Crime." In *Crime, Police, and the Courts in British History*, edited by L. A. Knafla, 285–99. London, 1990.

Peccianti, D. "Gli inconvenienti della repressione dello stupro nella giustizia criminale senese: Il dilagare delle querele nel '700." In Berlinguer and Colao, *Criminalità*, 477–515.

Pelaja, M. *Matrimonio e sessualità a Roma nell'Ottocento*. Bari, 1994.

Pellegrino, B., and M. Spedicato, eds. *Società, congiuntura demografica e religiosità in Terra d'Otranto nel XVII secolo*. Galatina, 1990.

Pellizzari, M. R. "Alfabeto e fisco: Tra cultura scritta e oralità nel Regno di Napoli a metà Settecento." In Pellizzari, *Sulle vie*, 99–152.

Pellizzari, M. R., ed. *Sulle vie della scrittura: Alfabetizzazione, cultura scritta e istituzioni in età moderna*. Naples, 1989.

Peri, V. "Chiesa latina e chiesa greca nell'Italia postridentina (1564–1596)." In *La Chiesa greca in Italia dall'VIII al XVI secolo*, 3 vols., 1:271–469. Padua, 1973.

Peristiany, J. G., ed. *Honour and Shame: The Values of Mediterranean Society*. Chicago, 1966.

————, ed. *Mediterranean Family Structures.* Cambridge, 1976.

Perry, M. E. *Crime and Society in Early Modern Seville.* Hanover, N.H., 1980.

Pescione, R. *Corti di giustizia nell'Italia meridionale.* Naples, 1924.

Peters, E. *Torture.* Oxford, 1985.

Petropoulou, C. "Lingua e dialetto nella Grecia calabrese: Aspetti linguistici e culturali." *ASCL* 59 (1992): 153–72.

Petrovitch, P. "Recherches sur la criminalité à Paris dans la seconde moitié du XVIIIe siècle." In Abbiateci et al., *Crimes,* 187–261.

Petrusewicz, M. *Latifondo: Economia morale e vita materiale in una periferia dell'Ottocento.* Venice, 1989.

Pike, R. *Penal Servitude in Early Modern Spain.* Madison, Wis., 1983.

Pitt-Rivers, J. "The Kith and the Kin." In *The Character of Kinship,* edited by J. Goody, 89–105. Cambridge, 1973.

————. "Ritual Kinship in the Mediterranean: Spain and the Balkans." In Peristiany, *Mediterranean Family Structures,* 317–34.

————. *The Fate of Shechem or the Politics of Sex: Essays in the Anthropology of the Mediterranean.* Cambridge, 1977.

Placanica, A. *Il patrimonio ecclesiastico calabrese nell'età moderna.* Chiaravalle Centrale, 1972.

————. *Uomini, strutture, economia in Calabria nei secoli XVI–XVIII.* Reggio Calabria, 1974.

————. *L'"Iliade Funesta": Storia del terremoto calabrese-messinese del 1783.* Rome, 1982.

————. "I caratteri originali." In *La Calabria,* from *Storia d'Italia: Le regioni dall'Unità ad oggi,* edited by A. Placanica and P. Bevilacqua, 3–114. Turin, 1985.

————. *La Calabria nell'età moderna.* 2 vols. Naples, 1985–88.

————. *Storia della Calabria dall'antichità ai giorni nostri.* Catanzaro, 1993.

Placanica, A., and M. Mafrici, eds. *Il Mezzogiorno settecentesco attraverso i Catasti Onciarî.* 2 vols. Naples, 1983–86.

Pomata, G. *La promessa di guarigione: Malati e curatori in Antico Regime, Bologna, XVI–XVIII secolo.* Bari, 1994.

"Porter plainte: Stratégies villageoises et institutions judiciaires en Ile-de-France (XVIIe–XVIIIe siècles)." *Droit et culture* 19 (1990): 7–148.

Povolo, C. "Considerazioni su ricerche relative alla giustizia penale nell'età moderna: I casi di Padova, Treviso e Noale." *Atti dell'Istituto Veneto di Scienze, Lettere e Arti, Classe di Scienze Morali, Lettere e Arti,* 137 (1978–79): 479–98.

————. "Aspetti sociali e penali del reato d'infanticidio: Il caso di una contadina padovana del '700." *Atti dell'Istituto Veneto di Scienze, Lettere e Arti,* Classe di Scienze Morali, Lettere e Arti, 138 (1980): 415–32.

————. "Aspetti e problemi dell'amministrazione della giustizia penale nella Repubblica di Venezia, secoli XVI–XVII." In Cozzi, *Stato,* 1:155–258.

————. "Dal versante dell'illegittimità: Per una ricerca sulla storia della famiglia: Infanticidio ed esposizione d'infanti nel Veneto dell'età moderna." In Berlinguer and Colao, *Crimine*, 89–163.

Prodi, P., and C. Penuti, eds. *Disciplina dell'anima, disciplina del corpo e disciplina della società tra medioevo ed età moderna.* Bologna, 1994.

Prosperi, A. "'Otras Indias': Missionari della Controriforma tra contadini e selvaggi." In *Scienze credenze occulte livelli di cultura*, 205–34. Florence, 1982.

————. "Esecuzioni capitali e controllo sociale nella prima età moderna." *Politica del diritto* 14 (1983): 165–82.

————. "L'inquisitore come confessore." In Prodi and Penuti, *Disciplina*, 187–224.

————. "Missioni popolari e visite pastorali in Italia tra '500 e '600." *Ricerche di storia sociale e religiosa* 23 (1994): 29–44.

————. *Tribunali della coscienza: Inquisitori, confessori, missionari.* Turin, 1996.

Quaife, G. R. *Wanton Wenches and Wayward Wives: Peasants and Illicit Sex in Early Seventeenth-Century England.* London, 1979.

Raffaele, S. "'Essendo Real volontà che le donne badino all'onore': Onore e 'status' nella legislazione meridionale (secoli XVI–XVIII)." In Fiume, *Onore*, 143–54.

Raggio, O. *Faide e parentele: Lo stato genovese visto dalla Fontanabuona.* Turin, 1990.

————. "Costruzione delle fonti e prova: Testimoniali, possesso e giurisdizione." *QS* 31 (1996), no. 91: 135–56.

Raggio, O., S. Lombardini, and E. Muir. "Dibattito." *QS* 30 (1995), no. 88: 221–51.

Rao, A. M. *Il Regno di Napoli nel Settecento.* Naples, 1983.

————. *L'"amaro della feudalità": La devoluzione di Arnone e la questione feudale a Napoli alla fine del '700.* Naples, 1984.

"Registri di cancelleria di Luigi II d'Angiò per il ducato di Calabria." Appendix to *ASCL* 54–55 (1977–78).

Reinhardt, S. *Justice in the Sarladais, 1770–1790.* Baton Rouge, 1991.

Revel, J. "Microanalisi e costruzione del sociale." *QS* 29 (1994), no. 86: 549–75.

Reviglio della Veneria, C. *L'inquisizione medievale e il processo inquisitorio.* Turin, 1951; 1st ed., 1939.

Riddle, J. *Contraception and Abortion from the Ancient World to the Renaissance.* Cambridge, Mass., 1992.

————. *Eve's Herbs: A History of Contraception and Abortion in the West.* Cambridge, Mass., 1997.

Rienzo, M. G. "Il processo di cristianizzazione e le missioni popolari nel Mezzogiorno: Aspetti istituzionali e socio-religiosi." In Galasso and Russo, *Per la storia*, 1:439–81.

Riggio, A. "Schiavi calabresi in Tunisia barbaresca (1583–1701)." *ASCL* 5 (1935): 131–77.

————. "Corsari tunisini nel mare di Calabria." *ASCL* 7 (1937): 19–34.

————. "Schiavi calabresi nell'ospedale Trinitario di Tunisi." *ASCL* 8 (1938): 31–46.

————. "Un censimento di schiavi in Tunisia ottocentesca." *ASCL* 8 (1938): 333–52.

Robisheaux, T. *Rural Society and the Search for Order in Early Modern Germany.* Cambridge, 1989.

Rocke, M. "Il controllo dell'omosessualità a Firenze nel XV secolo: Gli Ufficiali di Notte." *QS* 22 (1987), no. 66: 701–23.

————. *Forbidden Friendships: Homosexuality and Male Culture in Renaissance Florence.* Oxford, 1996.

Rohlfs, G. *Dizionario dialettale delle tre Calabrie.* 3 vols. Halle, Germany, 1932–39.

————. *Dizionario toponomastico e onomastico della Calabria.* Ravenna, 1974.

————. *Dizionario dei cognomi e soprannomi in Calabria.* Ravenna, 1979.

Romeo, G. *Inquisitori, esorcisti e streghe nell'Italia della Controriforma.* Florence, 1990.

————. *Aspettando il boia: Condannati a morte, confortatori e inquisitori nella Napoli della Controriforma.* Florence, 1993.

Rosa, M. *Religione e società nel Mezzogiorno tra '500 e '600.* Bari, 1976.

————, ed. *Clero e società nell'Italia moderna.* Bari, 1995; 1st ed., 1992.

Rosoni, I. *Criminalità e giustizia penale nello stato pontificio del XIX secolo: Un caso di banditismo rurale.* Milan, 1988.

Rovito, P. L. *Respublica dei togati: Giuristi e società nella Napoli del '600.* Naples, 1981.

————. "Le riforme impossibili: Burocrazia e giurisdizione nella Calabria del '700." In *La Calabria,* 2:557–81.

————. *La rivolta dei notabili: Ordinamenti municipali e dialettica dei ceti in Calabria Citra (1647–1650).* Naples, 1988.

Rublack, U. "Pregnancy, Childbirth, and the Female Body in Early Modern Germany." *Past and Present,* no. 150 (February 1996): 84–110.

Ruff, J. R. *Crime, Justice, and Public Order in Old Regime France: The Sénéchaussées of Libourne and Bazas, 1696–1789.* London, 1984.

Ruggiero, G. *Violence in Early Renaissance Venice.* New Brunswick, N.J., 1980.

————. *Binding Passions: Tales of Magic, Marriage, and Power at the End of the Renaissance.* Oxford, 1993.

Russo, C. *Chiesa e comunità nella diocesi di Napoli tra '500 e '700.* Naples, 1984.

————, ed. *Chiesa, assistenza e società nel Mezzogiorno moderno.* Galatina, 1994.

Russo, F. *Storia dell'archidiocesi di Reggio Calabria.* 3 vols. Naples, 1965.

Sabean, D. "Aspects of Kinship Behavior and Property in Rural Western Europe before 1800." In Goody et al., *Family and Inheritance,* 96–111.

————. *Power in the Blood: Popular Culture and Village Discourse in Early Modern Germany.* Cambridge, 1984.

————. *Property, Production, and Family in Neckarhausen, 1700–1870.* Cambridge, 1990.

————. *Kinship in Neckarhausen, 1700–1870.* Cambridge, 1998.

Saint-Saëns, A., ed. *Permanence and Evolution of Behavior in Golden-Age Spain: Essays in Gender, Body, and Religion.* Lewiston, N.Y., 1991.

————. *Sex and Love in Golden Age Spain.* New Orleans, 1996.

Salazar, L. "La strage di Pentidattilo." *RSC* 2 (1894): 82–88.

Salisbury, J. *The Beast Within: Animals in the Middle Ages.* New York, 1994.

Sallmann, J.-M. *Chercheurs de trésors et jeteuses de sorts: La quête du surnaturel à Naples au XVIe siècle.* Paris, 1986.

———. "Alphabétisation et hiérarchie sociale à Naples à la fin du XVIe et au début du XVIIe siècle." In Pellizzari, *Sulle vie,* 79–98.

Sampers, A. "Primi contatti di S. Alfonso e dei redentoristi con la Calabria." *Spicilegium Historicum* 27 (1979): 299–318.

———. "Missioni dei redentoristi in Calabria dirette dal P. Carmine Fiocchi, 1763–1765." *Spicilegium Historicum* 28 (1980): 125–45.

Sánchez Ortega, M. H. "Sorcery and Eroticism in Love Magic." In *Cultural Encounters: The Impact of the Inquisition in Spain and the New World,* edited by M. E. Perry and A. J. Cruz, 58–92. Berkeley, 1991.

———. *La mujer y la sexualidad en el Antiguo Regimen.* Madrid, 1992.

Sannino Cuomo, A. L. "Il matrimonio in Basilicata prima e dopo il Concilio di Trento." In De Rosa and Cestaro, *Il Concilio,* 2:545–68.

Sannita, W. "Induzione farmacologica ed esperienze psichiche: Medicina popolare e stregoneria in Europa agli inizi dell'età moderna." In *La strega il teologo lo scienziato,* edited by M. Cuccu and P. A. Rossi, 119–40. Genoa, 1986.

Sarti, N. "Appunti su carcere-custodia e carcere-pena nella dottrina civilistica dei secoli XII–XVI." *Rivista storica del diritto italiano* 53–54 (1980–81): 67–110.

Sbriccoli, M. "Fonti giudiziarie e fonti giuridiche: Riflessioni sulla fase attuale degli studi di storia del crimine e della giustizia criminale." *Studi storici* 29 (1988): 491–501.

Scaduto, M., S.J. "Le carceri della Vicaria di Napoli agli inizi del Seicento." *Redenzione umana* 6 (1968): 393–412.

Scarabello, G. *Carcerati e carceri a Venezia nell'età moderna.* Rome, 1979.

———. "Devianza sessuale ed interventi di giustizia a Venezia nella prima metà del XVI secolo." In *Tiziano e Venezia,* 75–84. Vicenza, 1980.

———. "Progetti di riforma del diritto veneto criminale nel XVIII secolo." In Cozzi, *Stato,* 2:379–415.

Schleiner, W. *Medical Ethics in the Renaissance.* Washington, 1995.

Schnapper, B. "Testes inhabiles: Les témoins reproachables dans l'ancien droit pénal." *Tijdschrift voor rechtsgeschiedenis* 33 (1965): 575–616.

———. "Les peines arbitraires du XIIIe au XVIIIe siècle (doctrines savantes et usages français)." *Tijdschrift voor rechtsgeschiedenis* 41 (1973): 237–77; 42 (1974): 81–112.

———. "La justice criminelle rendue par le Parlement de Paris sous le règne de François Ier." *Revue historique du droit français et étranger* 152 (1974): 252–84.

———. *Voies nouvelles en histoire du droit: La justice, la famille, la répression pénale (XVIe–XVIIIe siècles).* Paris, 1991.

Schneider, Z. "The Village and the State: Justice and the Local Courts in Normandy, 1670–1740." Ph.D. diss., Georgetown University, 1997.

Schnorrenberg, B. B. "Is Childbirth Any Place for a Woman?: The Decline of Midwifery in Eighteenth-Century England." *Studies in Eighteenth-Century Culture* 10 (1981): 393–408.

Scholz, J.-M., ed. *Fallstudien zur spanischen und portugiesischen Justiz 15. bis 20. Jahrhundert.* Frankfurt, 1994.

Schulte, R. *The Village in Court: Arson, Infanticide, and Poaching in the Court Records of Upper Bavaria, 1848–1910.* Cambridge, 1994. German ed., 1989.

Scribner, B. "Is a History of Popular Culture Possible?" *History of European Ideas* 10 (1989): 175–91.

Seelye, K. "Concealing a Pregnancy to Avoid Telling Mom." *New York Times,* June 15, 1997, E-5.

Sharpe, J. A. *Crime in Early Modern England, 1550–1750.* London, 1984.

———. "Women, Witchcraft, and the Legal Process." In Kermode and Walker, *Women,* 106–24.

Sheppard, T. *Lourmarin in the Eighteenth Century: A Study of a French Village.* Baltimore, 1971.

Soman, A. "Les procès de sorcellerie au Parlement de Paris (1565–1640)." *Annales ESC* 32 (1977): 790–814.

———. "Deviance and Criminal Justice in Western Europe, 1300–1800: An Essay in Structure." *Criminal Justice History* 1 (1980): 3–28.

———. "Criminal Jurisprudence in Ancien Régime France: The Parlement of Paris in the Sixteenth and Seventeenth Centuries." In Knafla, *Crime,* 43–75.

———. "La giustizia criminale nel passato: Immagine e realtà: Il caso dell'Ancien Régime francese." In Cattini and Romani, *Potere,* 151–58.

Spadaro, C. M. *Società in rivolta: Istituzioni e ceti in Calabria Ultra (1647–1648).* Naples, 1995.

Spagnoletti. A. *"L'incostanza delle umane cose": Il patriziato di Terra di Bari tra egemonia e crisi (XVI–XVIII secolo).* Bari, 1981.

———. "Il governo del feudo: Aspetti della giurisdizione baronale nelle università meridionali nel XVIII secolo." *Società e storia* 55 (1992): 61–79.

———. *Storia del Regno delle Due Sicilie.* Bologna, 1997.

Spanò-Bolani, D. *Storia di Reggio Calabria da' tempi primitivi sino all'anno di Cristo 1797.* 2 vols. Reggio Calabria, 1891; 1st ed., 1857.

Spierenburg, P. *The Spectacle of Suffering: Executions and the Evolution of Repression: From a Pre-Industrial Metropolis to the European Experience.* Cambridge, 1984.

———. *The Prison Experience: Disciplinary Institutions and Their Inmates in Early Modern Europe.* New Brunswick, N.J., 1991.

Sponsler, L. "The Status of Married Women under the Legal System of Spain." *Journal of Legal History* 3 (1982): 125–52.

Sposato, P. "Note sull'attività pretridentina, tridentina, e posttridentina del P. Gaspare del Fosso dei Minimi, arcivescovo di Reggio Calabria." In acts of the *Primo Congresso Storico Calabrese,* 239–66. Tivoli, 1957.

———. *Aspetti e figure della riforma cattolico-tridentina in Calabria.* Naples, 1964.

Stanton, D. C. "Recuperating Women and the Man behind the Screen: *Caquets de l'accouchée* (1622)." In *Sexuality and Gender in Early Modern Europe: Institutions, Texts, Images,* edited by J. G. Turner, ch. 11. Cambridge, 1993.

Stern, L. I. *The Criminal Law System of Medieval and Renaissance Florence.* Baltimore, 1994.

Stone, L. "The Revival of Narrative: Reflections on a New Old History," *Past and Present,* no. 85 (November 1979): 3–24.

Storia del Vallo di Diano. 3 vols. Salerno, 1982–85.

Strauss, G. *Law, Resistance, and the State: The Opposition to Roman Law in Reformation Germany.* Princeton, N.J., 1986.

———. "The Dilemma of Popular History." *Past and Present,* no. 132 (August 1991): 130–49.

———. "Reply." *Past and Present,* no. 141 (November 1993): 215–19.

Szabo, D., and S. Pietralunga. "Ruptures dans le concept de nature au XVIIIe siècle: Essai d'interprétation des crimes contre nature dans la Léopoldine 1786." In Berlinguer and Colao, *Criminalità,* 93–145.

Tacchi Venturi, P., S.J. *Storia della Compagnia di Gesù in Italia.* Rome, 1910.

Tedeschi, J. *The Prosecution of Heresy: Collected Studies on the Inquisition in Early Modern Italy.* Binghamton, N.Y., 1991.

Tentori, T. "Social Classes and Family in a Southern Italian Town: Matera." In Peristiany, *Mediterranean Family Structures,* 273–85.

Tocci, G., ed. *Le comunità negli stati italiani d'Antico Regime.* Bologna, 1989.

Tolley, B. *Parishes and Parishioners in Württemberg during the Late Reformation, 1581–1621.* Palo Alto, Calif., 1995.

Tomás y Valiente, F. *El derecho penal de la monarquía absoluta.* Madrid, 1969.

———. *La tortura en España: Estudios históricos.* Barcelona, 1973.

———, ed. *Sexo barroco y otras transgresiones premodernas.* Madrid, 1990.

Tondo, F. "Proprietà ecclesiastica e clero ricettizio in un piccolo centro salentino tra XVII e XVIII secolo." In Pellegrino and Spedicato, *Società,* 277–92.

Torre, A. "Il consumo di devozione: Rituali e potere nelle campagne piemontesi nella prima metà del Settecento." In Tocci, *Le comunità,* 303–20.

———. *Il consumo di devozioni: Religione e comunità nelle campagne dell'Ancien Régime.* Venice, 1995.

Trasselli, C. "Du fait divers à l'histoire sociale: Criminalité et moralité en Sicile au début de l'époque moderne." *Annales ESC* 28 (1973): 226–46.

———. *Lo stato di Gerace e Terranova nel Cinquecento.* Vibo Valentia, 1978.

Trexler, R. "Infanticide in Florence: New Sources and First Results." *History of Child-hood Quarterly* 1 (1973): 98–116.

Trifone, R. "Diritto romano comune e diritti particolari nell'Italia meridionale." In *Jus Romanum Medii Aevi,* pt. V.2. Milan, 1962.

Turchini, A. "La nascita del sacerdozio come professione." In Prodi and Penuti, *Disci-plina,* 225–56.

Turrini, M. *La coscienza e le leggi: Morale e diritto nei testi per la confessione della prima età moderna.* Bologna, 1991.

Valente, G. "L'incursione turchesca su Nicotera nel 1638." In acts of the *Terzo Congresso Storico Calabrese,* 681–735. Naples, 1964.

———. *Le torri costiere della Calabria.* Chiaravalle Centrale, 1972.

———. *Calabria, calabresi e turcheschi nei secoli della pirateria (1400–1800).* Chia-ravalle Centrale, 1973.

———. *Dizionario dei luoghi della Calabria.* 2 vols. Chiaravalle Centrale, 1973.

———. "I Catasti Onciari della Calabria." In *La Calabria,* 2:727–45.

Vallone, G. "Il pensiero giuridico meridionale." In Galasso and Romeo, *Storia,* 10:297–333.

van der Meer, T. "Tribades on Trial: Female Same-Sex Offenders in Late Eighteenth-Century Amsterdam." In Fout, *Forbidden History,* 189–210.

van de Walle, E. "Flowers and Fruits: Two Thousand Years of Menstrual Regulation." *Journal of Interdisciplinary History* 28 (1997): 183–203.

van Dülmen, R. *Theatre of Horror: Crime and Punishment in Early Modern Germany.* Cambridge, 1990. German ed., 1985.

Vardi, L. "Peasants and the Law: A Village Appeals to the French Royal Council, 1768–1791." *Social History* 13 (1988): 295–313.

Vassberg, D. E. *Land and Society in Golden Age Castile.* Cambridge, 1984.

———. *The Village and the Outside World in Golden Age Castile: Mobility and Migra-tion in Everyday Rural Life.* Cambridge, 1996.

Villani, P. *Mezzogiorno tra riforme e rivoluzione.* Bari, 1977; 1st ed., 1962.

Villani, P., ed. *Economia e classi sociali nella Puglia moderna.* Naples, 1974.

Villari, L. "La Calabria nel viceregno austriaco." In acts of the *Terzo Congresso Storico Calabrese,* 175–97. Naples, 1964.

Villari, R. *La rivolta antispagnola a Napoli: Le origini (1585–1647).* Bari, 1967. In English as *The Revolt of Naples.* Cambridge, 1993.

———. *Mezzogiorno e contadini nell'età moderna.* Bari, 1977; 1st ed., 1961.

Villone, A. "Contratti matrimoniali e testamenti in una zona di latifondo: Eboli a metà Seicento." *MEFRM* 95 (1983): 225–98.

Vincent, B. "The Affective Life of Slaves in the Iberian Peninsula during the Sixteenth and Seventeenth Centuries." In Saint-Saëns, *Sex and Love,* 71–78.

Viscardi, G. "Magia, stregoneria e superstizioni nei sinodi lucani del Seicento." *Ri-cerche di storia sociale e religiosa* 14 (1985): 144–87.

———. "La religiosità popolare nel Cilento fra XVI e XIX secolo." *Ricerche di storia sociale e religiosa* 22 (1993): 7–46.

Visceglia, M. A. *Territorio, feudo e potere locale: Terra d'Otranto tra medioevo ed età moderna.* Naples, 1988.

Vissière, I. *Procès de femmes au temps des philosophes ou la violence masculine au XVIIIe siècle.* Paris, 1985.

Vitale, G. "Servi e vassalli nei testamenti della nobiltà napoletana fra XIV e XVI secolo." *ASPN* 112 (1994): 7–36.

Volpe, F. "Struttura dei libri parrocchiali fra Cinquecento e Seicento." In De Rosa and Cestaro, *Il Concilio,* 1:65–82.

———. *Il Cilento nel secolo XVII.* Naples, 1991; 1st ed., 1981.

von Lobstein, F. *Settecento calabrese ed altri scritti.* 2 vols. Naples, 1973–77.

Wegert, K. *Popular Culture, Crime, and Social Control in Eighteenth-Century Württemberg.* Stuttgart, 1994.

Weisser, M. R. *Crime and Punishment in Early Modern Europe.* Atlantic Highlands, N.J., 1979.

Wessling, M. N. "Infanticide Trials and Forensic Medicine: Württemberg, 1757–1793." In Clark and Crawford, *Legal Medicine,* 117–44.

Wiesner, M. E. *Women and Gender in Early Modern Europe.* Cambridge, 1993.

———. "The Midwives of Southern Germany and the Public/Private Dichotomy." In Marland, *Art of Midwifery,* 77–94.

Wilson, A. *The Making of Man-Midwifery: Childbirth in England, 1660–1770.* Cambridge, Mass., 1995.

Wrightson, K. "Infanticide in European History." *Criminal Justice History* 3 (1982): 1–20.

Zamperetti, S. *I piccoli principi: Signorie locali, feudi e comunità soggette nello stato regionale veneto dall'espansione territoriale ai primi decenni del '600.* Venice, 1991.

Zanelli, G. *Streghe e società nell'Emilia e Romagna del Cinque-Seicento.* Rome, 1992.

Zangari, D. *Le colonie italo-albanesi di Calabria: Storia e demografia, secoli XV–XIX.* Naples, 1941.

Zilli, I. *Imposta diretta e debito pubblico nel Regno di Napoli, 1669–1737.* Naples, 1990.

Zorzi, A. "Tradizioni storiografiche e studi recenti sulla giustizia nell'Italia del Rinascimento." *Cheiron,* no. 16 (1991): 27–78.

———. "Rituali e cerimoniali penali nelle città italiane (ss. XIII–XVI)." In Chiffoleau et al., *Riti,* 141–57.

Zorzi, D. "Sull'amministrazione della giustizia penale nell'età delle riforme: Il reato di omicidio nella Padova di fine '700." In Berlinguer and Colao, *Crimine,* 273–308.

Index

Library of Congress Cataloging-in-Publication Data

Astarita, Tommaso.
  Village justice : community, family, and popular culture in early
modern Italy / Tommaso Astarita.
    p. cm. — (The Johns Hopkins University studies in historical
and political science ; 117th ser., no. 3)
  Includes bibliographical references and index.
   ISBN 0-8018-6138-1 (alk. paper)
    1. Social structure—Italy—Pentidattilo—History—19th century.
2. Social values—Italy—Pentidattilo—History—19th century.
3. Justice, Administration of—Italy—Naples (Kingdom)—History—19th century.   4. Pentidattilo (Italy)—Moral conditions—
History—19th century.   5. Cuzzucli, Antonino, d. 1710—Death and
burial. 6. Orlando, Domenica, b. 1686—Trials, litigation, etc.
I. Title. II. Series.
HN488.P445A86   1999
306'.0945'73—dc21   99-13654
                                                              CIP